THE COMPLETE GUIDE TO ADVENTURE RACING

THE INSIDER'S GUIDE TO THE GREATEST SPORT ON EARTH

BY DON MANN AND KARA SCHAAD

A GETFITNOW.COM BOOK

HATHERLEIGH PRESS
NEW YORK

Hatherleigh Press
An Affiliate of W.W. Norton & Company, Inc.
5-22 46th Avenue, Suite 200
Long Island City, NY 11101
1-800-528-2550

Library of Congress Cataloging-in-Publication Data

Mann, Don, 1957-
    The complete guide to adventure racing / Don Mann, Kara Schaad.
        p. cm.
    ISBN 1-57826-064-7 (alk. paper)
    1. Adventure racing—Handbooks, manuals, etc. I. Schaad, Kara.

GV1038 .M36 2001
796.5—dc21

                                                                    2001039072

Cover design by Peter Gunther
Interior Design by Fatema Tarzi

Cover photos by Tim Holstrom

**All Hatherleigh Press titles are available for bulk purchase, special promotions, and premiums.
For more information, please contact the manager of our
Special Sales Department at 1-800-528-2550.**

Printed in Canada
10 9 8 7 6 5 4 3 2

"It's not the critic who counts…it's not the man who points out how the strong man stumbled…Credit belongs to the man who really was in the arena, his face marred by dust, sweat and blood, who strives valiantly, who errs to come short and short again, because there is no effort without error and shortcoming. It is the man who actually strives to do the deeds, who knows the great enthusiasm and knows the great devotion, who spends himself on a worthy cause, who at best, knows in the end the triumph of great achievement. And who, at worst, if he fails, at least fails while daring greatly, so that his place shall never be with those cold and cruel souls who know neither victory nor defeat."

—Teddy Roosevelt

TABLE OF CONTENTS

Have questions about this book? Visit the authors on the internet at Getfitnow.com.

ACKNOWLEDGEMENTS

Our sincere appreciation to every adventure racing organization and the Director, staff and volunteers of each race, particularly to the Gerard Fusil Company, The Raid Gauloises Organization and The Southern Traverse Ltd.

We are grateful to David Bauman and Tim Holstrom for their stalwart images that captured the rigors of racing, to Peter Field Peck for his patience and levity as he photographed the Odyssey Adventure Racing Academy participants and whose images have given visual life to our book, and to Andrew Flach, Kevin Moran and Fatema Tarzi for making this incredible project possible.

And without the help and encouragement from our dear teammates in life, Dawn Taylor-Mann and Jay Pearlman and their never-ending support, we would still be pulling our hair out.

DEDICATIONS

This book is dedicated to our Mothers and Fathers who have always been there for us.

I dedicate this book to my loving and devoted Mother who committed her entire life to her children and husband. Everything she did in life was for family. She instilled in me the importance of family, proving anything else is secondary. Mother, I love you very much and will think of you every day for the rest of my life.

Your loving and grateful son,

Don

CONTRIBUTORS

With gratitude, we want to recognize the following people who continually strive to drive the boundaries of their abilities and simultaneously have the patience to document their experiences and to share them with us:

Dale Blankenship, Steve Bozeman, Jack Crawford, Richard J. Corcoran, Rolf Dengler, Nick Freyer, Jane Hall, Jim Hertz, Alan Holmes, John Howard, Joe Johnson, Colleen Laffee, Danny Lucero, Brad Miller, Keith Murray, Dan O'Shea, Blain Reeves, Jeremy Rodgers, Nate Smith, Dawn Taylor-Mann, Peter Tempest, Tracyn Thayer, Greg Vogel, John Vonhof, Anne Wilson and Harald Zundel.

An extra dose of heartfelt thanks goes to Ian Adamson, Angelika Castaneda, Adrian Crane, Parker J. Cross, Juli Lynch, Debra Moore, Harry Gerewin, Jane Hall and George Wortley for their additional support and contributions to our book.

Finally, we are grateful to Gerard Fusil for his vision and insight in the conception of this incredible sport and to Nelly Fusil-Martin for her continued dedication to this sport.

PHOTO CREDITS

The authors and publisher would like to thank the following photographers for their invaluable contributions to this book.

DAVID BAUMAN: 53, 55, 57, 106, 113, 115, 162, 167, 171, 172, 182, 191, 229, 252, 264

TIM HOLSTROM: X, 20, 52, 114, 142, 158, 170, 189, 190, 206, 228, 234, 243

DON MANN: 11, 12, 17, 19, 33, 34, 67, 84, 85, 108, 117, 118, 140, 155, 163, 195, 231, 251, 255

MARTIN PAQUETTE: 13, 26, 178

PETER FIELD PECK: 1, 8, 10, 14, 22, 36, 39, 41, 43, 44, 45, 49, 60, 61, 63, 65, 68, 75, 76, 86, 88, 95, 99, 101, 102, 103, 105, 109, 110, 116, 120, 121, 127, 130, 131, 132, 136, 137, 139, 143, 145, 146, 148, 149, 150, 151, 153, 154, 157, 203, 204, 209, 212, 247, 248

KARA SCHAAD: 18, 31, 50, 81, 122, 156, 164, 169, 197, 207, 208, 240, 250, 257, 258

COLOR INSERT

The following photos are by Peter Field Peck.
Page 1—Mountain biking. Odyssey Adventure Racing Academy (OARA).
Page 2 Top—Cross-country trekking. OARA.
Page 2 Bottom—Ascending techniques. OARA.
Page 3 Top—Portaging skills. OARA.
Page 3 Bottom—Teamwork. OARA.

The following photos are by Tim Holstrom
Page 4 Top—Eco-Challenge (2000) Borneo.
Page 4 Bottom—Elf Authentic (2000).
Page 5—Eco-Challenge (1999) Argentina.
Page 6—Elf Authentic (2000).
Page 7 Top—Eco-Challenge (1999) Argentina.
Page 7 Bottom—Elf Authentic (2000).
Page 8—Elf Authentic (2000).

PREFACE

Considering all of the modern-day comforts and conveniences and myriad choices of extravagant indulgences that technology has forged, why do we feel the need to voluntarily hurl ourselves into a sea of hardship? We have evolved to a place and time of prosperity. Why are we captivated by the whims of adventure?

We have become a world of greater sophistication and intelligence. Technology has brought us closer, shortening the gap among countries and cultures.

Simultaneously, it has broadened our horizons and exalted our hunger for greater knowledge and exploration.

We want to know what's beyond our own city limits. We have the means to get there and are developing a profound curiosity for strange, faraway lands. Adventure sets the stage for internal exploration stimulated by new external incentives. In turn, a deeper understanding of the self and the surrounding world is achieved. A greater sensitivity is attained.

Once we experience an adventure, we typically surpass our expectations, assuming an invincibility that powers us to greater dimensions. When you set out to achieve a goal and you hit it, it's life-changing. The more arduous or far-fetched, the more satisfaction you incur. As we encounter greater physical feats, our emotional and spiritual facets merge into a powerful union that becomes unstoppable.

A multi-day adventure race emphasizes self-sufficiency requiring continuous concentration. The time that trickles by from the start to the finish weaves a separate universe lived by everyone involved in the experience. You become totally immersed and focused on one common goal—the finish line. Nothing else on earth is

more relevant. It becomes an oasis, a time out with valuable lessons attached to each day endured.

Living outdoors for days at a time inspires a variety of obstacles requiring immediate adjustments in order to continue the adventure. To succeed, you must surrender. You are stripped of all pretenses of today's society. There's nothing to hide behind. You are left with the real you. It puts everything into perspective. You realize what is important and what is trifling.

As long as we can move and breathe, we will challenge our ability to achieve, for achievement is the root of mankind. We are driven with this deep, fundamental aspect of our being. We define it in different ways depending on what is important to us. More and more of us are looking to take risks to explore the inner depths of the things that make us tick. We are climbing mountains, diving off distant shores, and trekking dangerous territory to discover what we are made of.

Exploration has shaped and defined our world. Adventure was a way of life for our ancestors. Day after day, they sought new frontiers and greater environments in search of freedom. Centuries ago, slogging through rugged terrain was a quest for independence. It was a matter of life or death. Today, it is a voluntary weekend pursuit. We are products of comfort and convenience seeking adventure as a luxury. We should recognize the good fortune of simply having the choice to stay home or to take off and explore!

In September 1999, *Time* magazine published a cover story on adventure, revealing our craving for greater risk and conquests. The author, Karl Taro Greenfield, described this attitude, "…at the end of a decade of American triumphalism abroad and prosperity at home, we could be seeking to upsize our personalities, our sense of ourselves."

Everywhere you turn, you find adventurous candidates clad with cargo pants and t-shirts woven with the latest in wicking technology, driving SUV's, with daypacks stuffed with survival gear, trail mix and the latest works of authors such as Jon Krakauer. The romance of adventure has hypnotized the masses. If we don't have the finances or the freedom, we cling to heroic stories of those who dared to take the plunge, vicariously experiencing a walk on the wild side. We daydream the possibilities of one day taking a trip, venturing beyond our familiar walls, and for many, the dreams are fueling an exciting new reality.

True adventure is about defining your own path. Drawing your own map. Going beyond your traditional rings of comfort. This belief has fueled the sport of adventure racing. One that is so complex, it is impossible to define in a single sentence. For this reason, we have written an entire book about it! Adventure racing captures the rigors of life, magnifies them, and conveniently packages them all into one and two-day races, three to four-day experiments, and expeditions spanning two weeks or more in length.

According to Gerard Fusil, "the father of adventure racing," the sport is a competition that "brings people into a different situation—not like normal life—which causes more stress than normal." Competitors experience extreme climate changes, close encounters with unusual animals, different means of daily survival, obscure sleep patterns…the variables are endless. "You are in a very different situation," Fusil summarizes, backed with the knowledge from more than a decade of race production.

As we move forward into an unknown future, one thing is clear: our potential is boundless. As adventure races continue to span longer distances, athletes continue to get faster, defying the daunting lengths. With our hiking poles firmly planted and our footsteps outlined in this new millennium, records continue to be shattered as tolerance for discomfort rises. The 10th edition of the Raid Gauloises in 2000 explored the sacred Himalayas as competitors raced most of the route above 14,000 feet. New disciplines are being added to adventure racing, upping the ante for talent and skill proficiency. Scuba diving was introduced in the 2000 Eco-Challenge in Sabah and instead of skimming the surface bubbles of white-water in a watercraft, race directors are asking athletes to use their own bodies as their vehicle as they swim through the rapids.

Will we ever reach the ceiling of our potential? Where do we stop? Or do we? Is there an obvious black line of finality? Or is our capacity infinite? How will we know unless we continue to push our limits? How will we know unless we dare to take ourselves to the ultimate edge of our abilities?

Life is about accomplishments. The highest honor we can achieve is to strive to fulfill a desire, and through diligent effort, attain a personal triumph. The reward is a magic carpet of confidence, in which we give ourselves an eternal ticket to ride. The more successes, the higher we fly.

What is life for, if we're not living it?

FOREWORD

BY IAN ADAMSON

Prior to meeting Don Mann for the first time I had formed a mental picture of him as a clean cut, square-jawed, barrel-chested guy with a ramrod-straight back and piercing gaze. After all, his reputation as an elite Navy SEAL preceded him! Consider my surprise when we finally crossed paths. We were paddling our canoes furiously down river in the not-so-Great Noreaster adventure race in 1998 and having a hard time keeping pace with a guy with wild ZZ Top hair and beard and a maniacal grin. Teammate Robert Nagle mentioned that this was Don Mann, and I almost fell out of the canoe as I gawked in surprise at this lean, muscular athlete who was clearly enjoying the process of the race and looked as if he had just come from a Grateful Dead concert!

Having the fortune to get to know Don through subsequent races such as the Raid Gauloises and his own Beast of the East, I am glad to report he is one of the most sincere, kind, dedicated and personable characters in the sport. He has a wealth of experience as one of the earliest US athletes in adventure racing and through teaching dozens of camps and hundreds of athletes over the years. Don brings a lot more to teaching than his expertise, however. In addition to being an elite endurance athlete, he has a contagious enthusiasm for the sport.

Enthusiasm is definitely something you need to compete in a race such as the Elf Authentic Adventure, as it has gained the reputation as one of the longest and toughest races out there. And out there it is. In the 1999 edition in the Philippines, I was making my way from the transition area on day nine to the most exquisite sapphire blue ocean and thought I had gone to heaven. More accurately, as my decrepit and depleted body was being carried across the dazzling white sand, I saw a vision framed, between the palm trees. This was Kara Schaad. Maybe it was the fact that I had just spent two days peering at my swollen feet stuffed into rollerblade shells, but most likely it was because the vision captured precisely my idea of paradise.

Kara was having her first taste of adventure racing, and a succulent morsel it was not. The vision she saw was the antithesis of mine, but despite the horror she maintained composure and peppered me with a concoction of interesting questions for her paper, *The Chicago Sun-Times*. Getting to know Kara over the remains of the race revealed an intelligent, articulate and altogether impressive adventurer. Evidently Chicago was not providing the spice that misery in the tropics could provide, and I knew immediately that she loved to suffer just like me.

The combination of Don and Kara's experience, passion and exceptionally clear writing delivers in great detail the nuances of the elements of adventure racing. Each chapter is brought to life with experiences from elite adventure athletes such as John Howard, and Angelika Castenada and is illustrated with great clarity.

The text provides essential reading for anyone wanting an introduction to the sport and provides comprehensive information for the more experienced athlete who wants to tackle longer races.

INTRODUCTION

For many years, my life has been consumed by physical fitness, training and racing. Before adventure racing, it was motocross racing, marathons, triathlons, ultra distance cycling and ultra distance running. However, no other sport has held my attention for so long and so intently as that of adventure racing. All of my training has been in preparation for "the race" that was in preparation for the "the big race". I've often dreamed of training and racing. I've eaten, not for enjoyment, but to fuel my body to train and compete, and I've spent most of my money on gear and travel. In doing so, I have been rewarded with some of the best experiences of my life.

I have so many profound memories of racing in far away lands, such as watching a condor with a 10-foot wing span fly just a meter over my head, or summiting a beautiful mountain, rappelling down canyons under waterfalls, riding and bonding with a horse in the lush green valleys of South Africa, laughing so hard because I was stuck in quicksand, riding 50 miles downhill through treacherous mountain passes, or swimming for 16 miles in the white-water of the Himalayas. Where else but in the sport of adventure racing would you be required to swim in a river with class four-plus rapids, in the middle of a 500-mile race?

I have had some very sad memories as well. I have had to tell some very talented, incredible athletes and good friends that they could not be on the race team because I did not think they were ready for a particular race. I have had to wrap up a friend's mangled hand after he came close to losing it in a climbing accident. I've experienced some great hallucinations, lost lots of muscle weight in races when my body demanded more fuel than I was providing it, and have suffered frostbite, nerve damage, and so many other overuse injuries common in the sport.

I can sum up the sport by saying that competing in an adventure race is like compressing a lot of life into a relatively short amount of time. You learn so much about yourself and your teammates, especially your strengths and weaknesses. You discover qualities in yourself that you would like to change and qualities you are happy to possess. You learn to deal with people in a wide array of circumstances. Your teammates may be crying, laughing or screaming depending on the situation, and you learn to handle the situation to the best of your ability. You find yourself in the role of friend, trainer, team captain, consultant, or maybe even "the hammer," the one who keeps the team moving as hard as it can effectively move.

The sport is a dream come true for the adventure-seeking athlete. It demands what all other sports combined can ever demand of an athlete. Adventure racing demands strength, courage, intelligence, organization, commitment, speed, teamwork, endurance, and an ability to compete without sleep. It also requires that you maintain a certain level of proficiency in many different disciplines including navigation, climbing, and biking, and continually adds new disciplines to the list, like whitewater swimming and canyoneering.

The reward of adventure racing is priceless. You compete in the open wilderness, surviving on what you carry on your back, problem solving with a group of friends and being challenged physically and mentally. Life just doesn't get much better than this.

After team 'Odyssey' returned from the Raid Gauloises in Patagonia, Argentina in 1995, I had a dream of bringing a similar type race to the United

States. I wanted to create an expedition-level adventure race in the United States. I wanted the race to be relatively free of the major logistical obstacles (i.e. cost, time away from home etc.) of the larger international races. I didn't see why we couldn't create a 350 mile plus grueling expedition race in the US that would take the competitors just 5 days rather than 10 days to complete and cost many thousands of dollars less. It would be as difficult if not more and the competitors would not have to spend a month or more away from home, family and work in order to compete. It is always hard taking months away from work and family to compete in multi-day competitions. It is also very difficult to raise the funds required to enter the longer events. I shared my dream with Joy Marr and Mike Nolan and in doing so, Odyssey Adventure Racing was born and the Beast of the East was created. Thanks to Joy's endless amount of energy and creativity and Mike's tireless efforts, Odyssey and the Beast, our first public race, became a reality. Since then, through meeting the demands of the athletes, Odyssey has produced dozens of other races. The Odyssey events are made possible by the tremendous amount of support we receive from our friends, families and volunteers including Dawn Taylor-Mann, Steve Kirby, Dr. George Wortley, MD, Bill Davis, Ph.D., Shannon Anderson, Jamie Webster, Tim and Dee Soyars, Travis Overstreet, Walt Rawle, Mike Nolan, Dr. Parker Cross MD, and Luther Papenfuss.

I would like to thank Kara Schaad for her many months of diligent effort. I owe my incredible racing experiences and knowledge that I have gained in the sport to the many fine athletes that I have had the privilege of racing with and against over the past 25 years. I also want to thank my friends and family for putting up with my non-stop training and racing mentality over the years.

I hope that you enjoy this book and that it benefits you in some way in this wonderful sport.

—*Don Mann*

Kettle Moraine, WI…The race began with a mass start. We set off into the nebulous pool, an army of soldiers hunting for the first checkpoint somewhere in the distance. As we plunged ahead in our plastic canoes, the blanket of darkness that cradled the unknown conjured my deepest, darkest fears.

Then just as we established a rhythm and found a comfort zone, it started to rain. Then it poured. Then it pummeled our world, interrupting our focus on what lie ahead. The storm that had been promised in the forecast paid us a violent visit as it came bearing vicious winds that blew us every which way but in our desired direction.

The rage of the angry sky changed everything. Not only did it stunt our speed and rate of progress, it extracted significant energy from our bodies and temporarily incapacitated our mental strength. It also made communication impossible.

The second checkpoint was a large boat with blinding lights, which was located right smack in the center of the chaos. To pass, we had to scream our team number and hope we were heard. We couldn't hear each other, but somehow, we were allowed to advance.

The inclement weather was a rude awakening to the race, but we were soldiers of fortune. So, we resigned ourselves to the cold, hard fact that it would rain for most of the daylong race, and onward we pressed with fortitude.

And hence, my world as I knew it would never be the same.

In the spring of 1998, I received a call from a perfect stranger. He had read about my fitness accomplishments in Chicago's local sports and fitness magazine and thought I would make a great teammate for the Pathfinder Challenge, the first adventure race in the Midwest. Feeling adventurous, as I often do, I agreed to do the race and secretly prayed that he wasn't some sicko who would jeopardize my enterprising spirit.

As fate would have it, we finished, and I managed to go unscathed in the process (except for the loss of a toenail!). Our goal was to have fun and finish, and we did. Consequently, I embraced significant insight into the quantities of my inner strength.

So, I embarked on an exciting new path of outdoor endurance activities, which conjured confidence and courage and other qualities very different from what I had experienced in the prior two-and-a-half decades of my life as a dancer and a fitness trainer.

One year later, I received a similar call, which resulted in an 18-day trip to the Philippines to witness and write about the inaugural Elf Authentic Adventure. Once again, I was deeply exposed to profound intrinsic qualities.

I knew I was on to something. That something was empowerment and that something has led me to many more competitions. That something has engendered greater courage to take on bigger and bolder tasks upon every personal race victory. Even when I couldn't finish a race, I managed to grow stronger and wiser. Through my disappointment, my emotional scars have actually provided inspiration and they have enhanced my drive to become better.

For every individual who has experienced both the agony and the ecstasy of training and preparing for competition and then confirming his efforts as he crosses the finish line, my balaclava goes off to you. As in the sport of adventure racing where preparation is key and teamwork is a necessary factor of success, the formulation of this book has been just that. Don and I have overcome many challenges, not to mention the enormity of what adventure racing encompasses, in writing this book. Just as the pleasure of sharing race stories with family and friends is a true reward for the race experience, so is the pleasure of sharing this book with you.

—*Kara Schaad*

WARNING:
ADVENTURE RACING IS A SPORT WHERE YOU MAY BE SERIOUSLY INJURED OR DIE.

READ THIS BEFORE YOU USE THIS BOOK.

This is an instruction book on adventure racing and its multi-sport components that are inherently dangerous. You should not depend solely on information gleaned from this book for your personal safety. Your climbing/paddling/biking/trekking safety depends on your own judgement based on competent instruction, experience, and a realistic assessment of your abilities.

There are no warranties, either expressed or implied, that this instruction book contains accurate or reliable information. Your use of this book indicates your assumption of the risk of death or serious injury as a result of adventure racing's risks and is an acknowledgement of your own responsibility for your safety.

*Teams coasteer at the Pathfinder Challenge Race (2000)
on the west coast of Michigan.*

ECO-CHALLENGE 1999
BY ADRIAN CRANE, TEAM ADVENTURE ONE, #44.

DECEMBER 26, 1999

The calling of names began in a meadow near Lago Correntoso in Patagonia, Argentina. As my name was called, I lifted my arms in joy. I had been chosen as the one to paddle our two team kayaks to the center of the lake; the other three members of team 'Adventure One' would have to swim out through the cold water, scramble into the kayaks and begin the 1999 Eco-Challenge.

From the center of the lake, hanging tight to a buoy at the left end of the flotilla of kayaks, I could see the line of competitors standing facing away from the shore. Suddenly, the distant line of standing figures dissolved as competitors sprinted to the water and swam toward the boats. The swimmers yelled for their kayak bound teammates. Tony, Val and Tom found me quickly at the end of the line and wriggled, dripping, into the kayaks. The race was on.

At the first portage, across a small isthmus by the Rio Correntoso, between Lago Correntoso and Lago Nahuel Huapi, a melee ensued as teams manhandled the heavy boats as we carried them up the steep narrow trail. The backlog of teams and kayaks pushed and jostled in hopes of saving meaningless seconds in this eight-day race! Tom received a paddle in the side of his head for his efforts. Five kilometers further a second portage was more civilized since the trail was wider and the teams more spread out. The team was ready to plunge into the cold dark water. We leapt. A few hard strokes saw us in the main current and a few more had us across and into the eddy on the far side. Valerie screamed from behind and Tony pulled her with him into the slower water. In the gloom of dusk and the confining view from the helmet that now tilted over my eyes, I struggled waterlogged to shore and clambered over boulders out of the river, glad to be done with the cold, wet water sports for a while.

Four mild-mannered horses were handed to us and we swung astride them and headed out, mindful that the crowd and flashing cameras might easily spook a horse. Three hours later we rode into the first checkpoint on the horse leg, Rancho El Condor. We now had a two-hour enforced halt for the good of the horses. Tony and Val took the first shift of tending horses. I suspect that Tony watched the animals while Valerie slept but since I was fast asleep at the time, I can't say. At the next checkpoint and another enforced two-hour halt, dawn was on its way. Tom and I tended the horses, and he kindly let me sleep again for most of our shift. We headed out for the third and final horse section up a sandy trail in the bright morning light. We rode the horses harder now, kicking up dust as we trotted down a green valley. We caught the Kiwi team 'Macpac' just as team 'Vail' caught us in their rush to regain lost time after a route-finding error. Our pack of eleven horses (the Kiwis were down to three since their woman broke her ankle after being thrown at the start of the horse section) threw up swirling dust from the loamy ground. Big white cliffs on the left reminded us that we were heading into the hills. After a long descent, we bid good-bye to our horses and in the warming morning, shouldered our packs and headed out on foot along a dirt road.

Finding water soon became a priority. The road followed an open valley and as the day wore on, we could feel the effects of the hot sun on our backs. The dirt road dwindled into a foot trail, which we followed past endless bluffs and streams. It was evening by the time we found the ridge by which we would climb out. Valerie was tired, I was sick from the heat and Tom was mad at our lack of pace. "Why aren't we running?" he would say. "Because we can't," we would reply. Failing to find a cabin marked on the trail map, we descended the trail a short distance back to a small meadow. Here we bumped into 'Team USA' and we all agreed that we should just head into the brush and tackle the climb out of the valley. We splashed across the stream and up into the thick woods on the other side. A hard hour's climb saw us reach the top of the ridge at dusk.

We hurried on to look over the ridge while there was still some light. Climbing the ridge with the map in my hand, I argued back and forth with Tom about the correct route. "If you'd stop and look at the map, we could figure this out." Tom, objecting to this comment, replied, "I'm out of here," and to our surprise set off alone. Tony, Val and I looked at each other. "Do we need to use the radio?" I asked just to fill the silence.

It was now dark. We lay out the storm shelter under a willow bush and lay down to sleep as three. "What happens now?" asked Val. "I think we just wait until he comes back," I answered wearily. "I can't believe this. I really don't want to quit." It was a cold, clear night and despite the breeze across our high ridge, we all slept in some way in the shelter of the bushes. It was not until I could see the light of dawn, which crisscrossed with willow branches, that I shook my head and sat up. "Let's go guys," I said as I reached over to shake Val and Tony. A hundred yards away we found Tom wrapped in a space blanket beneath another bush. Tony bravely said, " Come on Tom, time to go," as if nothing had happened. Tom stuffed his gear away and we set off across high rocky ground toward the col between Cerro Confluencia and Cerro Lago. In the light of day, we crossed the pass and descended into the forest on the far side. Tom and Valerie were both talking about quitting at Camp 1 in the valley below. I was resigned to it. Joined by a Finnish team and the remains of the Kiwis again, we fought our way along the poor trail until we reached the final descent to the valley. Here the trails coalesced and we descended quickly and made our way in silence to Camp 1 on the shore of Lago Gutierrez. Tony and I didn't want to voice our hopes of continuing for fear it would steel the resolve of Tom or Val to quit.

At camp we pulled out our gearboxes and went through the motions of continuing. We had checked in at 16th place so all was not yet lost if we could pull ourselves together. Tony sat with Valerie to persuade her while I retained a sense of normalcy with Tom. He sat on a gearbox eating rice from a plastic bag while I had chunks of corned beef on four-day-old French bread. An hour and a half later, we pulled on our backpacks and headed out. I held my breath until we were out of sight of camp. Nobody had quit. "Good job guys," I said in relief. Dark clouds were building over the hills to the west. As a group of four we headed around the end of the lake and then climbed uphill toward the fixed ropes that led to Col

Agostini and Cerro Catedral. Just ahead of us were the teams of 'East Wind', 'Eco Holland', Italy, and France. Another half-hour was lost as we waited our turn on the ropes. When two ropes did come free, Tom and I scooted up and Tony and Valerie came fast behind us. "This is more like it," I thought. We eyed the growing clouds but optimistically agreed with a mountain guide that it might just be an afternoon storm.

Above the vertical rope ascents, we worked our way up a wide gully on fixed ropes. A light rain began and I was thankful that I had put my jacket on earlier. We were moving well as we ascended into increasing wind and continuing rain. Regardless of one's clothing, a constant rain will find its way in. We were all feeling the cold and damp down our arms and backs as we climbed higher on the mountain. I looked up the long snowfields and dark patches of rock into the approaching dusk. "This could be bad if the wind keeps up," Tony said. "Yeah, I don't want to put any more layers on or they'll all be wet," I added.

On the left appeared the dull orange of a tent. We agreed to take a quick break as the wind was gusting heavily. The tent was already full with the French and Italian teams so we threw our own shelter over us and crouched in the lee of some rocks. With a sleeping pad on our backs as insulation and the bottom of the shelter sealed against the ground, the temperature began to rise in our little nylon cell. But any rise in temperature from our huddle was soon negated by the chill that seeped into our damp and now stationary bodies. As the gusting wind hit us, it forced a cold draft through unseen gaps in the rocks beneath us. We were going to survive all right but how ready would we be to race on? After a while, Tom investigated the orange tent and found it crowded but warm. Valerie opted to head in there, stripped out of her wet clothes and dashed into the tent. Tom followed. Tony and I were now reduced to two sets of body heat against the elements. We put a space blanket over our heads and settled in. Pulling the shelter tight around our feet to keep out the drafts, I discovered that it was now snowing. "Good Scottish weather," I said and began to relate climbing stories to Tony. The wind and snow continued.

Presently a climbing guide, Tom Marshall, arrived with another tent. Now he needed help to erect it. I slid out and braved the wind to hold poles and nylon tight against the howling storm. After a few abortive attempts, we got the poles in some semblance of the correct arrangement and had the tent up. I dove in to hold it down. Tony joined me and soon Tom Marshall crawled in with his big sleeping bag. I went out to retrieve the packs and secure our gear against the wind. I wanted my boots and jacket close at hand during a storm like this. Valerie came across from the crowded orange tent and we zipped the door for the final time. We sat with the wind roaring like a locomotive on the high ridges until it sought us out and then with the wild flapping of tent fabric, pushed the roof down to our faces.

"Wow, this is a good one," I said for the fifth time to Val and Tony. Tom Marshall, the mountain guide, hadn't cracked a smile for a long time, confirming the severity of the situation. I was wedged between Tom Marshall and his big sleeping bag and Valerie and Tony squeezed double into their bag. Our second team bag was in the big tent with Tom and eight other people.

We spent the night dozing, listening to the roar of the wind, the flapping of torn tent fabric, and the intermittent static-filled transmissions on the radio. Morning came with no improvement. Scott Flavelle (the climbing leader) asked on the radio, "What's it look like outside the tent?" Tom Marshall replied, "We'll go out and look when we get a break in the wind." Half an hour later Scott called back to find the answer. "Well Scott," Tom said unemotionally, "we haven't been able to get out yet—the wind won't stop." Two inches of snow were on the ground with many feet more blown into crevices and behind rocks. "Should we go up, down, or stay put?" we wondered. By early afternoon the wind began to abate. We forced our feet into frozen socks and boots and headed up as three teams behind Tom the guide. We had been in the tents for 14 hours. We traversed steep, rough rock and snow to the location of CP 9 only to find that it had been literally blown away and they had relocated it to Refugio Frey in the valley below. We followed a circuitous trail we made for the Refugio, thereby missing the traverse of Cathedral Ridge and CP 10, which we would now never reach. It was still windy and cold and nothing had begun to melt. The Refugio was an oasis of warmth; we ate soup and regrouped. It was four

hours to the next hut. "Let's go. We can make it by dark," I said. We could not catch the teams ahead of us that had visited CP 10, but we could keep moving and stay ahead of the teams behind that would be coming around the base of the mountains since the ropes and the high route were closed behind us by race management.

The route over low passes and lightly vegetated valleys was covered with snow. The recent roller coaster in our team fortunes, the rigors of the storm, the luxury of the Refugio; after all of this, the joy of being on the move again in beautiful surroundings was a relief. The route wound through woods where every bough was outlined with a white highlight. From the top of the last pass we could look down to where Refugio Jacob beckoned from its perch by the Lake. "Half an hour till we are warm again," said Valerie. "We'll make it by dark," I added. The successful crossing from Refugio Frey to Jacob had refocused our thoughts on the race instead of just survival. We ate spaghetti and slept for four hours before heading into the crisp night in search of the path to the next CP, the canoe resupply. The bitter cold of this night could have been easily countered with fresh, dry clothes. As it was, with wet shoes, socks and damp layers, we needed our physical efforts to keep the cold at bay. By the light of our headlights, we followed the intermittent trail to the summit of 'Paso Peligro' and then descended an icy trail, which led us down into the forest. With dawn, finding the route became easier and we briskly descended to the trails around the head of Lago Mascardi.

It was a bright and warm mid-morning when we arrived at the canoe resupply, CP 11. Teams that had headed around the lowland route while we were stuck in the storm were already strewn around the camp. Some had obviously pushed through the cold night without sleep and then spent several hours here recovering from their efforts. "Let's keep moving and use the good weather," we agreed. Working as fast as our tired selves would allow, we donned wetsuits and dry suits, ate pate and sardine sandwiches and pulled out the required gear for the next leg—whitewater canoeing followed by another mountain trek. Chastened by the storm we chose to take the 'real' tent instead of the storm shelter. Along with the rest of our mandatory gear, climbing equipment, and food, we paddled two heavily laden blue canoes away from shore. Our self-bailing inflatable sat so low that two inches of water was a permanent feature of the floor. This made for an extra heavy and un-maneuverable boat. We performed a few 360-degree circles before Tom and I got the hang of paddling the flat-bottom whitewater boats on the lake. Tom would paddle mainly on the left while I used every other stroke as a rudder stroke.

The 12 kilometers of Lago Mascardi passed swiftly and we turned the nose of our boats into the Rio Manso. A simple rapid led us into the small Lago Moscos before we hit the river proper. In the cold water we could see every rock on the riverbed ten feet below. We swung into the eddy that was CP 12. While I wrestled with my dry suit in order to relieve myself, Tony received instructions on the upcoming rapids. "Pull around the corner and then eddy left to the river guide's camp. They will show you where to scout the rapid." We pulled our thigh straps tight and paddled around the corner. Tony and Val paddled on. "Weren't we meant to stop here somewhere," Tom shouted from the front of the boat. "I guess they know what they're doing, we'll just follow," I shouted back, over the noise of the river. Suddenly Tony and Val and their boat disappeared. "This must be it," yelled Tom. I steadied the boat toward the center of the gap ahead and we paddled hard. The front of the boat dipped momentarily over the descending chute of water and then rose over a high wave of white.

The pounding current behind landed on the loaded rear of the canoe and stood the boat upright. I briefly wondered why I was looking at the sky. I hung on to the paddle as I continued downstream alone and without a boat and then calmly reached for the perfectly thrown rope that landed just ahead of me across the water. Contentedly hugging the rope to my shoulder, I let the current swing me to shore. I stood up, warm and reasonably dry in my dry suit, to the cheers of the assembled crowd of onlookers. "You are number one," accompanied a thumbs up from one sightseer. Tom valiantly paddled the boat back from the far side of the river where he had washed up. It took him three attempts before he could get back across the churning stream. Tom and I flipped twice more on the descent of the

rapids before caution saw us take a short portage around the last big white water. Not to worry though, I had already capsized in these rapid several years before! Moments later the roar of whitewater was gone and we were two boats on a peaceful river.

As soon as we paddled into Lago Hess, I declared, "OK guys, no more downhill water on the whole rest of the course. We are done." We paddled giddily across Lago Hess and found the entrance to the river up which we would paddle to Lago Fonck. The river silt had built a delta out into the lake so we entered between the low banks of the dark river directly from the center of the lake. Reeds hemmed the stream and tall trees canopied overhead. The water showed no discernible current. The evening light was reflected perfectly in the crystal river so the division between the brushy bank and its reflection in the still waters could not be easily seen. The gentle dipping of paddles was the only sound. Presently the river became shallow and the current increased. We paddled more diligently. As the sandbanks rose to meet us, we stepped out to pull the boats upstream. With every meander of the river, the deep slow pools got smaller and the shallows with their currents became more prevalent. As long as we could make progress towing the boats upriver, we would stay in the stream and not portage. I ran ahead to scout for rapids and soon reached the lake. "I have seen the lake and she is beautiful," I yelled as I returned. Tom and Tony manhandled the boats up the last rocky rapids to the docile channel leading into the lake. "We're through, great job," we said in congratulations to ourselves.

Dusk was already on its way. The days go so fast. In the last of the light, we turned onto the lake proper and spied a distant twinkle. It was the CP, still seven kilometers away across the lake. The cold weather bought by the storm was still with us and we endured a chilling paddle across the lake. On arrival at the CP, Tom and Valerie got the tent up while Tony and I cleared the gear from the boats and made ready for the next section. Team 'Stray Dogs' was right beside us, changing out of paddling gear. They had only a tent with no poles so they expected a cold uncomfortable night, compared to my hopes of a good warm rest in our tent. We crammed the whitewater gear into mesh bags, put on dry clothes, and repacked our backpacks from the dry bags we had used in the boats. Frost was forming on the pile of gear even before we crawled into the tent.

Our predawn departure managed to be delayed until dawn. "It is not worth heading into the bamboo in the dark—team 'Vail' took ten hours," was the dread-filled warning that slowed us. It was true that one had to find the only trail, and that progress without it would be interminably slow. We followed the freshly cut trail through some confused clearings and then upward steeply, exiting after a couple of hours onto an open ridge into the sunshine. We moved together with 'Stray Dogs' and 'Finland', enjoying the companionship of each other's teammates. We skirted the high point of the ridge and headed for a band of rocks up which lay a yellow handline. Each of us made the steep 20-ft. climb and then followed snowfields to CP 14, "Volcanico Ridge". The glaciated peak of Tronador, our next major challenge, stood large on the horizon.

To the east, a perfectly symmetrical volcanic cone rose through the clouds in Chile. Below us, the rocky ridge descended to a uniform sea of green—the bamboo forest. We headed down, aiming toward an unseen lake hidden in the forest. Tom led and I kept track of our course on the compass. Peering through the brush ahead of us, we followed lines of least resistance and occasional clearings until we stood looking down on the lake. We skirted the east end, crossed the outlet stream and contoured in thick bamboo forest. Tom plunged ahead keeping the stream valley, in which the next CP would be found, to the right. Our little column of eight, from the combination of 'Stray Dogs' and 'Adventure One', wound along in his footsteps. The steep terrain and tangle of brush made the river valley itself most uninviting. Even on the upper flanks of the valley the bamboo was thick and scattered with fallen trees. Downed trunks lay randomly, seemingly always at a height that could not be ducked under or easily climbed over. Occasionally, a large tree would lie in a convenient direction and provide a few seconds of fast but slippery progress. Thorns and splinters made their way through our gloves and tights. Shins were battered by wayward pieces of the tough bamboo that lay crossways to trip us. When we felt that we had gone far enough to descend to the CP in the streambed, we were treated to a muddy descent, grabbing at branches and bamboo to stop ourselves from careening down the steep hillside. We came out in the stream just a little early for the CP, but right on schedule to see 'East Wind' and the Finns crashing down the streambed.

From CP 15 a series of spectacular rappels took us down three tiers of cliffs to the valley below. The final overhanging descent dropped us into a small knot of cheering spectators. Once on the ground, I paused to check that I had indeed retrieved the race passport from the CP worker at the top of the rappels. I couldn't find it. I looked up to see my team disappearing down the trail. "Wait guys!" I yelled. They left. I ran after them only to find a trail junction at which someone said, "They went that way," pointing left when we should have gone right to Camp 2. Swearing under my breath, I ran up the trail until I caught up to a team—a French Team who were correctly heading out after having visited Camp 2. "No, your team went the right way," they said. I ran back down until I finally caught up. Out of breath I blurted, "You guys could have waited, I think I left the passport at the last CP." Agonizing over the lost passport, I endured a miserable and silent hike into Camp 2 at Pampa Linda.

Once at the camp I found the passport not in its rightful place, but in the back of the top pocket of my backpack. The sun came out and I took my shoes off and stretched my toes in the green grass of the field. Things were looking up again. From out of the team gearbox came the bread, cheese and tuna. As we each ate and checked our feet, we went through the gear list for the next leg. Axe, crampons, and more food were added to the gear that had just come out of our packs. Tom carried lots. I added the climbing rope to my pile. Tony stared at Valerie's climbing gear, not volunteering to take it. "Are you OK Tony?" I asked. "Yeah," he replied. "So, without stating the obvious," I said, "Tom and I have all the team gear, you have to take Valerie's, yes?"

We headed out as soon as we could. Tom loaded up on food to eat as we hiked away from camp. Gnocchi and baked potatoes swung in plastic bags from the back of his already heavy pack. Just out of camp a breathless Marshal Ullrich from 'Stray

Dogs' caught us. "We're going to stick with you, is that OK?" Our teams had spent many years racing with and against each other in endurance races. Louise, Ike, Mark and Marshal were good company and if they could stick with us, we would enjoy their company. A good trail led up the valley toward Paso Vuriloche and on across the border into Chile. Tom's bag of potatoes swung on his back as we headed up, but none of us had the appetite yet to eat them. At the top of the valley we crossed the col and entered Chile. Stopping to add clothes, as dusk came once again, Tom and Tony argued. We hurried to find the 'wide meadow' mentioned in the route instructions before it got dark. The meadow was marshy and crisscrossed with streams, validating our decision to put on our mandatory light shoes, in order to keep the mountaineering boots dry for the glacier ahead.

The dark line of the forest on the other side of the meadow hid the trail to a hut, which was CP 17. We found an enclosure and then a distant glow stick and smelled the wood fire that the CP workers kept burning. We eagerly crouched by the fire as we checked in and decided on the night's strategy. "It will be so cold up high that we should stop here a few hours," we agreed. Tom sat apart from the group, still pouting from the argument earlier. Tony and Valerie didn't want to chance annoying Tom anymore so they settled by the fire to rest. I asked Tom to put up the tent and crawled in for a warm sleep under the edge of a shared sleeping bag. At 3 AM Tony woke us. Everyone was moving slowly in the frosty morning, putting on boots and trying to eat.

We set off up the trail, which in the dark and with an early morning mist was difficult to follow. We made good progress as we all pitched in to search for it in those places where it disappeared in rocky open ground. Dawn found us high on the ridge, well on our way to CP 18 at the foot of Tronador's glaciers. "This may be the last water, let's fill up," I said as we passed a stream that dribbled down some rock slabs. Tony and Valerie produced one shared bottle between them. It was too late for me to even complain about their lack of water carrying capacity. I had two bottles and Tom had an 80-oz. Ultimate Sport Tank. We drank what we could, even though it was difficult in the cold, as

we knew that there would be no water once on the glaciers. At CP 18 there was a cool wind but the sun was high enough to give us warmth as we put on crampons and laid out the rope for glacier travel. My pack was pleasantly light without the rope or climbing gear—even though the wet shoes hanging off the back continued to mock my otherwise minimalist approach.

'Stray Dogs' and the Finns headed out first but we soon passed them as they rested. Tom played irritatingly on the rope, tugging and pulling it, much to Valerie's and my annoyance. At CP 19, we left our non-essential gear, as it was out and back from that point to the summit of Pico Argentina. We climbed on, the strong sun warming us and keeping us busy applying sunscreen. At the col between Tronador and Pico Argentina we paused to unrope and clipped into fixed lines for the final fun-filled pitches to the summit. As always, sitting on a mountaintop in the light breeze and warm sun made us forget our fatigue for a few minutes. Chilean volcanoes, Argentine lakes, the Rio Manso and distant pampas were all laid out beneath us. We noted the plaque "Herman Clausen, 1939" and then swung down the ropes back to the col. We rushed the descent back to CP 18, where Tom Marshall was a welcome sight. Keen to break from 'Stray Dogs' and the Finns, we hurried on and endured the long tiring descent on sore crampon-clad feet to Otto Meiling Hut, CP 23. At least we were ticking off lots of checkpoints today. We were all ready for a brief break and the chance to eat some 'hut food'—soup and pasta. Except for Tom that is, who sat obstinately outside mumbling about lost minutes. We paid for his fourth plate of food but it sat untouched. Tom chatted to a journalist. Twenty-five minutes later as we roped up he was still talking. He continued as Tony, Val and I stood and quietly fumed. He continued while he slowly set up his climbing gear and onlookers wondered what we were all doing! Satisfied that he had annoyed us enough, he joined our rope and we descended the rocky lip of the ridge, traversed a snow bowl, and glissaded down to dry rock and the end of the glacier. An enjoyable rocky descent down a steep hillside allowed us all to enjoy the freedom of being 'off rope'. Tony was having trouble with a sore shin that had taken a beating in the bamboo. He would have had more sympathy had he shared his troubles with me, rather than waiting for me to pry it grudgingly out of him. CP 24 at 'Paso Las Nubes' was on part of the 'Raid' course that I had raced in 1995. I knew that we now followed a good trail down to CP 25. We moved fast and hit CP 25, the start of the much discussed and hard to find horse trail with plenty of light left. We had separated ourselves from 'Stray Dogs' and the Finns and wanted to keep our lead. Tom looked across the Rio Alerce at the steep bank opposite and surmised that "Horses wouldn't go there." He led us downstream and we searched for a trail. "Eureka, here it is," I said. We headed up.

Climbing the indistinct horse trail we were pulled to the right, a heading that would lead us too high on the ridge and leave us above the large cliffs on the far side. Still, it was preferable to striking through virgin brush. Tom led with his heavy pack, hunting for scraps of trail and breaking brush with impunity. "If I was a horse, which way would I go?" he asked before heading upward. Valerie, Tony and I fought to keep within sight of him. Nearing the top of the climb, we came across a band of low cliffs, presumably the same rock formation that created the large cliffs on the far side. Here they were shattered into a giant's staircase and we ascended to the ridge top hoping for a quick view of the route ahead. It was already dark. We put the tent up and left Tony and Val while Tom and I scouted the terrain ahead, hoping to locate a good trail. "I've got it!" shouted Tom from somewhere off in the darkness below me. He returned to the position

Many miles were endured on foot in the inaugural Elf Authentic Adventure (1999) in the Philippines.

where I waited. "I hope you haven't forgotten the way back to the tent," he said. "Let's get a couple of hours sleep and then go," we agreed. Encouraged by the cold of the high ridge, I slept in every piece of clothing that I had.

Getting up at 2 AM was miserable as I had no clothes to add and all that I wore turned damp and chilling when I crawled out of the humid, crowded tent into the icy fresh air. Tom's trail didn't go far before branching and disappearing into meadows. We descended several times only to come across the cliff tops. Dawn was already in the sky before we had worked our way around the cliffs and were able to descend to the valley floor. In the early morning light, perhaps our last morning of the race, we picked up the pace. Open forest led us to the trail around Lago Huaca and down to the rudely hidden CP 26. We arrived through the thick brush protecting the checkpoint in tandem with the French team, with whom we had spent the night so long ago in the storm. The French donned their climbing gear for the next set of rappels and left before us. We followed them down to the long low angle slabs where the ropes were strung. Dragging the 11mm rope through the ATC (rappel device) was hard work. Reaching the bottom beside a small ice cave, we removed our climbing harnesses and packed them away in our already full backpacks. "There is not much left to do guys—just three more kilometers on foot and some paddling," I declared.

We hurried down to the lake in time to see the French already paddling away. We pumped up two of the inflatable canoes and threw our packs in as seats. Halfway across the lake I realized that my pack was sitting face down in three inches of water and its contents, including my personal passport, were getting soaked and heavy. I stopped paddling and with a precarious maneuver rearranged the paperwork to the top of the pile. We paddled around the curve at the end of the lake and beached, just as the French finished rolling up their deflated canoes. "They have ten minutes on us. Are they going to beat us?" I wondered.

We followed instructions and found a good trail. There was just three kilometers to hike down to the end of a long arm of Lago Nahuel Huapi, the huge lake on which we had begun the event seven days before. Once there, we would paddle kayaks for 15 kilometers to the finish line. Halfway down, the trail emptied onto wide granite slabs in the riverbed and followed them for awhile. As we got out into the open, we looked ahead to see any sign of the French—nothing. I turned to check the view and saw 200 yards behind the French slowly working their way down the boulder-filled riverbed. They had missed the trail. Tony, Val and I ducked back into the woods on the trail hoping that the French had not noticed us. Meanwhile Tom sat on the edge of the slabs and waited for the French team. The good trail continued and led us to the beach where 70 yellow kayaks lay waiting in hope for their teams to arrive. "At least we are not last—look at all these boats!" I shouted to Val. Tony and Val and the French team stuffed their gear into and onto the kayaks and set off into calm waters and a light breeze. Tom fiddled with his gear and we pushed off a 1/4-mile behind the others. "Two hours to the finish," we had been told. Tom paddled hard and as we approached Tony and Valerie he declared, "we are going to blow by them." And we did.

As we pulled ahead, I relaxed my stroke while Tom pushed to more frantic efforts. "I want to beat them, keep paddling," he urged. "Tom, we need to stay close," I said. Even during the wide exposed crossing of the 'Brazo de La Tristeza', Tom refused to slow down to stay close to Tony and Val.

The headwind and waves grew during our crossing but we were soon hugging the south shore and sheltered from the headwind. Huge rock slabs descended steeply into the cold, clear water. Waterfalls jumped from ledge to ledge. A small inlet hid a rocky beach and we pulled the boat on shore, while I put on a paddling jacket. My lack of paddling effort had left me chilled! I took my time so that Valerie and Tony were right behind us again as we pushed off. Tom paddled hard, I took it easy and Val and Tony were able to stay in touch. To distract Tom from my delaying tactics, I pointed out rock formations and asked nutritional questions on his habit of devouring packets of GU every 15 minutes. Perhaps he just had a sugar high! With the shore just 30 feet away I was no longer in fear of a long swim but I did wonder if Tom might beach us and run off. Ahead I could see the steeply descending ridgeline below, which lay the low wooded peninsula Llao Llao that hid Bahia Lopez and the finish.

We turned the final point and across a small-enclosed bay could see the beach, the finish line and the scattered dots that were the welcoming crowd. Tom dug even harder to try to reach the banner well before Tony and Val. I let him pull us forward for now. As we got within 50 yards of the beach and the finish, I leaned on my paddle and pushed the rudder hard around. Tom flailed forward, as I backstroked. We churned water until Tony and Val caught up. Then we sheepishly stroked for shore, thumbs up, crossing the finish line as four.

WHY DO WE DO THIS?

Let me tell you why we do this. You feel the wind on your skin. You smell the granite. You become part of nature again. You live by your wits, you work hard, you sleep when you have to, and you eat when you can. For a few days you live life the way it should be lived. No guilt, no fear, no second guesses.

Adrian Crane and his teammates Tony Molina, Valerie Molina and Tom Possert competed in the 1999 Eco-Challenge adventure race held in Patagonia, Argentina. After seven days, they completed the race in 16th place out of a field of 52 teams from 33 countries.

A NEW SPORT FOR A NEW AGE

Proper navigation is a crucial link to adventure racing success.

Adventure racing is a multi-discipline sport that requires individual will, endurance, survival skills, outdoor savvy, and teamwork. The ultimate challenge is the ability to withstand adversity in unfamiliar conditions on a course that is predominantly wilderness.

The most common team is a foursome comprised of both men and women, whose goal is to cross the finish line as one unit. However, soloists, duos, and teams of three are becoming more prevalent in races and the Raid Gauloises continues the tradition of a five-member racing crew with two willing souls for support. The team is successful if it visits a series of checkpoints in the proper order from start to finish and remains intact throughout the contest. If one member of a team is not able to complete an event, the entire team is affected. In order for the team to finish together, each individual member must be able to conquer the course. But, if one member suffers, the fate of the team is determined by the cohesiveness and team dynamics of the group.

Odyssey Adventure Racing introduced the solo category to U.S. races, taking away the team aspect of the sport by adding a whole new element of self-sufficiency and courage. In addition, teams can enter as a twosome or foursome to conquer the one, two, and expedition-length races Odyssey offers.

Adventure races are loosely staged. In order to finish a race, teams must pass through consecutive checkpoints at various locations on the course between the start and the finish lines. There are usually several routes between one checkpoint and another, and teams must strategize their best route. This means that teams must understand their individual and team strengths and weaknesses when designing the most effective plan for progress.

In some races, support crews provide valuable assistance that further enhances the team's destiny. The

THE COMPLETE GUIDE TO ADVENTURE RACING

assistants have their own motorized transportation, which allows them to arrive at areas of transition ahead of the field of racers. Their mission is to set up camp and prepare hot meals and fresh gear for their team.

Although a support crew is a crucial link to the team's success, it is not a requirement of an adventure race. In some expedition-style races, where a hand-picked crew of support is not an option, each team prepares their necessary gear for the race and packs it up in sturdy tubs which are transported by race officials to key locations along the course. Sometimes, however, even this luxury is not an option so you are forced to carry all of your food with you, and find all of your water (and maybe some food) along the route.

The traditional disciplines that make up an adventure race include mountain biking, extreme hiking, paddling, ascending and descending with the use of climbing equipment, and navigation. Beyond the staple modes of human-powered transportation, the possibilities are endless depending on the inspiration of the race director and the terrain of the course.

The duration of adventure races thus far varies from one-day sprints to two-week expeditions requiring both day and night navigation through harsh and challenging landscape. A successful contender is versed in a variety of sports, has internal drive coupled with team spirit, and is self-sufficient.

A large appeal of this sport is the profile of the adventurer. It is voluminous, encompassing anyone with drive and an adventurous spirit! Physical fitness and proficiency in a spectrum of outdoor sports provide the necessary nuts and bolts. Beyond the external factors, however, the internal resume is vast.

SELF-DISCOVERY UPON A VARIETY OF EXTERNAL INFLUENCES

EFFICIENCY

Are you a quick, keen decision-maker? Can you think on your feet? Are you organized and efficient? These details will enhance your experience if your answer is "yes". If organization is not one of your better qualities, "do or disqualify" becomes an appropriate theme. If efficiency has not been a part of your vocabulary, you will learn to respect it and enjoy the benefits it employs.

DISCOMFORT

Perhaps one of the most profound aspects of an adventure race is the discomfort it breeds. When you are out on a course, particularly for more than one night, your level of discomfort escalates as the hours trickle by. The dirt and sweat you accumulate magnify the cold hard fact that you are living outdoors. A bed of soft earth and maybe a cozy wall of boulders define your sleeping conditions. Your blankets are made from Mylar and plastic and oftentimes, your teammates. And, you can't control the temperature to your preferred degree. Furthermore, your usual eight hours of sleep are often reduced to three or less in each 24-hour period.

You are constantly eating on the run. Your energy output constantly tests your input. A typical "meal" might consist of jerky, trail mix, and Oreos. Eating becomes a necessity rather than a luxury. Meals are no longer a choice or a social endeavor, but a means of survival.

How much discomfort can you tolerate? How comfortable can you be in your own skin when your own skin doesn't want to stick around? To succeed, you must be able to endure tremendous distress. The fluffy

Careful decision-making will enhance your journey.

life you know at home is funneled into basic survival, the fundamentals of existence. In a nutshell, the racers who possess a high tolerance for pain and discomfort and are still able to perform at a high intensity become the victors.

Your treks through the wilderness take their toll on your feet, and when you finally get to sit down, you still have to exert effort. Your raw, colorful body parts become swollen and tender as a constant reminder of your immediate reality. Instead of catering to your wounds in the comforts of home, you are forced to test the upper limits of misery. Just how far do you think you can go?

Your tolerance becomes a blend of physical charity, mental stamina, and emotional stability. This is what adventure is truly about. Are you willing to abandon your normal living conditions for a chance to explore the depths of your true character? That's what racing really conjures.

DEPRIVATION

Did you ever pull an "all-nighter" in college in preparation for a grueling final exam, or to hone your partying skills? What was your performance like the following day? Have you ever been so tired that you began to hallucinate? Do you know what happens when you become sleep deprived? Cognitive thought processes progressively dwindle, memory escapes us, and hallucinations entertain our existence. Physically, our coordination suffers and strength and aerobic power are sacrificed. Sleep is essential if we want to encourage normal brain maintenance and regeneration and maintain hard-earned physical growth. But for the duration of an adventure race, sleep is merely a means to avoid complete physical and mental bankruptcy.

Do you know what it feels like to be dehydrated? Hypoglycemic? You will probably experience one or more of these situations in an adventure race.

ADAPTATION

At first glance, many of the variables you encounter as an adventure racer seem harsh and crude. But once you assimilate these factors, you develop invincibility to trivial things. Your ability to adapt improves. This characteristic enhances your racing prowess. An adventure race encompasses unforeseen challenges around every corner. Adaptation is paramount to survival.

These qualities are adopted over time and experience. If you are unsure of how you rate, never fear, the moment you step out into the racecourse, you will know. And for better or worse, you will understand. You will experience yourself in a raw and pure state, one that will not only shape your race, but also shape your own person.

Isaac Wilson and Robert Nagle claimed first place at the Beast of the East (1999) in Virginia crossing the finish line after 3 days, 5 hours, and 24 minutes of racing.

Participating teams covered nearly 350 miles of punishing terrain.

THE COMPLETE GUIDE TO ADVENTURE RACING

ADVENTURE RACING REWOUND

The history of adventure racing encompasses many paths. Adventure in itself has carved its own place in this world from the very beginning. The difference between then and now is the luxury of choice. In centuries past, adventure was written into survival, into daily existence. Tribes were wandering hunters and gatherers whose driving force was prolonged subsistence. Today, we are wandering hunters in search of a greater understanding of ourselves, each other, and the world that surrounds us. Today, we not only choose to be adventurous, we choose our adventures. We shell out the necessary dough, train and prepare, and then discover if we have what it takes to endure a quest of inner dimensions through external means.

Adventure racing sprouted from multi-sport races. In 1978, twelve athletes tested their physical prowess in the premiere Ironman triathlon. This all-day event stemmed from an argument over which athletic feat was the toughest—the Waikiki Rough Water Swim, the Around Oahu Bike Ride, or the Honolulu Marathon across the great island landscape.

The following year, New Zealand stepped up to the plate and the Alpine Ironman was born. Conceived in 1980 by Robin Judkins, the arduous race included skiing, mountain running, and white-water kayaking. In 1983, Judkins outdid himself by creating the Coast to Coast, a rugged tour of the South Island, which commenced on the Tasman Sea and finished on the Pacific Ocean. Competitors kayaked through white-water, road cycled, and ran through mountains to complete the course. This race first introduced an overnight race experience in the wilderness spanning two days, thus manifesting the infancy of the sport of adventure racing. In addition, the team concept was attached.

Multi-sport as a competition in New Zealand was a natural progression for the Kiwis. Therefore, it is no coincidence that the roots of adventure racing are imbedded in the country's history. As the sport became more appealing, Geoff Hunt, a committed racer himself, established the Southern Traverse, which like the Beast, has become a favorite among racers because of the authentic experience. Authentic because the race is designed by a racer for racers.

Simultaneously, the Alaska Wilderness Challenge tested the fitness of adventure enthusiasts in the Northern Hemisphere. The races began in 1983 and were void of the frills common in most races today. In this no-nonsense approach, each contender receives a map and a pat on the back along with a wish of good luck. Additionally, the topography of Alaska caters to the adventurer as Iditasport (a generic term for human-powered treks to Alaska's distant places, both in winter and summer) offers myriad adventurous competitions.

Intrigued by adventure, a French journalist named Gerard Fusil conjured his version of a multi-sport, multi-day odyssey in 1989 and titled it the Raid Gauloises. His terms called for five-person teams of mixed gender (at least one team member had to be female) who must start and finish his race as one unit. The race would last for several days, encompassing hundreds of miles of rugged landscape in a specific order that would be marked by checkpoints. Because of the Raid, adventure racing has made a solid mark in the world of sport and adventure and many credit Fusil as the "father" of this remarkable new contest.

GERARD FUSIL: THE FATHER OF ADVENTURE RACING

A journalist since 1968 and a radio specialist, Frenchman Gerard Fusil has also worked for the daily written press, magazines, and French television.

A distinguished reporter, he has dealt with economy, politics, and news items. He has written articles on war and sports (the Olympic Games, international tennis tournaments, the America Cup, sailing, twelve Paris-Dakar car rallies, six circuit exploration trips, three Camel Trophies, a Paris-Peking, several mountain races, and more).

Fusil has also participated in many multi-hull and single-hull races, and has crossed the Atlantic three times racing, breaking the record for crossing the Atlantic in 1981. He was one of the three-team members of Marc Pajot on the Elf-Aquitaine catamaran to cross the Atlantic in 9 days and 10 hours.

In 1987, Fusil came up with the idea of a major sport-nature adventure. Two years later, he organized the first Raid Gauloises.

He managed the organization until 1997, making this race the reference for sport-nature events throughout the following destinations: New Zealand, Costa Rica, New Caledonia, Sultanate of Oman, Madagascar, Malaysia, Argentina, South Africa, and Lesotho.

In parallel, he led incentive operations for companies and maintained occasional activity as a journalist.

He has acquired an international reputation in the world of adventure, as demonstrated by the numerous press articles and television and radio reports.

Fusil set himself the challenge to greet the year 2000 with the concept of an adventure race, which combines the great ideas of our times.

In 1998, Fusil developed a new concept of nature-adventure sport in total independence. Together with

his partner, the French company Elf Aquitaine, he organized the first edition of the Elf Authentique Adventure in April 1999 in the Philippines.

GERARD FUSIL, IN HIS OWN WORDS...

I have been a journalist since 1968 after being a journalism student in the best French journalism school in Paris, the "Centre, de Formation des Journalistes". I spent four years working for general information in daily newspapers as a rewriter, then two years for French TV, and then for the best French radio for information at the time, "Europe 1".

At the beginning, I was mainly working on economy and social affairs. Two years later, my dream came true when I became a "Grand Reporter". This denomination does not exist in the United States but in France that means you are the journalist sent to cover various and important events. You must be able to tell the true story while making it interesting for the listeners.

So, I have worked on a lot of events: crimes, wars, strikes, popular tennis tournaments (Flushing Meadows), and also the Tour de France.

One day, my editor asked me to cross the Atlantic with a professional sport crew on a large American sailing boat named "Ondine" to try to beat the record of the "Atlantic" between New York and Cape Lizard, the southern point of Great Britain. The job was to report and to be able to help. As I was myself a keen sportsman, I did it with enthusiasm. I became a friend of Marc Pajot, the French Olympic champion who later became the French skipper for America's Cup.

In 1981, I was one of the three members of his crew when we beat the famous record on a catamaran named "Elf Aquitaine". It had been huge in France and I was considered an adventurer! After that, I was the specialist for the big sailing events, for the Paris-Dakar race (the founder Thierry

Sabiene became my best friend), and for mountain events.

In 1987, I was at Cape Horn to report on a single-handed race around the world, the BOC Challenge. It was there that I got the idea to organize an adventure competition for people who would use only physical and mental strength and no mechanics. The idea was to do it in Terra de Fuego and let people progress like the Indian Patagons living there a few centuries ago.

Back to France, I wrote the idea, worked on the rules of the competition, and finally found a sponsor. I did the first reco-trip in November 1988 organizing it in south New Zealand. After that, I created my company, Gerard Fusil Management, and the sponsors signed with me, along with Patrick Brignoli, for financial aspects. Nelly Fusil, who was my wife and excellent at press relations, was in charge of communications.

I organized the Raid Gauloises until 1997 and continued to work as a journalist for Europe, and sometimes for French magazines and television ...too much. Finally, after a successful event in South Africa, we agreed to follow different roads.

In 1998, I signed a contract with the biggest French Company, Elf Aquitaine, to create a new event—The Elf Authentic Adventure. The concept of this new passion is total autonomy in the expedition and its preparation, more exchange with the people of the country, and a competition with the formula to bring fantastic competition to the best ones and a beautiful adventure for the beginners if they have real adventure spirit.

—Gerard Fusil

WHAT A JOURNEY!

Just 11 years ago, in the spring of 1989, we were in New Zealand, in the middle of nowhere, giving the final touches to the first Raid Gauloises. We already knew the disciplines; we already had 25 registered teams ready to follow us into a new adventure.

"Well, the starting line will be here, in between these huge mountains and the arrival will be there, along this lake, just in front of a tiny café." We were at the polar opposite of Paris, our home. Imagine driving a gigantic needle through Paris and into the Earth, and you would find, at the other end, the starting point of the event. All these images come back to me as if it had all taken place yesterday.

We were a group of crazy French people: Patrick Brignoli of Raid Gauloises Organization, Alain Gaimard of Arc Adventures, and the Fusil family. Our idea was to bring people back to a simpler life, to get them out of the cities and civilization, and to get them out of their routine.

The concept was, and remains to this day, very simple: a starting line, an arrival, and in between a progression in the wilderness with non-mechanical mediums (raft, canoes, horses, etc.) and with the only help of some maps, a compass, and a Raid-Book. To make the event a little more difficult, we built the concept around a team of five people; and to make the picture a little more glamorous, we asked for at least one woman per team.

In our minds, it was all about discovery and respect: discovery of another country and civilization, discovery of oneself and others; respect of nature and of others. Solidarity, pleasure, and joy were also part of the state of mind.

The event was not based solely on physical strength, but also (I would say at least 50%) on mental endurance and intelligence. The ranking was not the Bible because the event was not merely a race, but rather an expedition and a competition against oneself. To participate was the achievement. All along these years, I have had the same respect for the first and the last team, because maybe the most important thing is to manage to cross the starting line. It takes a lot of effort to raise a sponsorship, to train, to be mentally ready to compete, and to commit to a team.

All the values of the first Raid Gauloises remain.

At the beginning, it was not easy for us to make people understand the concept. I remember spending my vacation in Los Angeles talking about the Raid, this new event. People looked at me with big, round eyes: "What the hell is she talking about?"

The first American team joined the race in 1992. Now, a new competition inspired by The Raid Gauloises comes out of the blue almost every day. I am amazed. If you had told me this would happen when I was in the middle of nowhere 11 years ago, I would certainly not have believed it.

In the spring of 2000, we celebrated the 10th Anniversary of the Raid Gauloises. We brought people from all around the world to two magical places: Nepal and Tibet.

We will continue to do it in the same spirit; a spirit of physical and mental challenge; a spirit which is not much different from the one we know from daily life.

Were we so crazy? Finally, probably not.

What a beautiful journey it has been.

—*Nelly Fusil-Martin*

Once the Raid Gauloises was announced, twenty-seven teams accepted the challenge of the inaugural race held in New Zealand, sprouting a fierce addiction to an intriguing new sport. The passion, however, was initially confined to European enthusiasts until the word got out through a series of articles in the *Los Angles Times* about the 1990 Raid in Costa Rica. Staff writer John Markman was invited to compete on a team of journalists. His accounts, which began on February 21, 1991, captured the spirits of many thrill-seekers.

One in particular was an entrepreneur named Mark Burnett. The article became a catalyst for Burnett, an ambitious adventurer, who consequently flexed his creativity and gave rise to the Eco-Challenge. After competing in the Raid Gauloises as a member of team 'American Pride', Burnett produced the first Eco-Challenge in Utah in 1995. His reigning theme has always been health, the environment, and the quest for experiences avant-garde. In 1996, his race traversed the wild landscape of British Columbia and in 1997, the Discovery Channel embraced his race and televised a two-part, four-hour documentary of the annual challenge in Australia (1997), to Morocco (1998), and Patagonia (1999). The impact of television catapulted the popularity of the Eco-Challenge and introduced the sport to thousands and millions of viewers.

Today, adventure racing has established its place in the world of sport and adventure. It is firmly planted in a world that continues to change its face and character. Fusil's idea has evolved to a distinct new odyssey that incorporates humanitarian projects and cultural appreciation in an expedition of total independence. He calls it "The Elf Authentic Adventure". Along with greater immersion in the host country, competitors have total autonomy from the moment they commit to the second they cross the finish line. Co-ed teams of seven, four who race and three who support, have the luxury of three categories in which to race—extreme, adventure, or discovery. These categories reflect the abilities and spirit of each team.

Robert Nagle claims the coveted first-place trophy for the Raid Gauloises.

JOURNEY INTO THE UNKNOWN

Every month, new races are taking shape across North America and around the globe. In 1999, approximately 80 races were produced in the United States. In the year 2000, over 300 took place and the calendar of events continues to grow!

The sport continues to expand from continent to continent. There is certainly a worldwide passion for conquering the unknown. Now, the questions remain: "In what direction is this sport heading?" and "What is the fate of adventure racing?" As we navigate our way toward another day, another month, and another year, we are sure to discover clues to the destiny of adventure racing.

A profound intrigue of adventure racing is its embodiment of the unknown. For many of us, the ambiguity of the unknown is at once both frightening and exciting. The mystery of the race unravels as you progress along the course. Your inner workings are thrust to the surface in bare exposure to your team and even more strikingly, to yourself.

To further stir things up, the actual race course is not revealed until the pre-race briefing, which is held one to several days ahead of an expedition-style race and usually a few hours before a one or two-day race. Prior to arrival at the race start, you spend hours, days and months in preparation for your competitive trek. You learn what to prepare for and polish the skills of the team as a whole. However, you won't know what

exactly, or how exactly your efforts will be tested until you reach the site of the race.

Most adventure races embrace the traditional outdoor disciplines of trekking, mountain biking, paddling one or more of a variety of watercrafts, and ascending and descending a ropes course, each of which we have devoted an entire chapter to in this book. Finding your way around with a map and compass is rudimentary to adventure racing and we explore the art of navigation in Chapter 3. We have collected racing tips and stories from talented adventure racers across the world. Their experiences will become yours as you mentally digest each page of this book. We have also provided a discussion on training, perhaps the most important aspect of adventure racing. Nutrition and health, equally important topics, are explored and tips on adventure racing schools, finding a sponsor, and teamwork are given. And because support crews are integral to racing success, we have devoted a chapter to them as well.

Dave Zeitsma reveals the course of his (2000) Raid—The North Extreme.

However, in no way have we said it all. There are bookshelves full of information on mountain biking alone. The same goes for kayaking, hiking, and mountaineering. Likewise, exercise science is a vast subject that requires many lifetimes of study to truly understand human performance. We have made it our priority, however, to scratch a hearty surface and to provide you with a good understanding of each subject presented, while providing significant insight into the gripping new sport of adventure racing.

Beyond the traditional disciplines of human-powered transportation, your fate is in the creative hands of the director of your race. A good director will always throw challenging surprises into a race. Adventure racers have united with camels in the first leg of the 1998 Eco-Challenge in Morocco and jumped out of DC-3 aircrafts onto the arid plain of Madagascar in the 1993 Raid Gauloises. In-line skating has become a relatively popular mode of travel and so has riverboarding (bodysurfing white-water with a cutout surfboard). Spelunking (cave exploration) has been a part of many jungle races, and in the mountains, you could be glis-

sading (sometimes on your backside for many feet), hauling a mountain bike through snowfields, or picking your way up a peak with an ice ax. Anything goes! And you can be sure it will in this sport.

Beyond the scope of this book lies a vast wealth of information. These pages simply provide a guide upon which to learn from and use as a resource. To truly become the master of your own abilities, seek expertise from many sources. The more knowledge you obtain from myriad sources and the more experiences you acquire, the more finely-tuned you will become as an individual. A stronger, wiser, adventure racing individual.

Team Explorer celebrates a second-place finish at the Beast of the East (1999) race in southwest Virginia.

THE START—RAID GAULOISES, BORNEO, 1994
BY ANGELIKA CASTANEDA

Two hundred athletes, assembled by teams, each in their own uniform, were standing in the middle of a football field, waiting to be called to their start. Teams started in five-minute intervals. The local people, some reporters, and race officials in a helicopter, which landed earlier, were the only people watching this start in the remote jungles of Borneo.

We each had one last chance to compare ourselves with other teams and many thoughts raced through my mind: "Their packs are smaller than ours, how can they do it? Their water bottles are integrated into the backpack! They are using ski poles! Should I have taken mine? No! Yes, I think I should have. She looks so strong—I wish I had those legs and arms. Maybe I am too old for this. I am the oldest competitor. I should have thought of carrying that extra hat against the sun. This team has only running shoes—no hiking shoes. Maybe I should have. Why didn't I? I was thinking of doing it and then I didn't. I don't know why I am doing this—I am really too old. I don't think I have trained enough, why didn't I train harder?"

I was trapped in my feelings, like being submerged in an endless motion of the bubbling waters of a whirlpool. All I had to do was reach out and turn off the bubbles. Then, in the stillness of the restful water, my thinking was sharpened, my focus turned to the banner.

BANG! My team was running through the banner to commence our race. We were running, then walking at a fast pace. We made it! We were in the race! I was so excited, my energy flew like a roaring river. My adrenaline finally released and my endorphins were surging—nothing could stop me.

"WHERE WITH ALL"

The kind of gear you have is not nearly as important as using it properly and having it when you need it. It's what you do with your gear that counts.

Technology has superbly altered our potential for enjoyment in the great outdoors. Changes in clothing fabric have increased our ability to manage temperature control. Thermoregulation was hardly a common word in our vocabulary ten years ago. Gadgets of convenience have gotten smaller and lighter and we can go further and faster due to scientific breakthroughs.

In a race situation, however, your reigning asset will always be experience. Through actual time spent in the outdoors, you will quickly accumulate a repertoire of what works and what doesn't work. Ultimately, it all boils down to "where-with-all" and technique. So, strive to perfect your abilities and gain experience in adventure sports so that you can adapt to any environment and any equipment with flawless performance.

In preparation for a race, consider these questions: "If I take away all the latest materials and technology, what am I left with? Will I be able to cope? Will I be able to perform? Will I be able to excel?" It's what you know that matters most.

Every adventure race requires that each individual racer carry basic survival gear throughout the race course. This gear list typically includes:

• Knife with locking blade	• Headlamp
• Emergency blanket	• Compass
• Whistle	• Shell (windbreaker or Gor-Tex jacket)
• Waterproof lighter	• Fleece top
• Several Chem-lights	

Students practice night biking maneuvers at the Odyssey Adventure Racing Academy.

Place these items at the top of your purchase list and then once you own them, store them together in a nylon bag or plastic baggie so you will be organized and ready come race time. Beyond these rudimentary items, you may be required to carry more depending on the terrain, the weather, and the length of the race. In addition, you will need gear specific to each discipline for safety and efficiency purposes. The gear specific to each of the major disciplines involved in an adventure race will be discussed in the appropriate chapters.

The following list from Odyssey Adventure Racing provides an example of the gear you will need for a two-day self-supported, non-stop competition.

THE ENDORPHIN FIX TWO DAY ADVENTURE RACE GEAR LIST

EACH COMPETITOR MUST POSSESS:

BIKING GEAR: mountain bike; approved bike helmet; lights attached to bike—white front, red rear, battery life for 14 hours; repair kit (spare tubes, patches); pump. Clipless shoes may be staged with the bike. Recommended: bike gloves; map case; rear bike rack.

BOATING GEAR: personal kayak paddles may be used (but must be carried the entire race); Coast Guard approved life jacket (minimum Type III—no inflatable life jackets will be accepted); helmet (bike or climbing helmet OK); commercial grade throw bag (w/minimum of 50' of rope) one per boat; dry bag or waterproof container (garbage bags are not acceptable); knife and whistle within easy reach while on water. Skill certified required for every competitor.

CLIMBING GEAR: climbing harness; three locking carabiners, Figure 8 or ATC—no other devices will be accepted; climbing specific helmet, with lights after 7 PM (no bike or boating helmet allowed on climb); sling or daisy chain if you are going to hang your pack during the descent. Skill certificate required for every competitor, you need to be checked off with the gear you will be racing with.

TEAM/SOLO MEDICAL KIT: band aids; gauze; adhesive/duct tape; iodine/alcohol swabs; analgesic; iodine tablets or purifier for water purification. Amounts need to be reasonable for a two-day race.

MANDATORY GEAR: to be carried throughout the competition by each racer: lighter; knife w/minimum 2.5" blade (folding OK); whistle; head lamp/batteries; fleece (type) top; Gor-Tex (type) shell; land compass (one per every two competitors). GPS not allowed.

ODYSSEY PROVIDES: clue book and course directions; boats and paddles; ropes set-up; maps of course; communications; medical support; manned checkpoints; prizes and awards and pre- and post-race food.

PLEASE NOTE:

The Endorphin Fix is unsupported! Racers will carry all gear, food and water (water occurs naturally along the course) for the entire race. If you use your own paddle, you will have to carry it the entire race. Staging your shoes with your bike is allowed. There will be random gear checks for your mandatory equipment along the race route. There will be manned checkpoints. Time constraints will be in place; you will need to make the time cutoffs in order to continue officially.

The Fix encompasses over 125 miles of rugged West Virginia rivers, mountains, and cliffs. You will experience some of the most challenging, yet beautiful geography in the U.S. You will need certificates of your ability in whitewater and rappelling fixed ropes. Odyssey can provide a list of regional businesses to facilitate you in attaining these. Be prepared for a long, tough course in a habitat that can be extreme in its diversity. The course is designed to be run virtually non-stop.

THE SOUTHERN TRAVERSE GEAR LIST

This gear list for the Southern Traverse race in New Zealand outlines the specific items you need for an expedition-level race, including mountaineering gear:

AT ALL TIMES

REQUIRED TEAM EQUIPMENT

1x Sleeping bag (min.130 gm fill-weight)

1x Foam pad (hip to shoulder length)

1x 50 meter 9-mm climbing rope (dynamic)

1x Waterproof tent fly (3m x 3m minimum)

1x First aid kit (as per list attached)

1x H.E.L.P. beacon

1x Altimeter

1x Lighter

1x Pocketknife (blade length 5 cm approx.)

2x Compasses (Southern Hemisphere)

2x Glow sticks

3x Flares (minimum)

1x Mountain stove and accessories

REQUIRED PERSONAL EQUIPMENT

1x Survival blanket

1x Polypropylene or woolen top

1x Polypropylene or woolen pants

1x Fleece top

1x Fleece or woolen hat

1x Whistle

1x Headlamp

1x Waterproof jacket i.e. Reflex, Gor-Tex

1x Waterproof pants

1x Polypropylene or wool gloves

1x Fleece top (additional to other requirements)—minimum 100 weight

Note: additional clothing/equipment may be required for the compulsory list due to weather conditions.

MOUNTAIN TREKKING—NO GLACIAL TRAVEL

No additional equipment required

MOUNTAIN TREKKING—GLACIAL TRAVEL

ADDITIONAL REQUIRED TEAM EQUIPMENT

2x Snow shovels

1x Waterproof four-season tent with poles (capable of withstanding winds of up to 100 km per hour, suitable as a shelter for four persons)

ADDITIONAL REQUIRED PERSONAL EQUIPMENT

1x Pair of crampons—minimum 8 points with 2 front pointing

1x Ice axe (modern)—minimum length 45cm

1x Pair of boots/shoes suitable for attachment of crampons

1x Avalanche beacon (supplied)

1x Sleeping bag (minimum 130 gm fill weight)

1x Foam pad (hip to shoulder length)

1x Climbing harness (modern)

1x Climbing helmet (modern)

4x Twist lock or screw gate carabiners

2x Short prusiks 150 cm in circumference (minimum diameter of 5.5mm)

1x Long prusik 300 cm in circumference (minimum diameter of 5.5mm)

1x Modern rappel device

1x Pair of leather gloves

Note: Competitors must have practiced the art of anchor changeovers with slings (or daisy chains) and screw gate/twist lock carabiners (the two points of contact rule is mandatory, i.e. you must always be attached to the fixed rope system with two points). Rappelling will be done with a back up prusik or mechanical prusik.

You must also practice self-rescue with your spare prusiks, should you jam your system. A thorough check of all competitors' competency and techniques will be undertaken at registration. This will include roped glacier travel skills. Any competitor that fails to pass the minimum standard will not be allowed to participate in the rope skill section.

KAYAKING

ADDITIONAL REQUIRED TEAM EQUIPMENT

2x Double kayaks (minimum width 0.55 meters measured at waterline with combined weight of 100 kg, fitted with bow, stern and full deck lines. All boats should be fitted with bulkheads)

IF NIGHT PADDLING INCLUDED

2x Rear red strobe light (1 per boat)

4x Glow sticks (2 per boat, front and back)

1x Throw rope/bag (20 meter minimum)

ADDITIONAL REQUIRED PERSONAL EQUIPMENT

1x Life jacket (6.2kg positive buoyancy—international standard)

1x Wetsuit (3mm min., "Farmer John"style)

1x Whitewater/kayak helmet—international standard (required on river sections only)

Note: It is not compulsory to carry the 50-meter climbing rope unless specified, paddling between the hours of 21:00 and 06:00 is not allowed. If you are on the water just before 21:00, it is possible to camp on the shore until the time has elapsed. If you are found on the water after 21:00, there will be a time penalty of 15 minutes for every minute on the water after this time. After 21:30, teams will be disqualified.

Sailing may only be undertaken utilizing the minimum gear equipment list. Any introduced articles, e.g. windsurfing masts, will result in a time penalty.

Some kayaks will be rented to competitors, with paddles and spray skirts. Any damage or loss of the rented material will be the responsibility of the team.

RAFTING

ADDITIONAL REQUIRED TEAM EQUIPMENT

1x Throw rope/bag (20 meter minimum)

ADDITIONAL REQUIRED PERSONAL EQUIPMENT

1x Life jacket (6.2kg positive buoyancy—international standard)

1x Whitewater/kayak helmet

1x Wet suit (3mm min.)—must be worn

Note: It is not compulsory to carry the 50-meter climbing rope.

Rafts, paddles, repair kits will be made available to competitors. All additional material, which could damage the condition of the raft, is forbidden; no pieces of wood, screws, or other elements, which could cause friction, are allowed. Paddling between the hours of 21:00 and 06:00 is not allowed.

MOUNTAIN BIKING

ADDITIONAL REQUIRED PERSONAL EQUIPMENT

1x mountain bike only, with rear red strobe light (flashing light)

1x cycle helmet—international standard

Note: It is not compulsory to carry the 50-meter climbing rope.

a. Cycle helmets must be worn during the whole biking section. The competitors or assistants at transition areas will need to be prepared to handle all mechanical problems.

b. Equipment inspection:

At race registration, there will be a minimum gear inspection for the organizers to certify that every team meets the requirements of the race regulations.

Other gear inspections can occur at any time during the race. Any team not meeting the requirements, at race registration or at a control point, will be unable to proceed and could receive severe sanctions.

c. Forbidden equipment/items:

GPS and night vision devices are not allowed.

Additional windsurf mast or sail, or any additions on kayaks and rafts.

Performance enhancing drugs.

JUNGLE TERRAIN

Jungle terrain is a common element in many adventure races these days and there are specific items you will need to assist your journey through the tropical bush:

- Tweezers
- Extra waterproof socks
- Mosquito netting (for your head)
- Jungle hammock (a lightweight netting that fits easily into your pocket and gets you off the ground, where millions of little creatures lurk when sleeping)
- Salt and lighter (to expel leeches)

- Whistle (to assist communication in the double and triple canopies)

Additional gear will be required for safety and survival in accordance with the demands of each discipline and the type of terrain and environment of the host site of the race. The extent of your equipment will depend on the specific course of each race. Once you have registered for your race, obtain a gear list so that you can organize your things at home and purchase needed items as soon as possible. This will give you ample time to train with your gear and get used to its performance. This extra time will also afford you the luxury of knowing what doesn't work for your race.

GEAR CHECK

The gear check, which is your first responsibility after you have checked in, is a necessary safety measure for both you and the race organization. If you are well organized and have everything on the list, the experience is really quite painless. In addition, it provides an opportunity to ask questions about your equipment and particular setups for the course. If you are unsure about anything regarding gear or skills, do not hesitate to ask! This is the time to get everything straight and is also the place to get completely comfortable.

Many racers place all of their gear in a giant plastic tub. This is convenient and will save you many hassles and headaches when locating gear, especially when time is of the essence. Consider organizing all of your equipment in sections in your tub according to the course disciplines. Then pack your mandatory gear that you must carry at all times in the pack you will be racing with. Spend some time as a team double-checking each other before you head off to the gear check to assure you have everything you need.

GEAR TIPS

- **Know your gear**
- **Take the time to talk with knowledgeable suppliers at your local retail outfitter**
- **Practice with your gear before a race**
- **Make certain your gear is reliable**
- **Consider the weight issue. Go for lightweight but don't sacrifice performance or durability**
- **Safety, comfort, warmth, and the ability to stay dry are paramount**

CLOTHING

Your racing apparel provides protection against the elements of rain, wind, and cold temperatures and creates a layer of protection between you and the flora and fauna. Clothing enhances your comfort on the course. However, keep in mind that "comfort" becomes extremely relative in a race situation. Think instead: "How can I optimize my comfort on the course through clothing selection?"

IN COLD WEATHER

Hypothermia is a genuine concern in outdoor pursuits. In cold, wet temperatures, staying warm and dry is crucial. Proper apparel will insulate and protect your body from the environment and decrease cold and wet-related emergency situations. Layering is an effective strategy in cold weather. By wearing several layers of clothing, you trap air, which provides a barrier to the cold air to keep you warm. The more layers you wear,

the more trapped air you accumulate for warmth. In cold temperatures down to 32 degrees Fahrenheit, a moisture-wicking fabric next to the skin, layered next to a thin fleece and a shell as the outer layer, provide an effective system. Of course, experimentation is key. Train with a variety of mixed layers to determine what works best for you.

When you are performing in cold temperatures, your priority, in addition to staying warm, is heat dissipation. Make sure all of the layers you wear allow ventilation. As you become warmer from intense movement, you can peel your layers so you don't overheat but monitor your situation as you will rapidly lose heat from your sweat-soaked clothes.

In the cold, it is also imperative to remember what your mother told you—keep your head covered. Because of the high vascularity of our head region, more than one-third (up to 40%) of our body heat can escape from the head if it is not protected.

Ideal cold weather apparel is impervious to moving air and simultaneously provides adequate ventilation.

IN HOT WEATHER

In extreme heat, ventilation and breathability are key. Wear lightweight, loose-fitting, breathable shirts to keep cool. Also choose garments that are light in color. Stay away from dark colors, which absorb light rays.

When regulating the degree of wetness of your clothing, heat loss through evaporation is only effective when your clothes are completely soaked. Consequently, if you want to be cooler, wet clothes will make it possible. However, if temperatures are lower, do what you can to stay dry. Fabric properties affect the degree to which they absorb moisture. Cotton and linen material

quickly absorb water and are not quick to dry. For this reason, polypropylene fabrics are a popular choice among adventure racers for thermoregulation.

In an adventure race, not only are you working hard, but you are also carrying a heavy load and are covered in clothes from head to toe in many conditions. Your fitness level will reduce the intensity to some degree, which affects your core temperature. In addition, each of us has a unique internal temperature regulator. Hence, it is important to know how your body responds to various conditions. So pack lightly and think through the garments you choose for a race. Your clothing should protect you from hot and cold conditions by retarding heat loss in cold weather and reducing heat gain in hot, humid temperatures. In an adventure race, you will be living outside for days. You should be able to rely on your choices of clothing for longevity.

GENERAL GUIDELINES FOR FABRIC TYPES

NATURAL FIBERS

COTTON

- High water absorbency (bad choice when you are wet and cold).
- Great choice if you can assure you will stay dry.
- Save it for the post-race celebration.

WOOL

- Great insulating layer.
- Bulky for racing.

SYNTHETIC FIBER

POLYESTER AND POLYPROPYLENE

- Dries quickly.
- Lightweight.
- More expensive.
- Excellent first layer.

NYLON

- Found in wind and water-resistant (not waterproof) outerwear.
- Durable and lightweight.
- Dries slowly.

SPANDEX

- Stretchy.
- Dries slowly.

WATERPROOF/BREATHABLE FABRICS

- Polyurethane coatings (which you can purchase at an outdoor supplies retailer) maintain waterproofing but also retain moisture (sweat) inside of garment.
- More advanced techniques allow breathability so you stay dry inside and out.

THE COMPLETE GUIDE TO ADVENTURE RACING

LAYERING

Your premiere goal in a race is to stay warm and dry. So dress accordingly. Choose apparel that is lightweight, breathable, dries fast and preferably does not retain odors. Your first layer of clothing should possess wicking properties, which is the ability to manage moisture by keeping it away from your skin. Polypropylene is an excellent fabric for your clothing foundation and remember that dark colors absorb heat.

In colder weather, you will stay warmer and drier (dark colors dry quicker in the sun) by wearing dark-colored clothing. Light-colored clothing absorbs less of the sun's heat, which will keep you cooler on hot days.

Tights are popular in adventure racing because of the stretch-ability factor and the reduction of rubbing that causes painful skin irritation. Look for fabric that contains polypropylene, as breathability and wicking are equally important for the legs.

Always bring your Gor-Tex shell with you. You never know what conditions are in store for the race. The terrain encountered in adventure racing is extremely dynamic. A bright, warm, sunny day could turn into a freezing, rainy night. Always be prepared!

FOOTWEAR

Your shoes for the disciplines on foot should be lightweight but durable. Bring at least two pairs with you to a race. In one to two-day races that are unsupported, you will wear the same hiking shoes for the duration. In expedition-length races, you have the option of changing shoes at transition areas. Remember that your feet will swell, become tender, and have the potential to develop blisters and other painful properties. You may want to bring shoes of different sizes for different stages of the race. You may also want to consider bringing a lighter pair for easier terrain where you may be running and something more rugged for the harsher stuff. But the bottom line always boils down to weight. Every extra ounce adds up as the hours accumulate.

Consider the toe box. It should be flexible and your toes should have room to spare. When your toes get smashed against the toe box when traveling downhill, you want to minimize the trauma incurred. Make sure your feet are secured by the shoelaces. This will minimize slippage, which lessens the chances for blisters and battered toes.

The soles of your shoes play an important role. Traction is paramount. Many shoe manufacturers mix rubbers in the soles. Harder rubber has less grip but is more durable while greater traction comes from the softer rubber that wears out faster.

Breathability is also key in shoe selection. The drier and cooler you can keep your feet, the further they will take you. Look for mesh detailing in the shoes' upper regions. If you are worried about dirt and stones penetrating your shoes, wear gaitors.

Break in your shoes before you race. Wear them everywhere. Train in them until they feel comfortable. Make sure they are the shoes you want to race in.

SOCKS

Look for socks that provide:

- Maximum comfort.
- Perfect fit to avoid blisters and better fit in your shoes.
- Wicking properties to keep feet dry and blister-free.
- SealSkinz (available at most outdoor outfitters) are a secret of many top racers. They keep the water out while simultaneously allowing your feet to breathe. SealSkinz may be worn on their own, however, some athletes choose to wear a thin sock underneath.
- SmartWool socks are proven winners in adventurous pursuits.

DON'T LEAVE HOME WITHOUT IT—BY DEB MOORE

WORLD CLASS ULTRA DISTANCE RUNNER, BEAST OF THE EAST, ECO-CHALLENGE, AND IDITASPORT VETERAN

Here are a few of my personal favorites that I think are invaluable for the foot portions of most of the adventurous events I do:

Supplex nylon pants with zip-off legs and lots of pockets—if it's hot, they are shorts. In the cold, they are pants without adding much weight or taking up much space. They are also a little wind and water-resistant and dry quickly. As long pants, they can help protect against extreme sun and nasty brier patches. You can swim, paddle, climb, horseback ride, and hike in them.

Long-sleeve white or light Supplex shirt with lots of mesh venting, such as Ex Officio or RailRiders. This will give some sun, brier and poison ivy protection. If the sun is really bright, I stay cooler with a sleeve than having the sun hit my skin all day.

Knee-high gaiters and leather gloves are worth their weight in gold if there is serious bushwhacking of any length involved. Although they may seem like an extra, you can move through brush and briers so much faster if your hands and shins are protected. You can bust on through rather than carefully picking your way. Sometimes, people will say they don't care if they get all scratched up, but they still take longer going through. Another problem is getting the cuts infected in later stages, especially in water legs, which can derail your race. There is also less chance of poison ivy, poison oak, or nettles slowing you down. I like using my old climbing gloves with full fingers, but bike gloves with leather palms are better than nothing. For the real minimalists, at the Tucson Orienteering Rogaine race I saw some people just put duct tape up the shin part of their pant leg. If you don't wear glasses, sunglasses for day with clear lenses for night is a good idea for eye safety.

Hiking poles give added balance on difficult terrain so you can move quickly. Uphill, they provide good back support and allow your whole body to work to power you up and forward (arms, back, and abs). I usually just take one. I get most of the benefit of using two, but by using only one, I don't tie up both hands. This leaves one hand free for compass work if it's highly technical or to grab my water bottle, food, map, etc.

An Activent Gor-Tex shell is much lighter and takes up less space than regular Gor-Tex, with most of the waterproof performance. Since it doesn't have to be very cold to get hypothermia in these races, having it with you most of the time is a good rule. I also carry one or two (if I'm alone) garbage bags. In an absolute downpour, you can wear them over your shell. In a pinch, two garbage bags make a sleeping bag. If you are moving, it's pretty easy to stay warm, even in Alaska. But if you are forced to stop for some reason, you can get real cold, real fast. (In Tucson, the day temperature in the desert was 95 degrees or hotter, but at night in the washes, it went into the 40's.)

Lightest weight polypro balaclava and a Gor-Tex ball cap are a great combination. They are lightweight and take up very little space. Use the ball cap for sun or rain. The balaclava is very breathable and lightweight and can be worn as a neck gaiter, a watchman's cap, or as full head and face protection. A ball cap over your balaclava will keep you very warm and dry.

If cold weather is a possibility, a long-sleeve polypro or micro fleece shirt and a micro fleece vest will usually get you past mandatory gear check. This kind of combo gives you some flexibility for layering for different temperatures and typically takes up less space in your pack than a traditional fleece. I've tried just taking the vest but found that just a supplex shirtsleeve against the unlined Activent made my arms really cold.

For some types of races, Gor-Tex socks worn with a liner sock keeps your feet drier from outside water and inside perspiration. If your boots get soaked in river crossings, you can pop these on for a while to help your feet dry to reduce blistering and trench foot in longer races. In cold races, keeping your feet dry from perspiration is going to help them stay much warmer.

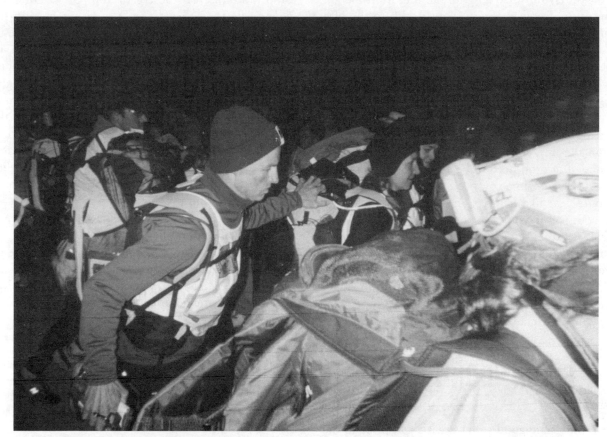

Geared up at the Ford Escape Wild Onion Urban Adventure Race (2000) held in Chicago, Illinois.

PACKS

When choosing the right pack to race with, consider three factors: your pack should be lightweight, it should be comfortable, and every pouch and compartment should be easily accessible. The size of your pack will ultimately be determined by the length of your race and the mandatory gear that you must carry. For example, if your race is supported with many stages and transition areas, you may not need a bag as large as you would for a two-day non-stop unsupported race.

While mid-size packs that have a 4,000 to 5,000 cubic inch range are ideal for weekend sporting trips, adventure racing is all about how much weight you

carry. In an adventure race, the typical size pack used ranges from 1,500 to 3,000 cubic inches with an average holding capacity of 2,500 cubic inches.

Equally important to how much you carry in a race is how you carry it. If you expect to race successfully for hours and hours or for several days in a row, you have to be comfortable. First, look for multiple adjustments on a pack. The shoulder straps should lie snugly but comfortably on your trapezius (upper back) muscle. A sternum strap is important to have for stability and also to support the potentially heavy weight that you will carry while racing. In addition, the hip belt should fit snugly across your pelvis.

The overall size of your pack is determined by the

GEAR

length of your torso. Before you venture out to buy a pack, measure your torso length spanning from the 7th vertebra in the cervical region (your neck), to the fifth vertebra of the lumbar region (your lower back). C7 is easily identified when you look down—it's the bone that sticks out most prominently. And L5 is the very first vertebra located directly above the pelvis.

This information will help you find the right size pack.

External pouches on your pack will make life a lot easier on the race course. Items like your headlamp, a knife, and your food need to be accessible so you won't have to stop every time you need to take a bite of food. Also, extra gear like helmets and poles can be stowed on the outside if you have mesh pockets and loops available. Furthermore, it is convenient to have extra mesh pockets and extra loops on the outside of your pack for used socks, shirts, etc.

Cold and wet is a familiar state in adventure racing. So, dress prudently to regulate your body temperature while racing and take the necessary steps to keep your things dry. First off, do not depend on the "waterproof" promise on the tag of your pack. Oftentimes, your pack can keep water in but not out, as most packs are not meant to be submerged in water. Your best bet is to start waterproofing from the inside of the pack out. Use Zip-Loc bags and dry bags to keep important things dry. Many racers group related items together like extra socks, gloves, and a hat and stuff them in a baggie and label it for easy identification. It is also a good idea to put your mandatory gear that you will not use regularly in one bag that is clearly labeled "MANDATORY GEAR". In addition, consider lining your pack with a garbage bag. This will aid your quest for dry things and provide a sleeping bag or raincoat if the need arises. Resign yourself to taking these steps prior to each race.

Solomon, Gregory, Dana and Lafuma packs are popular with seasoned adventure racers. They are all lightweight, have many extra pockets, pouches, and loops, and are comfortable for extended periods of wear.

EXTRA "DON'T FORGET TO BRING TO THE RACE" GEAR

These things are good to have with you prior to the start of the race. Once you arrive at the site of the race and learn the course at the pre-race briefing, you can make last-minute decisions about any extra gear that you may want to carry. Just don't get carried away! And always try on your pack with all of your gear and walk around with it before you get to the starting line.

- Sunglasses
- Ski goggles
- Swim goggles
- Sunscreen
- A variety of hats
- Bandanna
- Bug spray
- A variety of gloves
- Watch—investigate multi-purpose models with altimeter, barometer, and compass (Suunto and Casio are competitive brands)
- Map case

- Wet suit
- Extra bike shorts
- Extra athletic tops (jogging bras for women)
- Extra hiking/running shoes (one size bigger for swollen feet)
- Flip-flops for post-race relief
- Small bills (you never know what luck you may run into along the course. If you run into a small convenience store or even a soda machine, you will appreciate the few bucks you brought. If you are in a foreign country, a few bucks provide great bartering power)
- A waterproof disposable camera
- A toothbrush cut off just below the bristles
- Handy-wipes
- Extra cordage
- Gaiters (the low ones protect your ankles and feet from scree, twigs, snow, and other debris. The knee-high gaitors protect your entire lower leg and enhance body heat in alpine conditions)

GEAR TIPS TO LIVE BY

- Pack your heaviest stuff closest to your body. The further it is from you, the tougher it will be to maintain balance.

- A hip belt will be a lifesaver as you accumulate mileage. It transfers over three-quarters of your pack weight from your shoulders to your hips. This will reduce the fatigue to your other body parts. Also, consider the padding of your hip belt for ultimate comfort.

- If your pack doesn't have loops for a water bottle on the shoulder straps, you can easily make some with elastic cording.

- Train with your pack. This way, you will know if it is comfortable after several hours of activity and can be reassured that you will be comfortable during a race. If it is not comfortable, you can thank yourself for your discovery BEFORE you race.

- When packing, put the things you will use the least at the bottom, then work your way up with items you will need more often with the most frequently used gear on top.

- Try to stuff one-third to one-half of your food in the outside pockets, waist pack, and pants or coat pockets and put the rest towards the top of your pack.

- Consider packing your food in another teammate's pack for easy access!

- Get rid of extra containers, plastic, cardboard, or metal that can weigh you down. Many top racers go as far as clipping the extra tags and metal tabs on their zippers to save weight. However, this theory is prudent only if you are at the top level and are looking for one more edge to have over your competition.

- Secure everything before you head out. When you are riding, things can come loose and can be lost in a second, without being discovered until hours later—when it's too late. Bushwhacking can also cause gear to separate from your pack. So pay attention to your gear!

- Try to use headlamps and bike lights that work on the same size batteries.

- Everyone on the team should have equipment that utilizes the same size batteries, the same spoke size, wheel size, etc.

- Avoid redundancy. Make sure that only one person is carrying a first aid kit and only one person has a tool kit. Many teams travel with more gear than they need.

- Carry the smallest size pack possible. A big pack will create the urge to carry more gear.

- Tie wet clothing and socks to your pack.

- Look for a headlamp that is comfortable, lightweight, and durable. Illuminating power is key and the longevity of the light source is also a factor to consider. The further you can see and the brighter your path of vision is, the faster you can move. In addition, you want maximum burning power without a bulky load. Adjustability is important for flexibility of night vision and make sure you have a secure on/off switch that won't accidentally flip on during the day and waste your batteries.

GEAR

FINAL THOUGHTS ON GEAR

- Wrap duct tape around your trekking poles and around your bike frame.

- Stay warm. Bring an extra pair of socks and an extra pair of gloves. When one pair gets wet, change and tie the soggy pair to the outside of your pack to air dry.

- Bag balm, or udder balm, is a petroleum-based lubricant with antiseptic in it. It saves the feet and also helps manage cuts. Fill a film case with it and keep it handy as you race.

- Think through your hydration system. An extra water bottle, which you can attach to your pack straps, will lessen the time it takes to refill and treat water. As you pass by creeks or streams, you can simply scoop water into your bottle without stopping. If there are abundant natural supplies on the course, you can rely on the water bottle and less on a full, heavy bladder for your water. But don't skimp on water, particularly if you are not 100% positive about the course.

- Trekking poles are terrific tools when traveling on foot. Use them on trails and roads. Attach them on the side of your pack through the thick stuff, and take advantage of them when crossing water.

- If you know you will be pushing or carrying your bike as much or more than you will be riding it, consider bringing your hiking shoes and your cycling shoes. Or, bike and hike in one sturdy pair of shoes. It will make the time you spend on foot easier and more pleasurable.

- Keep a constant supply of food in your waist pockets and any other pockets that are handy.

- Keep anything that you might need in a pinch or supplies such as ibuprofen and personal items as handy as your food.

- Use dry bags to protect your gear while paddling.

- Remember that you will get wet and your clothing and equipment will get wet. Waterproof everything!

- Categorize your gear in separate bags and label each one for quick access.

Equine teammates require additional gear—Raid Gauloises in Ecuador.

A lesson in navigation skills at the Odyssey Adventure Racing Academy.

The art of navigation lies in the ability to assimilate your surroundings. A good navigator has a finely tuned sensibility to the world around him. He has the ability to get around without getting lost. And if he does get lost, he can find his way back with confidence. He is alert, aware, and always uses good judgment. Correct decisions are the result of careful consideration to countless details.

In the field of navigation, your position is always relative. It is simply an accumulation of distance and direction. Your sense of direction can be attributed to careful observation and an assembly of knowledge. Distance is synonymous with time. The more attuned your five senses are to your surroundings, the more success you will enjoy.

This culmination of know-how casts the foundation of adventure racing. Navigation, therefore, is the crucial link to adventure racing prosperity. If you don't know where you are going or how to find checkpoints along a course, fitness is irrelevant. All of your superior skills go down the drain. Climb the wrong mountain and you could miss a cut-off time, or risk the dangers of traveling un-scouted land and use up valuable energy and supplies.

It is truly empowering to be able to find your way through the wilderness with a map and compass and your own intuition. Mastering navigation is like learning a foreign language—you have to practice it and use it to get good at it. This chapter examines the fundamentals of navigation and provides insight on improving your role as a navigator.

THE MIGHTY MAP

A map is a graphic and symbolic representation of land as seen from above. Colors, numbers, contour intervals and lines of various thickness give clues as to the details of the land. In most adventure races you are normally given a topography map. A topography map shows the elevation of the land.

Planimetric maps show the world in a one-dimensional single plane. The road maps you purchase at the gas station or the trail maps that you obtain before a long hike describe in a one-dimensional language the ground as seen from above.

Nautical maps and charts provide detail as to the water, water's floor, water depths, and navigational aids for open waters and coastal travel.

Some maps you find in adventure racing are 20 years old or older. Pay attention to the publication date and take it into consideration when navigating. Some features may disappear while new ones take shape. Trails will change and new roads will alter the landscape. There are always going to be trails on your map that are no longer on the ground and there will always be trails you find that are not on the map. It is important to check your compass periodically when taking trails.

THE SCALE

Be sure to pay particular attention to the scale of the map. When given a number of maps, be sure to look at all of the scales on the maps. In the Raid Gauloises, we are given over 20 maps with different scales.

The relationship of an actual distance on the ground to a unit of measurement on the map represents a map's scale. A scale represents the degree of reduction expressed as a ratio. For example, a ratio of 1:25,000 denotes "one unit of measurement (on the map)" and is equivalent to 25,000 similar units on the earth's surface. A larger scaled map (1:25,000-1:75,000) reveals a small area in significant detail. A map of the United States would be represented in a medium size scale (1:75,000-1:600,000), and a small scale (1:600,000 or greater) may represent the hemispheres.

The map's scale is normally found at the bottom of the map. Be sure to study this scale during your map study. If you are going to cut up your map, be sure to keep the pertinent parts of the scale.

SYMBOLS

Symbols use small pictures, dotted lines, thick lines, thin lines, different color lines and different colors to represent the land shown on a map. Many symbols are self-explanatory but some can be tricky. For example, it is advantageous to take the time to learn the difference between a symbol for an unimproved road, which is a double broken line versus a trail symbol, which is a single broken line. Dark, continuous lines indicate more permanent features, whereas broken lines reveal less identifiable features. In addition, the darker and denser the coloration is on the map, the less crossable or "runable" it is.

Symbols are fairly consistent from map to map. For best results, seek the particular map you use for guidance to avoid any map mishaps. For quick reference, memorize the following color-coding:

BLACK	Man-made features
BROWN	Topographic features
GREEN	Vegetation features
BLUE	Water features
WHITE	Cleared land features
RED	Large roadways and survey lines
PURPLE	Map revisions that have not been field-checked

THE LEGEND

A map's legend, which can be found in the margins, outlines all of the crucial information provided on the map. Before you begin plotting checkpoints and devising your strategy, take some time to study this information. You will learn: who made the map and when; the amount of land covered; the name of the area and the names of the surrounding areas; you will be able to identify the UTM grid coordinates; you may find a key to map symbols and the map's scale, which will be located bottom dead center of the map along with the contour interval; and just left of the scale, you will find declination information. Also, you will see the date of any revisions on the map (usually found at the bottom left of a map) to get an idea of how up-to-date it is.

This information is all good to know and very useful when you are given time to do a detailed map study.

But this is not always the case. You may be getting your map just hours before the race and will consequently have to do your map study on the move or upon a stop. In all cases, you must always know where you are and which way you are traveling. If you travel too fast to be able to do this, you are going to get into trouble!

CONTOUR LINES

Contour lines represent elevation of the land. They are continuous, irregularly shaped circles that follow the same elevation as the land. The closer together the lines are, the steeper the terrain. Conversely, the further away they are, the flatter the terrain.

The key to interpreting contour lines is to compare them to the shape of the ground. As you become more proficient at visualizing terrain from contour lines, you will become a more skilled navigator. Spurs, knolls, and depressions are common features encountered in orienteering and the quicker you can identify these features frequently used as control sites, the faster you will be able to locate checkpoints.

Lines can be tricky, so understand their meaning and then study your map carefully to determine if the land goes up or down and if the route you choose is the best one. Remember, in adventure races, you will get copies of your maps, which are not always of good quality. Study it well but don't take it literally.

READ BETWEEN THE LINES

Always be aware of the mystery of the spaces between the contour lines. To become an advanced navigator, learn to read between the lines. For example, a contour interval of 40 feet might look innocent on your map, but when you see the land, you might encounter a cliff that is un-navigable.

Remember that the map doesn't show everything. Interpretation should always leave room for options. With those options, always have a back-up plan.

CONTOUR INTERPRETATION

- A contour line has no beginning or end. It is a continuous, irregularly-shaped circle.

- If you remain on the same contour line, you won't change your elevation.

- Contour intervals are the distance between contour lines. The interval is always written on the map.

- Elevation is marked on an index contour, which occurs every fifth line and is delineated by a darker line.

- U's and V's pointing to high ground indicate a gully.

- U's and V's pointing to low ground indicate a ridge or spur.

- The closer the lines are on a map, the steeper the terrain is and the further away they are, the flatter the ground.

- Lines that fall right on top of each other represent a vertical cliff.

- You are traveling uphill if you continue to cross lines of higher elevation.

- You are going downhill if the lines decrease in elevation.

- U or V of a stream will be pointing toward a higher line of elevation as they point upstream.

- Keep in mind, a stream or river may change from year to year. When you are racing, it may even be dry. Look for signs in the terrain.

- Contour lines that meet in a V (the V will point upstream) indicate a valley.

- U-shaped lines depict broad and gentle valleys.

- V-shaped lines reveal sharp, narrow ground with steep rises on either side.

- Pay attention to all of the lines around a point to determine if it is a valley or a ridge. Elevation and evidence of streams will indicate the type of terrain.

- A peak is illustrated by an "X" in the center circle of a series of contour lines.

PROMINENT TERRAIN FEATURES

SADDLE

The low area between two higher elevations is called a saddle. It is typically an easier pass through rough terrain. The representative contour lines on your map will resemble a figure eight.

VALLEY

Valleys are most often carved from river or stream erosion.

SPUR

Spurs are projections of land between aligned valleys formed by water.

DEPRESSION

A low area of land is called a depression when it is surrounded by high ground. Water and/or caves may be present in this terrain feature. A contour line will have tiny ticks that slope toward the depression.

RIDGE

A canting streak of higher ground is called a ridge. Travel on a ridge is typically easier than traversing lower ground. The view will give you a better picture of where you are, the ground may be harder, and up and down travel is usually less severe.

RIDGELINE

A ridgeline is the origin of all land features. It forms a dividing line of high ground between land features.

THE SLOPE CHANGES EVERYTHING

When determining the intensity and the time it will take your team to complete a hiking leg, you must consider the degree in which the land deviates from horizontal. A walk on flat ground, for example, will be a lot quicker and easier on the joints than hiking up steep slopes.

The "gradient" is an expression of the slope's severity. It reveals the rise and the fall of the land. It is important to consider this when determining your route. When examining your route, determine the gradient, which compares the vertical and the horizontal distances. To decipher gradient, first figure out the following:

Elevation change (vertical distance)—count the contour lines.

Trail length (horizontal distance)—use the map's scale.

Then use the following equation to identify the difficulty of the journey ahead:

$$\text{Gradient (ratio)} = \text{horizontal distance} / \text{vertical distance}$$

For example, say you want to know the gradient of the land in the next 1.5 miles ahead. Count the contour lines to figure out the vertical distance in that mile and a half (let's say it is 400 feet) then divide 7920 feet (1.5 miles) by 400 feet (the change in elevation). You will get a value of 19.8 (for simplicity, we will round it to 20). This means that the gradient rises 1 foot every 20 feet you move horizontally.

$$20 = 7920 \text{ ft} / 400 \text{ ft}$$

The gradient can also be expressed as a ratio of 1 in 20. The smaller the second number gets, the harder your hike becomes because you are gaining elevation at a quicker rate.

LATITUDE AND LONGITUDE

Lines of latitude and longitude intersect to form an imaginary grid across the earth. Latitude lines run east and west, and run parallel to each other designating distances north and south of the equator. The equator is equivalent to 0 degrees latitude and the north and south poles are at 90 degrees latitude. Latitude is stated in degrees north or degrees south.

Longitudinal lines run north and south in vertical lines and merge at both poles. They are expressed in degrees east and west in correlation with their distance from Greenwich, England, which is at 0 degrees longitude. Degrees of longitude are of the same value as you travel on either side of Greenwich until they converge at 180 degrees at the International Dateline.

Degrees can be broken down into minutes. For example, one degree is divided into 60 minutes. Sixty minutes is then broken down into seconds. This method provides an accurate means of locating and describing exact positions such as the CPs (checkpoints) in an adventure race. You can find these values at the intersections of lines and the borders of maps.

UTM COORDINATES

In 1947, the U.S. Army adopted the Universal Transverse Mercator (UTM) projection and grid system and in conjunction with GPS receivers have been able to find map coordinates in a much simpler fashion than by relying on lines of latitude and longitude. It is currently in use by the United States armed forces and is used to determine checkpoints in many adventure races across the globe.

The UTM structure creates 60 zones upon which the earth is divided. Each zone is 6 degrees wide in longitude and 8 degrees of latitude. The zones span from the latitude 80 degrees South to 84 degrees North and are identified in numerical order starting with 1 (one), which is on the International Date Line (180 degrees longitude) and proceeds east. The Polar Regions use the Universal Polar Stereographic (UPS) grid system.

Each zone is also assigned a letter from "C" to "X" with the exception of "I" and "O" to avoid confusion with "1" and "0" respectively. When reading UTM grid coordinates, we first examine "easting" which is the distance (in meters) eastward and then the distance north which is referred to as "northing". When looking at a map, you read right then up, or "in the door, then up the stairs". At the pre-race briefing, if the race organizer uses UTM grid points, your checkpoints will be located where the easting and northing coordinates intersect.

It is important to understand this system to properly plot your checkpoints on your race map. You will be given a series of numbers. Because we focus on small, specific areas when navigating the land, we will typically work with abbreviated values.

If you are given six digit numbers, that means you are covering a span of 100 square meters. Eight digits magnify an area to within ten square meters. All USGS topo maps that have been printed in the last three decades have blue "UTM grid tick marks" in the map's margin. When determining your exact location, each square is then further divided into one hundred boxes, which are created from ten tick marks going both east and north.

WHICH WAY IS NORTH

There are three definitions of North. **Magnetic North** is the direction a compass needle points. The magnetic force originates from an iron ore field off the coast of Baffin Island in Canada. **True North,** or geographic north, is represented by longitudinal lines to the North Pole. It represents one pivotal point of the earth's rotation. And **Grid North** is always at the top of your map.

The mechanics of a compass are simple: a needle is attracted to the earth's magnetic field and when it becomes aligned with these magnetic forces, it stops and points to a surrounding ring of degrees. Based on the needle's behavior, we can establish direction.

A compass must be accurate, generally within four degrees, to benefit your travels. You can perform a simple test with your compass to assure this precision by examining the motion of the needle. Petroleum oil or alcohol is sealed in the compass case to control the needle's motion. To test accuracy, quickly turn the entire compass 90 degrees. If the needle moves with the compass, or swings back and forth before pointing to north, the needle is insufficiently damped.

Fire roads and trails make navigation easier.

NAVIGATION

TO DETERMINE THE UTM GRID VALUE OF A CHECKPOINT, GO THROUGH THE FOLLOWING STEPS:

1. Look at the bottom of the map to find the easting of the UTM grid line (just west of the checkpoint).
2. Look at the margin on the right side of the map to find the northing of the UTM grid point (just below, or south of the checkpoint).
3. Divide the zone revealed by the easting and northing points into 100 boxes by marking ten equal ticks on the southern line and ten ticks on the western line.
4. Count the ticks from left to right until they are directly below the checkpoint.
5. Count the ticks going upward until you reach the one that is located on the same horizontal plane.
6. Draw lines to connect the dots and reveal your position.

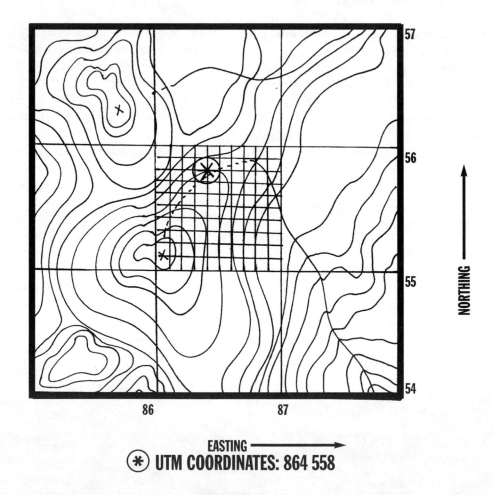

UTM COORDINATES: 864 558

I have been working with a map and compass for several years now. I have come to an understanding that navigating with these tools is a matter of the state of mind. During one race, we had a shot at the course record, but we allowed our judgment to stray. We didn't pay attention to our mind-set, and our navigation suffered for it. Our mistake cost us several hours of time, and a lot of extra burned energy trying to catch up from our mistake. The moral of the story: your mind-set can make or break your navigation.

—Jack Crawford

THE COMPLETE GUIDE TO ADVENTURE RACING

A CAUSE FOR A COMPASS

To avoid deviation, or error in your compass, avoid metal (including belt buckles, picnic benches and other places not so obvious), radios, flashlights, batteries, power lines, railroad tracks, pacemakers, and the hood of a car. Also, consider geographic locations such as ore deposits, which can throw your compass off.

Remember the following values for general reference:

0 degrees   = North

90 degrees   = East

180 degrees = South

270 degrees = West

Understanding when and how to dial in a declination is a necessity. There are many different compass designs available on the market today. Make sure you read through the accompanying literature to understand the specifics of your particular brand before you head out on the field.

DECLINATION

A compass works in conjunction with magnetic north while maps use geographic north as a reference point. Unfortunately, the two are not aligned. Therefore, there is significant discrepancy when working with both a map and a compass. This discrepancy is called declination.

Declination is the difference between **magnetic north** and **geographic north** expressed as an angle. It is measured with true north as the starting point and is in degrees either east or west spanning up to 1,000 miles difference, depending on where you are in the world. For example, 0 declination, represented by the agonic line, runs along the western shore of Hudson Bay, spans the eastern border of Minnesota, runs through Chicago, down the western border of Florida, and right through Cuba. If you are traveling through the state of Alaska, it has an easterly declination of 30 degrees while the westerly declination of Maine is 20 degrees.

Accounting for correct declination is crucial to your racing success. It must be accounted for when using both a map and a compass. If it is not taken into account, your chances of staying on course and finding checkpoints is extremely limited.

There are several methods of accounting for declination when planning and finding your route. You can use an isogonic map, which charts the difference of degrees. You can draw lines of magnetic meridians on your race map. You can key it in to your compass, or you can factor the difference each time you determine a bearing.

- Isogonic map of North America
- Meridian lines
- Key in declination to compass
- Mathematical calculations

A declination diagram on your topographic map will allow you to determine the difference between magnetic north and geographic north. Many times the map will list directions for correcting, or transposing grid to magnetic north (map to compass) and magnetic to grid (compass to map).

Another method to compensate for declination is to draw magnetic meridians on your map. These lines will correspond with the declination diagram on your map. Once you know the declination of your location, you can draw compatible lines on your map. These lines will intersect the borders of the map, drawing the same line of declination at the bottom of your map. Westerly declination dictates lines that slant to the left, and the magnetic meridian lines of easterly declination angle to the right. All of your lines will be parallel to each other and spaced one inch apart. Finally, add an "N" for North at the top of each line to remind you of magnetic north.

As we know now, USGS maps provide the local declination in the bottom margin. Equipped with the information given in this chart, you can use also addition and subtraction to determine your position. Remember this acronym LARS:

Left **A**dd **R**ight **S**ubtract

Your base is true north. So, if your magnetic north is to the right of true north, subtract degrees. If magnetic north is to the left of true north, add degrees of difference.

For example:

1. Your compass does not have a declination adjustment.
2. You get a bearing in the field of 28 degrees.
3. Magnetic north is to the right of true north (which is revealed in the legend on your map).
4. The local declination is 4 according to your map.
5. Subtract 4 from 28 to get a correct bearing of 24 degrees.

If magnetic north were to the left of true north in the same situation, your bearing would be 32 degrees (28 + 4).

Your compass is the most important piece of gear you will use in an adventure race. It allows you to find north at any time and any place and points you in the right direction. A compass, however, does not reveal position and by possession, does not assure a 100 percent guarantee that you won't get lost.

Throughout history, the shape of a compass has changed dramatically. Even today, there are many types available. But the mechanism upon which a compass is effective has remained the same—magnetism. The needle of a compass responds to the earth's magnetic field.

Lines of magnetic force vary depending upon where you are on the globe. Near the equator they run horizontal, but are vertical the closer you are to the poles. Thus, the dip or magnetic inclination, which is the downward pull of one end of the magnetic needle toward the magnetic field, varies with location.

Depending upon where you are in the world, you will need a particular compass. A compass is balanced differently in the Southern Hemisphere than in the northern region. So, do your research and make sure you bring the right compass to your race!

Before you get to the race site, research your compass. It is comical and sad when new teams arrive to an international race with their old compasses. I had a good friend use his compass in the Patagonia Raid in 1995. When he arrived in the country, he noticed that the needle of his compass was not moving and that it was stuck to the plastic bubble. He had to go out and find a compass that would work to successfully navigate the race course.

— *Don*

THE COMPLETE GUIDE TO ADVENTURE RACING

ORIENTING YOUR MAP

To orient your map, you must situate your map so that the lines running north are pointing to actual magnetic north. Follow these steps to orient your map:

1. Place your compass on your map so that the edge of the base plate is in line with the direction you wish to travel. The direction-of-travel arrow on your compass should aim in the same direction.

2. Turn the map and your body until both the magnetic needle of your compass and the north/south lines on the map are parallel with each other.

3. The map is now oriented and you are aligned with the intended direction of travel.

OR

1. Set your compass to north (turn the dial to 0 degrees).

2. Line the edge of your compass on a north/south line.

3. Turn the map until the magnetic needle is aligned with the meridian lines.

4. Your map is oriented!

5. You should get in the habit of orienting your map every time you stop to do a map study.

NEXT...DETERMINE YOUR BEARING

Your bearing is your direction to a landmark relative to magnetic north. When taking bearings, hold the compass level and directly in front of you. There are three types of bearings upon which compass work is based: direct, reciprocal or "back", and finding a landmark.

IF YOU ARE USING A MAP

1. *To take a bearing*—Situate your compass on the map by connecting checkpoints (or two significant points on the map) with the edge of the base plate. Turn the housing until the meridian lines of the compass are flushed with the north/south lines on the map. Your bearing will be revealed at the index line on your compass.

2. *To plot a bearing*—First set your bearing at the index line on your compass. Position your compass on your map by aligning the edge of the base plate with the landmark you are plotting from. Turn your compass (the whole compass) until the meridian lines are synchronized with the north/south lines of the map. The bearing line will follow the edge of your base plate.

IF YOU ARE OUT IN THE FIELD

1. *To take a bearing*—Hold your compass directly in front of you and make sure it is level. Point it at the object you wish to locate with the direction-of-travel arrow aiming right at the object. Rotate the housing of your compass until the declination arrow is aligned with the magnetic needle. Your bearing will be exposed at the index line.

2. *To plot a bearing*—Set the bearing you want at the index line. Hold your compass in a level position directly in front of you. Rotate your body until the magnetic needle and the declination arrow match up to reveal your direction of travel.

We tend to veer off course when sensory references are severed. Fog, night navigation, and dense woods can easily obscure our judgment when making navigational decisions. Consequently, it is a natural tendency to travel in circles in a clockwise direction. To avoid this potentially disastrous situation, use your compass.

1. Take a bearing in the direction of your target.
2. Scout the land in front of you and choose a distinctive landmark somewhere along your bearing.
3. Go to that landmark.
4. Repeat the same process until you reach your desired destination.

To avoid lateral drift, perform several short runs instead of one long trek toward your target. In addition to forward focus, keep an eye on where you started. If you lose sight of your intermediate target, you can always use your starting point to re-establish your bearing.

IF YOU DISCOVER THAT YOU ARE OFF COURSE

1. Take a back bearing from the point at where you are to the place you just came from.
2. The back bearing should be 180 degrees from your original bearing. If it isn't, move to your right or left until you are on track.
3. Continue progress toward your original bearing.

If there are no visible landmarks, send a teammate ahead and use him to maintain a correct path, and then spread out in a single file line while progressing forward.

It is imperative to be familiar with your position at all times. Keep constant track of your pace and the distance traveled and keep regular tabs of the time it takes you to travel from point to point. All team members should have an idea of the pace. The average pace count for 100 meters is 64 to 68 paces. (See Chapter 4 for more on pacing.)

Practice taking bearings before heading out into the wilderness.

THE COMPLETE GUIDE TO ADVENTURE RACING

WHERE ARE YOU?

TRIANGULATION

Use reference points when possible. In fact, it is good practice to have more than one known reference point as often as you can. The more reference points you have, the more precise you can be when calculating your position. You will have accuracy if you have 3 positive reference points.

To determine where you are in the field, shoot a bearing to an obvious point like a water tower. The opposite direction is the reciprocal of that point. That bearing can be calculated by adding or subtracting 180 degrees to the first bearing. You can also look on your compass and locate a point directly across from your forward bearing.

Shoot a bearing 90 degrees east and another one 90 degrees west of the water tower, which represents two more obvious points such as a peak or a sub station. The opposite direction of the bearings when intersected with the opposite point of the first bearing will reveal your position when lines drawn from those points intersect.

For more accuracy, draw more lines. But be aware that your lines won't always intersect at one point.

They will, however, reveal a general area of where you are.

IF YOU ARE LOST...

DO:
1. Cast aside your ego, stop, and confess you are lost. Pressing on will only send you further off course.
2. Scout the area and/or retrace your steps to your last known point.
3. Regroup and double-check your strategy before moving forward.

DON'T:
1. Argue with your teammates and run away in disgust.
2. Bang your head against a tree and stomp the ground with your feet.
3. Fill yourself with negative thoughts.
4. Quit.

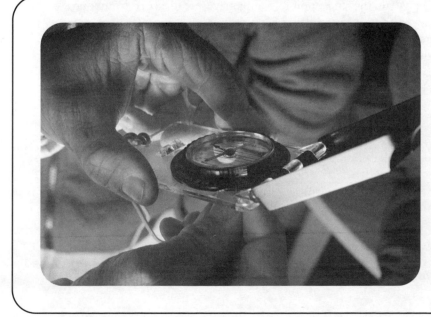

The fastest and easiest way to compensate for declination is to purchase a compass equipped with a declination arrow that can be adjusted according to where you are. It comes with a tiny key that you use to calibrate your ideal setting. Simply follow the instructions included with the compass. Once declination is set, you won't have to think about it for your entire race.

**NAVIGATION**

THE DAWN OF A CHECKPOINT

As darkness drops, we turn on our headlamps. Ahead of us, we can see a procession of head-lamps. There appears to be two teams traveling together, just like us. Their pattern of lights sug-gests that they are uncertain of where to go. Like fireflies gone berserk, their beams bounce back and forth, up and down the slope. Then they are still, then moving quickly, still again, then backtracking. We see this as a decided advantage since we are now totally relying on nighttime navigation.

Our advantage is Aric, an absolute expert navigator, especially at night. We turn our lamps off and move quickly through the dark, circling around the teams in silence. I feel as though I am on some military training exercise—on an ambush of the enemy or an escape from captivity. It reminds me of playing GI Joe with my brothers when we were kids.

We make good time and move out ahead, leaving the aimlessly wandering light parade and eventually stopping for water and food. Then, after picking and nibbling at our race fare, we are moving again.

We proceed on a steep downclimb along jagged cliffs that dropped drastically into a small val-ley. Aric thinks that the checkpoint is just beyond a cliff-lined ridge directly in front of us. So we head down and then up the cliffs, sporting some wonderful bouldering moves that challenge me to think about hand and foot placement. I like the mental puzzle. It breaks up the monot-ony of the endless miles placing one foot in front of the other. I feel balanced and strong.

As we climb to the highest point, the ever present Raid Gauloises banner which flaps in the wind like the flag of a newly discovered continent, is not to be seen. Our exhausted silence says it all. We are in the wrong place. There is no checkpoint here. After a careful map study, our error is revealed—we had traversed too far down into the valley and came up one ridge too far, just south of our destination.

We look north to where we are supposed to be. The full moon illuminates the peak as if to tease, "Over here, dummies." Suddenly, our minds seem to unload all of the exhaustion we have denied conscious access to for the past nine days. Fatigue pours into our muscles, our bones, our brains and our souls. Thus, we crawl to the checkpoint, completely spread apart from one another. I'm so tired. I'm so hungry—hungry for food my pack cannot offer me. We have not crossed a water source in five hours and my Camelback is sucking air.

My mind keeps yelling all of these things to me. "You're tired Juli," it says. "You're hungry, your legs are spent, you have no water. You haven't slept in 24 hours and you won't get any sleep for at least 12 more. ARE YOU STILL HAVING FUN?"

My eyes, however, register the soft oranges and pinks of a sky welcoming the rising sun down in the valley, far across the horizon. As we reach the summit, it seems as if I am above the sun. I know though that the sun will spend the next few hours creeping up toward me, passing over me to warm my tired muscles and re-energize my soul. I close my eyes to feel its gentle warmth and pop an energy bar into my mouth. Suddenly, it tastes delicious.

Then Robert from team 'North Face,' with whom we have been traveling breaks the silence. "Hey, I can see the next checkpoint from here," he exclaims. He is on top of a tall, thin mono-lith to the south of the summit. As we join him, we too can see the checkpoint. We are down the slope at a run.

— *Juli Lynch on the Raid Gauloises, Patagonia 1995*

STRATEGY: DETERMINING THE BEST ROUTE

Good navigation boils down to keen route finding and there is almost always more than one route to take. There are many variables to consider when designing your route. First, consider your team. Physically, your team is only as strong as the weakest member is. Keep everyone in mind! From a technical standpoint, each teammate may possess certain skills, which collectively will engender higher success. Be clear about the assets and liabilities of each person to effectively pool the most correct knowledge.

It is a good idea to elect a navigational leader. In addition to the responsibility of locating checkpoints, utilize your leader as a coordinator at times to encourage discussion and to gain multi-perspectives on your situation.

The predominating task is to seek the quickest route of travel. I like to have a primary and a secondary navigator. In races that use passports, (i.e. the Raid, the Beast, the Fix,) it works best to have one teammate reading the passport and staying in constant communication with the primary navigator reading the map. I also like to have someone on the team keeping the time and pace. And all team members should be involved with the map study and in the conversations. If the team gets lost, it should not be the sole fault of the navigator, but of the entire team. If you cannot travel linearly, decide what will be your alternative route. Always have a back-up plan. There are several factors which will influence your choices: "run-ability" or the ability to move quickly over terrain; obstacles such as steep slopes, water, thick vegetation, canyons, out-of-bounds areas such as private property, or forbidden roads; technical details like paths, handrails, catch points, and

attack points; fitness levels; and navigational proficiency.

Time and energy are the two most prominent variables which dictate your decisions. Which is better—a meandering but well-traveled path, or a direct but physically demanding cross-country route? The right choice lies in the culmination of the challenges of each route and the corresponding distances. Elevation gain and loss also present a significant challenge. Ascending and descending sloping terrain utilizes tremendous energy and if it can be prevented, it will save time in the long run.

Consider your travel in terms of elevation gains and losses. In other words, if your path of travel must take you up 20 meters, then the ascent is unavoidable. However, if the next checkpoint is at the same altitude, it may not be necessary to waste energy roaming up and down to find it.

Consider this general rule: Every 15 meters of elevation gain absorbs the same amount of time and energy it takes to run 100 meters on level ground. Use this "formula" when determining your ideal route.

OBTAINING ACCURACY

The navigator's job is to minimize ambiguity and to restrict the radius of uncertainty to within meters, not miles.

- The most effective practice is frequent assessments of position.
- Aim for large landmarks.
- Use baselines for your route of travel.

NAVIGATIONAL DEVICES

Aiming off involves purposeful deviation. For example, if you are trying to reach a checkpoint on a trail and want to be sure you catch it, a deliberate route off course to the right by several degrees will take you to the trail. Once you hit it, you will know to turn left and within several degrees, reach your destination.

Utilizing landmarks to fence in your target is referred

to a **bracketing.** If you encounter one of your brackets, you will know to turn around and head in the opposite direction toward your destination. Brackets also serve as a reinforcement to correct navigation. If you reach one, you are assured that you are moving in the right direction.

A **handrail** is a distinct feature that parallels your

course, and can provide a reliable guide to get you from point A to point B. Obvious examples of handrails are rivers, fences, and power lines whereas more difficult handrails are ridges or "vegetation boundaries". Handrails allow you to concentrate on your racing. Once you locate one, stay with it and power on!

A **catch point** will provide a location at which you will leave the handrail. This easy-to-identify point is found on your map and marks the beginning of your next "run". Catch points are often referred to as **collecting features.** No matter what you decide to call it, they intersect your route and could include a pond, river, trail or even a road. These points are numerous and extremely helpful. Take advantage of them!

"SENSES" OF DIRECTION

Use your eyes, ears, nose, and sense of feel to assimilate natural clues to your position. The more attuned you are to the environment, the swifter you will become as a navigator.

- Listen for babbling brooks, rivers, highway sounds, wind blowing through sheltered terrain, and the chatter of race volunteers and supporters at checkpoints and transition areas.
- You can smell the ocean. The aroma of a campfire can also be detected the closer you get to a campsite or transition area.

- The temperature drops the higher you travel.
- The air becomes thicker and heavier the closer you are to water.

PRACTICE MAKES PERFECT

- When you are on a road or trail, compare the contour lines of a topography map with the actual terrain you are on. Practice correlating map to land and land to map.
- Participate in an orienteering meet. To locate a race in your area, do a search for "NORTH AMERICAN ROGAINE CALENDAR" on the web. You will be directed to a slew of information on orienteering meets and find myriad contacts.
- Create a course and go do it. Plot some checkpoints on a map and try to find them. *Keep them to a radius of only a few miles on your first few training sessions.
- Go to an adventure racing academy. You can spend many hours learning from navigational experts, gaining both classroom and practical experience. At the Odyssey Adventure Racing Academy, participants spend approximately 16 consecutive hours doing map and compass work both day and night.

NAVIGATIONAL TOOLS

ALTIMETER

An altimeter provides vital information to your position. While your compass locates north, your altimeter shows elevation. You can compare your altimeter reading with elevation on your map to assess your location.

The weather greatly influences your altimeter. Therefore, it is important to adjust it at a known elevation before you start your race. It may even malfunction while out on the course. If this happens, reset it at your next known point with the precise elevation.

An altimeter also allows you to keep track of your progress and estimate future performance. You can calculate your rate of ascent or descent through regular inspections of time and elevation during your trek.

GPS

A global positioning system is rarely used in adventure racing as it takes away a significant chunk of the challenge. However, when courses are extremely arduous, a GPS is a helpful tool and therefore may be required in a race.

The GPS is a combination of satellites, a ground control system and navigation sets, which are installed in vehicles of transportation and carried by its users. Through rings of information that circle the earth, grounded systems pick up the information and translate the signals into valuable details about your position. It provides accurate information on your position based on latitude and longitude or UTM coordinates, altitude, velocity, and various other clues to your desired destination.

Because the GPS is so accurate, and gives precise information on a course, it has been considered a form of cheating in an adventure race and is grounds for disqualification if discovered (if forbidden in the race).

The first American team to compete in the Raid Gauloises traveled 24 hours in a circle. So after one day of work, they ended up in the same position as where they started!

Power lines are excellent handrails and provide open terrain for easier cross-country travelling.

HELPFUL HINTS

- For best results, every team member should have a role in navigation. Divide duties so that everyone knows the plan of attack and everyone is paying attention. For example, the head navigator will look for landmarks and orchestrate the strategy, another person will keep the bearings, another will count paces, and someone else may keep track of time and direction of travel. The more heads in the game, the better your team's chances of staying on track. Far too many instances have occurred where teams blow right past important landmarks because the only team member who has a clue of the team's position and where the team is going is the navigator.

- Designate your "Second in Command" navigator. He can double check decisions and alternate leadership with the chief navigator.

- When you are lost, admit it and regroup. Don't be stubborn in this game. It will only hurt you and your team.

- Backtrack to your last known position if you are lost. No matter how grueling the idea is, you will save time with this tactic instead of traveling further off course and risking disqualification.

- When your vision is severely restricted, in conditions such as dense jungle, scouting is key. Keep accurate track of distance and bearings. In desert situations, it is extremely crucial to pay close attention to distance and pace.

- Be particularly careful when navigating at night. Getting lost in the dark is about as bad as it gets in an adventure race. Trust your compass!

- Be 100% sure of your path of travel each time you leave a checkpoint and transition area and then verse each team member on your route before you venture out. Leaving a secure point along the course in haste is a waste of time.

MARINE NAVIGATION

At sea, there are several methods you can use to navigate your route. When any substantial landmarks are out of sight, and you are determining your course based on distance and direction alone, you are using "dead reckoning" techniques. In order for this method to work, you must pay attention and keep a detailed record of your progress. Dead reckoning is based on an initial point, which is ascertained from a known point—usually an object on shore, also referred to as the point of departure. From this point, the distance traveled with the corresponding time is recorded systematically.

Currents can inhibit your most valiant efforts if you are not familiar with how they affect your performance. If you are caught in a side-wind, the current can carry you completely off course. The best defense in this scenario is experience. Practice paddling in strong currents. Move in a variety of directions to familiarize yourself with your handling. Determine how far off your intended course a current carries you. Be aware of the force you exert and an estimated speed you travel in the varying conditions. This experience will be invaluable when you are in a race situation.

Another helpful practice is measuring your speed under various conditions. The more acquainted you are with your pace, the more effective you will be under pressure.

Declination is also a factor to consider when navigating open water. In dead reckoning situations, your compass is your lifeline. Be sure to calculate the variation before shoving off and don't forget it as you navigate your route.

When you lock a known point, look for something unique and preferably resistant to tides. A lighthouse or some other man-made structure is a good choice.

Another method, called piloting, utilizes bearings and ranging to find your way. A bearing is a direct line between a reference point and an object or landmark. They are crucial when determining your position. To determine your exact location, you can take two or more bearings, draw them on a map, and the intersection of the lines from your bearings will reveal your current position.

Once bearings are set, a route can be created. Landmarks such as islands can be used as markers of progress and to keep you on course. These landmarks can also be used for "ranging" in which you line up a smaller landmass with your final destination to keep you on course. Ranging keeps you on track. If your features remain in line, you are on course. When the two features fall off-line, it is an indication that you are paddling off course. This practice also provides motivation as it creates benchmarks of progress. These small victories will keep you mentally on track.

Good navigation always involves careful observation, stringent attention, proper planning, and flexibility in cases where things don't go as originally intended.

A DAY AT THE OFFICE

We were at the top of this mountain pass and the rain was coming down so heavy that we felt we needed scuba gear, and I remarked to the team, "No way are we going to get down this valley as the river will be too dangerous to cross." Well, we started down and by this time, we were catching the other team, so we made sure we had lots to eat and then tried to sneak around them by crossing the river and going down the other side. That didn't work when three of the team got swept downstream and only managed to escape when they caught hold of a tree sticking out over the river. So, we decided we would just rush past them.

We caught them as they were looking at the map and they were totally surprised. For the next half-hour, we crashed through the bush, sliding down little cliffs and going at a speed that was more suitable for a 10K race. Anne was at the back and all I could hear at the front was all this swearing and cursing. Eventually, the other team lost two of its members and had to stop.

By this time, we were well down into the valley and the route was supposed to cross the river, which looked more like a raging torrent, overflowing its banks and filling up the valley floor. The next few hours we preceded downstream, crossing numerous side creeks (which themselves had become major rivers). And we crawled across slippery logs with the water lapping our feet.

Just as it got dark, we came to a spot where the river ran up against large cliffs, blocking all down river progress. We had to return upstream and then try to clamber up vertical cliffs. We had just managed to find an easier spot when it became completely black. The rain was still almost solid and the U-shaped valley was filling up with water.

We descended back down beside the river and kept going. Then we came across an area where the river had completely overflowed and filled up the valley floor. I didn't say anything. I just waded into the water and started swimming. Well, we were swimming amongst the tops of ten-foot high trees in the dark. After about four big swimming sections, the oldest member of our team commented, "Another one of those and I am done for." So we had a talk and decided we better have some hot food. We got out our stove and with our last dry match, got the stove going. Then it went out.

—*John Howard*

While walking to the next checkpoint, a team with two Americans and one Brazilian caught up to us. They had been lost for an hour and a half. One of them told me that his strategy was to see what kind of shoe one of the New Zealanders (who were dominating the race) was wearing and to try to track him through the jungle. Unfortunately, he grew convinced that the New Zealander had changed shoes. Hence, he was unable to follow this strategy.

—*Jim Hertz on the Expedition Mata Atlantica in Brazil*

Swamps are frequent obstacles to overcome in adventure races.

Many miles are endured on foot in an adventure race. At first glance, this discipline may seem simple, but the endless hours accumulated on the trails, in the bush, skirting a riverbank, in the river, and up and down steep slopes can take its toll. Efficiency is paramount. Knowledge of proper foot care is also a key component to successfully finishing a race.

FOOT CARE IN ADVENTURE RACING

In many cases, an adventure race is won on foot. The team that can outlast the grueling consequences of endless slogging through harsh conditions is the one that takes home top bragging rights. "Fast cars need good tires," Gerard Fusil says. In order to continue proper function, the feet need to be taken care of. And, in an extreme race, you create extreme medical conditions. So the feet need extra attention and a specific regime to increase their longevity on a course.

"Every morning, I check my helicopter before I get in. If I check it after it has a problem, it does me no good," Fusil commented as he emphasized the importance of foot care in an expedition-length race. Regular maintenance of the feet is crucial to adventure racing success. Each of us has unique feet. Therefore, we each have unique reactions to the conditions we expose our feet to and we each have our own method of taking care of them. Based on information you gather and through experimentation, you will be equipped to determine the right care for your feet in an adventure race.

The following excerpt from the book, Fixing Your Feet, *by John Vonhof provides insight to the important details of foot care in the sport of adventure racing.*

FOOT CARE BASICS

Most of us know first-hand the agony of blisters. Just one can ruin an otherwise good day—whether on a training run or during a competitive event. The blister may be on your heel, the ball of your foot, between the toes, or on the tip of a toe. No matter where, blisters have the ability to reduce a fast adventure racer to a slow adventure racer, a slow one to a shuffler, and a shuffler to a walker. What are the basics of foot care for adventure racing and what are the best ways to prevent and treat blisters?

You need to recognize that you and you alone need to find what will work on your feet. That goes for what you put on your feet and how you treat blisters. Others can give suggestions, but what works for them may not work for you. Much of your training should be done in race gear, with the shoes and socks you will race in, and with the packs and other gear in the approximate weight you will use in the race. This avoids subjecting your feet to new stresses on race day.

Blisters are very predictable. Take four elements: moisture, friction, heat and cold, all common to your feet when you run, increasing the likelihood of a blister. The longer these elements exist on the feet, unattended to, the greater the risk. So, what can we do to reduce one or more of these elements? Before one can solve the dilemma, one needs to understand the problem.

Adventure racing doctor Billy Trolan MD, in his Outdoor Research *Blister Fighter's Manual* defines our skin and blisters as follows: "Our skin is designed to protect the rest of our body against temperature extremes and infections. Divided into two layers, the epidermis (outer) and the dermis (inner) constitute the main parts of the skin. Between the two is the Basement Membrane Zone or BMZ, which acts as the glue that holds the two layers together. Blisters form when the "glue" that holds the layers of skin together break down. A space forms between these layers which fills with fluid." The glue zone is like two-ply tissue paper and is the most common area of blister formation.

Trolan identifies four primary causes of blister formation:

> *Heat*—Hot temperatures cause a thermal reaction that breaks down the glue between layers of skin. Heat buildup can be caused by the wrong material in socks, hot ground surfaces, non-vented shoes and friction.
>
> *Cold*—Decreased blood flow to the skin makes it more fragile.
>
> *Moisture*—Moisture is absorbed slowly, either from water entering the shoes or from sweat on the feet. Water may enter the shoes from streams or other sources, or is retained against the skin by non-wicking socks and non-venting shoes.
>
> *Friction*—Two surfaces rubbing against each other cause friction. Friction may happen between the feet and socks or socks and the shoes, or because shoes are too tight, a bunched-up sock or even sand or dirt that gets into the shoe.

Understanding these four elements that cause blisters, whether independently or in combination, is key to preventing and eliminating blisters. Most adventure races are unique and failure to heed common sense advice can cost you dearly.

It was the ninth day of the inaugural Elf Authentic Adventure race in the Philippines. The race was progressing at a pace much slower than the race organizer, Gerard Fusil, had intended. The rain had been relentless. The wet season was wetter than usual. Consequently, much of the jungle floors were extremely soggy and the rivers were high.

Under a burning sun not far from the coast of Suribao, a flare blazed through the sky. Its cutting trajectory signified a plea for help from team 'Spie' and team 'Pharmanex', the top two teams who had been battling for the lead off and on for the majority of the race. Their feet were destroyed. Despite their toughness and many miles of experience, the Philippine terrain had gobbled the hard-earned calluses and stalwart epidermis of the majority of the eight feet.

—Gerard Fusil

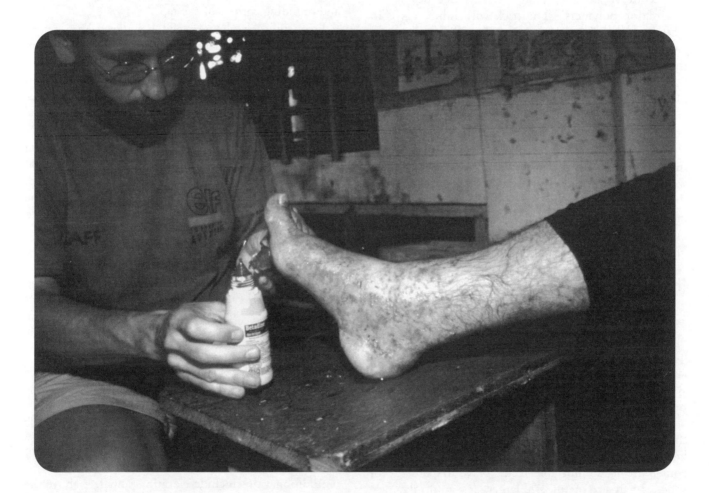

THE FIRST LINE OF BLISTER DEFENSE

There are several blister-reducing options that should become our first line of defense. Proper socks are a key priority. Moisture-wicking socks are available from almost every sock manufacturer, and given a choice, should always be picked before an all-cotton sock. Two pairs of socks or double-layer socks offer an inner layer that moves against the outer layer, reducing friction to the skin. Try several different types of socks of various weights and fabrics.

Lubricants are next on the list. Most runners grew up using a lubricant, usually the age-old standby— Vaseline. Another favorite is Bag Balm, a salve with healing properties. Newer, state-of-the-art lubricants may contain silicone, pain-relieving Benzocaine, or antifriction polymers. The trick with lubricants is to reapply them frequently, being sure to clean off the old layer before another application. Remember though, that lubricants and grit don't mix. The grit will quickly become an irritant, then a hot spot, and then finally a blister. If your skin becomes too tender from the softening effects of the lubricant, then powders may be better for your feet.

Powders can help reduce friction by absorbing moisture. This reduces frictions between the feet and the socks. Dry skin is more resistant to blister formation than skin that has been softened by moisture. Beware of powders that cake up and cause blisters. A good powder will absorb many times its weight in moisture. Simple and readily available cornstarch also works.

THE SECOND LINE OF BLISTER DEFENSE

The second line of defense includes a variety of options. Proper footwear, skin tougheners, taping, frequent sock and shoe changes, proper hydration, correct lacing techniques, and gaiters all contribute to the prevention of blisters. Some of these options may be more important for your feet than others.

Well broken-in footwear is important. Good outer soles for traction, enough room in the toe box, a strong heel counter that grips your heel, and quality insoles all contribute to comfortable feet. Have a spare tire of shoes, a half-size or full-size larger, as a multi-day race progresses and your feet swell. Different thicknesses of socks can make up for the initial looser fit of the shoe.

Skin tougheners work three ways. They coat the feet for protection, toughen the skin, and if using tape, help the tape or blister patches adhere better to the skin. Tincture of Benzoin is commonly used; however, if it gets into a cut or open blister, it will be momentarily painful. It is important to recognize that one's feet are also toughened as they are conditioned to the stresses and distances of adventure racing through proper training. Another way to toughen the skin is to go barefoot, even running barefoot, in gradual stages to toughen one's outer layer.

Taping provides a barrier between the skin and socks to reduce friction. There are specific methods of taping toes, the balls of the feet, heels, the bottoms of the feet, between toes, and even the whole foot. Duct tape is commonly used, but Johnson & Johnson's Elastikon tape works well and is porous. Making the tape stick involves cleaning the feet well, using a tape adherent, and rounding corners of the tape.

Frequent sock changes will help keep the feet in good condition. Wet or moist shoes and socks, from water or constant sweating can cause problems over time as the skin softens, maceration occurs, and skin layers separate. Changing the socks also gives opportunity to reapply either powder or lubricant and deal with any hot spots before they become blisters.

Maintaining proper hydration helps reduce swelling of the feet, often common after hours of running, so the occurrence of hot spots and blisters is reduced. When you become fluid and electrolyte deficient, the skin loses its normal levels of water and easily rubs or folds over itself, leading to blisters.

Adjusting your shoelaces can relieve friction and pressure over the instep and make footwear more comfortable. Shoes that are too tight in the toe box or too loose in the heel can be adjusted by using different lacing techniques. Several alternatives to shoe laces are commonly found in running stores. These include thin elastic laces or laces with an inter-locking lock.

Racers should consider wearing gaiters to provide protection against sand, dirt, rocks, and grit. These irritants cause friction and blisters as shoes and socks become dirty. The gaiter's typical weak point is the strap under the shoe's arch. Plan ahead for equipment failure by finding alternate ways of attaching gaiters to your feet or by carrying an extra strap.

Additional tips include elevating your feet above the level of your heart when resting to reduce swelling, and taking off your shoes and socks to air your feet whenever possible.

HOT SPOTS AND BLISTERS

A hot spot is an area that becomes sore from rubbing, and without treatment will develop into a blister. Usually, there is redness in the center and possible stinging or burning sensations. Hot spots can be protected with tape or a blister patch product. Using a lubricant will provide only temporary protection. The hot spot must be covered to protect it from further rubbing. Try to determine the cause of the rubbing and eliminate it. Change socks or shoes or cut a small slit in the shoe to eliminate the pressure point.

A blister forms when the outer layer of skin receives friction, which causes it to rub against the inner layer of skin. As the outer layer is loosened from the deeper inner layers, the sac in between fills with lymph fluid. As the outer layer is cut off from oxygen and nutrients, it becomes dead skin. If this outer layer bursts, the skin loses its natural protective barrier. A few minutes of protecting a hot spot can save hours of lost time later.

The blister should be drained if it is in a weight-bearing area and larger than three-quarters of an inch in diameter. Use an alcohol wipe to clean the blister's skin. Then use a sterile needle, or a pin sterilized by passing it through a flame, to make several small punctures in the blister's edge. A small knife with a scissors can be used to make a small "V" cut in the side of the blister where ongoing foot pressure will force fluid out of the blister. Use finger pressure to drain the blister. Clean and dry the skin before applying a blister patch.

Cloudy or hazy blister fluid indicates infection. Drain the blister and apply antibiotic ointment.

Recheck the blister frequently. Do not drain a blood-filled blister.

If the blister's roof has ruptured, with either the skin torn off or held only by a flap, carefully cut off the remaining skin, clean the area and apply antibiotic ointment. If you choose to skip the antibiotic ointment during your run, remember to apply it after the race.

BASIC BLISTER PATCHING

Blister patching techniques include the use of Spenco 2nd Skin or Blister Block applied directly over the blister, whether or not the roof is still attached. 2nd Skin needs to be held in place with tape or Coban self-adherent wrap. An application of Tincture of Benzoin or other tape adherent to the skin will help the adhesive-backed Blister Block better adhere to the skin.

You can also use duct tape or Elastikon tape for blister patching. Apply a piece of toilet paper or tissue over the blister to prevent the tape from sticking to the blister's roof. You can substitute a piece of duct tape cut in the blister's shape and applied sticky-side to sticky-side to the tape over the blister.

The use of Tincture of Benzoin or a tape adherent to the skin around the blister will help the patch better adhere to the skin. Allow the tincture to dry before applying the patch. Apply a thin coating of Vaseline or powder to any uncovered sticky areas before putting on your socks. Avoid getting the tincture into the blister or any open cuts—it will burn.

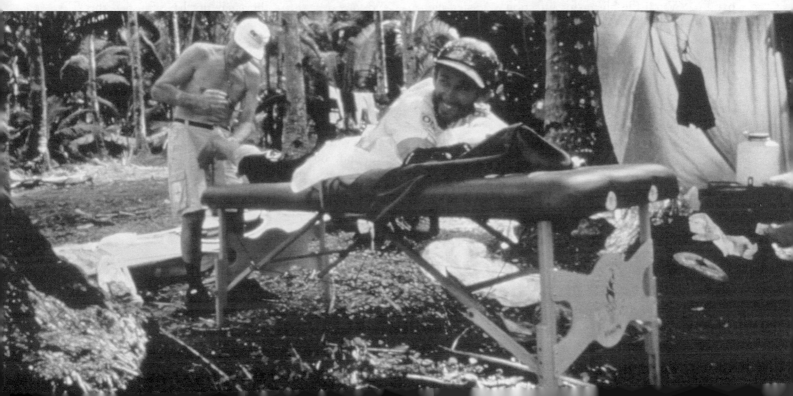

EXTREME BLISTER PATCHING

For those participating in multi-day events, there are several extreme techniques to prevent and treat blisters. An extreme method of preventing blisters is to apply a tape adherent to the feet and then a liberal application of a silicone lubricant. Then put on good moisture-wicking socks, either single or double-layer. If your socks have a large toe seam, put them on inside out to avoid getting blisters on the tops of your toes.

Extreme taping of the feet can be used both for prevention and treatment of blisters. Use either duct tape or Elastikon tape to tape any problem areas. This may include the balls of the feet, the heels, or any combination of these areas. Clean the feet with an alcohol wipe before applying a tape adherent to the area to be taped. Round any corner edges of the tape and apply the tape to the problem areas. Apply a thin layer of lubricant to the edges of the tape to neutralize any adhesive leaks.

Remember to smooth the tape as it is applied. If you overlap the tape, be sure the overlapping edge is in the same direction as the force of motion. Practice taping before training runs. Trying to learn how to tape during a competitive event is asking for trouble.

Extreme blister treatment can also involve using a syringe (without a needle) to inject Tincture of Benzoin into a drained blister and then immediately applying pressure to make the blister's roof adhere to the base skin. Be forewarned: this method produces short, intense pain when the Benzoin contacts the new skin. An alternative is to inject New-Skin Liquid Bandage. It does not seal the blister as well or as long, but is less painful. Watch the blister for infection. A safer alternative is to dry out the blister overnight by injecting zinc oxide into the blister. Cover the sealed blister with Benzoin or Instant Krazy Glue to help the tape or blister patch better adhere to the skin. If using moleskin or adhesive felt over the blister, use a disposable razor to shave the small tiny fibers, which can catch on socks and exert a pull against the blister.

TEAMWORK AND FOOT CARE

Adventure racing is a group activity in which teamwork is vital. Your team is only as strong as its weakest member and as fast as your slower member. As you train and race, your team will learn from each other's strengths and build on each other's weaknesses. It may sound easy, but this aspect is rated as one of the most complex and difficult of all adventure racing components. Each team member must have some degree of skill at all disciplines. This includes foot care.

Patty Hintz, a member of team R.E.A.R., participated in a 2-day adventure race in the Shasta Trinity Alps. She recalls,

"The mileage for the running section was about 35 miles and one of my teammates had a problem with blisters. Being an experienced ultra-runner, I brought along extra Spenco 2nd Skin. When she said she had blisters, I had no idea we were talking both heels, both forefeet, and multiple toes on each foot! We had three different types of tape to put over the second skin. I first tried moleskin—but a few miles later it was off. Next was cloth tape, but it did not hold either. Finally, I remembered the duct tape in our team's mandatory gear. I don't know how she managed, but she said her feet felt 100% better. She was able to continue the race and the duct tape never came off."

This story is important in that Patty had anticipated foot problems and was prepared. She knew the value of 2nd skin and knew how to apply tape to the feet. She also knew how to improvise. If she had been on a team where no one knew how to properly drain blisters and tape over them, they may not have finished the 2-day event.

Patty says that, "Later we talked about what caused the blisters. She had great socks made for running to reduce friction. Her shoes had plenty of break-in time and fit her properly. I personally think it was not enough experience with time on her feet. I honestly feel if your shoes fit you properly, you wear appropriate socks, you buy the right type of shoe for the way you run, and you spend time breaking a new pair of shoes in before you race in them; blisters are going to come until your feet have enough distance and time to toughen up. Until then, I'm a firm believer in duct tape."

FOOT CARE KITS

There are two types of foot care kits. The first is a basic self-care kit for keeping your feet healthy and the second is to carry with you during adventure races. Each is equally important. A basic self-care kit for good foot treatment does not have to be large. This kit is meant to be used at home before an event. The following items are basic. Add to the kit as necessary for your particular conditions.

- Toenail clippers
- File or emery board
- Foot powder
- Moisturizer cream
- Pumice stone

For 24-hour or longer adventure races, particularly where there is limited or no crew for support, make a small foot care kit to carry in your packs. The quantity of each item depends on the number in your team and length of your race. The following items are recommended:

- Tincture of Benzoin
- Alcohol wipe packs
- A small Swiss Army-style knife with scissors, or

nail clippers, and lighter or matches for blister puncturing

- Small container of tape adherent
- Small container of foot powder
- Small container of lubricant
- Your choice of tape(s) wrapped around a pencil or around container of powder or lubricant
- Plastic bag with your choice of blister materials and several pieces of toilet paper or tissues

You may consider other options to include in the kit based on your personal foot problems or injury history.

- Lightweight ankle support
- Pads for metatarsals, arches, or heel pain
- Heel cup

Whatever you carry in a foot care kit, know how to use each item. Each member of the team should know how to tape his/her feet to prevent and fix blisters. Each team member should work at finding what is best for his/her feet—lubricants or powders, two pairs of socks or one pair, double layer socks or single layer, how to lace shoes for specific foot problems, and how to find the best fitting shoes. It is the responsibility of the whole team to be sure each member is adequately trained in proper foot care. It can mean the difference between a good race and in just finishing—or even not finishing.

After looking at the 7 toenails I lost in the Raid, my teammate Angelika Castaneda said to me, "Don, why didn't you remove your toe nails? I always remove mine before racing." Some people go so far as removing their toenails and sewing the skin together so that they don't grow back. This might be a bit excessive. But, you do need to be sure the day of the race that your toenails are trimmed down so they don't pull off.

—Don

EFFICIENCY

All of us learned how to walk in our first years of life. By now, most of us take it for granted. To make the most of this skill in competition, there are several techniques that will enhance your foot performance, which consumes a large portion of many adventure races.

Efficiency is the net result of input versus output. To be efficient, the amount of effort put into a task should be low, while simultaneously yielding a high output. Think of your body as an automobile. Your goal is to reap the highest mileage per gallon. You want the biggest bang for your buck.

In human movement, we consider the amount of energy that is required to perform work. Ease in movement takes less effort, and consequently, reduces wasted energy, which is non-productive. So what does it take to be efficient? There are several factors to consider.

Movement economy is critical to the amount of work you accomplish compared to the amount of effort you put forth, particularly when you engage in endurance sports of ultra-long distances. Your ability to utilize oxygen is key.

Other factors that affect your economy of movement are technique, posture, and muscle fiber. To walk faster, take smaller steps and keep your arms close to your body. Once you develop speed and are not totally taxed by it, increase your stride by a fraction. Develop speed at your new pace until you are efficient and repeat the process until you find your ultimate speed at your ideal stride.

Posture also affects efficiency. Strong torso muscles will effectively transfer power throughout your body. They will also hold up longer, which lessens your chance of unnecessary fatigue and tension. Moreover, a strong core will better accommodate your pack.

The ratio of muscle fibers in your legs will determine whether you are better at power or endurance. The fast-twitch ones will generate quick and powerful bouts of movement. Conversely, the slow-twitch fibers will carry you through long legs of trekking. We are born with a specific ratio, which predisposes our athletic destiny to a large degree. However, with steadfast training,

we can alter our ratio to a certain degree. This is where specificity of training comes in. If you want to be a fast trekker able to endure many miles at a time, trek fast for many miles at a time—OFTEN.

Mechanical efficiency is another factor to consider. To be efficient, you must overcome friction. The less friction involved in an activity inside and out, the more efficient you will be.

As we discussed earlier, you spend a good chunk of your time in an adventure race walking or engaging in variations of walking. It is easy to take this mode of travel for granted, however. The more efficient you are at it, the faster racer you will become and the more energy you will save.

Keep in mind, as your walking speed increases, your economy decreases. Consequently, you use more energy and are less efficient. Over time, with lots of practice, you can overcome this physiological dilemma.

Terrain greatly affects the energy cost of walking. Walking in sand takes twice the effort of walking on grass or a paved surface. Snow under your feet makes walking three times as difficult. If you are planning a race across a desert or one with a fair amount of glacier travel, gain experience on the terrain you will be racing on!

If the terrain encompasses a large gain/loss of elevation, you need to consider these factors as well. Trekking steep inclines offers a whole new set of challenges for your joints. The only way to become efficient on the slopes is to train on the slopes. If you live in the mountains—lucky you. If you live in an urban area or in a relatively flat community, your creativity will be challenged. But all hope is not lost. Stairs can be found in buildings and at your local health club. The treadmill can also simulate steep terrain. Train vertically on artificial hills on a regular basis and then take side trips to the mountains several times before your race. Your body and your teammates will appreciate it!

UPHILL

When hiking uphill, the key is to maintain a steady pace to the top. Don't burn out too quickly. Instead, "ration your energy" so you can get all the way to the top. In this case, strong legs and a powerful cardio system will enhance your ascent, but just like anything else, practice makes perfect. The more you get on hills and mountains and work your way up, the better you will become.

As you climb higher, make the task easier by taking in the natural beauty of your surrounding environment. Allow yourself to become completely immersed in the land. Before you know it, you will be at the top of your mountain. Don't fight the climb, instead, go with the flow. Work with the path of least resistance.

Take short steps as you lean into the hill. Be sure you have a steady foothold before transferring your weight upward. Place your entire foot onto the ground and avoid spending too much time walking on the balls of the feet. Change up your muscle access to keep your body as fresh as possible. To do this, alter your stride on a regular basis, vary your speed and your technique.

 **TREKKING**

DOWNHILL

While walking downhill seems as if it would take less effort than going up, it requires tremendous effort to keep yourself from tumbling downhill every time you take a step. This "resisting" or "braking" with good form and a safe tempo down a steep grade is very costly in terms of energy. Going down, you're fighting gravity just as you do when going up, only in a different way. Thus, deceleration is actually harder on the body, adding greater wear and tear over time.

- Before you descend make sure your laces are tight and toenails are closely trimmed (this should be done pre-race).

- Take short steps as you lean into the hill.

- Your walking poles will come in handy here.

But, be careful. Poles are designed to 'save your legs', but not at the expense of your shoulders! (See Chapter 7 for more techniques in downhill travel.)

SIDE HILLS

Avoid travel moving sideways on a steep slope whenever possible. It throws off sound mechanics and greatly challenges balance. This hastily uses energy and increases the risk for injury. Look for ridges or valleys to trek instead. The extra distance to get to a ridge is usually worth the energy saved and injury denied and is many times faster in the long run.

When trekking difficult terrain, use your poles to test the ground before you trod. Take your time, and be certain of your foot placement before progressing forward.

THE COMPLETE GUIDE TO ADVENTURE RACING

TRICKY TERRAIN

SCREE

Rock shavings frequently fall from the mountaintops creating talus and scree fields that are typically found between forests and peaks or sometimes within the forest. Talus is usually large enough to step on while scree is significantly smaller than our feet or even our big toe.

These fields may often be easier to cross versus thick brush. But be careful, loose rock and sharp edges can end your race quickly. When traversing talus, first be sure the rock is secure. Slowly place your weight onto the rock and keep an eye out for an escape route in case shifting occurs. Maintain considerable space among teammates to avoid injury from falling rock. If the rocks become dislodged, be ready to yell, "ROCK!" to alert your teammates to seek protection or get out of the way.

Be careful with your footing when traveling through scree. Your poles will serve you well as you progress uphill. When moving downhill, it may be possible to stride in a cross-country ski-like fashion. As you slide through the small rocks however, be aware of changing terrain or what may lie beneath the scree.

SAND

Traveling through sand is difficult because the surface sinks with every step you take. Take deliberate steps and work with the terrain as opposed to fighting it every step of the way. If sand travel is unavoidable, look for hard-packed areas to hike on.

SNOW

Always tread lightly when traveling across snow. Probe with your poles (or an ice axe, if required for the race) for thin layers. Breaking through could mean a sprained ligament or worse, a terrifying ride on a speedy stream underneath the snow. Keep an eye out for depressions and variance in the color or texture of the snow. The sound of running water will also provide valuable clues to safe travel.

Be extra cautious around trees and boulders. If you step too close, a serious fall could occur. Sturdy, waterproof mountain boots or crampons will provide greater traction in the snow. Also, it is a good idea to carry a rope for rescue and safe travel through tricky areas.

WATER

Before you take the plunge, explore your alternatives. Look for bridges, or natural river crossings like a firm path of dry rocks or fallen logs. If heading into the water is your only option, look for the safest place to cross. Take the time to study the water first, then loosen your backpack before you go in so that in an emergency, you can easily slide out of it. Place your poles upstream to determine the depth of the water and to hasten the possibility of being swept downstream. Feel with your foot for a steady spot before committing. Once you feel secure, plant your foot firmly. Progress one step at a time as you cross facing upstream. As you traverse the water, realize that it could change sporadically and tread carefully.

Odyssey Adventure Racing Academy participants get plenty of practice and race experience in the new River George area of West Virginia.

CLOSE-CALL IN PATAGONIA

BY JULI LYNCH, TEAM ODYSSEY

As darkness seeps across the landscape, we get a spectacular view back across the Nahuel Huapi Lake. The blackened ridges slide down into the deep midnight blue of the water. The lights of Bariloche dot the distant horizon like painted stars in an earthbound galaxy. Here, the moon waits for the total passing of sunlight before its grand entry. It's as if the sun and the moon have an agreement to honor each other's performance, to wait until one has exited west. For now we are immersed in a black that is pierced with the stars of a million planets. And then, it appears, over the silhouettes of the Torres, rising to take its place as a spotlight for our journey. Headlamps be damned. Our lunar lamp lights the way. We skip like children from rock to rock. Aric careens ahead, map in hand, compass poised. Marc and Mike follow, unsteadily.

It is midnight. We continue to climb. We are 14 hours into a ten-day race. I love the rock scrambling we are doing. A fixed rope here allows us to scramble up steep, slippery rock. My pack feels great. I hate my footwear. But I know exactly who to blame and keep my mouth shut. We begin to pass teams that have bivied out for the night. I almost step on one guy who has deposited his carcass right on the trail. The trail is unmarked but somewhat obvious by the footprints and fixed ropes. Aric, however, keeps a vigil of the map and compass. Don assists. I listen intently. We look upward to huge luminous peaks that seem to bend and beckon us. We climb on.

At 12:15 AM on Tuesday, December 5, we reach a spot that requires a couple of relatively easy climbing moves along some rounded rock. Aric climbs first followed by me and then Don. Marc and Mike are behind and decide to try a less difficult route 10 feet lower and 10 yards to the right. I hear the rock first and then Marc's cry, "Oh my god." There are sounds you have in your body's memory. Sounds that immediately produce images in your mind. Sounds that have only one meaning. The sound of boulders sliding, then crashing one upon the other means rock slide. Mother Nature shaking loose a tense muscle, relieving her holds on rocks that want to travel. Sometimes they leave without obvious warning, crashing down until they find a new place to dwell. Sometimes they crash down in the stretching, yawning and shaking of entire mountainsides. And sometimes we determine their departure, with a step or a placement of our hand.

My heart stops. My breath is held. My brain waits for the next piece of information. What it receives is an image of Mike being crushed under the tulage of descending boulders. I look at Aric. I look at Don. I say, "Mike." His scream shatters the thick silence that follows the settling of the rocks. "My arm. I broke my arm. Get down here you guys," Mike shouts. Relief surges through my body. He's alive. "Mike, we're coming. Stay there. Put pressure on your arm. We're coming," shouts Don as he takes charge. Marc is crawling up over the lip of the ridge. "Marc, you stay here. Juli, come with me. Aric, get the beacon and the flares," says Don. Don and I carefully crawl over the rock fall.

We reach Mike and in the darkness, I see only his hand. Flesh and bone and tendon exposed, mangled from his wrist. He is conscious. Don tears into the medical kit and gives me explicit instructions. He speaks to Mike calmly and with reassurance. Mike keeps apologizing to us, "Jules, I'm so sorry for this." "Mike," I say, "it's O.K., it's not your fault. You will be all right. We will take care of you." He is so calm and still. He allows Don to manipulate, bandage and secure his hand. Don keeps him talking by asking questions. Aric sets the beacon and sets off flares within 5 minutes. We yell to Marc to set up the tent. Aric constructs a splint out of a sock and sand and scouts a spot for a helicopter landing. We are lucky. Forty feet below us is a ledge with a sheltered spot for a tent. While Marc works on setting up the tent, a French team who has bivied below us climbs up and offers help. The have seen our flare. We get Mike down from where the boulder hit him and down to the tent. Then, we wait.

At 1:30 AM, out of the moonlit, star-filled Patagonia night comes the faint then stronger chop, chop, chop of a helicopter. We sigh deeply. We cover our equipment and our heads and wait for it to lower 2 medics. Don and Aric talk to the physician while I sit with Mike in the tent. He is cold. We have wrapped him in our jackets, bivies, and sleeping bag. He asks about his hand. I reassure him that he will be O.K. The pain is setting in. He's quiet now, no doubt reflecting, as he so often does. But this time I know it is a different reflection. A questioning, a rush of fear and the unknown.

The helicopter comes in a second time and drops a stretcher down. We walk Mike to the landing and Don gets him secured. The helicopter drops down one more time and Mike disappears as he is lifted into the night. I hear the mountain sigh and I know at that moment that I am blessed to have Don and Aric as teammates. I say a prayer to Mother Earth. I thank her for sparing Mike's life, not daring to ask her why, but instead accepting that her mountains offer many gifts, which we will never understand.

CROSSING WATER

HELPFUL HINTS

- **If the water is fast flowing, cross in a tight group to utilize each other's support. If you form a line, put the weakest person in the middle, the strongest person upstream and link elbows with each other.**

- **In extremely fast, shallow water, form a huddle and lean into each other as you progress across the water.**

- **In treacherous waters clip into a safety rope. Many races will have one already set up if the water has any danger zones.**

- **In general, narrow streams are deeper.**

- **Once you are safely across and know you will be trekking dry land for awhile, change your socks and clip your wet ones to your pack to dry.**

PACE

Achieving the right pace is crucial to longevity in this discipline. Before you set off in competition, calculate your pace. To do this, walk a triangle based on bearings of 90-degree increments. Set a bearing of 90 degrees and walk 100 paces, each step counting as one pace. Turn at a ninety-degree angle to your right and walk 100 paces at a 180-degree bearing. Turn ninety-degrees again and walk 100 paces at a bearing of 270-degrees. Upon your 100th step, you should end up in the exact same spot as where you started. This process will reinforce your pace so you become extremely familiar with it in a race.

- In a team situation, appoint one person to keep track of team pace. This is particularly effective when you are close to a change in direction or to a major landmark.

- On average, it takes 64-68 steps to travel 100 meters.

- To estimate the distance of your average step, stand with your feet together and then lean forward. Allow one foot to naturally come forward to prevent your body from tumbling to the floor. The distance between your feet is a close value of what your average pace is. This information will assist you in determining how many steps it will take to get to a particular destination.

PACING STRATEGIES

When estimating the length of time it will take to conquer a hiking leg and then actually hiking it, you must have a realistic sense of your abilities! Only you know your body best.

Most authorities will suggest a conservative average pace (hiking with a heavy load on your back) of 2 miles per hour and an additional hour for every 1,000 feet of elevation gain.

So, for example:

Say you want to cover 10 miles with an elevation gain of 2,000 feet. Divide 10 (miles you want to the hike) by 2 (average walking pace) to determine your estimated time, which equals 5 hours. Now factor in the elevation gain, which is an hour for every 1,000 feet. In this case, add an extra 2 hours. The estimated

total time it will take you to hike 10 miles at an elevation gain of 2,000 feet is 7 hours. WHEW! Add the various footwear possibilities, the weight of your pack, your level of fatigue, hydration and nourishment levels, the weather, the type of surface you are on, and the thickness of the vegetation and you can easily understand the intensity (physical alone!) requirements of an adventure race.

This discipline tends to get overlooked because we assume we know how to walk so it won't be a problem in a race. However, many teams tend to fall apart on the trekking legs and conversely, in many cases an adventure race is won on foot. It is a good idea to do many hiking workouts as a team before a race. This training will provide ample opportunities to time your performance in various conditions and also to get a feel for team dynamics.

REST STEPS

Incorporating rest steps into your walking technique can be a lifesaver when trekking endless miles. It will help you find your pace and put off the onset of fatigue. Your pace will decrease as you pause between each step, but it will allow you to continue moving forward, which is the goal of a race.

First, focus on inhaling a large amount of air, and then take a step forward. As you exhale, keep most of your weight in your front leg to relax the muscles of your rear leg. Extend the front leg as much as possible to decrease the amount of effort it takes to hold your position. This transfers the load from the muscular system to the skeletal system. Repeat on the other side and strive towards a rhythm which you can sustain for hours at a time. Imagine climbing stairs with a pause between steps. As your right foot steps up, your knee extends and for a moment, your left leg dangles. If you exaggerate the motion, and slow down, you will be able to rest between each step.

When the air becomes thinner, and the terrain steeper, you may take three or four breaths per step. Maintain this conscious breathing to keep your focus and accumulate optimal energy through the oxygen you take in.

67

REST STOPS

An important but seemingly frivolous time to rest is shortly after your trek commences. It will allow you to loosen shoelaces, adjust your pack, assure your direction of travel and assess the team. After your initial stop, maintain regular communication with your team so that you can be efficient with your pace and the amount of stops you make.

Your subsequent stops will be for water refilling, eating, bladder and bowel relief, navigation, and resting your legs. Before you stop, decide as a team, how long you wish to break and designate a timer to keep track of the minutes. Once you are at rest, take your pack off or lean against a rock or tree to relieve some of the pressure on your back and shoulders. The extra tension that you create while enduring a heavy pack can zap your energy. If you have been traveling for many hours, elevate your feet to counteract the blood pooling in your legs and feet. Every chance you encounter to re-coup some energy, take it.

In addition, be aware of your collective water supply. Stop to refill your containers when everyone is almost empty. If one person has demolished his/her supply share until your stores are low. Otherwise, you will stop every hour, which sabotages your time.

A good rule of thumb is to take breaks every 1-1.5 hours. Remember you're in a race but also don't forget to take care of yourself and your team as you go. Experience is the best testament to rest management.

TREKKING POLES

Hiking poles can be a tremendous asset to your hiking performance. They distribute the load a little more evenly, taking some of the weight off legs and commanding more work from the upper body. They can assist you when hurdling over obstacles such as tree trunks or boulders. When bushwhacking, you can use them to push brush aside, and they make climbing hills and hiking descents more tolerable.

When trekking uphill, shorten your poles. As you ascend, plant your pole into the ground a short distance above you, then hoist yourself just past it. This technique requires a total body effort, which saves the legs and feet for the long haul.

Similarly, when traveling down a mountain, lengthen your poles longer than a normal span for flat terrain. In the same manner as uphill trekking, plant your poles a short distance in front of you to decrease the downward pull of gravity and hence lessen muscular exertion. Be careful, however, not to depend on the shoulder girdle too heavily. You can cause problems for yourself by the end of the race if you place too much stress on the shoulders. Practice before your race with poles to obtain a feel for your own technique that works the best.

The Leki Super Maluku poles are popular because of their ergonomically correct grip and flexible construction.

TEAM PACE TIPS

- Put the slowest person in the middle.

- Adjust your pace to average the slowest with the fastest.

- Maintain a 3-5 pace distance between each other.

- Call out branches, rocks and other potentially harmful objects to your teammates behind you.

- In the event of an injury, fatigue, or the need for faster speed, you can create a short-roping system. Simply tie a rope around the waist of the strongest teammate and around the waist of the speed-challenged teammate allowing 3-5 feet of rope between each person. To create the loops in the rope, use figure-8 knots so that you won't create a new situation to deal with!

TREKKING

BUSHWHACKING

The joys of bushwhacking are numerous if you're into peculiar vegetation and the discomfort it breeds. Which, if you want to enjoy success in adventure racing, is something you have to get used to. There are several techniques that adventure racers use to conquer thick brush. Some teams take running starts and dive and crash through it, making great time and even better war wounds. Other teams tread more carefully, as they cautiously choose their steps and move under and over thick branches and rocks. Some teams are so careful that they end up traveling in circles just to avoid the really creepy stuff!

Bushwhacking can take its toll on your joints. Take an uncertain step and your foot slides on the muddy floor, sending your foot in one direction and your body in another. Reach for an unsecured root to stabilize your body as you swing across a steep drop-off, and the consequences can be fatal. Never over-commit to a step or a handhold. Check and double-check the terrain before you move through it.

CONSIDER THESE TIPS

- First off, avoid the bush if possible. Travel can be five times slower in the thick stuff.

- Brush is always nastier closer to streams and rivers.

- Brush is generally less dense under heavier timber.

- If possible, traverse talus or scree fields as opposed to lush, more vulnerable terrain.

- Take the high road—ridges generally provide easier travel and are usually less vegetated.

- If a stream parallels your route—it may be easier to travel right through the channel. If you choose to do this, loosen your pack straps, use each other and your poles for stability and be extra careful on the rocks.

- Animals usually choose paths of lesser resistance.

- When bushwhacking, hold a branch for your teammate behind you while you pass through to avoid snapping him/her in the face.

- When trekking through mud or sand, space yourselves to avoid a serious tumble.

- Don't blindly trust tree trunks when climbing up a steep slope. By entrusting your weight in a tree, you could seriously jeopardize the fate of your working limbs and possibly your life.

In the colder months, vegetation is sparse, making bushwhacking much easier.

THE COMPLETE GUIDE TO ADVENTURE RACING

EXTREME TERRAIN

THE MIGHTY JUNGLE—TROPICAL REGIONS

The jungle is a frightening place if you don't understand it. But it doesn't have to be. Many expedition-level adventure races are held in tropical areas, thus jungle travel is inevitable. With some knowledge and common sense, you can safely race through the densely canopied terrain.

Tropical areas, commonly called "the tropics", are found in the areas of the world that lie between 23.5 degrees north and 23.5 degrees south of the equator. The equator bisects almost all tropical rainforests of the world. Rainforests, semi-evergreen seasonal forests, tropical scrub, thorn forests, and tropical savannas are all prevalent in these regions with annual rainfalls of 100 inches or more distributed throughout the year.

Vegetation is abundant in these areas. There are about 30 different foods you can safely eat in the tropics. Common edible foods you may find include: bananas, sugar cane, tropical almonds, water chestnuts, cashews, and many exotic fruits. Remember that food with a hard shell is safe to eat in its natural state. Of course, if you are not sure about a food, save yourself and your team from sickness by sticking to what you have in your pack.

In a jungle, it is really hard to move through the thick brush. You have to trust your compass and do an extremely good map study. One of the routes that offers the least resistance in a jungle is a waterway. Try to avoid cross-country travel by going directly from point A to point B. Take the smartest way, which isn't always the fastest initially (but eventually, you will save time and heartache).

If, by chance, you are near a ridge and you have a choice of going high or low, go high, on top of the ridge. It will have less vegetation, less streams and less swamps to cross than in the valley. You can also see more when you are up high and game trails are more likely to be found.

OTHER REMINDERS WHILE RACING IN THE JUNGLE

- Jungle movement is almost impossible to do at night. It is extremely easy to get lost. Try to avoid thickets and swamps.

- Be careful when you are touching bushes and plants. Black palm in Panama, for example, can cause cellulites, which can eventually lead to the need for amputation. Long thorn-like needles go right through gloves, boots and pants and can wreck havoc on your racing.

- Don't touch the animals! Poison Dart Frogs or Poison Arrow Frogs, which are bright blue, green, orange, and bright yellow in color are very dangerous—1/100,000 of an ounce of secretion from these frogs will kill any human being.

- It is really easy when you are moving through the jungle to focus on the trees immediately in front of you and not on the forest as a whole. Keep your focus and attention beyond the immediate flora. Look behind the immediate front. Look through it and look at the whole jungle. Try to get an idea of whether you are going up or down to see how the landscape goes. This practice is called developing your "jungle eyes". This will help you avoid a lot of scratches and bruises.

- Animals generally move towards water and clearings.

- Within 30 minutes of sunset, it will be pitch-black. The sun leaves quickly. Prepare for darkness with efficiency.

- Look out for falling trees. One of the biggest causes of death in the jungles of Panama is a tree falling on campers.

- Watch out for poisonous snakes. See section on snakes in "Merging With Nature."

THE DESERT—ARID REGIONS

In the desert, your knowledge of the terrain and the basic climactic elements and your ability to cope with the elements has everything to do with your success. Being smart applies especially to desert conditions. Work occurs early morning and late into the evening. During the day, progress is slower and rest is inevitable.

FIVE DESERT TYPES

Mountainous—recognized by scattered ranges, barren hills and typically separated by dry, flat basins. Sometimes a high ground might rise gradually or even abruptly from these flat areas to a height of several thousand feet above sea level. But they are still considered deserts. Rainfall is infrequent. But flash floods can happen.

Rocky Plateau—rock outcroppings provide shelter from the sun and have "cisterns" which collect water after it rains.

Sand Dunes—usually completely void of plant life. Travel is extremely tough.

Salt Marsh—in arid areas, the insects are incessant. Bites are highly likely, which can lead to infection. Terrain can be corrosive to gear and skin.

Gebel (highly dissected terrain) or "Wadi"—found in arid areas. Formed by rainstorms that erode soft sand and carve out miniature canyons. Forms a maze as it twists and turns. Shelter is available, but don't take a wrong turn or you will have to back out the same way you went in.

THINGS TO REMEMBER IN A DESERT OR AN ARID ENVIRONMENT

1. Low rainfall.
2. Little water.
3. Intense heat—mirages are a common phenomenon.
4. Intense sunlight.
5. Wide temperature range.
6. Cold temperatures at night, hot temperatures by day—up to 140 degrees.
7. Sparse vegetation, hard to find cover.
8. Sand storms are possible—have wrap-around goggles or glasses.

Heat gain is caused by hot temperatures, direct sunlight, direct blowing winds, reflective heat from the sun rays coming off the sand, and conductive heat from direct contact with the sand and desert rocks which average 30-40 degrees hotter than the air. In addition, the intense heat and sunlight increase the body's need for water. At night, the drop in temperatures can range close to 100 degrees going to 140-50. If you are not prepared, the consequences could be extremely uncomfortable and even dangerous. So, try to move faster in the early and late hours and more slowly with plenty of breaks during the daytime.

If you get caught in a sandstorm cover your eyes, your mouth, your nose and ears. Mark the direction you have been traveling, and just lie down and wait for the storm to go by.

MIRAGES

As light is refracted through heated air rising from a surface of sand or stones, an optical illusion, called a mirage, occurs. A mirage will make an object that is one mile away appear to move. Mirages make land navigation difficult because they obscure natural features by making them blurry. If you are not sure if you see a mirage, get to higher ground (10 feet or higher) if possible so that you are above the super-heated air close to the ground (that's the only place where a mirage takes effect) to correctly assess the terrain.

IN THE DESERT

- Light levels in desert areas are usually more intense than other geographical areas. Nights are usually crystal clear, making it easy to see other teams, flashlights and checkpoints. But, if moonlight is not available, visibility is extremely limited.

- Regardless of the type of desert, the conditions provide the same challenges: it is difficult to find food, water, or shelter. Physical movement is very difficult and so is land navigation. Seeking shelter is also difficult, as there is virtually nothing to provide cover from the intense heat and sun.

- The key factor in arid area survival is understanding the relationship between physical activity, the air temperature and water consumption. The body requires a certain level of water for activity at certain temperatures. If a racer were working hard in the sun at 110 °F, that person would normally require 5 gallons of water per day. This may be an unlikely goal to accomplish. Regardless, you need plenty of water to survive an adventure race, so drink as much as possible as often as possible.

IF WATER IS SCARCE

- Don't eat. Whatever you eat requires water for digestion. It is better to save your water for cooling.

- Thirst is not a reliable guide for water needs. A person who uses thirst as a guide will only drink 2/3 the amount of water needed for normal hydration and health.

- At temperatures below 100°F, try to drink 1 pint of water every hour.

- At temperatures above 100°F, try to drink 1 quart of water every hour.

This practice may be impractical during racing, but strive towards these guidelines. Drink in regular intervals to remain cool and decrease sweating. Even if water supply is low, take constant small sips to stay cool. Conserve your sweat by reducing the intensity of your activity during the heat of the day and try to move faster at night and early morning.

In addition to heat hazards, arid area hazards include insects, snakes, thorn plants, cacti, contaminated water, sunburn, eye irritation, and climactic stress.

To lessen the impact of these hazards:

- Wear gloves.
- Visually inspect an area before you sit down and shake anything out that comes in contact with the ground before you move on.
- Always pay attention to where you put your hands and feet.
- Always assume that water is contaminated and treat everything you drink.
- Use lots of sunblock paying close attention to your lips.
- Cover your eyes and head.

The worst conditions I've ever experienced in racing occurred at the X-Games in Baja, California. It was 140 degrees Fahrenheit. These difficult conditions almost killed the racers. John Howard, worried about the safety and lives of the racers, asked the race director to cancel the event. The sun would bake our packs and hydration systems so that when we would drink our boiling water, we would burn our lips, our tongue and our mouth. Then the water wouldn't even dissipate. It felt like this hard rock inside our guts. Everyone became dehydrated.

To make matters worse, there was no cover for shelter or shade. It was literally a survival situation.

Robyn Benincasa was resting under a bush with her two male teammates who were passed out. I brought my teammates to the same bush. Then my teammate Johnny passed out. As Robyn, my other teammate Juli and I were talking, we would be interrupted every couple of minutes by blood-curdling screams as our teammates' limbs would lock up. The three of us who were awake would massage it out; then they would go unconscious again. When the person would scream, he would jump up and his face would hit all of the bushes and he would yell, "AAAAAHHHH" as one of his limbs would lock. Soon, most of my teammate Johnny's body was seized with muscle cramps. Both of his calves, both quads, his right forearm, which locked the thumb out of joint, and his neck locked up which caused his head to turn violently to the left. At that point, his eyes rolled into the back of his head and he passed out again.

—*Don*

NATURES PEAKS—ARCTIC REGIONS

Regions where the temperature of the warmest month of the year does not exceed 50°F are categorized as Arctic regions. Sub-Arctic regions are those areas where the mean temperature of the warmest four months of the year does not exceed 50°F. Mountainous and high elevation areas of temperate regions also have extremely cold weather. Training and racing in cold weather dictates abundant knowledge of the area for safety.

In addition to cold temperatures, wind chill increases the hazards of cold regions. This effect is caused by moving air on exposed flesh. For example, a fifteen-knot wind coupled with a 15°F temperature elicits an equivalent chill factor. Changes in weather and temperature occur very quickly in these regions, so be prepared to stop. Remember that the body can lose heat a lot easier than it can produce it. Plan accordingly!

TRENCH FOOT/IMMERSION FOOT

Trench foot is the result of lots of hours and days of exposure to wet or damp conditions at temperatures above freezing. This problem is very common in adventure racing. Once your feet are completely saturated with water, they are more susceptible to blisters and sores, skin softening and pain.

Your feet become cold, swollen, and look waxy. They feel heavy and numb and it is very hard to walk. If you are caught with a severe case of trench foot, the nerves and the muscles may sustain major damage. Upon worsening, the flesh dies and gangrene sets in. Amputation is inevitable.

The best prevention: keep dry socks with you. At least once a day, wash your feet and change your socks. Use a substance like Hydropel to help the feet repel moisture.

COLD-WEATHER TIPS

- **Sunburn occurs more often at high altitudes than low altitudes.**

- **Snow blindness is caused by the reflection of ultraviolet rays from the sun as it shines on a snow-covered area. The following symptoms may occur: the feeling of grit in your eyes, pain when moving your eyeballs, watery eyes, and headaches. Permanent eye damage can occur with eventual blindness if not treated. To treat, bandage eyes until symptoms dissipate. To prevent, protect your eyes with dark glasses or goggles.**

- **Stay hydrated.**

- **Wear lightweight, loose layers. The volume of air trapped between your layers creates the insulation.**

- **Don't dress too warmly. Dampness decreases the insulating quality of your clothing and as the sweat evaporates, your body cools.**

- **Tie wet clothing to your pack when you are moving.**

THE NEED FOR SPEED

Generally, if your team is well into a race and feeling fresh and you encounter easy terrain, running is a sensible option. Speeds above 5 mph warrant running as opposed to walking for greater efficiency. So, if you are traveling at a fast walking pace, consider running.

WHEN TO WALK AND WHEN TO RUN

The premiere objective in an adventure race is to cover a set distance in the shortest amount of time. Your speed is a consequence of two interdependent variables of your stride: length and frequency. Stride frequency is the number of steps you take each minute. Stride length is the distance between each step.

As running speed increases, stride length will increase more than frequency will increase. At slower speeds, running velocity will increase as the stride is lengthened. As a runner improves to higher-level speed, only then is stride frequency a factor.

Reciprocally, when you increase your walking speed, stride frequency is more predominant than stride length. When you walk, one foot is always in contact with the ground. Therefore, it would be very ineffective to lengthen the stride in an attempt to get faster. This fact also explains why it makes more sense economically to run when you reach a speed at which your stride needs to lengthen and be efficient at the same time.

Ultimately, you will walk or run at a pace that requires "minimum effort".

To maximize efficiency, an optimal balance must be achieved. Your weight, frame, strength, flexibility, coordination, timing, and rhythm affect your final product.

GOING THE DISTANCE

A mile is a mile is a mile, right? Wrong! A city mile is different from a country mile. A Himalayan mile is far more demanding than the trails of the Rockies and the Rockies are different from the Appalachians. Your miles will vary depending on the weather, altitude, landscape, fitness, and the time of day.

GETTING IN SHAPE TO TREK

Get used to lugging a heavy backpack around. The extra load will take its toll on your neck, back, and shoulders. Develop the stamina as well as the awareness of possible areas of rubbing and chafing. If your pack isn't right for you, your training days will reveal any problems.

The key is to acclimate to your shoes, pack, and even the apparel you will be wearing for the race. Specific training tips will be covered in the Training Chapter.

RACE WITHOUT A TRACE

In order to preserve this glorious playground we call Earth, and to ensure the destiny of this sport, it is paramount to race without a trace. Be prepared for your endeavor. Be sure you know what you're getting into, have the right equipment for it, and if you require dependence on natural resources, respect the fruit that nature bears.

Strive for zero damage of the environment as you race through it. Travel in single-file lines. When not on trails, trek on ground least susceptible to damage. Let nature be. Restrict your souvenirs to memories,

photographs, and stories. Let wildlife be. Don't provoke the animals. Whatever you take in, take out. Keep track of your food wrappings. In fact, get rid of the packaging of as many items as possible before the race. It will save time, weight, and effort during the race.

Act responsibly just as you would if you were a guest in someone's home. When outside, you are nature's guest. Pick up after yourself, if you make a mess—clean it up, and leave things the way that you found them.

MERGING WITH NATURE

Under the normal conditions that we humans have set for ourselves, we are at the top of the food chain. However, when exploring the great outdoors, we make ourselves vulnerable to the millions of creatures that call it their home. Remember that you are treading on their territory. With knowledge, tolerance, and levity, you can minimize any outdoor annoyances caused by your temporary neighbors.

INSECTS

A common scenario humans must tolerate in the great outdoors is bug bites. In a race situation, your experience will be more enjoyable if you are prepared for an attack. Preventative measures such as covering your body parts when trudging through the bush, using a repellent, and ingesting substances such as vitaminB₁ to sour the way you smell to the bugs, will lessen your discomfort. Once bitten, a tough mental state, and an over-the-counter antihistamine and skin lubricant will allow you to continue to race.

*See the health section for details on first aid care.

REPTILIAN CREATURES

To lessen your chances of a snake encounter, pay particular attention to your environment, especially at dusk and dawn. Watch where you step, reach, and climb. Keep in mind slithery reptiles are ectothermic, or "cold-blooded". When it's cool, they want to be warm, so you may see one sunning itself on a rock or a road. When it's hot, they stay cool in the shade under logs, rocks, and in crevices.

Wearing pants or gaiters is a common practice for snake-phobic folk. Your trekking poles can also come in handy. Use them to predetermine your footsteps and to move a snake out of the way if necessary.

If you come across a snake, back away without taking your eyes off of it. If it rattles, move quickly. Once you have distanced yourself, keep your eyes open and continue along the racecourse. Most bites occur when you step on a snake.

There are no steadfast rules that determine whether or not a snake is poisonous. To remain injury-free, just try to avoid all snakes all of the time.

TO LESSEN THE BURDEN OF INFECTIONS AND WOUNDS FROM INSECTS AND OTHER CREATURES

- Carry insect repellent and use it.

- Close off your clothing, tuck your pant legs in, roll down and button your sleeves and collars, and wear gloves if you can. Many times, you may need to wear a mosquito head net so that you can sleep safely. If you don't have protection, you can smear mud on your skin for protection.

- Insects come out mainly at night.

- Try to avoid stopping by swamps.

- At least once a day, look for ticks, fleas, leeches and other insects. Keep them off of you as much as possible.

- Try not to lie or sit on the ground.

- Treat your clothing with insect repellent.

- Leeches can be found in wet underbrush.

- Whenever you put your shoes or clothes on, shake them out first.

- Try to avoid stopping near ant hills.

- Always protect your feet when in the jungle. Even in the water.

- Be aware of sharks in estuaries. They have been found in jungles.

- Coral—dead or alive—can cut your skin and cause bad infections.

- Use your trekking poles to probe in front of you while walking through jungle waters.

One common rhyme to remember:

"Red touch yellow, kill a fellow.
Red touch black, venom lack."

In case of a bite:

1. Try to stay calm and positive.
2. The bite will be excruciatingly painful within seconds of a lethal encounter. Anticipate pain and swelling.
3. Clean the area with water.
4. Get to a doctor as soon as possible.

25-50% of venomous snakes will actually inject poison. But that's no reason to let down your guard.

MAMMALS

When we race through the wilderness, we share the same space with hundreds of thousands of other living beings. The largest and perhaps the smartest are bears. Although bears have a ferocious reputation, they eat a diet full of fish, berries, and grass. They are playful creatures but they don't like surprises. If you intrude on a bear's domain, he won't be happy. If a sow feels like her cubs are in jeopardy—watch out! This is not surprising considering that just about every species on this planet will protect their home and young under any circumstance.

If you stumble upon a bear in the wilderness, maintain your distance and try to be calm. Stick close together to create an image of enormity, which might deter the bear. Bears have terrible eyesight so they might think you are too mighty a match and retreat. If he sniffs the air, he knows you are nearby and is assessing the situation. If he becomes animated—by exhibiting his enormity or moving his head about—he wants you to leave. Do it. But, by all means, don't run away, bears can outrun the fastest Olympic sprinters in the world. If you make a mad dash, he will most likely run after you.

If you hold your ground, wave your trekking poles high in the air, talk softly, and stay calm chances are, the bear will scamper away. Counter Attack, a bear-repellent that is similar to pepper spray, may be a tool you will want to carry in the wilderness. If this is the case, keep it readily available and make sure you are upwind and precise when you use it.

TREKKING

Bears have an incredible sense of smell upon which they thrive. They can smell a human a mile away. But, their life agenda is not hunting humans. While you are in bear country, make lots of noise. Talk loudly, sing, or blow your whistle at regular intervals. Let your presence be known. When you are near water or out on a windy day, nature's sounds can mask your best efforts of noise making. Pay attention. Be aware of rivers, natural food sources like berry patches, and keep an eye out for animal droppings and animal tracks.

When you enter a new valley, blow your whistle loudly for several seconds to announce your team to the creatures that roam there.

Bears and many other wild animals are much like us in that they have good days and bad days. Sometimes they are easy-going and sometimes they get irked for no good reason. We cannot predict the moment they choose to fly off the handle any easier than we can control the behavior of our significant other!

Part of the fun of racing in the wilderness is the close proximity you obtain to creatures of the wild. If you maintain keen awareness, have a base of knowledge about your temporary neighbors, and can remain calm in case of close contact, your stories will be great fun to share when you reach safe ground.

Remember that bears are not the only furry creatures out there. Moose, elk, caribou, mountain lions, and many other animals share the wilderness and require acute attention in an encounter. Don't get too close and if an animal charges, get behind a tree or some other tall, wide, solid object.

THE CRITTERS ON MY FACE

BY ANGELIKA CASTANEDA

This is an excerpt from the account of a ten-day Expedition Competition, the Raid Gauloises. The team was the first American all-women team. Five women finished the three hundred fifty-mile race through the jungles of Borneo in eight days and six hours. The disciplines in this ultra-distance event included: hiking, climbing, rafting, canoeing and spelunking.

The jungle had overtaken us and we were at its mercy. We had lost our only lifeline to civilization, the little path along which barefooted headhunters were chasing their prey a mere decade before.

With only dim sunlight filtering through the impenetrable foliage of the high jungle canopy, finding the hidden trail had become a matter of survival.

We searched for the hatchet marks commonly engraved by indigent hunters. Finding these navigational aids savages would help us speed up the slow progress of chancing our way through the jungle.

Then, as the daylight quickly expired, darkness penetrated our claustrophobic world, and the forest became enveloped in an eerie silence of solitude. Just as suddenly as the light had fleeted, and the silence had come, nightlife ignited in a cacophony of exuberant chirps and whistles unique to the rain forest.

With little option, I embraced the sounds, listening intently to the frogs and other mysterious creatures that sang their rhythmic tunes in an ear-numbing exchange of volleys. The music of life played a symphony for us intruders from another world, a great variety of magnificent overtures that stifled our thinking.

With our senses smothered under the weight of the night's pitch-blackness, our compass had become our only guide. Our headlamps were only a single finger probe into the vast three-dimensional world, where all we could see were the assembled shadows of the ghostly-green dew-laden bush. Our fatigue painted strange apparitions before the theatre of our minds.

There was no option but to endure the trial, with no advantage to complaining about it. I embraced these images, making them my own special treat.

In the drudgery of my imagination, we trudged for hours, for days, and for nights. My obsession to find the path and see an opening out of our predicament developed first into yearning and ultimately into naked despair. Eventually, a catharsis of spirit came upon me, and I was left with nothing except humbling acceptance for adaptation to this world that we had inherited.

My mind took flight into its own fantasy world—how much I missed my beloved mountains, my private room in the farmhouse of my childhood, from which I could see the open fields of the valley.

But reality kept checking in on us as the rain kept up its persistent drizzle, conspiring to keep us constantly wet. The cold kept us moving, lest it gained a grip with its icy, hypothermic fingers. That night we walked for more heartbreaking hours than I can bear to remember. Finally the darkness and its comrades had their way. Fatigue and fear of becoming hopelessly lost convinced us to stop, and wait out the time until the first rays of light would come to our aid.

The five of us huddled under a big tree, embracing each other in search of warmth and rest. The rain continued to pour, big dollops of water fell on us periodically as little leafy reservoirs over-filled their capacity.

Sleep was impossible as spasms of shivering cold racked us to the bone. Desperate for respite we took turns lighting our few emergency compost wood sticks. All our heads formed a makeshift roof as we bent over the tiny flame that gasped for kindled life.

With a few more sticks added, our miniature bonfire got going, and we were immediately released by the euphoria of imagined protection. The illusion of creating a home environment out of these glowing embers was as real to us then as a great raging hearth would be to the city dweller disconnected from Mother Nature. We lay on the soaked ground with no protection, embracing each other, sapping and sharing strength as we stared

longingly into the little flame, rooting for its courageous fight to survive the hostility of falling water.

My thoughts drifted out of the bounds of my body. I saw myself from a distance, a girl with her eyes sealed against reality, the escape of her soul seeking peace.

It was then that utter exhaustion changed its roll from persecutor to ally. Rest soaked us up like a sponge that had been crisply dried. My mouth fell open and my head turned upwards to the sky as the rain drops sprinkling my face.

With my eyes closed I embraced the picture of the little flickering flame, holding on to the soothing image as though losing it would seal my fate to be lost here in the darkness forever.

Then new senses took over. Where our bodies were touching I felt the electricity of life, where energy and warmth flowed from one to another in a trickling stream that strengthened the whole to a degree that vastly outmatched the sum of its parts.

Suddenly I felt a feather light touch on my face, distinctly different from a drop of rain. My senses, sharpened by survival power, and my body, numb from exhaustion, cannot agree how to react—I cannot move. Instead, I embrace life, and simply let the touch be.

Another and then another light touch follows, as if someone is tickling me with a feather. In my mind I reach out with my hand to strike my face, swatting the offending insect, but in reality I could not care any less and do nothing.

The light pats seem to be associated with mushy sliding movements, almost like someone caressing me with delicate light strokes of a feather's tip. They generate a pleasantly peculiar feeling.

My thoughts dwell a while on that perception, and I remain at ease in a healthy version of denial. This interruption from my thoughts of warmth and sleep among puffy, soft pillows could have bothered me, but I did not want to be troubled.

Again, I embraced the circumstance.

Ouch...! A little sharp bite zaps me out of dreamland.

Then again, another bite! "No...!" I roar inwardly.

Although I anticipate what my tormentor could be, I could not move and I did not want to move.

The symphony of the jungle's night music had receded as the pouring rain had blanketed over it. I had almost forgotten that we were in the domain of creatures very different from ourselves.

Another bite, and then another! Indignant about the assaults, but still too transfixed by acceptance to react, I hone in on what I'm feeling.

The slimy sliding movement halts close to my open mouth, and a few seconds later I feel the final anticipated sting that confirms my theories about who the critters are…

I'd accepted that my face was their battlefield, and they'd won the fight. Defeated by their relentless efforts I turned my thoughts back to my dreams, my white soft and puffy blanket...

I could fight them later, I decided, but just not now...

A little later I could take them on, but now I would sleep...

And so the leeches continued to bury themselves into my skin.

The most intense pain I've ever experienced came from a tiny electric caterpillar that was on a tree that I had gently touched. Aware of black palm, I thought I was being careful. But, I just barely put my finger on this tree to rest for a moment, and as soon as I did, I felt this shooting pain up my arm, I broke into a cold sweat and then collapsed to the ground. I thought for sure I had been bit by one of the many poisonous snakes found in the jungle.

I looked at my hand to see the snake bite—but didn't see any. Then I looked at the tree and found a one-inch caterpillar that knocked me off my feet.

—Don

EQUINE TEAMMATES IN ADVENTURE RACING BY JULI LYNCH

So, you have taken on a race that includes an equestrian event. This means that not only will you have to become a proficient rider, but also a proficient horse person who is capable and confident in the care and maintenance of horses. The most ideal environment for establishing this proficiency will be with an accomplished horse person, who is willing to take you and your teammates under his/her wing to teach you the essential elements of riding and horse care for adventure racing.

Often, it is difficult for an accomplished horse person to know where to start or how much information to give you. My experience tells me that time is of the essence when training for an adventure race and while a lifetime of experience with horses may sound like a great place to start, most of us only have time to devote to the most critical learning.

In an adventure race, the terrain is often rough and the horses, stock grade breeding; or in the case of the 1998 Eco-Challenge in Morocco, of Arabian breeding, known to have a full, springy movement. Consequently, it will be of great benefit if you can "sit a horse", which is an old western phrase that means you can get on any breed of horse and "stay on".

If you have little to no experience riding a horse, begin with instruction in English riding. Most international races will only accommodate this style of riding. In the United States, riders can usually choose from English-style or western-style riding. Western-style is the technique that cowboys use. The saddle is larger than an English-style saddle and typically the reins are held in one hand in order to use a "neck rein" technique for steering and bending the horse. This allows the cowboy to use the other hand for roping. Watch an old John Wayne movie to witness Western-style riding. Watch the movie "National Velvet", to see English-style riding.

English-style riding offers a smaller saddle and requires two hands on the reins. The advantage of learning this technique first allows a smooth transition to Western-style riding and more importantly, most international races use some style of English saddles and English reins. In the 1995 Raid Gauloises in Patagonia, we used an "Argentine" saddle that was a deep-seated English saddle. In the 1997 Eco-Challenge in Australia, we used an English saddle with English reins. In the 1998 Raid Gauloises in Ecuador, we used a western/English combination saddle with western reins, whereas the 1996 Raid in Lesotho used English saddles.

THE BASICS

Locate an English-style riding instructor and sign up for a minimum of ten lessons if you are a first-time rider. Your instructor should cover all of the following basics with you:

- Preparing a horse for riding (brushing, hoof cleaning, etc.).
- Leading a horse and safely tying a horse to a tree, fence, and picket line.
- Proper saddling and bridling a horse.
- Catching a horse in a field.
- Putting a halter and lead rope on a horse.
- Mounting a horse (from both sides—don't underestimate the number of cliff ledges you will ride along).
- Proper lengths of stirrups. Know how to do this quickly on all types of saddles (English and Western).
- Signals for walking a horse forward.
- Signals for stopping a horse.
- Signals for turning a horse in both directions.
- Signals for backing a horse.
- Signals for asking a horse not to trot.
- Proper hand position at the trot (not hanging on horse's mouth).
- Ways to ride the trot (posting, standing in stirrups, sitting). Note: In my opinion, standing in stirrups is the most comfortable and safest position for adventure racing. Learn to balance your hands on the horse's mane, neck or front of the saddle.
- Ways to ride a canter and a gallop. Even though the canter and gallop are rarely used, a runaway horse *will* gallop. So know how to ride this gait!

- Transitions: Walk to trot, trot to walk, walk to canter, canter to walk, trot to canter and canter to trot.

- How to fall off at a moving gait and land safely (as possible).

- How to stop a runaway horse.

- Trail riding (while learning in an arena is safer, to truly be an adventure racing equestrian, you must be comfortable trail riding).

- Practice all gaits on the trail. Practice bushwhacking (off trail), practice mounting and dismounting and running alongside a horse while leading it.

- If possible, ride a horse across a stream. Learn how to confidently get a horse to cross wooden bridges and bodies of water.

The type of equestrian event that your team will compete in will determine the level of care that will be required of you. One-day events usually entail a few hours of a ride-and-run, which require general horsemanship skills. A multi-day event on the other hand will typically involve 2-3 days of horseback riding with virtually no assistance from the outside other than mandatory vet checks.

The equestrian section of the 1995 Raid Gauloises in Patagonia lasted for three days, which included two nights with our horses. That meant that we had to be fully prepared to camp with horses as no assistance from the race organization was provided. On the second night of camping, half of the teams we camped with lost their horses in the middle of the night because their horses broke free from their tie-downs. Our team had a decided advantage in the morning because our horses remained tied down. We were able to ride off while the other teams (six of them!) were stuck chasing their steed that were running freely across the pampas.

YOUR HORSE IS ANOTHER TEAMMATE

1. Plan to stop at every water hole, puddle, stream, river, trough and bucket to water your horses.

2. A good feeding strategy for your horses is to stop every 30 minutes to allow a couple of mouthfuls of forage. At night, camp in a field where your horse can graze through the dark hours. *Get as much information on the feeding of the horses prior to the race so that you know what to

expect. Some races will supply grain and hay at the camping spots, while others require you to carry grain with you and some rely on the natural vegetation.

3. Be aware of lameness in your horse. Get a feel for your horse at a trot. By standing up in the stirrups you can come to feel your horse's rhythm. If your notice that the "feel" of the rhythm suddenly changes at the trot, all other circumstances remaining relatively the same (terrain, speed, horse's energy), you may have a lame horse. If this may be the case, get off and lead your horse at a trot a circle in both directions. A lame horse in motion will step lightly on the sore leg and his head will rise simultaneously in an effort to take weight off the leg, giving him a bobbing action with his head. So what do you do if your horse is lame? Gently lead him forward, allow your horse to stand in cold water when the opportunity arises, and count on the rest he will have at the overnight camp spots (most races will not allow you to ride at night).

4. When your horse is tired, like a human, he will slow down. Allow your horse to rest just as you allow your team to rest throughout the day.

5. If your horse begins to pant, cool him off with tepid water applied to his head, neck, legs, and buttocks. Avoid dumping water on his kidney area (lower back) and be sure you don't use cold water, which could cause your horse to go into shock.

6. If you notice your horse continuously looking back at his belly or trying to kick at his belly, he may be colicky (he may have a bellyache!). If this is the case, hand-walk him until you reach the next checkpoint then notify the race officials.

If you anticipate racing for one full day or more with horses, seek a teammate with horse experience—it will benefit all living beings on your team!

WHAT TO WEAR FOR THE RIDE

- Bike shorts will soften your ride.

- If you wear your trail running shoes on your horse, ride with only your toes in the stirrup. Never shove your entire foot into the stirrup. Your typical racing footwear lacks heels and can easily slip through the stirrup creating a potentially life-threatening situation if you cannot release your foot.

STRATEGY

Once you have your horses and are on your way, keep in mind that navigating from horseback is different that navigating on foot. Horses cannot cross swamps, but they can traverse fairly steep terrain and forge rivers that would sweep humans under foot. A healthy horse can trot 5 miles/9km per hour. Most races will forbid galloping the horses to guard against teams running them into the ground. Strategically, it is wiser to maintain a steady trot than to engage in bursts of galloping anyway.

If you have little or no experience riding a horse, begin with instruction in English riding.

Study your map well and consider the terrain in front of you. If there are worn horse trails heading in your desired direction, use them. Horses are intense creatures of habit and will be far more willing to move forward if they are following a trail. If you are unsure of the terrain, send a foot guide ahead. *I was almost buried by a horse in a marsh bog in Ecuador because it appeared to be solid footing.*

Let the horses determine who will lead, not the riders. Horses will quickly establish a hierarchical arrangement amongst them. If you are traveling in single-file, watch for signs of agitation or aggression (kicking, biting) between the horses and place them so that the leader they accept is first in line. Place the slowest one somewhere in the middle, not at the end. Place the kicker or non-aggressive or amiable one at the rear. Place the boldest and most aggressive at the lead. He can be a bit ahead of the others and play scout. Don't hesitate to switch riders and horses. Not all horses get along with all people and vice-versa.

If your ride is a ride-and-run, let your horse carry the runner's gear. Horses will follow people on foot, so don't hesitate to have a runner out front setting the pace. However, when you encounter steep terrain or when crossing rivers, place the runner at the rear of the group and have him or her "tail" the rear horse. That is, have them hold onto the rear horse's tail (make sure he is not a kicker!). If you are concerned about the horse kicking someone, you can rig a long line from the horse's saddle back to the runner. Be certain that you can quickly release the line in the event of an emergency situation.

Do not hesitate to have the entire team dismount and lead the horses on extremely steep terrain. You will save time in the long run and prevent the gear from slipping forward or back and prevent the horse from losing his footing. A good rule of thumb is that if you are sliding backward while sitting your horse on an uphill or sliding onto his neck on a downhill, get off and walk.

There are many water crossings and bridge crossings when riding cross-country. Remember, you are dealing with herd animals, so it is imperative that the first horse in line is your bravest and boldest. And you, too, must be brave and bold, for the slightest hint of doubt at a water or bridge entrance will be recognized as fear by your horse, which signals danger. Ride toward the water and bridge crossing confidently and don't stop to investigate unless you have a safety concern. Forge ahead with a squeeze of your legs and a *cluck cluck* sound. Talking to horses really does work as long as you are reassuring. Yelling at them rarely achieves the objective. When progressing as a pack, keep the horses nose-to-tail for such crossings and the ones behind the lead will barely notice what they have done once they have crossed.

If you have the opportunity to swim with your horses, know that horses are great swimmers as long as they are left alone. In other words, start the horse upstream from where you want to land, stay on his back and give him his head (don't try to guide him with the reins). You are safest wrapping your arms around his neck and encouraging him on by squeezing your legs. Avoid dismounting and swimming alongside or in front of him. A hoof could kick you.

Most adventure races will have mandatory vet check and mandatory rest stops. At the vet check, your horse's vitals will be monitored (respiration, heart rate, dehydration index, etc.) and he will be checked for injuries, saddle sores, lameness, etc. If the veterinarian determines that your horse is too tired to continue, you may have to remain at the rest stop longer than the required time. If the veterinarian determines that your horse is unable to continue at all, they may or may not provide you with another horse. My experience has been that it depends upon the reason why the horse is unable to continue. You will have to make a good case to convince the officials that your horse's inability to continue is not your fault.

HAPPY TRAILS

The horseback riding section of any adventure race is a critical opportunity for the team to get off their feet and rest. It is a time when the team can rehydrate and catch up on calorie consumption, a rare moment in adventure racing. By being prepared and confident in your riding skills and being comfortable working with and caring for horses, the team will enjoy the experience. Like it or not, for a given amount of time, those four-legged beasts are part of the team. Strategically, they can create a huge advantage for you if you are prepared. This is because horseback riding is typically the one skill that most teams have the least amount of experience with.

So mount up and ride off toward the sunset with your team. Adventure racing is the ultimate challenge of skill, endurance, teamwork and strategy. It is only fitting that it be shared with the beauty, power and magnificence of the horse. Happy trails!

Mountain biking demands adventure, bravery, spirit, and skill all wrapped up into the package of a single soul. The hills are fierce—and there are plenty of them. You constantly teeter the fine line between crashing and thrashing. Power is essential throughout the ride.

Single-tracks, sharp turns, steep drop-offs, and varied degrees of inclines are sprinkled with boulders, gravel, sand, mud, and trees, evoking a constant flush of adrenaline that fuels your fears. You can always get off and walk. Nature is at your fingertips and the beauty is always there for the taking. But it's more fun to experience it on wheels.

Years ago, mountain biking basically meant riding downhill really fast. You would take a chairlift or throw your bike in the back of a truck and head to the top of a mountain so you could hammer down to the bottom. We've come a long way.

THE RIGHT BIKE FOR THE JOB

When purchasing a mountain bike, go to a reputable shop and discuss your specific needs with a knowledgeable salesperson, preferably one who is enthusiastic, a racer, or someone who is familiar with the sport. Describe adventure racing and the particular regions where you are interested in racing. Establish a relationship. Your visit is not a one-time stop. You want to be comfortable with the people and their business practice because you will be coming back for maintenance, repairs, and possibly upgrades. If you are lucky, you may even be able to find riding partners at the shop through employees, riding clubs, or events sponsored by the store. Down the road, you may even consider soliciting the shop for sponsorship.

COMPONENTS

In many adventure races, a hybrid or a cycle-cross bike may be your best bet. In any case, your off-road bike should fit you well, be light-weight, dependable and durable. Most importantly you need to be very familiar with your bike. The level of components you choose will depend on your bank account and will determine the efficiency of shifting and braking. Many pros will not use anything above XT. Some find that XT components are even more reliable than the more expensive XTR.

BRAKES

The kind of brakes you use depend on your skill-level and patience for maintenance. Disc brakes are a powerful option; however, they are a high maintenance bicycle part and more expensive. They function through a caliper system that hugs both sides of the wheel hub. The advantage with disc brakes is that they have excellent stopping power, which is very nice on the steep downhills and they do not clog up with mud. If you do end up bending or breaking a disc out on the trail or in a race, there is a very good chance that you have lost that brake.

V-brakes are identified by their long arms, which squeeze the rims to stop. V-brakes are fairly easy to repair on the trail. It is easy to carry and replace spare brake cables and pads. The latter is typically the more traditional choice of brakes.

SUSPENSION

Deciding between full-suspension and front-suspension is a common quandary. If you want rigid frame performance but somewhat of a soft ride, look for seat posts that have suspension on them. The spring in the seat post responds to trail conditions on demand. You can ride easy and enjoy a plush ride, or ride hard and get a damper-controlled ride (a damper controls the compression/rebound effect of your suspension through a hydraulic component). They take the edge off by giving a little suspension to your ride.

Another option is a head shock, or rear shock, which you can turn on and off. This flexibility allows comfort when suspension is on but doesn't interfere with your speed when turned off. This hard-tail design is a popular option for adventure racers.

Full-suspension is obviously more comfortable on the long and multi-day rides, but they are heavier than the hard-tails. With a full-suspension bike, there is also another piece of the bike that can break while riding with a hard-tail. Full-suspension bikes do not transfer all of the rider's energy to forward motion. Many full-suspension bikes can rob a portion of energy from a rider and transfer this energy to the up and down movement felt when riding with full-suspension.

TIRES

Learn about your course for tire selection. It's a good idea to have a collection of different tires for different purposes. For example, there are tires with forward-facing scoops, or wide blocks that stretch straight across the tire. These aren't good in mud. The mud cakes up in it causing mud slicks, which makes the bike heavy and kills its gripping action.

If you know you will be riding mostly fire roads and less technical trails, look for tires that will "float" on top of the gravel. The same tires you use on the trails of one race may slow you down in the predominantly gravel roads of another. Skinny, knobby tires cut through terrain, and fat flat tires float on top. Soft rubber tires don't wear very long, nor do they stick well in the rain. Harder rubber is better for the vast majority of riding.

THE COMPLETE GUIDE TO ADVENTURE RACING

When placing your tires on the rim, be sure to pay particular attention to the way the arrows are pointing on the tire. And be sure you are aware of how much tire pressure your tire is capable of holding. I do not like to try and save money by purchasing inexpensive tires. Tires need to be strong and lightweight, which typically means more expensive.

CLIPLESS PEDALS

Similar to ski bindings, clipless pedals allow you to attach your feet to your bike through shoe-mounted cleats that connect with spring-loaded teeth on your pedals. Utilizing clipless pedals creates a direct transfer of power from your muscles to the pedals. They allow a smoother pedal stroke, which leads to greater efficiency. It is relatively easy to adopt the pedals. A common fear

Choose a bike that is durable but remember that weight is an important factor in multi-day races.

is the inability to unclip in case of a fall. To unclip, simply rotate your heels outward, away from the bike. With a little practice, you will develop confidence and better riding technique.

Clipless pedals are not always advantageous in an adventure race. There may be situations in a race where you will have to walk or carry your bike for several miles, in which case your biking shoes may not be the right choice of footwear. It's a good idea to bring both kinds of pedals to a race with shoes that work with both of them. In one race we had to walk our bikes for the majority of a "70-mile ride". In a race up in Alaska, we ended up walking 30 of the 100 miles. There are clipless bike shoes that you can walk and ride in, however they are normally not meant to be walked in for any considerable distances.

THE SEAT

If saddle comfort is an issue, which ultimately it is when you spend hours and days in the biking legs of a race, consider the seats that are cut away, and filled with gel. The design supports your sit bones, while providing relief for your more vulnerable parts. Many manufacturers produce these ergonomically compatible seats, which effectively enhance your riding comfort. If you want to decrease the fatigue in your back and smooth out your ride, you may want to consider using a suspended seat post. These are relatively inexpensive and much cheaper than buying a full-suspension bike.

TRANSPORTING YOUR BIKE

If you are racing overseas, consider the wear and tear of shipping. Or, if you plan on racing in an area with extreme terrain such as the tundra of Alaska, you may want to pull out your old beater from the back of the garage (if you don't have one, ask your neighbors).

When traveling with your bike, seek an airline that will let your bike fly free. Another option is to UPS or airmail your bike to the first location you will visit in the host city or country. Compare pricing for the least expensive option.

To ship your bike, pack it in a hard case for the best protection. You will need to disassemble several bike parts to pack it correctly.

BIKE LIGHTS

Get a good system that has a strong riding mount on both your helmet and your bike. The beams should be easily adjustable. A lot of the pros use a three-beam system on the bike, 8/12/21 watt bulbs, and an 8-watt beam on the helmet.

Stay centered on the trail when riding at night. There could be all kinds of obstructions that you can't see. Stay in the middle of the trail. Keep a low body position and be relaxed and ready to move your head out of the way to avoid getting whacked by a tree branch that you don't see coming.

Going uphill or places where you don't need a lot of light, turn off your lights to save your battery life. In many cases, you can ride without lights. Full moons illuminate the sky enough for you to usually ride without your lights. But, be alert and ready to act fast. You can't see the terrain in front of you as clearly as you can in daylight, so be ready to assimilate the ground in an extremely fast mode.

Keep in mind, at night, your average speed is slower, repairs are slower, and food breaks take longer.

Everything takes longer at night. When you stop, use your flashlight to save your bike lights.

Don't skimp on lights. Invest in a reliable system that you will feel comfortable using in a race. Cheap lights offer less light so you cannot see as far or go as fast. NightRider illuminates the trail as bright as daytime but it is a costly and heavy system. Once again, skill versus weight becomes an issue.

BIKE LIGHT TIPS

- **Change bulbs on bike lights. Use two low beams instead of high beams for longer battery life.**

- **Always bring spare batteries.**

The thing to realize about lights is that sometimes you need a lot and sometimes you need a little, both on foot and on your bike. The weight penalty of lights is in the batteries, not really the lamp. On foot, you do want a decent headlight. I like the Petzl Duo because you have a high beam and a low beam, allowing the batteries to be stretched a lot further while still having a high beam available if needed.

On the bike, get a decent bike lamp but set your headlamp up to work on the helmet (adjust the head strap and put some sticky back Velcro on the helmet if needed). The headlight will be your spare, which is mandatory on the bike legs anyway. If things get technical, use them both at the same time.

The bike light need not be high-tech. Most of the technological advances are based on rechargeable batteries and really bright light for use in traffic.

A high-tech light on low beam or a low-tech light on D cells or a 6V battery will give similar light power and will work for seven hours, enough to get you through a night that includes few enforced halts. A fancy light system with high beam is best, but the low-tech solution with the added headlamp on your helmet works well.

Remember, for the best differentiation of the terrain, you need the location of the light source to be as far away as possible from your eyes. On foot, holding the headlamp in your hand will help on rough trails, and it is imperative not to rely solely on a helmet-mounted light while biking (that is why bikes should have a light bracket down by the front hub).

—Adrian Crane, Team Odyssey/Hi-Tec Adventure One

THE COMPLETE GUIDE TO ADVENTURE RACING

FOOTWEAR AND APPAREL

SHOES

The premiere feature of a cycling shoe is the stiff sole. The rigidity enhances your efficiency, which would otherwise get lost in needless flexing of a softer shoe. In addition, the stiffness supports your foot, which helps prevent aching feet.

If you buy a pair with shoelaces, take extra precautions to tuck them in to avoid an unnecessary crash as they get caught in your cranks. You may need to purchase a couple of different pairs of bike shoes. For typical mountain bike races and off-road triathlons it is best to have a pair of shoes that fit snug and not hinder circulation.

In an adventure race, you may get to the bike section that is up in the mountains and need heavy socks to keep warm. Or the bike leg might be on day 5 and your feet are so swollen that you need a size and a half larger than you would typically wear.

EYEWEAR

Always protect your eyes! Dirt, sand, bugs, branches, and the sun's UV rays can be harmful in many ways. Find a pair that fits firmly on your head so that once they are on, you forget they are there. Be sure that you have a clear lens that you can use for night riding.

APPAREL

Thermoregulation is paramount throughout the race and the mountain biking leg is no exception. Although you are moving faster and creating a larger breeze, you are working harder and muscles work best when they are not over-heated. Wear polypro next to your skin and extra-breathable fabric in any additional layers.

Cycling shorts that are form fitting prevent chafing and offer protection from saddle-related soreness and rubbing. Try out various shorts to find the right comfort and style of chamois.

Bring extra bike shorts. The bike legs tend to be very long and grueling. The extra pair may be just the thing that allows you to sit down for the last 20 miles.

If you are wearing loose-fitting pants, make sure they are tucked away from the possibility of getting caught in your pedals. Better yet, stow them in your pack and stick with biking shorts or tights.

If your bike shorts are really wet from the last bike leg, roll them in a towel and keep rolling and unrolling to squeeze the moisture out. This will dry the shorts enough to put them back on.

HELMETS

All helmets must abide by the standards of the Federal Government's Consumer Product Safety Commission (CPSC), and should be in good shape. Make sure your helmet fits snug. Put one hand on each side and try to teeter the helmet from side to side. If it moves, tighten the straps and check the fit pads to make sure they are the right size. Buckle the strap and open your mouth wide as if you were to scream or yawn. You should feel the helmet dig into your head. If it doesn't, tighten your straps. Hopefully, we will someday have a helmet that meets all of the needs for an adventure racer. There are some races which require the racer to have 4 helmets: a bike, climbing, whitewater and horse helmet.

GLOVES

Gloves cushion your hands, which provides some relief on long rides. They also protect your hands when you fall. The kinds of gloves you wear are based on personal preference. If you want to keep cool and enjoy the greatest dexterity, short-fingered gloves will suit you well. For added protection and warmth, invest in the long-fingered variety. It would be nice to find a good pair of cushioned gloves that work for you while riding, trekking with poles, paddling and/or climbing.

PREVENTIVE MAINTENANCE AND REPAIRS

Bicycle maintenance and repair is an important aspect of riding and a nebulous one for many of us. Know your bike before entering an adventure race. If you haven't experienced a breakdown on the trails, count yourself lucky. Unfortunately, luck only goes so far.

There is an art to bike repair. And, as is the case of any craft, it takes persistence, practice, and patience. Take the time to learn from an expert. Investigate workshops in your area, and be proactive in your quest for knowledge. When you take your bike to the shop for a tune-up or a repair, watch, listen, and learn. Talk to the mechanic, ask questions, and empower yourself so you can be self-reliant on the trails and in a race.

Your mountain bike is an investment in your training and competitive performance. To get the largest return on your investment, it is wise to take care of it by paying it the proper attention and care it deserves. Every three months or so, you have the oil changed in your car. Likewise, every couple of months (or less if you ride every day) some preventive maintenance on your bike is in order. Every year, you may decide to take your car to your mechanic for a tune-up. Similarly, it is a good idea to take your bike to a mechanic for an annual tune-up.

In addition to quarterly and yearly maintenance, a quick check of your bike parts before and after each ride is sensible.

Chris Scott reviews bike maintenance and repair with Odyssey Adventure Racing Academy.

TUBE AND TIRE TALK

Bicycle flats are the most common problem people have with their bikes. Aside from bad luck, the second most common cause of flats is under-inflation. Usually, 40 to 50 pounds of pressure is enough to prevent a flat, depending on your weight and how much you are carrying. In adventure racing, you carry more cargo.

Consequently, more weight on the bike means more tire pressure is needed. Most of us will hover around 50 pounds of pressure.

WHEN YOU HAVE A FLAT

If you don't have enough tire pressure, you will probably end up with a pinch flat. When a tire with inadequate pressure hits something hard, it pinches the tube between the tire and the rim causing a 'snakebite' flat, which flattens the tire almost immediately.

To fix the flat: First, disconnect the wheel from the bike (knowing how to disconnect the brakes is important and one of the first mechanical tasks you should learn when you purchase your bike). Current mountain bikes come with quick release wheels. This means that no tools are needed, as a clamping mechanism holds the wheel to the frame.

Be certain that all of the air is out of the tire. Use your tire levers to pry the tire off the rim and remove the tube. Then, identify the cause of the flat. If you take one tube out and put another tube in without checking for the cause, you are bound for more flats. There may be a thorn or piece of glass that caused the first flat and it will continue to create flats until you find it and remove it.

Inflate the tube, find the hole in the tube, and then locate the source in the tire. Next, inflate the tube just enough to make it round, put it inside the tire, and put the valve of the tube through the hole in the rim. Then, you can usually pry the tire on one bead at a time by hand, typically starting at the valve hole and working your way around.

Once you have the tube and tire on, inflate slowly to about 10 to 15 pounds. Then make sure the tire is properly seated on the rim. Once it is, inflate to full pressure. Don't exceed the recommended pressure printed on the sidewall of the tire.

FIXING A FLAT WITH A CUT TIRE

If your tube rips and you are without a spare or patches, there is hope. Find the puncture, then rip the tube apart at the hole and tie both ends in a knot. The ride will be bumpy, but you will be able to inflate the tube enough to finish the race. You may have to stop every now and then to refill it, but you will be able to continue riding.

If the tire itself is damaged, the problem may be remedied with a tire boot—a hard piece of plastic adhesive, which goes on the inside of the tire to hold it together and keep the tube from protruding through the hole in the tire.

For a quick fix, if it is apparent that a thorn or a nail caused a flat, take four to six inches of tire off the rim on both sides of the flat. Pull out the part of tube that has the hole in it, patch it, and re-stuff it in your rim.

OTHER MOVING PARTS

Your chain is composed of 55 eight-piece links. Keep them clean and well lubed, and they will remain happy and perform at their best. If you ignore these bike parts, they will become dry, dirty, and worn, which increases friction and the vulnerability of your cogs, chain rings, and rear derailleur. Clean your chain whenever it looks dirty and make sure you lubricate it once it's clean. In addition, if your chain sings while you ride, it's asking for a lube.

Grip shifts are an optional component. If you must have them, keep in mind, they take a lot of energy, especially when they start to stick. If you have too much lube in the shifter body, it makes the action really slow. When this happens, use a degreaser and clean the body with warm soapy water. Then lightly lube the spring, the spring cavity, and the cable path, paying attention to both shifter halves.

When brakes start getting worn, move them up toward the tire. The bottom of the pad usually has more material left on it than the top.

TOOLS TO TAKE TO THE RACE

- Spare tube.
- Patch kit.
- Pump.
- CO₂ inflator.
- Spoke wrench—will get your wheel round and true to finish your ride.
- Tire levers.
- Folding Allen-wrench with a flat and a Phillip's head screwdriver.
- 6" adjustable wrench.
- Open-ended wrenches—7-14 mm
- Needle-nose pliers.
- Duct tape.

- Chain tool—The ability to put a broken chain back together will keep you from having to walk home. Crashes often damage the rear derailleur. Having a chain tool will allow you to bypass the derailleur and make a single speed bike by putting the chain on one of the rear cogs and cutting it to the right length so you can keep going. You won't be able to use your gears, but you will be able to continue riding. Simply take the chain off the system and shorten it to the proper length so it will fit around the middle cog in back and the middle one in front.

A CLEAN BIKE IS A HAPPY BIKE

Clean and lube your bike as often as needed. Any time you ride in diverse or harsh conditions, your bike will appreciate a good wash. Take care of your bike and it will take care of you. Take it to a do-it-yourself car wash (keep the high pressure streams away from ball bearings) or dip a scrub brush into a bucket of water mixed with a grease-cutting soap. To clean the drive train and your pedals, use a stiffer scrub brush. Dry your bike with a towel and then coat all areas of metal on metal with lubricant. Don't forget: sand and salt are your bike's worst enemies.

- Cleaning solvents are convenient. Keep in mind, however, you can't fly with them. Purchase your supplies in the host city or country of your race.
- WD40 prevents rust and gets things loose. Spray your frame, then wipe it down.
- Grease is for your moving parts. A Teflon-based lubricant such as Tri-flow or Finish-Line are tried and true.

TEAM STRATEGY TIPS

- Pick one person to be in charge of bike maintenance.
- Coordinate bicycle parts so that they are all from the same manufacturer. All team members should have the same tires, tubes, and spokes.

INDIVIDUAL TIPS

- Water bottle cages are a handy place to stow food.
- Tape power gels to bike frame.
- Tape batteries to bike frame.
- Tire strips prevent tubes from getting punctured.

When you buy cables, purchase a bundle so you have spares for frequent replacements. You should replace your cables every few month if you are riding consistently, especially in wet conditions.

I was the bike mechanic for the Raid in Ecuador. The organization provided us with very inexpensive "Indian" bikes that were not ready for the prescribed rugged course. These bikes broke 15 to 20 times throughout the competition. I rode in the back and when a teammate broke down, I gave that rider my bike, fixed the broken bike, and caught up to the next rider having problems. I carried the tool kit and this plan worked well. The first rider stopped at every intersection to ensure that if we became separated, we would not end up going in different directions.

Mike Nolan, Team 'Odyssey' manager, was our mechanic in South Africa. He meticulously prepped all of the team's bikes. When we arrived at the CP, we were so happy to get off our feet and on to the bikes. The ride started up a mountain pass. The temperature was increasing as we ascended into the higher altitudes. I heard a pop, then another pop. They were like gun shots. But it was just a combination of Boyle's Law (as temperature and elevation increase, so does the tire pressure), and Murphy's Law taking its toll out on us. That race we had over 20 flats. And to make matters worse, we ended up carrying/pushing our bikes for a good 40 miles.

It is so important to have a good mechanic on your team. Mike Nolan took care of so many potential bike problems for our team that would have resulted in many extra hours of slow riding and/or pushing the bikes.

—*Don*

THE COMPLETE GUIDE TO ADVENTURE RACING

REGULAR MAINTENANCE SCHEDULE

BEFORE THE RIDE

TIRE

- Check tire pressure. Tires are porous, just like our skin. They sweat air. Low tire pressure is the number one cause of flats.
- Check treads.
- Look for any cuts or foreign objects in the tire walls.
- Be sure the wheels are true. Lift your wheels one at a time and give them a spin. If the wheel does not move freely, it may be rubbing on a bike part, most likely your brake pads.

BRAKES

- Brakes should be properly aligned.
- Make sure brake pads are not rubbing the tires or riding above the rim.
- Check the brake pads for wear. Look for the wear indicator marked by the manufacturer.
- Check brake lever tension. You should not be able to squeeze the lever completely.
- Adjust cable length if necessary.

CHAIN

- A dry chain is a dysfunctional chain. Make sure it is well lubricated before you set out. To lube, first remove superficial grime by turning the pedals backward with one hand while you hold the chain with a rag in the other hand. Next, apply lubricant to the chain while you continue to pedal backward. Make sure you target the entire chain. Wipe the chain down again to remove excess lubricant from the chain, as the extra solvent will attract dirt.
- At least a week before your race, put a new chain on your bike. Then ride it all week to break it in and stretch it. Your shifting will be a lot smoother, and there is a lot less chance of your chain stretching and breaking during the race.

OTHER

- Go through all of your gears, shifting from high to low. Make sure your derailleurs are working smoothly.
- Secure quick release of brakes, wheels, and seat.

- Listen for loose parts by bouncing your bike in place.
- Make sure your handlebars, stem, and headset are tight.
- Secure all gear attached to your bike.
- Check your bike lights.
- Double check your tire pump and repair kit for essential tools.

AFTER THE RIDE

- Sweep away any collected debris.
- Check your tires.
- If your bike is dirty, wipe it down or take it to a do-it-yourself car wash and hose it down (avoid a direct stream on the greased parts).
- During a race, have your support crew clean your bike as much as possible (if no support, take a minute yourself).

EVERY THREE MONTHS

- Check wheels and bottom bracket for lateral play.
- Check gears.
- Clean and lubricate brake and derailleur cables (replace if worn).
- Clean and lubricate chain (if extremely dirty, take it off and soak it in a solvent).
- Check gripping action of brakes.

ANNUAL CHECK-UP

- Disassemble the bottom bracket, headset, hubs, and pedals, and clean and grease the ball bearings.
- Assess alignment of frame.
- Replace any parts that assist in keeping bearings grit-free.

At least one month prior to your race, take your bike to your mechanic to make sure all parts are in working order. If possible, make it an interactive experience by taking the time to hang out with your mechanic. When you leave the shop, put some miles on your bike. The weeks leading up to the race will leave time for your parts to loosen a bit and allow you to get comfortable with the adjustments.

WHEELS

TOOLS THAT A SUPPORT A CREW SHOULD NOT BE WITHOUT

Screwdrivers—
    Phillips head—several sizes
    Small blade—3/16"
    Medium blade—1/4" - 5/32"
Crescent Wrenches—150 mm (6") and 200 mm (8") models
Ring spanners to fit specific areas of bike—6 mm - 17 mm
Barks wrench (hexagonal head)
Open-ended wrenches—6 mm - 17 mm
Allen wrenches—4 mm, 5 mm, and 6 mm
Pliers
Small vise grip
Hammer (10 oz metal)
Rubber mallet
Hacksaw (sometimes the only choice for repairing your bike)
File (to fix rough edges)
Punch
Floor pump with gauge
CO_2 inflators
Spoke wrench
Crank extractor
Free wheel extractor
Chain whip
Chain rivet tool
Cone wrenches
Bottom bracket tool
Head set tools
Brush (3/4" - 1")
Grease
Oil
Cleaning solvent (purchase it when you arrive in the host state or country)
WD40
Chain lube
Towels
Spare parts (cables, spokes, lights, and spare batteries)

THE COMPLETE GUIDE TO ADVENTURE RACING

A WORD ABOUT GEARS

The lifespan of your headsets, bottom brackets, hubs, and free wheels decrease once introduced to dirty water when riding.

Nine cogs in back and three in front are standard today. Most riding situations can be negotiated in the middle chain ring in front. The beauty of this ring is that you have full use of all the rings in back. The small chain ring is often referred to as the granny gear for climbing (your middle chain ring coupled with the lowest gear in back will also assist a climb). The larger chain ring is for letting it rip on open road.

Caution:
If you are using the smallest chain ring in front, never use the smallest cog in back.

Likewise, if you are in the biggest chain ring in front, do not use the biggest cog in back.

This practice puts the chain at an extreme angle because it is going from inside out or outside in, placing a great degree of stress on the drive train. When you ride fast—small to small—there's no tension and the chain is very loose and dangles about. Big to big creates an incredible stretch on the chain, which can destroy the derailleur.

ACHIEVING PROPER POSITION

It is crucial to achieve the proper fit on your bike—comfortable and relaxed—in order to negotiate tricky terrain. The perfect fit will elicit a smooth ride. Conversely, the wrong fit can set you up for some serious consequences. You are more likely to crash because you cannot maneuver as well, you will sacrifice power, and you increase your risk of injury—particularly to the knees, which is the most common place of injury for cyclists.

There are three important positions to consider when adjusting your bike for the proper fit: the vertical position (seat height), the fore/aft (horizontal) position, and the handlebars. Achieving the correct adjustments will allow you the greatest efficiency and power in your pedal strokes. Your ideal position will be a compromise of ideal settings for ascending and descending.

SEAT HEIGHT

When you straddle your bike with your feet firmly planted in the ground, there should be at least three inches of space between the top tube and your pelvis. You don't want your anatomy coming in contact with the bike's anatomy. More importantly, when you are riding, your knees should be slightly flexed at the bottom dead center of your pedal stroke (between 10 to 15 degrees). The more extension you achieve in your knee, the more power you will have going uphill. Conversely, a more flexed knee will make the downhill easier.

Ultimately, try to achieve the fullest extension possible while still maintaining a slight bend in the knee. If you are sitting too high, your hips will rock from side to side when pedaling and you sacrifice power. If you are too low, you place undue stress on the joints. The goal is to allow your ischial tuberosities (your sit bones) to rest firmly in the saddle when you are seated.

HORIZONTAL OR FORE/AFT POSITION

The horizontal position is defined by the body's distance from the seat to the handlebars.

While riding, you should be able to maintain a stable spine. In other words, you shouldn't have to round forward or assume an exaggerated angle at the waist to reach your bars. In addition to losing efficiency, an improper position can cause knee pain, back pain, and saddle-related soreness.

If your lower back is strained when you ride, you may be riding with the seat too far back. Sit too close and you lose power and aerodynamics by sitting too upright and too far forward away from the bottom bracket. Ultimately, the closer you are to sitting right above the bottom bracket, the more power you can generate.

In addition, your torso can lend power if placed in the right position. As mentioned earlier, the correct position should allow you to sit "heavy" with your sit bones placed firmly into the saddle. If you can maintain a comfortable, neutral alignment while riding, you will decrease pain and injury, and improve your riding efficiency.

HANDLEBARS

Your bars should be set at saddle height or about an inch below. Ride with your hands shoulder width apart. Many mountain bikers ride with the handlebars at the same height as the seat. Riding with the bars lower gives you a more aerodynamic edge. Adjusting them higher lends to a more upright position, taking some strain off the back and neck.

Yes, the Beast of the East did it to me not only once, but twice in the same night. I flipped over my handlebars twice in one night. The second time, I just laid there because it was the most comfortable I had been since the race started. Bad combination: no sleep, single track, night, dim light, and LOG!

—Blaine Reeves

EFFICIENCY

THE PEDAL STROKE

The top priority of any cyclist is to obtain optimal pedaling efficiency. This efficiency comes from maximum propulsion with minimum extraneous movement. If all of your power is directed toward your pedal stroke, an efficient technique can be established. Strive for a "spinning" motion as you ride. Your pedal strokes should feel smooth and circular in motion. Avoid choppy, sharp strokes, especially as the terrain gets steeper and you experience changes in the surface you are riding on.

There are many factors that determine efficiency:

First, strive for equilibrium between your cadence and traction. It will take some time to embrace the correct gear that correlates with the terrain. Once this is accomplished, your performance will greatly improve.

Your position on the bike (which changes often according to the terrain) also affects efficiency. For example, when climbing, it is most efficient to shift your weight forward to achieve the greatest power. On the downhill, your weight should be back for efficient descents.

Every 100 revolutions or so, use one leg predominantly to transmit force and let the other one enjoy the

ride so it can relax a bit. Then switch off to the other side. Your legs will get a break, and you will eventually pick up speed. This technique also makes you a better rider to establish a smooth cycling technique.

When riding in a standing position, avoid dropping into the pedals. Remember that all of the force you are sending into the pedals comes right back to you through your joints, which makes for painful souvenirs in the long run. It also takes away your power as you mash the pedals instead of turning circles.

Consider the force pattern of a complete pedal stroke. It begins at the top at the twelve o'clock position. Peak force occurs one-quarter of the way through a revolution at 90 degrees. Ultimately, the longer you can hold on to that peak force, the more effective you become.

Take advantage of the multiple gears on your bike. Make them useful by doing a lot of small shifting while you're riding to maintain a consistent cadence.

PEDAL STROKE PERFECTION

1. Push down to the six o'clock position of the stroke.
2. Before the pedal reaches the bottom, pull back on

it as though you are scraping mud off your shoe.

3. Pull up as you focus on driving your knees toward the handlebars or your chest.

4. As the pedal approaches the top of the stroke, push forward on it.

The goal is to smooth out the four points. Think circles. Create a circular movement with your feet and continuously strive for a spinning motion. Try to avoid "feeling" any one part of the stroke.

If you begin to feel tired in your lungs, slow down your cadence. If you begin to feel tired in your legs, speed up the cadence and ride in an easier gear.

TRACTION

The key to mountain biking is mastering traction. Traction is the amount of friction between your wheels and the surface you are riding on. This friction is the result of the balance between too much force, which discourages traction, and too little, which encourages a fall.

The amount of horizontal force depends on the degree of vertical force. In other words, if all of your weight is over the front wheel, the back wheel loses traction and vice versa.

On paved roads, pump up your wheels to gain speed as traction is of little concern. However, off-road, you don't need as much air in your tires. Learn what tire pressure works best for you depending on the surface you ride on, your weight, and your abilities.

Read the terrain and look ahead to attack a route with the proper gear and the most ideal riding surface. Give yourself as much time as possible to choose the right gear for maximum inertia. Staying one step ahead will also give you more flexibility with the line you choose to ride.

TERRAIN

In most adventure races (expedition-style), you ride more fire roads, trails, and sometime paved roads and less single track.

SAND

There is no reason why you should crush your brakes and force yourself off your bike in a flailing nose dive because of a change in terrain. However, certain surfaces, such as sand, have a way of triggering the synapses in our brain that make us want to brake. The most effective way to conquer sand is actually the opposite of our innate reaction—barrel right through it. Upshift to a higher gear to enhance your power and shift your weight back in the saddle for added traction. Stick to your guns, breathe easy, and plow right through it.

If you encounter a long stretch of sand, continue pedaling, even if you slow down. Do whatever you can to maintain traction in the back wheel. Pull up on your bars as if you are attempting a wheelie and keep your weight as far back as possible. If there is any navigable way out to the side of the trail, try to take it. But, whatever you do, try to keep moving. It is almost impossible to get moving again once you have stopped in the sand.

Before you lay your bike to rest, clean off any salt build-up and check your parts. Remember that salt and sand are the bike's worst enemies and it's up to us to protect it.

SNOW

Riding in snow is rare in an adventure race. However, you can never be too prepared for the mysteries of this sport. And, if you live in an area that hosts all four seasons, the wintertime is no exception to your outdoor training schedule. Make sure you dress appropriately, and switch to special snow tires to accommodate the fluffy, sometimes icy terrain.

As you ride, avoid any sudden movement and be careful with your braking. Don't go too fast and be extra sensitive to the slippery terrain. If your wheels spin out, lay off your pedal strokes until you have full control. Oftentimes, if you encounter snow in an adventure race, you will carry your bike. If you know this ahead of time, figure out a good carry system prior to the race start.

MUD

If you will be riding through muddy trails, decrease your tire pressure. However, be careful not to lower it so much that you get pinch flats. The lower pressure lessens the chances of crashes on slippery roots and rocks.

Ride through mud in a seated position. Standing doesn't work in mud. You need to keep the rear wheel loaded at all times while in the mud. Run one gear higher than you normally would in dry conditions. It reduces your torque to the back wheel and it will slip less.

Before you use your brakes when it's muddy or wet, pulse one lightly to try it, and then drag your brakes on to test them. This will clean the rims so when you need the brakes, they will work.

When you accumulate a lot of muddy water on your chain, it takes the lube away, which leads to problems. To prevent this from happening, lube your chain before and after every ride with a good wet-weather product, and change or adjust your brake pads after every ride in mud.

TECHNIQUES

BALANCE

Before you learned to walk, you learned to stand on your own, without the support of a wall or your parents. Similarly, before you ride effectively, practice good balance on your wheels. Our equilibrium hinges on neuromuscular control. The coordination of the eyes, ears, and kinesthetic receptors allows us to remain upright. Our eyes scope out and process the spatial relationship of objects in our visual field. The ears perceive head movement through the canal system of the inner ear, and receptors located in the muscles and the tendons give us awareness and feedback regarding the position of our body in space.

In an adventure race, your dynamic balance is constantly challenged in the mountain biking legs. Quick reactions to constant changes in the forces that surround you will keep you on alert. Correct timing of muscular contractions is crucial. As you master your equilibrium, your response times will improve, and extraneous movements will cease. Good balance will also decrease the chance of injury on your perilous trek.

Imagine yourself on a technical climb. To effectively maneuver around obstacles, or to recover from a gnarly encounter with one, good balance will keep you upright. It can mean the difference between countless spills accompanied by unwanted injuries and loss of time, or a flawless ascent. Good balance allows you the luxury of careful planning because you have more time to assess the trail ahead. It also gives you more options, and with better balance, you can conquer tougher terrain.

To master your equilibrium, practice balancing at a standstill on your bike. Relax your body, bring the cranks parallel to the ground with your dominant foot forward and then make adjustments as your body and bike unite in an attempt to tip over.

As you add speed to the picture, get used to how your body feels on the bike. Become familiar with weight shifts forward and backward, up and down, and side to side. Get to know what happens when your body changes positions.

Start off riding slowly as you perfect your balance. Then, as you increase your speed, balance becomes easier.

A WORD ABOUT POSTURE

The torso connects the upper body to the lower body, the right side of the body with the left, and the back with the front. Smooth, fluid, coordinated movement is dependent upon a trunk that is stable, yet able to bend and flex according to the demands imposed on it.

Power and speed hinge on the stability of the trunk. Without the ability to control forces exerted upon it, the trunk is useless, and therefore greatly hinders performance. Injury is also more likely to occur in a weak torso.

Maintenance of neutral alignment is key. The spine has two natural curves to it. In the lower back, there is a small inward curve in the lumbar spine, and in the cervical vertebrae (the neck), there is another. There should not, however, be a sweeping forward flexion in the thoracic vertebrae, or at the waist.

The effects of stress, fatigue, and gravity encourage flexion at the waist. Surrendering to these factors promotes compression on the spine, pain and injury, and poor performance. To prevent poor posture and alleviate pain throughout the torso, focus on the strength of the surrounding muscles.

The best way to improve your torso position for riding is to practice good posture while you ride. Be aware of the position of your pelvis. Try to feel heavy in the saddle while seated, and find a neutral place when standing. This neutral place is somewhere between the two extremes of an anterior pelvic tilt and a posterior tilt.

Practice pulling your abdominals inward, opening up your chest, and keeping your shoulders back and down away from your ears. Finally, strive for a neutral head position. When the terrain gets tough, or when we are fatigued, we have a tendency to drop the head. When in doubt, retract the neck, coaxing the head straight back into a better position.

GENERAL TIPS TO CONSIDER WHILE MOUNTAIN BIKING

- Keep your head up.

- Where your eyes go, your bike goes. If you look at an obstacle, you will hit it. Your front wheel will usually hit whatever you are looking at. As hard as you try not to look at a treacherous object or will it away, it's not going to magically disappear. Acknowledge and accept the hindrance and maneuver your way around it.

- Scan the terrain. Look for problems and obstacles in your way. Once they register in your brain, focus on where you want to go. Logs, rocks, and other bumps can actually define your path as you pick a line that goes through and around them. Veteran bikers scan 30 to 40 feet ahead. Novice riders stay closer to home at about 10 to 20 feet. Adjust with your speed. The slower your speed, the closer you scan. If you are going fast, you may scan as much as 100 feet ahead.

- Plan your maneuver before you get there, but feel your way through it.

- To achieve maximum results, be present. Be committed to the moment. Effective trail riding demands total awareness.

- Breathe! We tend to hold our breath when the going gets tough. It's a natural response. But this natural response causes tense muscles, decreases energy flow, and usually sends us flailing off our bikes. Relax and focus on your breath for optimum performance.

- Combine your instincts with experience.

- Try to find the path of least resistance. Go with the terrain instead of fighting it.

- Concentration is paramount. "Off-road cycling is a very balanced effort between concentration and relaxation," says Danny Lucero, Odyssey's bike specialist.

- The most common mistake is to get nervous, look at the scary parts, then go to the scary parts and crash.

- Insist on a good fit on your bike.

- Always keep a light touch on your handlebars. The front brake (controlled by the left hand) does most of the stopping, and the back brake (right hand) controls the ride.

Strive for a balance between exerting enough power and losing traction as you climb hills.

CLIMBING

The art of ascending involves good balance, stamina, and perseverance. A good set of lungs is an essential asset that will enable you to climb with finesse. Powerful legs will make the ride even easier. Above all else, keep your weight over your front wheel.

It is crucial to find the gear you wish to climb in before you hit the hill. So, know what works and get there before you begin to chug up the terrain. Even though you may feel like you're going nowhere fast as you spin your heart out, your granny gear most often will offer the smoothest, cleanest ride.

If you want to go up, you have to get down and lean toward your bars. Many beginners make the mistake of sitting upright with more weight emphasis on the rear wheel. This way-back position reduces the weight on the front wheel, which causes a loss of traction and increases the chances of stopping.

Shift your weight forward, closer to the hill, so that your pelvis is directly over the nose of your saddle. This will aid in balance. If you get it too far forward, however, you will lose traction in the back wheel. Too far back, and you lose balance. As always, practice makes perfect. Lower your chest to the stem and increase traction by pushing the handlebars down as the terrain gets steeper. Try different positions as you ascend a hill until you find the right position for you.

Don't let your ego surpass your ability. The last thing you want is to spend yourself completely up a hill and zap all of your energy. If you need to get off and walk, do it. But, remember that pushing your bike up the hill isn't always easier. If you decide to walk, make sure your bike is on lower ground so you exert the least amount of effort.

CLIMBING TIPS

- Try not to sit back down when the grade is steep, or you may stall out. Wait until you have a break in your climbing and then sit.

- Shift back to an easy gear when you return to a seated position.

- Heavier riders do better by spending more time in the saddle to climb. Lighter riders will find greater success by standing more.

- Most novices don't stand often enough and when they do stand, they are up too long.

- Avoid "motoring" the hill by going as hard as you can all the way up. Find a steady pace as you ascend, where you are just below your pain threshold. You can pedal at an amazingly slow cadence and stay upright. On tougher hills, you may want to go a little slower than you may be tempted to go to save energy getting up and over. Once you get to the top, you want enough energy to keep going at a good speed.

- You can get a lot of extra traction on technical climbing if you are standing and lifting your front wheel over large rocks and ledges.

- Don't anticipate the top. When you're riding up an endless hill with too many switchbacks, take them one at a time. Make it your goal to get to the next bend. Climbing is a repetitive act. It is only putting one foot down and pulling the other one up, and doing it over and over until you get to the top. Develop a mantra to get from one turn to the next. It becomes a total mind game that you play.

- On a long climb, try to find a rhythm and stick it out as you adhere to that cadence. Try to stick close behind another rider as you climb. When the other rider stands, it might be a good time for you to stand. Tell yourself that if he can do it, you can do it. Also remind yourself how much fun it will be to blast down the hill. There is nothing more exciting than flying downhill. The steeper your climb, the more rewarding your descent will be.

- If you're having a hard time climbing, let your teammate push you by placing their hand on your lower back.

- When you're riding really steep hills, you don't want to ride on the inside corner. More often than not, the insides are steeper than the outside. So take the more gradual outside climb.

- Most of all, enjoy the feeling of true power and enjoy the view!

DRILLS

During training, use these drills to find a balance between gaining enough power as you push up the hill and losing traction:

Find a steep hill with some loose surface. Shift into your lowest gear and attack it. Get out of the saddle and try to go up the hill as hard as you can. Force your rear wheel to begin breaking free. After you develop some proficiency out of the saddle, do the same thing in a seated position. This will encourage you to learn how much pedaling force you can apply before losing traction.

Here's a variation:

Ride into the hill in your lowest gear, and creep up as slowly as you can. Pretend you are an airplane on the verge of stalling. Pick the smallest cog that you can ride up the slope and repeat the previous drill. Pay attention to the stalling point. Work on the sense and loss of traction both in and out of the saddle.

This series of drills will show the two different extremes. Going into a hard gear where you are barely in control and ready to stall, and going in too easy of a gear where your exertion exceeds your progress will create a keen sensitivity of both ends. Once you know what those ends feel like, strive for a balance between the two.

When you are ready to come up out of the saddle, keep in mind that you use twelve percent more oxygen and your heart rate goes up about eight percent. Standing is harder on the legs because they provide locomotion while supporting you. However, standing also changes your leg muscle access, allowing different muscles to fire while others rest and can delay fatigue, allowing you to stretch during extended climbs.

DESCENDING

On your descent, get back in the saddle, hold on for dear life and let it rip! Okay, so this may not be the best advice, but it was probably your first instinct the very first time you came head to head with a threatening descent.

The part about shifting your weight back, however, is true. In fact, it is the most important part of your downhill attack. This maintains rear wheel traction and enhances your balance.

When you descend, bring your pedals to a three o'clock and nine o'clock position, lift your weight off the saddle so that your hips hover just above it, and extend your elbows and knees, but keep them loose to act as suspension. Everything is flexed for shock absorption, and the more relaxed you are the better.

A common tendency is to suffocate the bars with a death-grip as gravity pulls you down the moutain. Try to resist this temptation. Otherwise, your hands and upper body may experience agonizing pain, keeping you out of the action for a day or more.

QUICK DOWNHILL TIPS

- Don't go too slow.
- Go as fast as you can to gain speed for the next uphill or obstacle.
- Look for smooth lines.
- Try not to death grip the bars. You only need to have a light grip.
- Try not to brake as often as you think you need to.

CORNERING

Try to put your weight to the inside and pedal through the corners. If you are attempting a sharp turn, put your leg out to help you get around. A low and wide stance will keep you upright and on the course.

Some riders will put all of their weight on the outside pedal to carve the turn. Many riders will drop the outside pedal, but if you also put weight into it, you will make a sharper turn. When you come into a turn, approach it wide and brake without skidding. Then cut inside across the corner and exit wide. This will reduce the sharpness of the curve and minimize the amount of leaning.

When you're on the inside of the turn, lean. Press down on the grip that's on the inside of the turn and angle the bike over. Don't worry about gaining lean— as you gain confidence, you will naturally slant more. The key is to slowly build speed and lean. Too much of one or the other will cause skidding.

A good drill you can do on easier ground to build confidence in your turns is to find an object like a bush and practice cornering it over and over until you gain confidence and develop a feel for angle and speed.

Approach corners wide, then cut inside across the corner and exit wide.

THE COMPLETE GUIDE TO ADVENTURE RACING

The faster you ride over path obstructions, the smaller your movements need to be to clear them.

JUMPS

Logs, roots, and rocks create obstructions on the trails. The fast guys will hit a bump at full speed (fueled by confidence, of course). They stand up high over the bike, which raises their center of gravity, then they pre-load the front end by staying high, pop the front wheel up just in time to clear the obstacle, and hit it full on.

Once you get your body to peak height and the front wheel goes over the bump, the bike will come up to your body. The bigger the jump or bunny hop and the faster you approach it, the more the rear wheel will kick under you.

To clear a little log in the trail six to eight inches high, approach it with enough speed so that if you don't pedal for two feet before it, you will still clear it. Approach the log with both legs equally flexed, and your crank arms parallel to the ground. Stay seated with all of your body parts relaxed. Unweight your front wheel while holding it steady by shifting your body to the rear from the ready position. When the front wheel hits, let the bike come toward your chest and absorb the impact with your elbows and your knees. If your elbows are loose, they will bend upon impact. When your front wheel hits the ground on the other side, return your arms to the original position. This pushes the bike forward away from you, and helps bring your bike over the obstacle.

Then return to the center of the bike while un-weighting the rear wheel. When you're riding over something, use your dominant leg to apply force. Try to have that leg apply pressure to get up and over the obstacle. Use a lot of upper body motion. When your front wheel is midway over an obstacle, use your pedals to lift the back wheel over it. You can ride over obstacles, jump over them, or roll over them.

With fast speed, smaller obstacles become insignificant. The slower you go, the more work you have to do to conquer an obstruction in your path. The faster you go, the smaller your movements need to be to get over the obstacle.

GIMME A BRAKE

Effective braking is the result of anticipation, and anticipation stems from experience. Beginners don't brake correctly. Too much rear braking causes the bike to lock up and skid, which rips up the trails (upsetting environmentalists) and causes you to lose control. Experienced riders use their rear brake to skid on purpose, as a skill, not a mistake.

Once your rubber skids, you cannot brake any harder. It's more efficient to keep applying a braking force to a spinning wheel. This is the reason why new car owners want anti-lock braking systems. However, you don't have a fancy system on your mountain bike. Instead, you can apply a series of tiny, micro-braking actions. This is a technique called feathering

Figure out a hand position that works best for you. Some riders use just their index and middle fingers on the brakes and put their other fingers around the handlebars. Some riders just use their index fingers to brake. Practice with the one that works best and keep in mind that it may change depending on the terrain and how much force you need to brake.

When you brake, you're not only braking with your brakes (of course your brake levers and cantilevers are the most obvious parts of stopping), but you also stop your bike by gripping the seat with your thighs and moving your weight back as you brake. Use all of your bike and body to brake. This is the finesse of mountain bike riding.

Brakes aren't only used when you want to slow down. They can keep you in control and can also help you build speed. Alternate squeezing and releasing on a long descent, and if you lay off the brakes sooner when coming out of a corner, you'll notice that you will gain more control.

HITTING THE BRAKES

Brake hard at the last possible second right before you start to skid. Then as you skid, release your brakes. Why shouldn't you brake earlier? You'll lose too much speed. Why not later? Locking up the brakes is inefficient and you'll lose control.

Can't remember which is which? Think R–R, right is rear. Consequently, your left hand controls the front wheel.

Brake hard when the ground is hard and brake soft when the ground is soft.

Don't think of braking as just something to do with your hands. Think of it as a whole process. Start off with a weight shift. Get out of the saddle, bend your arms, and keep the weight off the front wheel to prevent an 'endo' (end over end) fall. Use the trail to slow yourself down without braking.

Get into a rhythm while you ride. Let your front wheel roll freely over a log or drop off. Don't put your brakes on. If you do, you will probably go over the handlebars.

Skidding represents bad technique. Learn to use your rear brake more than the front brake.

One of the major reasons your bike may perform poorly when braking is pad residue on your rims. If this is the case, clean your rims with steel wool. Seventy percent of your braking power comes from your front brake, the other 30 percent from your back brakes. Figures change, of course, as conditions change.

Muddy terrain decreases your rear stopping power more than it wipes out your front. You can change how much braking power you get at either wheel by shifting your weight forward or backward.

Finally, keep an eye on your brake pads. If they are worn unevenly, they will interfere with your efficiency.

CRASH COURSE

Everyone does it, but no one ever really asks for it. We all crash sooner or later.

Most often, we crash because we lose confidence or brake unnecessarily, creating a harder ride for ourselves. Learn to trust yourself. Stay loose and relaxed as you ride. Tension forces mistakes to happen and it also sucks up your precious energy.

To lessen your chances of eating dirt, heed the following tips:

Don't be afraid to walk. You have to know your limits. Don't be afraid to walk anything that is beyond your skill. You don't want to have to leave the race because you broke an ankle or got knocked unconscious. Walk whenever you don't want to ride.

Practice caution. In an adventure race, you are always on unfamiliar trails. The trail is not necessarily safe. Don't assume anything. And don't assume others won't be coming your way. There may be hikers or other bikers heading in the opposite direction as you. Be alert and aware and use your peripheral vision.

Exhibit grace and finesse. Don't give this up for speed. If you do, it will be very likely that you will crash. Keep your form and style as you gradually develop your skills. Increase your speed over time and avoid getting romanced by all of the obstacles on your path. Typical off-road fare includes: water puddles, mud holes, "banked turns", tree branches, loose rocks, ruts, roots, sudden drops, and nasty inclines that devour your lungs and make you beg for mercy every time you make a turn. Pick your line and sail along it.

Keep your distance from the person in front of you. A good rule of thumb is one foot per mph. So, if you're going six mph, give the biker ahead of you a good six feet.

Most often, our lack of confidence gets us in trouble. Many times, this occurs because we try to mimic someone else's speed or style. Find your own style and trust yourself. Ride at a level that you enjoy, while still remaining competitive.

DRAFTING

On long, steady roads, drafting can save upwards of 27 percent of your energy. Take advantage of this as a team when you have the opportunity. Approach your teammate when he is steady and smooth and maintains a constant cadence. Be aware of your surroundings (i.e. riders pulling back) and then alert your teammate that you are falling in line. Make sure you keep several inches between your front wheel and the back wheel of the person you're drafting behind. Focus ahead and strive for a moderate speed as you maintain pace.

FROM "AN ODYSSEY OF THE EXTREME"

BY ANGELIKA CASTANEDA

...Finally, after hours of struggle through the green labyrinth, we have a big surprise. A paved road appears, we suddenly feel reconnected to civilization. A new drive of energy and hope gushes up from deep within our embattled spirits. We don't talk; words are not needed. We are one spirit, fully committed to a single goal—winning.

Like warrior hunters employing all our senses to assess the situation, we look left-to-right, pausing, listening, and then back right-to-left. Nature tells us nothing. We turn to our maps, and decide to follow the road to the right. How pleasant and easy this smooth road feels. Soon we come to an incline and as I attempt to shift to a lower gear, I notice the grip-shift on my handlebar is broken; I cannot shift at all. Stuck with only one gear—a downhill gear— steep grades will be impossible. We create a makeshift towrope from a bungee cord and attach it to my handlebars.

Despite being pulled by this bungee cord, we all waste vast amounts of energy. The hills are extremely steep, and pedaling against my big gear becomes a major task. We climb numerous hills, each time praying that it's the last one. But each time, the road only dips away and climbs out over another crest. We begin to wonder whether this

desolated road leads through the dense forest at all. This smooth, paved road that seemed like such a relief has become a living nightmare.

Like any other hill, we zoom down this next one, drafting each other at incredible speeds. Mere inches separate us. When the downhill ends, we pedal hard to take advantage of the momentum, hoping it will push us over the next peak. Most times it doesn't, and the slog to the top is a gutwrenching ordeal. I try to stay as close as possible behind John's rear wheel, maintaining my highest level of concentration.

But, for just a split second, I forget about my broken gears. Over my many years of competition, I have conditioned myself to use the gears as an automatic response to the terrain. I attempt to downshift and the bike does not respond. Then like a slow motion movie, I become a mere observer, watching myself slam into John's bike.

I've encountered real danger several times in my life, and there is a definite similarity in all those brief moments just before a serious accident. In a split second, I anticipate how it will happen; the scene unfolds in my mind. It's an attempt by nature to warn me of the inevitable in a last desperate hope that I will find a way out or be able to fall in a better position.

My whole body, mind, and soul scream "STOP"

THE COMPLETE GUIDE TO ADVENTURE RACING

as I start to fall. Every hair stands on end and every pore slams shut. I feel my eyes open wide and my mouth gulps one last gasp of air. It fills my lungs and a strange kind of noise—a howl-like scream of terror and disbelief—mingles with the rush of air. Every muscle fiber instantly jolts tight, soft tissue turning to granite. My fingers spread wide to break the fall. Like soldiers on the front line of an ancient battlefield, they must be sacrificed first in the body's battle plan to protect. My spine, chest, and shoulders coil to absorb the shock. Brain and body whirl in high-speed synchronization, working as a well-trained team, each member struggling to preserve the rest.

As I extend my arms to the right, attempting to regain balance, my foot becomes stuck in the pedal, wedged between John's wheel and mine. I can't pull it out from between both wheels and I tumble over John's rear wheel, crashing into the gravel on the road. There's no bounce; instead, I hit the ground like a sack of rocks and my world cartwheels around me. In the melee, I see my right knee flopping around, reacting as if it's not part of my body. I hear my ligaments shredding and ripping.

The tumble ends and I try to stand up, hoping the sight and sounds of devastation were just an illusion. Not feeling any pain, not recognizing the wounds and injuries, I almost make it up, but my knee collapses and I fall again. Like a soldier in midst of battle, I feel stripped of my most important weapon—my healthy body.

How far behind is the enemy? We are in first place, but how much time is left before they reel in the intervening distance? Keith, who is a doctor, sits down at the curb, his head buried in his hands. He has no instruments to help me; there is nothing he can do. We cannot go on. What can be done? The 'quitting' strikes my mind and I refuse to entertain the thought. I search for solutions.

My usually soft-spoken voice becomes loud. I order my teammates to stand me up, put me on the bike, hold me from falling, push me on my way, and let go so that I might be on my way. I hook onto the bungee behind John and pedal with the good leg. My injured one becomes a hitchhiker, rid-

ing along on the opposite pedal. I see it as a stranger, a parasite that refuses to assist, as it limply moves to the steady motion of the task. It looks like a life-sized rag doll, limply circling a mindless series of flops.

A brief glimpse over my shoulder assures me that we are still in the lead. Fifteen miles of frantic pedaling and we remain in front. Then approaching water, I scream to Keith and John to go way ahead so that they can steady me when we halt…

…After what seems like a week in hell, our boat plunges into the ocean, quenching the searing heat. John and Keith pick me up and carry me to the boat. My body is quivering uncontrollably. As we start to paddle, my agony turns to ecstasy. We are in the last mile. A glowing grin of victory breaks onto my face. We have won.

In the midst of cheering, I am whisked away to the hospital. Try as I might to resist, my eyes are closing, dark clouds tumbling into my vision. All sounds dim and fade; the last vestiges of my resistance break…

…Where am I? What is going on? I can't move! I'm in a foreign bed with a ceiling I've never seen before. I touch a white gown that envelops my body. Then, as though she had read my mind, in the softest, warmest voice I have ever heard, my sister Barbara whispers close to my ear, "For five long hours you have been in the operating room."

Then my fingers find something big, solid and cold lying on my chest. I lower my gaze and see the medal around my neck. This chunky, round disk radiates like the sun in its magnified evening splendor. It is solid gold and it is resting on my heart. With eager fingers I gather it slowly. I close my eyes and recall the combat that brought it to my hand— the ecstasy and agony that became wed when the battle was won.

Angelika, John Howard, and Keith Murray combined their talent to win the ESPN Extreme Games adventure race in New England, 1996.

TOWING SYSTEMS

HERE ARE SOME TIPS:

- Use 550 cord or nylon webbing.

- Using a sturdy piece of plastic tie material, secure a 1-2 inch loop to everybody's handlebars on the team. This is just in case this person needs to be towed at some point in the race. Secure this plastic loop with duct tape or riggers tape.

- Somebody on the team needs to carry a piece of 550 cord or nylon webbing with them. Secure a bungee hook on to the end of this cord/webbing.

- When a person is in need of tow, loop one end around the tower's seat post and hook the other end on to the handlebars of the person being towed.

- Anticipate the tow. Before you begin to climb, the tower hands off the end of the tube to the 'towee' to tie in. When finished, the 'towee' unclips the tubing and hands it back to the tower.

Take care to avoid the possibility of the towing parts getting caught in your rims or other bike parts. Hence, practice first! Ideally, you should not have to stop and get off your bike to manipulate a towing system.

If towing is not an option, or one of your teammates needs some extra oomph, ride alongside him and place your hand on his lower back. The key is to stay balanced and find the path of least resistance to ride on.

These methods will help equalize the strengths among the team. If you are the weak link, don't hesitate to take advantage of these techniques. If you are the strong link, practice your pushing and towing skills so you are ready to perform if the situation arises. In a race, everyone has their ups and downs so it is advantageous to practice towing and pushing one another in every situation so you have experience come race time.

Two inner tubes tied together make an excellent towing system if used on the back of the seat post and front of the headset.
—Blain Reeves

Put a rack on your bike behind your seat, secure a fishing pole to it, then attach a 550 parachute cord and pull.
—John Howard

BIKE RACKS

Bike racks create a favorable option for carrying necessary supplies out on the field. While you won't place your entire pack on the bike rack, you can decrease a considerable percentage of the weight you carry in your pack by transferring it to the rack. This will take the load off your back and a lot of pressure off your pelvic floor during a race. A system that works well is to keep all of your gear in a dry bag in your backpack. When you get on your bike, remove the dry bag and attach it to your bike rack. This leaves just a close to empty pack and your hydration system on your back. Most bike racks can only safely hold up to 20 pounds.

Make sure your rack is durable and secure to the bike and when you attach your gear, secure it well.

GOING THE DISTANCE

The best way to get in shape for biking is to bike. Mountains provide grueling terrain to conquer. Going up requires tremendous power. Going down demands total body strength and balance.

Ride whenever possible. Use your bike for transportation when running errands, when visiting friends and family, and traveling to and from work. Ride often enough that the task becomes second nature. You will develop a keen awareness of the nuances of your bike. Riding frequently will also create a need for frequent maintenance and inevitably, you will face repairs. The more experience you have with the ups and downs of riding, the better your experience will be in a race.

On days when you don't have a lot of time to train or when the weather just won't seem to cooperate, try a spinning class. In less than an hour, you can perfect your spinning technique and work on power intervals. In addition, a class provides a nice change from the solitude of riding alone.

There are also many complimentary workouts you can do to enhance your riding. See Chapter 11.

Biking strength trumps finely-tuned technical skills in an adventure race. Your ability to pedal hundreds of miles is what really counts. It is also important to know field repair and have a sure-fire towing system rigged for a race.

GET IN-LINE ... IN-LINE SKATING, THAT IS!

TO SKATE IN AN ADVENTURE RACE

The first edition of the Elf Authentic Adventure in the Philippines required teams to travel 101 kilometers on skates through the rough roads of southeastern Samar. A tenacious team from Malaysia demonstrated remarkable navigational abilities through the jungles—on many occasions they even traveled barefoot! Their skills eventually secured a fourth-place position overall in the 12-day race. However, the skating leg was a short-term threat to their racing destiny.

The foursome had set off at an uncertain pace, which was confirmed as they crossed a bridge and endured a nasty fall by one teammate. Consequently, the team resorted to hike the rest of the leg which made for a much slower pace than if they were skating.

Team 'Spie Kiva', on the other hand, was strong throughout the race including the lengthy skate leg. In fact, they were able to put a sizeable distance between them and team 'Epinephrine/Pharmanex', who had been breathing down their backs for many days of the race. Their swift performance afforded the opportunity to make a crucial cut-off for the last leg of the Elf Authentic Adventure. Team 'Spie' boarded their Subirans (2-person sailboats) and confidently set off for the finish line which was 103 kilometers on the other side of Leyte Gulf.

Team 'Epinephrine/Pharmanex', however, just missed the 2:30 PM cut-off, which forced them to rest at the transition area until 5:30 AM the following morning. Hence, the distance between the top two teams increased, which sealed the victory for team 'Spie Kiva'.

When asked how the "roller" leg went at the first Elf Authentic adventure race in the Philippines, Matteo Pellin of team 'Spie Kiva' proclaimed, it felt "like a massage."

EQUIPMENT

SKATES

A good pair of skates will increase your ability to perfect your skills, achieve maximum, controllable speed, and decrease your injury potential. The primary mechanics of in-line skating involve lateral motion as opposed to movement on a linear plane. Consequently, the lateral support of the skating boot is a key feature to look for. Your ideal boot should fit snugly around your ankle and the liner of the boot should hug your lower leg.

For ultimate speed and power, your body will assume a forward lean as your ankles, knees, and hips flex to accommodate fast forward motion. A good boot will allow ease in ankle flexion, which places the rest of the body in an effective position to skate fast. When trying on skates, get into a skate-ready position and note the degree of ankle flexion. Your ideal position will allow you to balance and feel comfortable.

WHEEL CHARACTERISTICS

Durometer (hardness)—Recognized by the symbol "A" accompanied by a number that represents the hardness of the wheel. The softer wheels get a lower number, while the harder wheels earn higher numbers. Softness offers better traction and a smoother ride. Harder wheels provide less traction and encourage better slide. The terrain you will encounter in your race will dictate the hardness of the wheels you will use.

Size—Big wheels mean big speed. The bigger your wheels are, the faster you can skate. Typical wheel size for recreational skaters is 72 mm. For adventure racing, opt for a larger size.

Profile—The profile, or the width of a wheel, will also affect your skating speed. Narrow profiles create faster speeds while the wider profiles provide greater stability.

Core—The core, made from urethane or plastic, secures the wheel and the bearings together and keeps the bearings anchored. Lighter wheel cores make for lighter wheels, which roll faster.

BEARINGS

Bearings are rated ABEC (Annular Bearing Engineering Council) 1 through 5. The higher the rating, the more tolerable the bearing, hence, faster speed results. Most skates are rated between 1-3 while the hard core speed-skates are generally rated between 3-5.

For best results, maintain your wheels and bearings, just like you do the rest of your equipment. Wipe down your bearings with a soft, dry cloth, particularly after a jaunt through sand or water. Before every outing, and most importantly before your race, test your wheels and bearings. Hold your skate in one hand while you swipe the wheels with the other. Each wheel should spin freely for more than a few seconds before slowing down and eventually coming to a stop. If they don't, take the bearings off your skates and clean them. If you don't want to do it yourself, you can take it to a skate shop for a service accompanied by a nominal fee.

ROTATING YOUR WHEELS

The inner edges of your wheels take a bigger beating than the outside edges. To assure the greatest performance from your skates, the wheels should be rotated regularly. When you notice wearing on the inside of your wheels, it's time to rotate them.

First, label your wheels right and left and 1-4. For example, the wheels on your right skate should be numbered starting with the front wheel, R1, then R2, R3, and R4 for the back right wheel. Label the left wheels the same way. Next, use the skate tool that came with your skates to detach the wheels. Switch sides with the wheels (right goes on the left skate and left on the right) and swap 1 with 3 and 2 with 4. Most importantly, make sure the wear of the wheels is on the outside.

PROTECT YOUR PRECIOUS PARTS

The object of a race is to be swift and fast. To accomplish this on skates, you want to be protected. ALWAYS WEAR A HELMET. Your life could be over in a matter of seconds if you spill and knock an unprotected noggin. Kneepads will guard against injury and boost your confidence with tricky turns and other slick maneuvers. Wrist guards will protect all those important bones in your hands (if you wear wrist guards, don't skate without knee pads—when skaters wear wrist guards only, they are actually more prone to wrist damage because they rely too heavily on the only protected area—the hands and wrists—to catch the fall), and elbow pads will soften any blows to the arms.

It may seem laborious to suit up with your skating armor, but you will skate faster with more confidence and less risk of injury. Practice getting in and out of your protective gear and skates so that you can be fast in and out of skating transitions.

IN-LINE SKATING TECHNIQUES

In every athletic endeavor, balance is crucial. In-line skating is no exception. In addition, before venturing out of your driveway (much less a race) be sure you can stop, turn, and fall properly. Knowing how to stop is the most basic skill you need when skating. This expertise will give you confidence and allow for better control in tight areas and sloping terrain. The ability to turn effectively will give you more options in your path of flight—you won't be limited to skating straight lines! And, knowing how to fall correctly will save you from serious injuries, which leads to race disqualification.

STOPPING

There are four common methods of stopping on skates:

1. The first, and easiest way to stop is to snowplow by angling your toes and knees inward the same way you would on snow-skis.

2. A more popular technique of stopping involves the heel brake. This one requires a little more balance. To use the heel brake, first cease your stroking and transition into a gliding motion. Slide your right foot forward, then bend your left knee and drive your right heel into the ground to activate the brake. Practice this method until you can quickly come to a stop.

3. The T-stop can reduce speed or allow you to stop without the use of the heel brake. To execute this technique, you simply form a T-position with your skates and drag the wheels of your back skate in a position perpendicular to the front skate. This method requires more skill so make sure you are proficient with the heel brake first.

4. Finally, you can stop by turning, IF you are comfortable turning while on the move. In an adventure race, this technique is not usually necessary. Therefore, proficiency of the other three methods will be most useful.

TURNING

There are several ways to turn on skates. The easiest is to look and point in the direction you wish to turn. For example, if you want to turn right, stabilize your body on your right skate-leg, look to the right and reach or punch your left arm in the same direction.

The left leg will naturally follow and you will turn in a lunge-like position (bend the right knee and keep the left leg straight).

Another way to turn requires a bit more agility. For example, if you wish to turn to the left, brush your left skate-leg behind your right as you glide (or actually lift and step) the right leg in the direction of the turn (in this case, to the left). This method may need more practice, but eventually, it produces greater speed and fluidity.

Practice turning by skating in a giant, continuous circle. Travel in one direction for several turns, then switch and skate in the opposite direction. Once this feels comfortable, execute a figure 8 pattern in both directions.

FALLING

Learn to fall properly and you will lessen your chances of serious injuries. When you lose control, exaggerate knee flexion and thrust your hips forward until you drop to your knees. Your kneepads will absorb most of the shock of the fall. Momentum will carry your upper body to the ground at which point you can break the rest of the fall with your hands (make sure you don't lock your joints—rather let them "give" upon contact). Practice falling until you feel confident of your skills.

EFFICIENCY

Always keep your knees flexed and weight balanced. If you lean too far back, your skates will slide forward and you will fall on your backside, or worse, your head. If your weight is too far forward, you will lose momentum and speed.

As you gain confidence, proficiency will follow. Practice skating with your pack fully loaded with racing gear and plan several skating workouts with your team to witness your collective abilities before race day.

Elf Race, Philippines

During the canoe leg of the Eco-Challenge in British Columbia (1996), we traveled along really long finger lakes that lasted forever. Well, as it often happens, day turned into night and we began to get very sleepy. Sleepy enough that I almost had one of my teammates flip our boat in the dark of night with no one around for miles. The good thing was he didn't flip the boat, so we decided to stop and take a snooze along the banks of the lake.

We must have slept for an hour-and-a-half only to be awakened by a 2,000-pound short-horned bull standing right over us. In fact, the bull was snorting while nibbling at the end of my teammate's sleeping bag. After waking, my teammate attempted to rid himself of the 2,000-pound terror, but the bull continued to snort and began to scuff the ground with his hoofs. Needless to say, my teammate got out of his bag—and so did the rest of us.

It was the closest I had come to using the mandatory jumbo bear pepper spray. I'm glad there were no camera crews around at that time to film us—a couple of big, tough adventure racers barefoot and practically naked, defending themselves with a can of pepper spray.

—*Blain Reeves*

AQUEOUS ADVENTURES

Paddling is a staple in adventure racing. The form of transportation and the characteristics and personality of the water will change from race to race, but the basics are universal. You may paddle calm fjords in a canoe with your entire team, or in a peculiar boat indigenous to the country you race in. You could find yourself battling class IV rapids in an inflatable raft. Or, you might end up riding 10-foot swells along the coast of a tropical beach.

CANOES

The possibilities are numerous. Your job is to become a proficient paddler with knowledge of various size canoes, which can be classified into one of four categories: recreational, touring, white-water, and cruising. Each type of canoe capitalizes on speed, maneuverability, and stability, emphasizing one of these three factors, depending on its purpose.

The longer the canoe, the faster it will travel. A smaller boat is easier to maneuver. Wider canoes are more stable than narrow ones. A deeper boat (the vertical measurement from floor to gunwale) carries more and stays drier.

The bottom profile of a canoe can vary from a flat bottom (most stable) to a V-bottom to an arched bottom (least stable). Canoes also come "rockered" (the ends are out of the water) for greater manipulation.

The sides and ends of a canoe also vary, depending on maneuverability and stability.

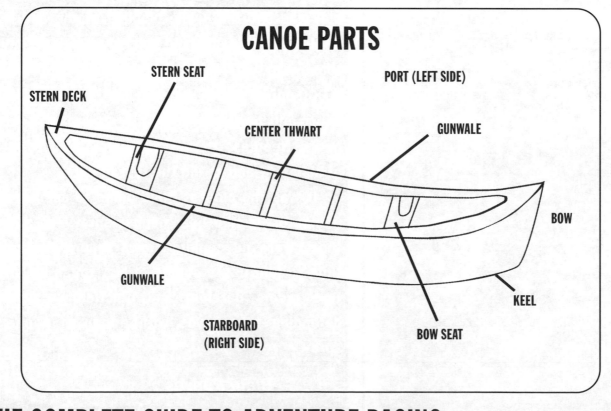

CANOE PARTS

STERN SEAT · STERN DECK · PORT (LEFT SIDE) · CENTER THWART · GUNWALE · BOW · GUNWALE · KEEL · STARBOARD (RIGHT SIDE) · BOW SEAT

KAYAKS

There are a variety of kayaks available depending on the type of water you will negotiate.

Performance is determined by the shape of the kayak. In an adventure race, if you use a kayak, you will probably be in the sea kayak.

Many paddles have a feathered option which allows for greater aerodynamics when the blade slices through the wind. To make this work, include a subtle flick of the wrist upon each revolution.

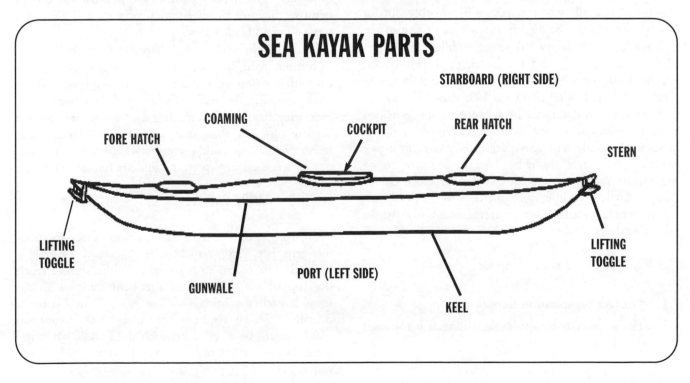

SEA KAYAK PARTS

STARBOARD (RIGHT SIDE)

COAMING

FORE HATCH   COCKPIT   REAR HATCH   STERN

LIFTING TOGGLE

LIFTING TOGGLE

PORT (LEFT SIDE)

GUNWALE   KEEL

PADDLES

The ultimate paddle for an adventure race should be very lightweight and comfortable to use for extended periods. There are many variables to consider such as your paddling style and technique, the type of water you will be in, and the type of boat you will use (its length and the height of the seats). But unless you have a bottomless bank account, you will probably opt for one paddle that can be used in many race situations.

There are basically two types of paddles: the single-bladed canoe paddle and the kayak or double-bladed paddle. Both types have their advantages and disadvantages; a double-bladed paddle is best suited for kayaks and inflatable watercrafts. In a canoe, a single-bladed paddle is easier to maneuver the boat. However, a double-bladed paddle will provide greater power in a race situation and, therefore, it has become popular among top racers. When racing, your goal is to move fast. A double bladed paddle will elicit power upon each stroke, whereas a canoe blade alternates a power stroke with a recovery stroke.

A kayak paddle is not appropriate when:

1. The race organization forbids it.
2. The watercraft is unsuitable (the craft is too high or the gunwales are too high).

3. The conditions are unsuitable (i.e. the course takes you through very narrow or shallow waterways).

Paddles are constructed of a variety of materials including fiberglass/carbon fiber, wood, and plastic. Fiberglass/carbon fiber paddles are popular these days because they are the lightest, strongest, and have the most efficient blade shape.

The most hydrodynamic shapes are the "propellers" or former "wing" paddles, which are highly asymmetrical with a scoop on the upper lip of the blade. These blades provide the most efficient paddle stroke; however, they require some getting used to as the stroke is slightly different than that used with a conventional blade. Whichever paddle you decide to use, it is paramount to practice with your paddle before the race.

FITTING A CANOE PADDLE

Sit upright on the deck or on a floor, place the paddle grip between your legs, and extend the blade upward. The throat of a straight paddle should reach the top of your head and the bent paddle's throat should reach the bridge of your nose. When you are actually paddling, your control hand, which is your top hand, should be at eye level with the handle when the blade is immersed and the paddle is vertical in the water.

When you hold the canoe paddle, space your grip hand and the shaft hand approximately shoulder-width apart. Your arms should be almost straight. This will encourage greater muscular access from the larger muscles of your upper body—the back muscles. In addition, you will paddle with greater efficiency, as the blade will stay vertical longer.

When the elbows are flexed, movement stems from the muscles of your arms, which is not efficient. Conversely, straight arms encourage more power as the movement originates in the torso and back.

FITTING A KAYAK PADDLE

To get a general idea of the length of paddle that is ideal for you, consider the following test. Stand with the paddle perpendicular to the ground and directly in front of you and extend your dominant arm upward without elevating your shoulders. You should be able to hug the edge of the top blade with your fingers for a good fit. The paddle is too long if you cannot drape part of your fingers over the edge of the blade. It is too short if your wrist can flex over the edge of the paddle. Most of us will use a kayak paddle that is between 220 and 240 centimeters long.

Keep in mind that this test is only a base of reference. You may be more comfortable with a paddle that doesn't fit this test based on your body shape, paddling style, or the type of watercraft you will use. Ultimately,

you should be able to paddle with a neutral but relaxed posture. If you have to greatly alter your technique to accommodate the paddle (i.e. leaning over the gunwale to immerse the blade), you will lose efficiency and set yourself up for injury.

When you grasp an object, an oval shape melds comfortably with your hand. Therefore, an oval shaped paddle shaft permits ease in your grip, which reduces tendon and joint pain. However, if you perform numerous strokes that require the blade position to be altered, an oval shape could be a disadvantage. In this case, you may prefer a round shaft for flexibility. As you plant the blade in the water in various positions, you can alter the blade angle to suit a particular stroke without twisting your wrists in awkward positions as you would with the oval shape.

Here are a few tips to help improve your grip on the paddle:

- Keep the shaft as dry as possible. Use drip rings—and adjust them appropriately.
- For better grip surface, take #400 sandpaper or fine steel wool and sand the shaft where you hold it. (With fiberglass shafts, be careful not to rise up the glass fibers. They will irritate your hands.)
- Take an inner tube from a bike or tennis grip-tape and wrap it around the part of the shaft you hold onto.

PERSONAL SAFETY

The Coast Guard requires anyone in a boat or kayak to wear a Personal Float Device (PFD) on their bodies while on the water. Not only will it save your life, but it also acts as good insulation in cold water.

THERE ARE 3 CATEGORIES OF PFDS:

TYPE I

This PFD is an off-shore life jacket with a minimum buoyancy of 22 pounds. It is completely appropriate for abandoning ship on high seas. And since the ratio of one pound of flotation for each ten pounds of body

weight is considered ideal, it is more than adequate for most people. They are extremely safe, but very bulky and tough to kayak in as they restrict your movement.

TYPE II

The Type II PFD is a cheaper version of Type I. It doesn't have as much buoyancy but it is designed to do the same job under less extreme conditions. The flotation capability is less, and they are almost as clumsy as Type I. Paddlers generally avoid Type I and Type II PFDs.

TYPE III

If designed properly, this PFD is ideal for kayaking, canoeing, or rafting. The Coast Guard sometimes refers to these as flotation aids more than life jackets. They are not really meant to support an unconscious castaway. But either way, they do guarantee a minimum of 15 and a half pounds of flotation.

More than likely, you will look for a Type III jacket. When you choose your PFD, try it on and go through all of your movements. Check for comfort and be sure it won't chafe you, restrict your movement, or rub your neck or under your arms. In some cases, you could be paddling for 24 hours, so you want to avoid as much discomfort as possible.

When you are picking out your PFD, be sure you have a jacket big enough to fit over all of your clothes. It goes on the outside of all of your jackets, shirts, sweaters, etc. But more importantly, make sure it is fitted to your body so that it won't rise over your head if the shoulders of the jacket are pulled up. Inflatable life jackets are much less bulky and lighter in weight. The problem with these PFDs is that they are not always reliable. And there is a good chance that these PFDs can become punctured prior to the boat section of the race.

PFD TIPS

- The right length for a kayaker is a "shorty", which comes right down to your last rib.

- PFDs have a shelf life. The life is reduced considerably if you put weight on it. If you rest your boats on the jackets or sit on them—every time you compress the foam of your PFD, you reduce its buoyancy.

- Every time your PFD is in the heat or sunlight, buoyancy is reduced.

- Natural attrition is a yearly buoyancy loss of three percent. So, every few years get a new PFD!

- The Coast Guard does not allow you to sew anything to a PFD as it reduces its buoyancy. The only modification that is allowed is the attachment of a whistle, which is mandatory on the water. At night, it is easy to lose track of other kayakers. If you tip, blow your whistle three times. If you hear three short whistle blows, it is usually a signal to help a distressed paddler or boater.

- Although you cannot sew anything to your jacket, you can cut the belt lengths and the ties so it fits you and it is a good idea to put reflective adhesive tape on it. You can also create a drain hole in the pocket of your jacket. If there is none, it is likely to fill up with water.

HELMETS

Your helmet should fit securely on your head and should be comfortable at the same time. Oftentimes, your bike helmet will provide the necessary protection in an adventure race.

AUDIBLE SIGNALS

On the water, the Coast Guard recommends that your whistle or audible signal is audible for half a nautical mile. It is a useful tool when trying to locate your team, and it is also an effective means of communication to let oncoming boats know you are nearby. When you are in a kayak, you are extremely low in the water, so it is hard to be seen. When purchasing a whistle, stay away from police whistles and make sure the one you obtain won't disintegrate in water.

Serious kayakers get a small freon-charged horn from a bicycle or marine supply store. They can be heard up to a mile away, only weigh a few ounces, and fit in the palm of your hand. If this is a route you wish to take, get 100 blasts per replaceable cartridge. When paddling, keep it in an easy, accessible place like your outside pocket to obtain immediately when needed.

STAYING AFLOAT

BAILING YOUR BOAT

Eventually, water gets into the boat and you will need to bail. Or, if you tip upside down and your watercraft fills with water, you will need to get the water out before you get back in it. The best bailer for this job is an empty Clorox bleach bottle. Find one that is rounded and very rigid with a good size handle and a cap that screws on and off. Keep the cap on it and cut the bottom off to make a scoop out of it. Fishermen have been successfully using this method for decades.

If all you have to worry about is a slightly leaking hatch, a slightly leaking skirt, or a little water in your kayak, use a giant natural sponge. They are most absorbent and wear well. A synthetic bilge sponge from a marine store will also work if you can't find a natural one. To use, simply let it sit in the bottom of the boat and every now and then squeeze it out over the side of the boat. (A sponge also offers the ladies a way to discreetly urinate in the boat while paddling. When the woman paddler squeezes out the sponge, all her male counterparts need to know is that she is getting rid of excess water in the boat.)

Don't forget to attach a lanyard to your bailer and tie it to your boat. There's nothing worse than being upside down while watching your bailer float away, leaving you with nothing to bail your boat.

PUMPS

Self-contained electric bilge pumps made just for kayaks are easy to use, and large ones move a lot of water. The drawback to this kind of power is that they break down a lot, they are additional weight, and you have to install and maintain them.

Many of the British kayaks come with a diaphragm pump mounted on the aft hex. The advantage to this method is that the pump is always there when you want it and it only takes one hand to operate it. The disadvantage? It only displaces a small amount of water.

The cheapest, most common method of pumping is through a hand-held bilge pump that you can stow down in front of your spray skirt's tunnel and pump away when necessary. They are about 18 inches, tough but lightweight, and depending on the model, will move six to ten gallons a minute. You probably will never see an electric bilge pump in a boat at an adventure race.

LINE

You will also need end lines, also called "painters," which are short ropes tied to the end of the canoes. They are usually used to tie the canoe to shore, to stabilize it when it's on a vehicle, or to tow it. Use polypropylene line at a minimum of three-eighths of an inch and at least fifteen feet. Any line you use in the water should float, and this line will. When you paddle, stow the line in a safe place so you don't become entangled at a bad time.

THROW BAG

A throw bag is an essential piece of gear that you will need on the water. It is most effective when thrown from the shore. They can also be used for unpinning a boat from a rock, creating a tag line, or for lining a boat through a rapid too extreme for your team to run. Be sure to keep the rope tightly coiled in the bag when not in use to avoid potential catastrophes. The rope should be an asset when in trouble and not a hindrance when things are calm.

KNIFE

Place your knife somewhere on your life jacket where it is easily accessible. You want to get to it and use it as quickly as possible in adverse conditions. A knife may be used to cut a snagged rope or possibly one that is wrapped around a body part. In an emergency situation, be swift but careful. It is unnecessary to create further misfortune by slicing flesh or your watercraft (use caution in an inflatable!).

DRY BAGS

If you want to be certain that your gear will stay dry on the water, pack it in a dry bag and secure it to your watercraft with a carabiner. Some racers wrap garbage bags around their packs and secure them to the craft, but, inevitably, your pack will get wet this way.

If you are in a one to two day race, garbage bags may be a preferred option when considering the amount of weight you will haul around the racecourse. If you compete in a longer race with support, you have the luxury of more options. In this case, you may decide to use a dry bag.

SAILS/KITES

In some race situations, teams have rigged makeshift sails to their boats to enhance their speed on the water. Obviously, if wind is present, this may prove efficient. To do this, tie your boats together and then use whatever material is available for a sail. A jacket or garbage bag will work, or if you are prepared, a few yards of nylon fabric will do the trick. Use your paddles or trekking poles to stabilize the sail. If you are not comfortable with these, use thick tree branches or hiking poles.

Team 'Spie' prepares for 1 and 1/2 days of paddling in the Samar Sea during the Elf Authentic Adventure in the Philippines.

IAN ADAMSON'S GEAR TIPS

Ian Adamson has claimed first place rights in both the Raid Gauloises and the Eco-Challenge and holds a World Record for paddling the most miles in a sea kayak in a 24-hour period.

THE DRY SUIT

Although a wetsuit can be worn in 48-degree water, putting on enough rubber to keep delicate body parts from turning blue severely constricts movement and makes you look like the Pillsbury Dough Boy. Dry gear has the advantage of being lightweight, comfortable, unrestricting, and very warm.

A dry suit does just what it says—it keeps you dry. How much of you it keeps dry depends on the design, but typically everything between your neck, wrists, and ankles is spared unwanted dampness. It should also be noted that dry suits can hold a large volume of air, something which can be quite advantageous as it provides additional buoyancy if you end up out of your boat. Unless you intend to do some really extreme paddling and want to spend a thousand dollars, then you are best off sticking to a regular suit.

DRY TOPS

Dry tops are best adapted to kayak paddling since they are basically dry suits that end at the waist. They are also considerably cheaper than dry suits since they do not need the waterproof zipper to allow you to get in and out of them. The best tops have a spray skirt cuff that helps prevent water cascading down between the dry top and the skirt.

DRY PANTS

Although these creations are available, they can be a serious liability to paddlers since they have been known to fill with water, which can hold you down under rapids and restrict movement when swimming. Without getting into a debate on the merit of dry pants, I would recommend spending a few extra dollars and getting the full dry suit if more cold protection is required.

UNDER LAYERS

Underneath any dry suit, one should wear an appropriate layer of thermal to insulate you from the cold of the external water (something a dry suit doesn't do very well) and to transport sweat away from your skin. The material weight will depend on how hard you paddle, how cold it is, and how much time you are likely to spend in the water. For proficient paddlers who are likely to be splashed and not submerged, a layer of 100-weight polypropylene is sufficient. If you are in an open boat or spend lots of time making like a fish, then a layer of fleece should be added. One down side of most dry suits is that they keep moisture in just as well as they keep it out. Because of this, conditions that are conducive to perspiration, such as cold water on a sunny day or strenuous exertion, may cause a build-up of water on the inside of the suit. The solution is to pony up a few extra dollars and buy a Gor-Tex dry suit.

POGIES

For the uninitiated, a pogy is a close relative to the glove, adapted to wrap around a paddle shaft. Pogies are made to fit kayak, canoe, and rowing blades and come in a variety of designs.

BOOTIES

If you have ever tried to portage your boat or scout a rapid with numb feet, it can be quite a nasty experience. Not only does it upset your balance, but also makes gravel surfaces seem more like broken glass than rock. This is where booties come in handy. The best paddling booties are low profile so they can fit inside a low deck, well-soled with a grippy rubber for traction on slippery rocks, and high enough on the ankle to overlap a dry suit or wetsuit leg. Thicker booties come with a side zipper since the thickness of the neoprene and snugness of fit precludes pulling them over your heel.

HEADGEAR

Apart from your helmet (you are wearing one, aren't you?), a fleece or neoprene headband or beanie can be worn. For really cold water or extended submersion, a neoprene hood works well. These cover either your head and ears or all the way down to your shoulders, if it is a diver's style hood.

When thinking cold water paddling, think like a skier. Similar principals apply, such as most heat is lost from your head and your extremities feel the cold first. With this in mind, chemical hand and foot warmers are a boon. Small disposable warmers can be attached with the ubiquitous duct tape to the paddle shaft adjacent to your grip position or placed inside your booties. They won't last as long as for skiing since water conducts the heat much faster than air, but they certainly work for a while.

If you don't already use a seat pad, consider using one in the cold. Not only do they add comfort layers to your derriere, they add thermal insulation, something that is much appreciated when sitting inches from near-freezing water. Most outdoor retailers sell ready-made seat pads, but less-expensive ones can be cut from closed-cell foam purchased at a discount store.

CANOEING ON LAKES AND RIVERS

The first skill you will need to master in paddling is boat entry. When boarding your canoe, launch the canoe and bring it parallel to the shore. Place it in deep enough water so that it will float when you put your weight into it. In moving water, the upstream end needs to be held tight to the shore to keep the canoe from spinning into the current. In really shallow water, walk the canoe from shore to ankle deep water.

Cargo is always loaded first. Trim the canoe with your gear to equally distribute the total weight in the boat. Then to enter the canoe, put the paddle across the gunwale with the blade facing the shore. Face forward, grasp both gunwales and lean the canoe to shore until the paddle blade braces the shore or the bottom. Transfer your weight slowly onto the bottom center of the canoe. Place one foot at a time and always strive to make three points of contact when boarding.

As you board the canoe, enter directly into your paddle position right where you will sit or kneel. For maximum stability, kneel. Kneeling is sitting with your knees down. Spread them as far as comfortable for increased stability and paddle power. Lean back against the seat or the fort and aim your toes to the stern or flex them underneath you to elevate your ankles. You will probably alternate between the two positions and even come up with your own variation as you become more comfortable in the canoe.

If you choose to sit, foot braces will improve your paddling efficiency—just as they do in a kayak.

The ideal position to paddle in a canoe is on your knees. To soften the experience, kneepads are extremely helpful. You can wear them on your knees or glue them to the inside of the boat (make sure you use non-absorbing foam with a non-slip surface).

When paddling tandem, the stern paddler generally gets in first. The stern stance is generally wider and more stable. If you prefer to sit, some canoes are designed with low-mounted bucket seats for sitting. While the paddler's stability and reach is reduced, the sitting position is a lot more comfortable for long paddle sessions. In a race like the Raid where you paddle for two to three days, it is pretty unlikely that you would be on your knees the entire time. A great option is to sit in calmer waters and rise up on your knees when you hit white-water.

To successfully complete a paddling journey, you must perfect your paddle strokes, be able to read water, and be proficient in safety techniques.

PHASES OF A PADDLE STROKE

THREE PHASES OF A PADDLE STROKE

There are three phases of the paddle stroke: the catch, propulsion, and recovery. The paddle enters the water in the catch phase at a right angle to the direction of travel. During the propulsion phase, the canoe moves in your intended direction. During the recovery, the paddle could be in or out of the water. The paddle should come out of the water at about hip level.

In tandem situations, the paddlers need to paddle in sync with one another. The bow paddler sets the pace and the rear paddler tries to match every stroke. The paddles need to enter and exit simultaneously in order to reach maximum efficiency.

Time, communication, and honest effort create a winning formula for successful teamwork.

In a canoe, the bow and stern paddlers paddle on opposite sides of the boat from one another. This technique prevents unnecessary instability and reduces any tippy sensation and promotes stability and increases the efficiency of the two person team. Both paddlers should either sit or kneel. The closer the partners work in complete synchronization, the faster and more efficient they will paddle. This differs from kayaking, where both paddlers paddle on the same side of the boat.

CANOE STROKES

BASIC CATEGORIES AND TERMS

There are three categories of paddle strokes: the power stroke, the turning stroke and the bracing stroke.

Paddlers use the terms "onside" and "offside" when discussing paddling on different sides of a canoe. Onside is the side of the boat where the soloists' hands are during the forward stroke. The opposite side of the boat is the offside. When in a tandem situation, the terms are determined by the bow paddler's position.

The "control hand" is determined by the hand that is on the grip of the paddle. This is the hand that controls the blade. The thumb on the control hand is called the control thumb. The hand that is used to hold the shaft of the paddle is the shaft hand.

POWER

FORWARD STROKE

The forward stroke or power stroke is the primary stroke used when paddling a canoe. In addition, greater efficiency occurs when the arms remain extended throughout the stroke. To be most effective, the paddle should be parallel to the keel line and as close to the canoe as possible.

Carrying the stroke farther back just wastes energy by lifting water and turning the canoe.

REVERSE STROKE

The reverse stroke is normally used to stop the boat's forward progression. It is the opposite of a forward stroke. The difference is that in the reverse stroke, the catch occurs just behind your hip. Once you catch the water and rotate your torso toward the bow, backward movement is created.

TURNING

J-STROKE

The J-stroke is a modified version of the forward stroke. This stroke is to be used when you need slight adjustments. The amount of "J" that you put into the stroke all depends on how much of an adjustment you want to make. To perform a J-stroke, simply begin the stroke as though it were a forward stroke. As the paddle comes back toward your hip, ensure the blade is fully below the water line and push it away from the boat. You may find that you will need to make many minor J-strokes to keep the boat on line. This stroke takes practice to perfect.

THE DRAW

The draw stroke can either move the canoe toward the paddle, or in a tandem situation, can turn the canoe to either side. To perform a draw stroke, simply pull yourself toward your paddle while keeping your control arm as stiff as possible and bend your shaft arm only slightly. The power phase of this stroke is complete as your boat nears the blade. Once the boat and the blade are close, think of sweeping water under the boat. Take the paddle and sweep the water under the boat. Be sure that you keep your paddle in a vertical

PADDLING

position while performing this stroke. You may find that you will need to make many short draw strokes to get your boat where you want it.

THE PRY

As the forward stroke and the reverse strokes are opposite from one another, so are the pry stroke and draw strokes. The pry stroke moves the boat away from the paddle. It helps to visualize using a pry bar or pushing water away from your boat when performing this stroke. To perform a pry stroke, keep your paddle parallel to the boat's keel and the shaft of the paddle angled slightly under the boat. Then rotate your body toward the paddle, keeping both arms just slightly bent. These strokes are short. The paddle must remain completely vertical in the water when performing the pry stroke.

In a canoe, the stern paddler is responsible for most of the steering although the bow paddler can make quick on-the-spot steering corrections. The stern paddler can perform a stern-pry stroke or a stern-draw stroke if corrective steering strokes are required.

SWEEP STROKES

The sweep stroke turns the bow of the canoe away from the paddle and maintains the forward momentum. The reverse sweep stroke turns the bow toward the canoe but slows the forward momentum. When paddling tandem, the two paddlers perform opposing strokes. One paddler will perform a sweep stroke while the other paddler will simultaneously perform a reverse sweep stroke.

To perform a sweep stroke, place the blade vertically in the water alongside and toward the bow of the boat. Keep both arms straight and rigid while rotating your body sweeping the blade in a semi-circle back to the stern of the boat. Your torso, head, eyes and paddle all move simultaneously.

BRACING

High bracing and low bracing are good strokes to practice and to know. These strokes should come to you instinctively when you need them. They will keep you dry and in your boat.

HIGH BRACE

To perform a high brace, hold the paddle over your head. Be sure to keep your elbows low to reduce the risk of shoulder injury. Use the power face of the paddle as you slap the paddle against the water.

LOW BRACE

To perform a low brace, hold the paddle at chest level. Use the off power face of the paddle as you slap the paddle down against the water.

TIPS

- **Practice these strokes on flat water first so that you understand them. Once you establish efficiency, progress to moving water.**

- **The rivers provide a gamut of challenges. In addition to paddling stroke savvy, you have to know how to read the river and how to read the water. The faster the water flows, the greater the kinetic energy—the greater the force it creates. Hundreds of thousands of pounds of force can be created against a pinned or trapped person in a boat. It is imperative to under-**

stand the characteristics and environment of moving water in order to fully respect it.

- **Take a river-paddling course to learn about moving water. It is impossible to fully grasp paddling techniques and to experience the true power and force of rivers through a book.**

- **Always use strokes that will keep your boat moving, preferably toward the next checkpoint. Unless of course, you want to stop.**

ANATOMY OF WATER

FACTS ABOUT RIVERS

1. Rivers flow downhill from higher ground to low country. This is how the terms upstream and downstream originated. If you are upstream from your teammates, you are above them. If you are below a strainer (fallen tree), you are downstream and in the clear from it.

2. As you view a river downstream in the direction of its flow, river right is the right bank and river left is the left bank. These are standard directions to use when determining a route or navigating rapids, and they don't change if you are looking upstream. They remain set in accordance to your position facing downstream.

3. When the water is flowing swiftly but there are no rapids, the best place to be is in the center of a current. This is where the fastest water flows. You will travel the same speed as the water when you are not paddling. To improve efficiency and control, paddle faster than the speed of the moving water. This is particularly important as the water flows at quicker rates.

4. Keep your eyes on the direction and place you want to go. Just as in mountain biking, where your eyes go, you will go. So keep your focus off obstructions in the water. Instead, look at a safe place to paddle toward.

5. When approaching a bend in the river, aim for the inside as early as possible. This will influence your success in turbulent waters. Keep in mind, when a river bends, the fastest water shoots to the outer perimeters of the bend. A river bend right means fast water left.

A lazy attack will send you toward undesirable hazards and will prevent a prudent survey of the forthcoming path. Angle early to give yourself extra time to make good decisions and obtain ideal positioning in the water.

When in doubt, get out and scout. If you are unsure of the water and your ability to negotiate it, paddle to shore and assess the situation from dry land.

EDDIES

Eddies are calm spots along the river's edge caused by water that backfills behind protruding natural features. For example, a large protuberance from the shore such as a boulder will interrupt the downstream channel of water. This causes the water to flow past the object and then swirl upstream behind it. These pockets are great bailout points that provide an opportunity for rest, regrouping, and scouting proceeding runs.

If you want continued, forward progress with high efficiency, don't get caught in an eddy, it will slow you down. However, if you need a resting spot to regroup or strategize with your team, an eddy is a good place to be.

HOLES

Similar to eddies, holes are created from obstructions—most often rocks—in the water. The rock will usually be partially submerged in the water with the top portion exposed. As water reaches the rock, it is divided and flows around both sides. Downstream, a vacuum is created by gravity as water is sucked behind the rock, forming a hole. The magnitude of the hole's strength is determined by the characteristics of the rock—it's size, shape, and depth of submersion.

PILLOWS

Pillows reveal a smooth, shallow mound of moving water, covering a structure just below the surface. This mound is usually not deep enough to paddle over. A white-wave just in front of the pillow or a depression just downstream is a clue of trouble upstream.

When you see a white-wave, there is probably a pillow right behind it. Avoid it!

HYDRAULICS

A hydraulic can be identified by water that flows over an obstacle and lands on surface water below, creating a depression. Downstream surface water rushes upstream to fill in this depression, creating a vertical whirlpool effect. When a hydraulic is large enough to trap and recirculate a boat, it is referred to as a "keeper".

A powerful hole will "keep" you if you capsize. The surge of the water pushes you up and then pulls you under in a perpetual and dangerous manner.

If you consider yourself a novice in this discipline, do whatever it takes to avoid these danger zones. In a race situation, potential dangers will either be acknowledged and discussed in the pre-race briefing or excluded from the course.

You may have seen footage of Robyn Benincasa at the Raid in the Himalayas. She was swimming the hydrospeed board and was caught up in a hydraulic. Many boaters and swimmers have died in hydraulics. The only thing you need to do if you are ever so unfortunate to be caught in one is to either swim down below the hydraulic and away from it, or swim down low and out to the side. If you do not do either, you will most likely not get out of the hydraulic alive. I suggest that you learn to recognize them and stay clear.

STRAINERS

Strainers are a serious hazard in fast water, especially if you have been dumped from your boat. They are fallen trees, which filter water and can trap your body if you become entangled. Strainers can also be fences, brush, or drainage gates. The force of moving water can pin people against these strainers, resulting in serious consequences. If you encounter a strainer, move on to your stomach and swim towards it. As soon as you reach it, pull yourself onto it in one, quick motion. Your best bet? Avoid strainers.

BROACHING

A broach occurs when the current pushes a boat sideways against a solid object, such as a rock. To guard against broaching, lean the boat toward the object to allow upstream water to flow under the boat and lift it around the obstruction.

V-FORMATIONS

The waves of a river are choreographed by rocks, submerged obstructions, and by the pitch of the river bottom. When reading water, look for V-formations. They mark the channel between obstacles. V's are a surface feature of the river formed by two parallel obstructions, usually two rocks, indicating a clear, deep-water path that you can safely paddle through. As you travel downstream, try to aim the bow of your boat right at the center of the V.

Water lines formed off the obstructions join downstream, which point the way for you to go. So, simply point your canoe into the V's. This habit should keep you free from trouble. The sharp angle of the V will always point downstream. In gentle currents, the V's will be small. In racier water, the V's will be more pronounced.

WATER LEVELS

Water levels dramatically affect the dynamics of a river. Heavy storms or spring runoffs can alter an easy trip down the river to a challenging ride. On the other hand, when water levels are low, typical Class IV rapids may become quite easy to manage, as their characteristics become less fierce. The race management will know what levels you will be facing and will run the race accordingly. If they don't mention the water levels, ask so you know what to expect before you get to the water.

BOAT HANDLING

FERRYING

To get from one side of the river to the other without getting swept downstream, a crossing known as a "ferry" is employed. The ferry uses the water's energy deflected off the side of the canoe. This force, balanced against upstream paddling, results in movement of the boat across the current. Ferrying is helpful to line-up for downstream V's or for maneuvering around hazards, such as rocks and strainers.

The key to a successful ferry is both boat angle and speed. To ferry upstream, typically the easier direction, point the bow of the canoe upstream and toward the shore you wish to reach. Hold the angle as you paddle using forward strokes. This makes it easier to see the current and make adjustments.

If you are doing a solo ferry, power across the water with strong forward strokes, each one ending with a J-stroke or pry for correction. In a tandem ferry, the bow paddler provides the power, while the stern paddler does the correcting to maintain a good angle. In either case, strive for a small angle as you cross. That way, you will have more control of your boat position. Relax as you paddle, using the least amount of strokes possible to get to the other side.

Depending on the water movement and your expertise, your angle of ferry will vary. The greater the angle, the faster the ferry. However, speed comes with a price. Your potential to tip increases with the angle.

While maneuvering a ferry, your strokes will usually be determined by the direction of wind or currents, as you paddle on the side of the natural power source. If you are in a canoe with a canoe paddle, you will usually paddle on the downstream side.

EDDIES

EDDY TURN (GOING IN)

To approach an eddy, you must cross the eddy line that delineates the border between two distinct currents. The domain of this line can be recognized by tiny whirlpools and bubbles. Inside the line, the water is calm. But on the fringe, your stability is lessened. Approach the eddy at a 45-degree angle. The key to entering an eddy is to aggressively lean into it and paddle hard to create a turn. Once the bow has passed the eddy line, the force of the water on the stern will swing it into the eddy.

Give yourself enough room so that you can enter the eddy at a 90-degree angle. Paddle aggressively using forward strokes and occasional prys to stay on track. Generate enough speed (greater than the speed of the current) to cross the eddy line. Drive the bow hard across the eddy line. If you do not paddle with enough momentum, the strong currents of the main channel will push you away from the eddy. Once your bow has entered the eddy, lean hard in the direction of the turn.

EDDYING-OUT

Situate yourself so that you are aiming upstream. Start paddling vigorously and then cross the eddy line at a right angle. Prepare to brace upstream and continue paddling with force.

STRATEGY

- When training or racing with other boats, stay in sight of one another! The lead boat should always be able to see and recognize river hazards.

- Upstream V's indicate rocks, often forming in front of them.

- The river is usually faster on the outside of a bend. When you approach obstructions, set your course in advance, using good ferry angles.

- Whenever in doubt, get out of your boat and scout the river. If the water is too difficult to handle, portage to a calmer area.

- Make sure the river doesn't disappear in front of you. If it does, it could be a drop or a waterfall. Get out, scout, and portage. Only run it if you know you can make it.

- If you capsize, do not stand in the river. Foot entrapments are almost always 100 percent fatal. When your foot gets stuck under a rock, the waves knock you down and your chances of survival are nil. Instead, stay on the upstream side of your canoe and keep your feet up. Never stand up in moving water unless it is less than knee deep.

- If you are on a river and you see a sign with broken arrows, portage. Solid arrows equal a preferred course. Broken arrows equal an optional course.

PORTAGING

Anytime the water becomes too intimidating or downright unsafe, you may have to get out of your boat to progress along the race course by means other than paddling. There will also be sections of a race where you will be with your boat and missing one essential component—the water. In these situations, portaging comes into play.

CARRYING

Lifting your kayak or canoe can be done with one or two people. First, make sure all of the heavy gear is out of it. If two people lift a kayak with heavy gear in the middle, it could damage the kayak. If the boat is light enough, one person can carry it while the other takes the gear.

If the boat is extremely heavy, you will have to haul it by holding on to the lifting toggles. Take short breaks when necessary. Switch sides often and switch bow and stern positions to delay fatigue.

LINING

To line your boat, attach a rope to one or both ends and walk along the shore with the boat in the water.

Keep your PFD and helmet on, in case of a fall.

Portaging your boat isn't always easy, but it may be your only option at various points along a race course.

THE AMERICAN WHITE-WATER AFFILIATION
INTERNATIONAL SCALE OF RIVER DIFFICULTY

CLASS I —EASY

- Few or no obstructions, all of which are obvious or easily missed.
- Fast moving water with riffles and small waves.
- Risk to swimmers is slight.
- Self rescue is easy.

CLASS II—NOVICE

- Straightforward rapids with wide, clear channels that are obvious without scouting.
- Occasional maneuvering may be required, but rocks and waves are easily missed by trained paddlers.
- Swimmers are seldom injured and group assistance, while helpful, is seldom needed.

CLASS III—INTERMEDIATE

- Rapids with moderate, irregular waves are present, which may be difficult to avoid and are capable of swamping an open canoe.
- Complex maneuvers are necessary in fast current and narrow passages.
- Good boat control is paramount.
- Large waves, holes, and strainers may be present, but easily avoided.
- Strong eddies and powerful current effects can be found, particularly on large volume rivers.
- Chance of injury to a swimmer is low, but group assistance may be needed to prevent long swims.

CLASS IV—ADVANCED

- Presence of intense, powerful rapids requiring precise boat handling in turbulent water.
- Depending on the river, there may be long, unavoidable waves and holes or constricted passages demanding fast maneuvers under pressure.
- Risk of injury to swimmers is moderate to high and water conditions may make rescue difficult.

CLASS V—EXPERT

- Extremely long, obstructed or violent rapids which expose the paddler to above-average risk of injury.
- Drops may contain very large, unavoidable waves and holes or steep congested chutes with complex, demanding routes.
- Eddies may be small and turbulent and difficult to reach.
- Scouting is mandatory.
- Rescue is difficult, even for experts.

CLASS VI—ALMOST IMPOSSIBLE

- Difficulties of class V carried to the limits of navigability.
- Nearly impossible and very dangerous.
- Risks are high and rescue may be impossible.
- For teams of experts only, at favorable water levels after close study and with all precautions.

KAYAKING

KAYAK FIT

When making your kayak fit, you need solid contact with your feet, your knees, your hips, your rear, and your back. It should be loose enough for comfort, yet close enough so that by flexing your feet and thighs, you become one with the kayak. The balls of your feet are the direct transmitters of forward force from the body and paddle to the kayak. You have to adjust your foot pedals or the bar so that your knees are touching the under sides of the deck and your lower back, from the waist down, is gently pressed into the back of the seat. The heels should be close together and the toes should be turned outward. Your feet should not quite be 90 degrees to your ankles. To determine comfort, sit this way for 15 minutes—if your feet or legs go to sleep, readjust to give yourself more room. Spread your knees to gain balance. You need to adjust your kayak prior to paddling. Adjustments are very difficult to do while out on the water.

Balancing and leaning are usually done through your knees in a kayak. The farther apart you can place your knees without discomfort, the better your side-to-side balancing will be. They should just touch the deck near the sides of the boat. If the angle is comfortable, and

not cramped or awkward, place some thin padding on the under side of the deck for cushioning. If they do not make contact with the deck, add thick pieces of foam to fill the spaces. You can also place a heel pad to support your heels, kneepads where your knees hit and padding next to where your hips go.

When you paddle, avoid sliding in the seat. The back supports usually involve a cushion strap on a seat back to create proper fit. They shouldn't be any higher than absolutely necessary, so try to keep them in contact with your lower back. If your boat seat-back extends too far above your lower back, it will restrict your upper body motion and should be changed.

SPRAY SKIRT

Ironically, the part that keeps sea kayaks worthy—the component that keeps water out of your boat—is the part that frightens most people. A spray skirt seals around your waist and around the boat to keep water from coming in, keeping your lower body dry and warm and keeping you and your boat safe. To avoid trouble, simply keep the release tab within eye and hand reach!

ENTERING AND EXITING THE KAYAK

When getting into and out of a kayak, your center of gravity is highest. Because of this, your kayak is most unstable. It's best to get into your kayak in six to eight inches of water. This prevents damage to the bottom of the kayak. Bring it alongside the beach and stand in the water between the boat and the shore, facing the bow. Place your paddle behind your back and lay its shaft across the boat's aft deck, just behind the carrying and perpendicular to the boat's center line.

Get used to using your paddle as a stabilizing bar. If you feel anxious or clumsy, practice getting into and out of your kayak on stable ground, such as your lawn. Put your kayak on the lawn and practice maneuvering, using your paddle as a stabilizing bar. Don't do this on anything hard if it's a Kevlar or fiberglass boat.

When practicing this technique (entry or exit) on the water, your kayak has to be close in and parallel to shore. If the wind is blowing onto the beach with any strength or if there is excessive wave action, you won't be able to use this. Instead, you will probably have to get into the kayak on land and then push yourself into the water.

WET EXIT

Practice capsizing, so if it happens while you're out paddling, you will be prepared. When you are upside down, don't let go of your paddle. Or better yet, tether your paddle to your kayak so you won't ever have to worry about losing it. Then reach down for your spray skirt by placing your hands next to your hips and sliding your thumbs around the coaming until you feel the loop of your spray skirt. Grab it and pull it toward you to release. Slide out of the boat as if you were climbing out of a pair of pants. When you are out, hold on to the kayak (and your paddle if not tethered) and surface.

Under no circumstance, should you let go of the boat. Always hang on to your boat.

In surf or breaking seas, maintain your hold while staying upwind of the boat. A sea kayak can knock you unconscious if it hits you. No matter what the condition of the sea is, your best bet is to keep a hold on your boat in its capsized (inverted) position until you are ready to bail it.

A swamped kayak right side up is inherently unstable. And it can take on more water. By keeping it upside down, you minimize the amount of water it can take, while maintaining an air pocket that helps improve buoyancy. If you have to swim your kayak, keep it upside down.

STROKES

For 100 percent paddling efficiency, keep the paddle blade at right angles to the direction you're traveling. As the angle changes, your efficiency will fade. Keep the shaft vertical to the water surface when moving forward or in reverse, and keep the shaft horizontal for sweep strokes to turn the boat.

Instead of moving the paddle toward the boat, focus on moving the boat toward the paddle.

There are myriad strokes you will use to maneuver your watercraft in an adventure race. The ultimate goal is the same as it is for every sport: efficiency. Maximum power with minimal effort should be your objective.

To achieve maximum power over a long period of time, it is imperative that you learn proper technique. Paddling is an upper body exercise. Your torso is your power center and your back, predominantly the latissimus dorsi, is the driving force. Your arms are there to connect your back to the paddle, nothing more. You shouldn't use your arms or place too much stress on your shoulders as you paddle. It is not an arm exercise. Successful paddling is the product of back and torso camaraderie.

Before you learn proper stroke technique, focus on your posture and the basic mechanics of pulling in a seated position. Spinal stability is paramount. As you flex forward at the hips, don't let your spine break at your waist. Likewise, when you pull back, keep your spine in neutral. Focus on keeping your shoulders back and down away from your ears to keep your chest open and try to stay relaxed. Focus on the horizon as you propel yourself forward.

Hamstring flexibility is also a factor that affects your ability to paddle efficiently. The more flexible your hamstrings are, the further forward your reach will be, allowing you to generate more power. Also, you won't fatigue as quickly and your legs will remain more relaxed. Allow your lower body to be "one" with the boat.

THE FORWARD STROKE/POWER STROKE

This stroke creates forward propulsion and will be the primary focus of your paddling. Hold the paddle with your arms comfortably extended about shoulder-

width apart. Think about making a box with your arms and the paddle and move within the box. Hinge at the hips as you reach forward and dig your paddle into the water. Pull with your back and use your torso to rotate toward the direction of pull. Once you reach your hips, slice the paddle out of the water and repeat.

Peak force should occur mid-stroke—about the time your blade passes by your knees. For ultimate power, maximize your torso rotation. To do this, twist your body so that the arm in front reaches as far ahead as you can comfortably extend it. When you "catch", or enter the water with your blade, the body will recoil which contributes power to your stroke. Simultaneously, as the stroke is executed, the recoil also rotates the opposite arm forward to perform the same maneuver. As this push-pull effect is polished, you gain efficiency in your technique. At the crux of the stroke, your torso muscles are firing the hardest.

Keep your strokes smooth and even, and close to your boat. Maintain steady pressure and grip the paddle loosely. A tight grip will only take away precious energy you would rather use toward propelling yourself forward. Breathe with each stroke and strive for a comfortable rhythm that you can sustain for a long duration.

Your shoulders should not feel the burden of endless strokes if you are paddling correctly. They will assist the motion, but should not carry it. Be particularly sensitive to their vulnerability in strong currents, as it is easy to injure the shoulder joint.

THE REVERSE STROKE

In many cases, the ability to maneuver your watercraft backwards is just as important as moving forward. The reverse stroke is basically the opposite of the forward stroke.

THE SWEEP

A broad, brush stroke will turn your boat in the opposite direction. It can be used to "correct" your power strokes when you stray off your intended direction, or to maneuver around obstacles as you draw a half-circle in the water. To perform a sweep stroke, lean forward and catch the water as close to the bow as you can. Sweep the blade out away from your boat and around to the stern in a semicircle pattern. While you do this, lean into the sweep to tilt the opposite side of your boat up. Rotate your torso and keep a strong, straight arm to pull the paddle through the stroke. At the same time, push forward with the same foot. As the blade comes around, your body will move back to an upright position.

If you are using the sweep to correct your course, insert a sweep stroke between forward strokes.

STEERING

To control the direction of your boat, the blade of your paddle can be used as a rudder, but should only be used for extreme corrections as it dramatically slows the boat down. As you are moving forward, plant the blade in the water by the stern and hold it there until you have corrected your line of travel.

THE PRY

The pry stroke allows you to move laterally away from objects such as rocks or when shoving off from a dock. As you hold your paddle in a normal position, rotate your torso in the direction that you wish to move away from. Drive your blade into the water as close to the boat as possible (driving face inward). Push with your lower hand and pull with the upper hand to move the boat sideways away from the point where you initially planted the blade.

THE DRAW

The draw is the reverse of the pry stroke. Start in the same fashion as the pry with your paddle in a normal position and your body twisted toward the side. Plant your paddle two to three feet away from the boat (power face toward you and fully immersed) and pull yourself toward the paddle. As you move closer to your paddle, push out with your upper hand to facilitate the movement. To ensure lateral motion, keep the power face parallel to the side of your boat. If you lose sight of the blade's position, the sideways motion will break.

To connect several draw strokes, keep the blade in the water. At the end of the draw, when the paddle is vertical, turn the blade a quarter so that the driving face is angled toward the stern. Slice the blade through the water away from your boat until you reach your starting position. Twist the blade back so the driving face addresses your boat and then pull yourself to your paddle again.

THE J-STROKE

A power stroke that begins or ends with a draw or a pry can be used to turn your boat.

THE COMPLETE GUIDE TO ADVENTURE RACING

PADDLING TIPS FOR ALL WATERCRAFT

- Aim for waves in 90 degree angles.
- Avoid as many waves, rocks, and other obstructions a possible. They all slow you down.
- When faced with an obstruction, keep paddling until you are well clear of it.
- If you tip, make yourself as small as possible. Thrashing about extends your surface area and wastes energy.
- If you find yourself approaching a hole or hydraulic, your natural instinct will be to shy away from it. If the water is coming at you and you lean away from it, you will tip. Instead, lean

- INTO the water's force and paddle through it.
- Always tether your paddle to your watercraft—particularly in the ocean or large, volatile lakes.
- Hold your paddle so that you have 90 degree angles at your elbows. To find the correct position, put the paddle on top of your head and place your hands on it so that they are directly over your elbows.
- Balance is a big key to paddling success.
- Torso stability is advantageous to powerful paddling.

RESCUE

Before you venture into the unknown, it is prudent to know what to do in case of an emergency. Water is an extremely powerful entity. Respect its powers and be prepared to rescue yourself or others at anytime.

It is wise to schedule a swift water rescue course every year to perfect and review your skills.

SNAG LINE

A snag line is used to rescue a victim whose leg is stuck under a rock. *Before you attempt a rescue, scout the area and create a keen awareness of your surroundings. Then, when you are familiar with the scene, proceed carefully with the rescue.* Two people, one stationed on either side of the river, are needed to create a snag line. Two ropes are also needed. First, position one rope underwater and then walk upstream with the second

rope belayed around your hips until you can catch the rope under the victim's body. Keep walking upstream until the rope catches the person's feet. Essentially, you will make a "V" with the rope to release your teammate's foot. When the victim is untangled, the first rope will provide a "catch" for him, where he can then be safely hauled to shore.

THROW BAGS

It is mandatory to have rescue equipment with you when on the water. A throw bag, simply comprised of a small bag which houses 50 to 75 feet of polypropylene rope (which floats) three-eighths of an inch in diameter, is an invaluable part of your life-saving gear. To save a victim with this bag, the rescuer holds on to the end

of the rope, which is always protruding from the bag, and throws the rest of the rope in the bag to the victim.

In an underhand motion (as if you were pitching a 12-inch softball), toss the bag directly at your teammate. If you offshoot at all, aim just slightly upstream. Before your journey, practice throwing the rope and always stuff the rope back in the bag. Never coil it. When you are in your watercraft, secure it to the seat or thwart so that it is easily accessible.

CAPSIZED

If you flip, and inevitably you will if you spend enough time on the water, your first move is to position yourself upstream of your watercraft. Hold onto it and gain your composure. If you are in water that hits below your knees, stand. Raise one end of the canoe until it is above the water's surface, and then push down on the opposite end of the boat while lifting one gunwale to break the water's suction. If the canoe is still upside down, raise the canoe out of the water. Let some seconds elapse so the canoe drains, then roll the canoe to the upright position.

If you are by yourself in deeper water, begin by placing your hands on both gunwales of your upright boat, near the wide section of the canoe. Your hand placement may vary due to the canoe width, stability and arm length. There should be space available for your body in the section to be entered.

Push down with both hands and use a strong kick to lift your body upward until your hips are across the nearest gunwale. Roll onto your back and sit on the bottom of the canoe before bringing your legs in. Hand paddle the canoe if necessary to retrieve your paddles and gear. Swamped canoes may be paddled to shore with paddles or hands and can be bailed out from land.

BOAT OVER BOAT

Hold the gunwale on the opposite side your teammate is reentering to stabilize the boat.

Tandem partners can help each other out.

In a situation with two boats, where one is capsized, do a boat over boat rescue. In this situation, the two people in the water work first. The weaker swimmer will swim to the canoe that is still upright, while the other gets on the tip of the boat. Their efforts are then united to line the capsized boat perpendicular to the rescue boat, forming a "T" and remaining in the position at the bottom of the "T".

The rescuers at the top of the "T" who are in the boat, hold onto the capsized boat while the other paddler then pushes down on his tip of the boat to break the vacuum. This action raises the end near the rescuer's boat up and out of the water. More than one person may need to push down on the end of the boat if one person is not heavy enough. Create a seesaw-like motion to get all of the water out of the boat.

Keeping the boat upside down, the rescuers pull the boat up and across the craft until it balances on their gunwales to form a plus sign. As you do this, be careful not to pinch your fingers between the two boats. The capsized paddlers should keep hold of the canoe as it is pulled in and then move to a stable position on the rescue boat. Once the boat is drained, the boat is flipped upright while still balancing on the gunwales. The rescuers then slide the canoe into the water without losing contact; they stabilize the craft gunwale to gunwale with their own boat. The capsized paddlers can then reenter the canoe.

PADDLING

COMMON SENSE REMINDERS

- When you are tossed from your boat, keep your knees tucked toward your chest and get your feet up toward the water's surface and away from possible entrapment as you swim or float toward calmer water. Face downstream and try to stay close to your boat on the upstream side (to avoid being sandwiched between the boat and a rock!).

- Never stand in moving water! Riverbeds are uneven and a foot is an easy object to lodge into small, hidden crevices underneath the water. Once a foot becomes entrapped, the force of the current will push the attached body until it is face down in the water. At this point, it becomes difficult to be seen.

- Foot entrapments usually happen in gentle waters where you can easily stand up. If the water level hits your waist or higher, you're setting yourself up for trouble if you try to stand. If you must stand in water, find a spot where the water hits your knees or lower. But keep in mind, standing in white-water is typically unlikely, as the water is too swift to be stable.

- Also, avoid attaching anything that may dangle from your body. It is too easy to become tangled with river obstructions.

HAUL SYSTEMS

If a boat is stuck, you have several options to set it free:

1. Try the simplest method first—push the boat. **If that doesn't work...**

2. Tie a rope to the boat and try to pull the boat free with the rope. First, make sure you anchor the other end of the rope to a fixed object such as a thick tree trunk. You will then pull from a position between the tree and the boat. *Make sure you are secure as well!* **If that doesn't work...**

3. Create a taut rope between the boat and the anchor and then pull from the middle of the line. This method applies more pressure to the boat in an attempt to dislodge it. **If that doesn't work...**

4. Create a Z-line. You will need two ropes and a carabiner for this method. The strength of a Z-line is double the other options because the tension runs through a pulley. The rope that is attached to the boat is tied to a carabiner with a figure 8 knot. The second rope is laced through the carabiner. One end of the second rope is anchored to a fixed object such as a tree and the other is belayed around the rescuer's hips. **If the boat is not freed with this technique...**

5. Rig a second pulley system to piggyback the first pulley. The rope end which was belayed to the rescuer's hips is knotted to a second carabiner and then a third rope is anchored to a tree, laced through the second carabiner and belayed around the rescuer's hips. This piggyback gives you a 4:1 strength ratio to free your boat.

BEWARE:

- Don't forget about the power of the current!

- Always position yourself upstream from the haul system.

- Be prepared for victory. When the boat comes free, be ready for it and watch for failure of the rescue gear.

- Always pay attention to your footing and body position.

EMERGENCY

Hypothermia is likely if you are in the water and exposed for a long period of time. The "HELP" position (Heat Escape Lessening Posture) and huddle position can minimize heat loss in cold water. The HELP position protects the highest areas of heat-loss in your body: head, neck, underarms, and groin area. This technique is possible only when wearing a life jacket. To adopt this position, cross your legs at your ankles and pull your legs toward your chest. Cross your arms at your chest, taking care to protect the area under your arms, or hold your neck with your hands for additional protection to keep your head out of the water.

The huddle position involves a group of paddlers clustered (together) to conserve body temperature. This is more efficient than floating alone. When huddling, body-to-body contact is critical. Form a circle, place the smaller, weaker paddlers inside, and wrap your arms around one another.

COMMUNICATION

Rivers are extremely noisy, which makes communication a challenging task. To effectively communicate with your teammates, use these basic visual cues:

1. Pat your head with your hand to ask if your team is okay. If they are okay, they will pat their heads to signal that they are fine.

2. A paddle perpendicular to the ground signals things are "ALL CLEAR".

3. A paddle held overhead and parallel to the ground is a universal signal to "STOP".

FROM: "SABAH 2000 ECO-CHALLENGE" BY HARALD ZUNDEL

Following the jungle trek, we confronted the race's white-water swim and a sampan paddle down the rapids.

A sampan, Malaysian for "one piece", is a wooden canoe built from a single tree. The sampan looks like a rowboat and is very heavy. This section of the course included a dark zone—if we did not reach a specified point on the river, we had to stop on the shore by 5:30 PM and camp until 6:00 AM.

Unfortunately, we did not make the cut-off time. Our boat, caught on a rock, quickly filled with water, and we thought our race was over. We did not immediately see a way to free the boat and empty the water. Luckily, we found a solution—the team moved to one side of the boat and pressed our entire body weight on it. We were able to level the boat, and in doing so, prevented more water from rushing into it.

Next, we bailed together until all the water was out of the boat. We finished bailing and then had to figure out how to get the boat off the rock. I went ashore with one end of a towrope. The other end was tied to the boat. While the rest of the team struggled to keep the boat afloat and stable, I used the rope and pulled toward the shore.

Our plan worked. Much to our relief, we had rescued the boat. Although we made it to the shoreline just ten minutes before the cutoff time, we hadn't made it to the cutoff checkpoint.

So, we camped out in the rain. We flipped the boat and scooted underneath it to have some cover from the rain. At 6:00 AM the next morning, we were back in the boat and after only one hour of paddling, we reached the cutoff checkpoint—that's how close we came the night before! At least we managed to save the boat, thus keeping the team in the race.

STRATEGY BY COLLEEN LAFFEE,
WORLD RECORD HOLDER IN EXTREME KAYAKING

- Learn how to get in and out of your boat efficiently. Determine the best place and the best system to stow your gear (if it is not attached, it is lost).

- Make communication and cooperation with your paddling partner your first priority.

- On the river, look for the most efficient way through the water. In flat water, this means staying out of eddies and seeking the fastest current. When the river bends, the faster current is on the outside. In white-water, avoid holes, large waves, and eddies which will slow you down. In wave trains, situate your boat on the shoulder of the wave, rather than the peak (the center of the wave has a current, which actually moves upstream). In larger rapids that are on a bend in the river, you may want to stay to the inside of the bend. The current will be slower, but the rapid will most likely be less intense and you will be more likely to make it through upright.

- Wind can wreck havoc on any waterway. On a lake, staying close to the shoreline is most effective. In the ocean, if there are islands, work from one to the other. Stay as close as possible to the other boats, especially your teammates! In some cases, it is best to rig the boats together to maintain stability.

- Know how to get in and out of your boat even when partially or completely full of water.

- Make time in the flat water. Don't worry about making time in the rapids. Your main concern in white-water is keeping your boat upright and out of trouble.

- Practice paddling with your teammates before the race in the appropriate craft with your intended paddle partner. Find out who should steer and who should captain.

- Try different stroke rates and rest methods. It is a good idea to take turns resting so that someone is always paddling. Think forward progress! The person who is resting can bail the boat, eat, and drink.

- Try different paddles and paddle combinations to decide what feels the most comfortable and what system is the fastest.

- Rest in the current, not in an eddy, or take turns resting and paddling.

KAYAKING Q & A WITH IAN ADAMSON

Q: In adventure racing, I have seen photographs of kayaks or canoes towing each other. Is this legal? Why?

A: Towing is legal in most adventure races since these competitions require teams to work and stay together. If paddlers on a team are not evenly matched, someone is tired, or there is more than one boat and they are of different speeds, towing keeps the team together and increases their net speed.

In the ESPN X-Venture Race, each team had one single and one double sea kayak for the three competitors. Our team rigged a tow bungee to pull the single kayak when we couldn't match speeds between the boats. This had the effect of slowing the double down, but it increased our average speed above that of the single alone.

Q: What is the best way to navigate or steer straight on the open water? What happens when you hit rough water, turbulence, wind chop, or waves?

A: Open water navigation can be tricky due to the effect of tidal currents, wind waves (chop), swells, and turbulence. To maintain the best course in the open water, you need to evaluate the effect of the conditions on your course. This is often a direction other than that which the kayak is pointing.

If moving across the current, take notice of a fixed object, such as a hill on the far shore, and adjust your course depending on which way you drift in relation to it. Inevitably you end up pointing the kayak up current of the fixed point, although your course across the ground is towards it.

Wind waves will also push a kayak around noticeably in the direction of the wind. This is in addition to the effect of windage (the wind on the paddler and the boat). When going across the chop, you may have to steer into each wave to prevent being knocked sideways, and then steer away from it down the back side. You will end up steering a serpentine course through the waves, but it will help you maintain your balance and speed through the water.

Q: How much kayaking experience must I have before I attempt a one-day adventure race and a multi-day race?

A: Most one-day adventure races have short kayaking sections designed to accommodate beginner paddlers. The Hi-Tec Adventure Race Series supplies small inflatable kayaks that you sit in or on and are virtually unsinkable, bar multiple punctures. Basic kayak experience, which can be gained in a few hours practice, will get you through a race.

Kayaking in a multi-day race is on another level completely. I have experienced some extreme conditions that require expert level skills to be negotiated safely. In the 1995 Eco-Challenge in Maine, the first leg of the race was a 130-mile paddle which included Grade III wild-water at night, in open canoes, in the wilderness, with no moon. Large stretches of open ocean are also common, including surf entry/exit conditions, large swells and strong winds. Consequently, it would be foolish and possibly dangerous to attempt a multi-day race without extensive experience and practice. The flip side is that the paddling in a long race can be spectacular and exciting!

*The ropes course in an adventure race often
requires a long vertical progression up a
rope where you never touch the rock face.*

The sites of the rope courses in adventure races are spectacular and always unforgettable. The key to successful travel in this discipline, aside from lots of practice, is to trust your equipment and the people who rigged the course (once you have double-checked everything yourself!). Every time you attach yourself to a rope, check your equipment and the rigging system with your own eyes. Once you develop this confidence, you create a freedom that allows you to perfect your skills.

CLIMB ON!

A free climb is accomplished when you reach the top using only your hands and feet, or other parts necessary to move you upward. A rope is used only for protection in case of a fall. It is not employed to ascend. If at any time you use equipment for assistance, to rest for example, you are not free climbing.

Aid climbing involves the use of equipment to progress upward. It is most common in an adventure race to ascend with equipment, the least of which involves a hand ascender rigged to a fixed rope to assist a climb up a steep incline. A more arduous ascent may encompass a long, vertical progression up a rope where you never touch the rock face.

The use of equipment generally depends on the steepness of the terrain. To determine the difficulty of a climb, a rating system has been developed:

CLASS I: Rugged hiking

CLASS II: Rock scrambling

CLASS III: Steep scrambling

CLASS IV: Easy climbing with frequent exposure. A rope is used on the more challenging areas and a fall could be fatal.

CLASS V: Climbing with a belay which involves a rope. Protection is used to reduce the length of a fall. This category is broken into subgrades.

This rating system has gotten more and more complicated over the past several years as elite climbers continue to shatter the upper limits of what we comprehend to be most difficult. Hence, the levels are constantly skewed. For adventure racing purposes thus far, your experience will undoubtedly range from rock scrambling over boulder fields, maneuvering on fixed ropes up precarious terrain, to ascending a fixed line using techniques involved in aid climbing.

The design and function of equipment has allowed us to accomplish adventures that were once virtually impossible for man to comprehend. In an adventure race, your equipment is an essential element of the race. Take the time to investigate the right stuff and invest accordingly.

EXCERPT FROM "THE CROCS ARE EDIBLE AREN'T THEY?"

BY IAN ADAMSON

On the 1997 Eco-Challenge in Queensland, Australia

As we traversed the canyon rim, a truly spectacular sight unfolded. Thousands of feet of climbing rope were stretched out through the waterfalls and cliffs tormenting the river. A long rappel beside a thundering shoot of water led into the canyon, flattening out to a short traverse across slimy wet boulders. An equally treacherous jumar ascent led to a second traverse to the edge of a large round pool with waterfalls leading into one side and out the other. A final jumar ascent followed the inlet waterfall back out of the canyon on the other side.

The sound of crashing water was deafening but I could still hear my teammate Jane's whoops of delight as we bounded down the first rappel. Welcome relief for our crusty bodies came from sheets of spray from the adjacent waterfall, which also maintained a healthy growth of algae on all exposed surfaces. We had full trust in the riggers who had set the ropes after experiencing their work last year in British Columbia. The otherwise perfidious footing was made relatively safe with carefully placed ropes and fixed anchors.

ESSENTIAL EQUIPMENT

SEAT HARNESS

Don't leave home without it! A harness is a necessity when ascending and descending. It is your lifeline. It acts as a chair by distributing some of the load into your backside instead of being completely concentrated around your midsection. It also provides the device for which you tie into fixed ropes in a climb, rappel, or tyrolean traverse. This is an extremely important detail! You must tie into the waist belt. If you don't, you will be in for a ride of your life—most likely your last.

Good fit is essential. The waist and leg loops are your areas of concern. When fitting your harness, your waist strap should be comfortably snug. You want to be able to breathe comfortably but the waist should be tight enough not to slip over your pelvis, in case you flip upside down.

Likewise, the leg loops should be taut but comfortable. The worst situation you could create for yourself is to frivolously tug on your leg loops. This may have dangerous consequences, such as the cut of circulation in your legs, increasing the risk of fainting.

There are four basic categories of harnesses: alpine, big wall, sport-cragging, and competition. The alpine harness is a good choice for adventure racing, as it is relatively light (ounces add up to pounds, and pounds add up to a lot of misery). The alpine harness also has droppable leg-loops for ease in quick relief, and is non-absorbent and adjustable.

There are two basic seat harness designs. The leg-loop style is the most common. This style connects the leg loops and waistband with a "belay loop", which is a rugged webbed ring used for belaying and rappelling.

The other style looks and fits like a diaper. A "diaper-like" leg loop wraps under your body and is easily adjusted with plastic clips. This harness is popular because of the ease in adjustments—especially for women. When nature calls, you can disconnect the leg loops without taking the harness off.

When choosing your harness, try it on and pull the waist straps up as high as you can. Adjust the leg loops from this position. Then tie in and hang for awhile to assess your level of comfort.

The distance between your waist strap and your leg loops is called the "rise". In most cases, it is adjustable, and the rise usually determines the gender difference in a harness.

A vital component of safety is buckling in. It is of the utmost significance that you double back your strap through your buckle after the initial threading to secure your waist strap. This practice is so important that it is included in your safety check each time you travel up or down.

Once in operation, check your harness after every use. If you identify even the tiniest imperfection, toss it and purchase a new one. Your life is not worth risking to save a few dollars. Harnesses are made of a polyamide (polyester fiber) material which ages naturally upon contact with air, even if it is not used or stays in a box. With age, the strength of the fibers remains the same, but the elasticity diminishes.

CHEST HARNESS

A chest harness is necessary in aid climbing. You will need to secure gear to it and it will keep you upright in case of a fall. It helps stabilize your upper body, particularly with a heavy pack on your back. It also encourages relaxation as you climb, as you don't need to use your arms as much.

If the climb is short, you can makeshift a chest harness out of webbing by tying two loops together. To use, slip your arms through the holes with the knot in back and secure the other ends in front with a carabiner. Make sure it is not so loose that it could slip off or too tight that it could asphyxiate you.

The only way to know the ideal fit is to experiment in your training. Climb several times with different degrees of fit. Most often, a snug fit is advantageous when you climb. It will keep you closer to the rope, which enhances efficiency. If the webbing is too loose around your chest, you will be too far away from the rope. Consequently, when you ascend, you will use extra energy to first pull yourself in towards the rope and then upward, as opposed to moving straight up.

ROPES

While it is unlikely that you will have to set up line in a race, it is good practice to know all of your gear. Climbing ropes come in a variety of sizes, length, and materials and are either static or dynamic. They start at 8 mm in diameter, then progress to 8.8 mm, 9, 10, 10.5, 11, and 12 mm.

No-stretch or low-stretch ropes are static. They were initially used for cave exploration and rescue work. If you are doing fixed line work, such as expedition-style climbs, these ropes are effective because they don't stretch.

Recreational climbing, however, utilizes dynamic ropes that stretch. Dynamic rope combines strength and elasticity to absorb the impact of a fall. In an adventure race, you could encounter either kind.

For safety purposes, take care of your harness. Heed the following tips to remain safe on treacherous terrain:

- **The effects of UV light are destructive according to the color of your webbing and the quality of the UV light. Discoloration is a sign of damage—throw it out.**

- **Chemicals or corrosive products destroy the safety of your harness—throw it out.**

- **Small cuts and abrasive forces from climbing lessen the strength of your harness.**

- **If your harness is exposed to sand, it can penetrate the webbing and cause micro-tears, which could lead to breakage of the tape under tension.**

- **If your harness is dirty, wash it, preferably by hand with soap for delicate textiles. Let it drip-dry.**

- **Check your harness before every use. Check the webbing, the buckles, and the function.**

- **A harness has a natural lifetime of five years. If you use it often, the lifetime decreases. Excessive use, which causes abrasion, falls, and sun discoloration, can all speed up the aging of your harness.**

The protective headgear for climbing and rappelling primarily guards the top of the head against falling rocks and debris. Therefore, the focus of protection in a climbing helmet is in the center. Adjustable helmets provide flexibility in terms of comfort and fit. In addition to comfort, look for a helmet that is lightweight.

THE COMPLETE GUIDE TO ADVENTURE RACING

KNOTS

Do you remember when you learned how to tie your shoes? The knot we use to keep our shoes intact is probably the most fundamental in the entire western world. In the sport of climbing, there are several knots, which should also become second nature.

There are three basic classifications of knots:

1. Single knots are tied using a single strand of rope to create a "simple" knot.

2. Retraced knots follow the route of a pre-existing knot with a second strand of rope or the tail of the first.

3. Knots on a bight involve a double loop of rope.

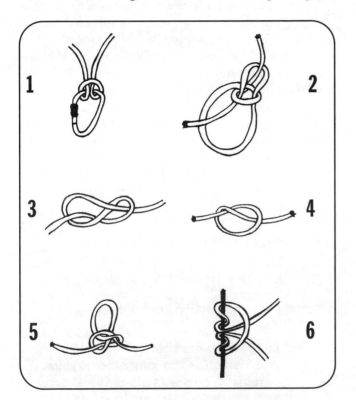

These following knots will come in handy on a race course:

1. *Munter Hitch*— easy attachment to a carabiner.

2. *Single Bowline*—creates a fixed loop (that will not slide) at the end of a rope.

3. *Figure 8 Knot*—a "stopper knot" that creates a stopping point at the end of a rope.

4. *Overhand*—this stopper knot prevents a rope from sliding through a hole.

5. *Butterfly Knot*—creates a loop in the middle of a rope.

6. *Prusik Knot*—for back-up when going up and down on the ropes.

ROPE TIPS

• Wet rope equals danger. They are difficult to manage. They become heavy, are difficult to tie, and freeze easily. Wet ropes are 30 percent less effective in strength than dry ropes, and they hold fewer falls.

• Always purchase equipment that has been tested. The standard in the U.S. is UIAA. They test gear to meet standards.

• Only use climbing ropes for climbing. Don't use it for towing purposes or any other task but to climb. You will sacrifice your safety!

• Dirt, chemicals, and sun shorten the life span of a rope.

• For best results, store in a rope bag. Ropes used on occasion should be replaced every four years. Used every weekend—two years. Used at climbing gyms—every couple of weeks. If in doubt, replace.

• "Dry ropes"—Some companies will treat ropes with a silicon-based or Teflon-based coating. The treatment improves abrasion resistance of the ropes and reduces friction of the rope as it runs through carabiners. They cost about 15 percent more than untreated ropes.

• Always check the rope before you use it.

ASCENDING AND DESCENDING

HARDWARE

CARABINERS

Carabiners are a staple tool when working on the ropes. They also come in handy in various other race situations, such as securing gear in a boat or rescue situations. These "metal snap-links" are available in different shapes and sizes.

LOCKING CARABINERS

The first carabiner you will need is a "locking" one. Any time you are attaching a main device to your harness such as a rappel device or ascender, you want to use a locking carabiner. Any critical life situation commands attachment with the "locker".

Locking carabiners that are heavy and large are made specifically for rappelling. General purpose locking carabiners are smaller and lighter. They may be harder

to use, but they save weight. The lock also comes in many different designs. You will find auto-lockers, spin-ball, twist-lock, and super-locks, which are all designed to make locking the gate a no-brainer. Your personal preference, which will probably be based in part by how quickly you can clip and unclip, will ultimately determine what you use. Use what is most comfortable for you.

The lock can be a metal collar that is screwed tight over the gate (the opening), or a spring-loaded mechanism that locks automatically. In either case, the carabiner is unlikely to open. You will always use this one with your belay device. Anytime your life is in the hands of a single carabiner, a locking one is paramount. If you are in a situation, however, without a locking carabiner, two can be used. Be sure that the gates are placed in opposition and they form an "X" when purposefully opened.

There may be occasions where you will need other carabiners for other functions. However, most race requirements call for locking carabiners. In which case, it makes the most sense to use them for other functions rather than carry a whole slew of carabiners.

CARABINER TIPS

- **Load carabiners along the major axis, which is the long side. If your carabiner is loaded along the shorter side, or the minor axis, it could actually fail in a fall.**

- **A carabiner's gate "open strength" is less than half of its gate "close strength".**

- **Keep them clean and free of grit. If you have dropped a carabiner 20 feet or more—toss it.**

- **Check for cracks before use. Toss it if you see any.**

HAND ASCENDERS

This device is used to assist any ascent that requires a fixed rope. To install the ascender onto the rope, use your thumb to pull the cam (the working catch) downward, then lock it on the body of the device to keep the cam open. Then put the rope into position inside the ascender. Unlock the catch so it is free to push up against the rope. To release the ascender from the rope, slide the device upward along the rope while simultaneously pulling the cam back by working the catch.

The mechanical ascender latches (or bites) onto a rope through the use of a metal cam. The cam then allows you to ascend steep terrain. To progress, slide it upward (it moves freely). When you hit your full reach, lock the device in place by weighting it and then pull yourself higher. Continue this process until you get to the top.

To care for ascenders, wash and rinse in clean water, dry with a towel and keep away from corrosive or aggressive chemicals.

OTHER TYPES OF ASCENDERS

The Petzl *Tibloc* ascender is lighter than the "old standby," but also smaller; so it is best used attached to your chest harness so that it may slide freely up the rope.

A *no-handle ascender* can be mounted to your body, used in conjunction with a handled ascender on top. They save weight and are becoming more popular, particularly in vertical ascents.

A new system is available called the *Pompe*. This consists of a rope clamp/grab foot-loop combination, utilizing a reduction system, which gives you a mechanical advantage 30 percent higher than the regular standard techniques. The sliding foot loops attached to the croll make the climbing speed slightly slower, but they make climbing a single rope easier. The Pompe is advantageous if you are doing long climbs and carrying a lot of gear.

The *Grigri* "automatic belay device" made by Petzl has a spring-loaded cam that pinches the rope in an event of a fall but is also easily released. It is most effective when used as a belay device. The Grigri allows you to go up or down with ease. For best results, use with a handled ascender—with the Grigri attached to body and the handled ascender on top.

RAPPEL DEVICES

The *figure 8* device, as the name suggests, looks like the numeral eight. It allows a smooth transition. Therefore, the braking hand is crucial to control the descent. It is durable and very safe. Friction is provided simply by running the rope through the device.

The *ATC (Air Traffic Controller)* device is popular in adventure racing. It is multi-functional in climbing. Consequently, it is a good choice when the weight of your gear is a factor. It works on the slot principal, whereby the rope wraps through and around the device. It is lighter and more compact than the figure 8.

ACCESSORY CORD

The industry standard is 7 mm cordage. A 6 mm cord will hold your body weight. But, when you are hanging 150 feet off the ground, you are safer with the 7 mm size. Eight mm is a tad too big and doesn't have the same clamping power.

ASCENDING AND DESCENDING

WEBBING

Nylon webbing is very versatile in climbing pursuits. You can make ascenders, foot loops, and chest harnesses from this material. The 9/16" size is a good width. One-inch width webbing also works but can become a bit heavy and bulky. When purchasing your webbing, get more than you think you'll need. You will save yourself an extra trip to the store and the extra length can be used for a variety of purposes.

ETRIERS AND DAISY CHAINS

Daisy chains are premade with loops, which are girth-hitched to the harness and provide a variety of tie-in points. You will need one for each ascender if you use the two-ascender climbing method. The drawback: it is slightly heavier then the webbing and can't be custom designed for your body. Etriers are webbing foot ladders. Ultimately, webbing and cord still prevail as the lightest, cleanest, and most specific material when designing your ascending system.

GLOVES

When you work with ropes, it is wise to protect your hands with gloves. Without them, your hands will suffer burns, blisters, and cuts that will be very painful and hinder your racing performance.

Leather gloves are most effective on the ropes. You need a rugged material that will protect your hand from the friction you create while ascending or descending. You can find a good, inexpensive pair at a gardening or hardware store.

> Talk about ascents—try being in the shoes of my teammate Tom Meier as he ascended a wall full of poison ivy (which he is allergic to) and then stirred up a nest of ground hornets and got stung several times. And this all happened the very first of five days in the Beast of the East!
>
> —*Blain Reeves*

FUNDAMENTALS

BELAYING

Belaying is a fundamental part of climbing. In simple terms, a belay is a rope that connects the climber to an anchorperson who is the belayer. The belayer is there to stop a fall. To be most effective, a belayer is experienced and provides a solid anchor to oppose the forces of a falling climber with sufficient friction, or creates a "stopping" force to halt the fall. The rope courses are normally run by experienced climbers who will usually take care of the belay. But don't show up underprepared for your descending or ascending task, knowing that they are there to help you. Their number one priority is your safety—not to do your job for you.

When getting started on a vertical ascent, keep the rope taut (via your belayer) for a smoother, easier climb.

COMMUNICATION

The following terms are used to communicate on a climb. It is crucial to verbalize your intentions before you make a move on the ropes. Problems can easily arise if everyone involved in an ascent or descent is not ready or is unaware of the situation.

The climber or rappeller calls out "on belay?" to confirm that the belayer is ready. The belayer replies "belay on" when all systems are go. Then, the person moving up or down the rope yells "climbing" or "rappelling" to signify that he is ready to progress. The belayer confirms the start by shouting "climb on" or "rappel on".

ROCK SCRAMBLING

Most of this type of climbing is instinctive. Think like a Billy goat. The goal is to move efficiently without injuring yourself or falling. When traveling with your team, pace yourselves at least ten feet apart to avoid a people slide if the top person falls and also to avoid falling rock and debris.

Footwork and balance are critical factors to master if you want to become a competent climber. Your lower body should do most of the work—it is bigger and stronger than your upper body.

Use your eyes to climb. Scan the rock and plan your next move before you execute it. Check out your handholds and footholds and make sure they are secure at all times. When you are ready to progress be efficient with your movement. Don't take too small of a step, which wastes energy, but don't take too large a step either—you will sacrifice balance and use too much energy. Be deliberate and swift. Fluidity will make the most of time and energy.

DOWN CLIMBING

Most of the time, you will face outward when descending "for best visibility". Always keep your center of gravity low by keeping your knees soft and relaxed. Keep your hands low and stay balanced. As the terrain gets steeper, turn your body sideways and try to keep a good eye on the ground below. If you are faced with steeper angles, turn toward the rock, keep your weight and hands low and try to avoid leaning away from the landscape.

ASCENDING AND DESCENDING

DEFYING GRAVITY: ASCENDING WITH THE AID OF FIXED LINES

In certain areas of the race course, there may be spots that are too difficult or too dangerous to travel without the aid of a fixed line. To encourage secure travel, a rope is anchored to the terrain to allow safe progression with greater ease.

Depending on the slope of the terrain, there are several methods that could be employed in an adventure race.

FIXED LINE WITHOUT DIRECT AID

In a situation where free climbing is possible but a fixed line is available, you may decide to attach an ascender (which attaches to your seat harness with a carabiner and rope or a daisy chain) to the rope. You climb under your own power, but have the safety backup of your equipment.

In case of a fall, you are immediately caught. To ensure your safety, double-check the line for a continuous, smooth feed through the device. If there is too much sag, a shock load may strip the sheath off the rope and send you for a ride. To avoid this, don't forget your backup knot. Use an overhand knot or a prusik attached to a carabiner for backup.

FIXED LINE WITH DIRECT AID ON EASY SLABS

As the terrain gets steeper, you will need to use your ascenders to pull yourself up. This is where a big handled ascender comes in handy—especially with gloves. You may not need to engage foot loops in this case. In most situations you will be able to walk up the slab, pulling yourself up as you go. This is easier and faster than using foot loops, however, have them handy in case the slab becomes too steep or if you have over-estimated your abilities.

FIXED LINE WITH DIRECT AID ON HARD SLABS

On steep terrain, the best method will require two ascenders and two-foot loops. The ascenders slide up the rope and are attached to your harness by a sling and your weight is essentially on your feet. To make upward progress, you "walk" up the wall as you alternately slide your hand ascenders up the rope. This method also works on a free-hanging ascent.

You will need:
- 1 Seat harness
- 2 Etriers
- 2 Ascenders
- 2 Daisy chains
- 3 Carabiners

Backup knots are clipped into a separate fourth carabiner.

FIXED LINE WITH DIRECT LINE ON OVERHANGS

On a vertical cliff, you will ascend a free-hanging rope. This situation is very popular in adventure races. To climb a fixed line, there are several methods to choose from.

The first method which we just discussed simulates the motion employed on a VersaClimber machine found in health clubs. It is versatile in several climbing situations and is quite easy to use when negotiating the lip of an overhang. This method only requires one harness, which saves weight in your pack. The only downside to the VersaClimber is that it is a more difficult technique to master and it is harder to support your upper body while ascending.

An efficient technique for vertical work utilizes one ascender for both hands which is also attached to double foot loops. Then, a one no-handle ascender is anchored to the rope and attached to both the chest harness and the seat harness. To make upward progress, the knees are tucked into the chest, and then the top ascender slides up the rope until the arms are extended. Then you "stand up" in the foot loops, which bring the arms back into your chest. This method resembles the motion of an inchworm, and some racers call it "the frog".

You will need:
- 1 Seat harness
- 1 Chest harness
- 2 Ascenders
- 2 Foot loops
- 1 Daisy chain
- 4 Carabiners (one for backup knot)

THE COMPLETE GUIDE TO ADVENTURE RACING

On steeper ascents, two ascenders may be more advantageous if a full ascending system and appropriate rig is necessary. There may be spots where you can ascend as you "walk" up the rock face, assisted by the upward progression of a hand ascender. There will also be portions of your ascent where you are hanging freely and the only contact you have with the world as you know it is with the rope.

MAKING THE RIDE EASIER

Anytime you can get your body weight over your legs, use it and you will be more efficient. These climbing methods respond better to finesse as opposed to power. Technique, balance, and flexibility reign. The techniques you choose depend primarily on comfort and efficiency. Try both in your training.

Don't be afraid to rest when you need to. It is frivolous to waste energy by holding onto your weight when it is not necessary. Your equipment can hold your weight so you can rest in place without holding on. It may take a little time to overcome the notion that you don't have to hold on while you rest. As with all of the other techniques and disciplines involved in an adventure race, it takes time and practice to become comfortable and proficient.

In a situation where you need to get back to the bottom of the climb, clip in to your backup knot, and replace your low ascender with a rappel device. Stand on the foot loops of the top ascender to transfer your weight to the rappel device. Remove the backup knot and use the top ascender for a rappel backup.

If the race director lets you use whatever you want in terms of gear, you can create a system with nothing but webbing, cordage, and carabiners. If you are proficient with knots and climbing techniques, then you have greater flexibility in the climbing system you use in a race. Stick to traditional systems if you are a novice climber.

When putting together your climbing gear, decide what percentage of the weight in your pack you want to dedicate to climbing. The weight you carry in a race effect has a direct effect on your performance.

THE CLIMBING FINALE

Often, the toughest part of an ascent on a fixed line is overcoming the lip at the very top. When you are close to the lip, clip into a backup knot. Then use a jerking motion to move the ascender past the lip. If this doesn't work, remove the ascender and place it higher on the rope. Remember: always use backup. Don't ever put your life in the fate of a single piece of gear. When overcoming the lip, stay calm and try not to waste energy. It is easy to struggle and get frustrated, which only leaves you exhausted once you are free.

RAPPELLING: GRAVITY RULES

Descending a rock face while safely attached to a rope is pure exhilaration. When rappelling down a high cliff, your entire body weight is attached to a rope and is dependent upon an anchor to keep the rope fixed for the entire route while you skillfully maneuver yourself downward. Once you develop the confidence to safely identify a secure anchor, rope, harness, and braking system, you can stow your trust in the rappelling system and dance with gravity.

CHECK ALL THREE PLACES OF ATTACHMENT

First, check your harness to assure all your safety straps are doubled through. Make sure your connection to the rope is secure, and make sure the anchors for the rope are safe. The anchor should be checked in two locations, which should be joined by a sling. Develop a system that becomes habitual each time you rappel. Check the anchor, the point where you are clipped in to your harness and the harness itself.

THE RAPPEL SYSTEM

There are four components to a rappel system. They are the anchor, the rope, a method of creating friction, and the rappeller. The elements are interdependent and each one plays an important role in the success of a rappel.

A secure anchor, the core of which everything is attached, is the crucial piece of the system. A sound anchor is attached to two or even three separate, usually natural, objects. This way, if one anchor fails, you still have one or two to rely on. The anchor will be set up for you in a race, but it is a reassuring and prudent practice to inspect it yourself before you descend.

The rope you use should be in good condition. Climbing ropes are dynamic, as their construction provides elasticity as tension is applied to them. This cushions a fall to some extent, lessening the impact of the experience. The length of your rappel will determine the length and weight of your rope, especially if you have to maneuver over several plateaus or cliffs to which the rope conforms. If you are rappelling straight down a rope, the ride will be easier and faster. This is where your braking system is most critical.

The braking system is simply a means of providing friction on the rope, which in turn allows you to control the speed of your descent. Your success depends on the friction device and the mastery of your braking hand, which is situated behind the hip of your dominant hand.

The ideal position to rappel should be comfortable and effective. Sit down towards the ground until your legs are perpendicular to the rock. Your feet should be about shoulder-width apart with your knees slightly flexed. Allow yourself to look downward from time to time to formulate a picture of where you are going. Most importantly—relax! The tighter you are, the more awkward your trip will be.

On less aggressive angles, your rappel will be nothing more than walking backwards to the bottom. On steeper terrain or places where the rope hangs freely over a cliff and several yards away from the face, you will sit in your harness and work your way down in a free rappel.

To begin, obtain a stationary position by placing your hand behind your lower back. This position places the rope at an angle, which halts any rope movement. To glide down the rope, push it away from your body, creating a 90-degree angle in the rope as you laterally extend your arm. This will allow the rope to feed smoothly through your braking device. A smooth technique integrates continuous, fluid arm movements outward for speed and inward for control of the speed. To enhance the comfort and fluidity of your rappel, don't forget your leather gloves! As your pace increases, so does the friction and accompanying heat. Protect your hands with thick, leather gloves.

As you descend, move slowly with steady control. Don't bounce or leap. If you get stuck because your gear or outer clothing layer gets caught in the braking system, it's a good idea to keep your knife handy so you can easily cut yourself free. Just be certain you don't cut your rope (which is your lifeline) in the process! Even a mere kick can be fatal when in contact with a taut rope.

To finish your rappel, look for a safe spot that is clear from rock fall and dangerous ledges and assume a stable stance. Make sure there is enough slack in the rope to work with and then clear it from your braking device. Shout out "off rappel" to signal your teammates and race personnel to proceed. While you wait, get yourself organized for the next leg of the race—eat, drink, and savor the brief time to relax.

Caution:

Make sure you use locking carabiners that are locked in place before you descend. Arrange the carabiner so that the gate is visible. This practice will reduce the incidence of a fall, as you will be more aware of your carabiner's status.

ASCENDING AND DESCENDING

TYROLEAN TRAVERSE

A Tyrolean traverse can be the easiest discipline you will encounter in a race, or the hardest, depending on the angle of your ride. To prepare for a traverse, the guides at the races will usually help set you up. This process usually involves no more than two locking carabiners and a daisy chain. As always, once you are clipped in, check your anchors, the point where you are attached to the rope, and your harness. If you are confident of your gear, then all it takes is some nerve, a little gusto, and sometimes a whole lot of upper body oomph.

If you are traveling on a decline, a strong push off the wall you are launching from will send you a good distance down the line. If you slow down and don't make it to the other side, you may have to tap into your strength reserves. Wrap your legs around the rope and cross your feet at your ankles while you pull your body, hand over hand, until you reach a ledge with solid footing where you can safely unclip. If the traverse is a good distance, you will have to contribute even more upper body strength.

If you are moving upward from start to the finish, hopefully you have practiced your pull-ups! It takes a tremendous amount of upper body strength to pull yourself up a rope. To conquer this set-up, wrap your feet around the rope and cross your feet at your ankles. Then hand over hand, pull yourself to the top. As always, when working with ropes, make sure your hands are protected.

SAFETY ON THE ROPES

On walk-ups of less-severe angles, the only gear you may need is one ascender that clips in, aiding your ascent. But get used to the rule: Never trust your life to a single piece of gear. In an adventure racing situation, many factors stack up against you in terms of efficiency. You become tired, fatigued, hungry, and generally less aware, which can lead to mistakes. Therefore, it is crucial to maintain a "continuous analysis" of your ascending system. Double and triple check everything involved in your system.

Upper body strength comes in handy in a tyrolean traverse.

INDOOR CLIMBING WALLS

Although your climbing experience in an adventure race may not be very technical, there are several benefits to practicing on an indoor wall:

- Convenience
- Builds self-confidence and trust
- Enhances experience
- Builds total body strength

- Carries over to rock scrambling and maneuvering around natural objects
- Helps finesse on less-harsh angles to climb

If you cannot get to a crag easily but have quick access to a climbing wall, take advantage of it. The more you wear your harness and work with climbing gear, the more comfortable you will become with your equipment in a race. Additionally, your overall climbing prowess will improve.

THINGS TO REMEMBER

Adaptability is key. As an adventure racer, you should be able to adapt to whatever you are faced with in a race. "Gravity is judge, jury, and executioner," says Dave Weinbach, OARA climbing guide and instructor.

Never simply trust the rope system. Double-check it yourself—always.

You should have full control of your body on the rope. You should be able to go up or down with ease. A vertical environment is either up or down and you should have full command of this environment.

A HIMALAYAN ODYSSEY

TEAM 'ODYSSEY' COMPETES IN THE 10TH EDITION TRANS-HIMALAYAN RAID GAULOISES

Team 'Odyssey' was one of 10 U.S. teams that competed in the tenth annual Raid Gauloises competition. A total of 69 teams representing 18 countries began the expedition, which encompassed roughly 500 miles of terrain across the great Himalayan landscape. In sharp contrast to the conservative Hindu and Buddhist influences, the city of Kathmandu seemed to be filled with international athletes, media and Raid personnel. Everywhere you went, you ran into groups in matching team shirts and Solomon backpacks.

Team 'Odyssey' and the other American teams stayed at the Radisson Hotel, which is a very luxurious and modern hotel compared to most in the city. One thing became immediately obvious; the Nepali people are gentle, respectful people, always eager to take the extra steps to ensure satisfaction. In hotels, restaurants and shops, the locals are not happy unless they have pleased you in every way possible. Even though the Raid teams took over the hallways and filled the rooms with bike boxes, trunks and other gear, the hotel staff was friendly and helpful in transporting the heavy trunks and maneuvering around the mounds of race gear.

During one of the first nights there, several of the team members left at 10 PM, in search of a seamstress who could construct four bike cases in a pinch. After their second stop, they found a tailor who agreed to stay up all night and consequently, the bags were ready the following morning.

The cooperation of the Nepali people was especially helpful because of the enormous amount of pre-race wrangling. Registration and gear check-in, which took place in the gardens of an impressive renovated Hindu palace, took nearly 7 exhausting hours. The following day, the 69 Raid teams attended a packed race briefing at a modern convention center in Kathmandu, where they received maps and course details. Nepal's Minister for Culture, Tourism and Civil Aviation, as well as other Nepali dignitaries and Raid officials welcomed teams and media representatives. The briefing reached an enthusiastic peak with the announcement of each of the 69 teams.

Teams listened carefully to Patrick Brignoli, President of Raid Gauloises, as he addressed the crowd. He called the course the "wildest landscape in the world," but promised that it would be the kindness and friendliness of the Tibetan and Nepali people that participants would be impressed with. He also discussed the difficulties in setting up the race, particularly in working with the Chinese government for access into the Autonomous Region of Tibet. He warned participants about the need to comply with all rules in order to respect and protect the Tibetan individuals who worked hard to make the competition a reality. Taking hundreds of Westerners into this politically oppressed country required that everyone follow the rules. We were warned, for example, not to take pictures of the Tibetan Dalai Lama, as this is considered a serious crime.

After the briefing, Team 'Odyssey' members carefully dissected the maps and the competitor handbook as they plotted their course and strategy. The next morning, Mike, the captain of the support crew, supervised the team as they organized their gear into trunks and individual backpacks—an agonizing chore because of stringent weight requirements imposed for the flight into Tibet. Therefore, the team was forced to leave behind what were thought to be essential items, such as food, clothing, and tents.

Next, the team met for a strategy meeting, in which each section of the race was studied. The team made important decisions regarding gear selection for each section, logistics, assignments and goal setting. Later, everyone enjoyed a great meal in the hotel's restaurant, and loosened up after three very long days of pre-race preparations.

TIBET

So, with the countless gear checks, administrative wrangling, and the packing and repacking completed, the team set off for the next leg of this incredible experience. The excitement in the air was palpable the morning the teams boarded themselves and their gear on buses, ready to begin their trip to China's Autonomous Region of Tibet. Flying from Kathmandu to Lhassa, through a special chartered arrangement made by the Raid organization, the teams were treated to views of Mt. Everest, the tallest peak in the world, rising through the clouds at 29,000 feet.

Arriving in Lhassa, the teams passed through shanty-lined streets and past several run-down hotels, before arriving at the large and rather well-appointed Grand Hotel. Here, they were welcomed by Tibetan dignitaries, treated to a banquet dinner, and entertained by a traditional Tibetan opera and dance troupe. The dancing Yak made big points as he maneuvered through the crowd, as did a Nepali tourism official, whose exuberant rantings left the international audience cheering and laughing.

The next four days leading to the start of the race were designed for acclimatization purposes. The first day, teams traveled over 10 hours along the Friendship Highway, a rocky dirt road that winds through the barren, stark Tibetan landscape. Stops along the way included the Kamba La Pass at 15,700 feet, which was marked with billowing prayer flags and a stunning view of immense Yamdrok Lake. Late in the day, the buses arrived in the village of Gyangze at 13,091 feet. Here, the group toured the Palcho monastery, which has been home to Buddhist monks since the early 1400s. After a long day of traveling, the teams arrived at Shalu Valley for an overnight camp. The bone-numbing cold made everyone very aware of the increased altitude.

Day two of bus travel took more than eight hours and brought teams through dramatic mountain passes, past hundreds of tattered prayer flags, and to Shekar Dzong at an altitude of 13,800 feet.

At the barren, windy camp at Shekar Dzong, teams hurriedly set up tents and cooked meals. Because so many of the competitors were feeling ill, the prolog (or dress rehearsal) scheduled for the following day was canceled; giving teams another day to adjust to the elevation. The next day, they reorganized and repacked gear for the race start in the morning. In the cold of the night, the camp began to sound like a tuberculosis ward, as teams fought the effects of the altitude and dust-blowing winds. Despite the cold, wind, dust and aggravated lungs, competitors were ready to begin what they had come for. The beginning of the most celebrated Raid Gauloises ever.

—Dawn Taylor, Team 'Odyssey' Reporter

THE OTHER HALF

Your support crew, as the name suggests, provides the team's strong shoulders upon which to lean, collapse, or receive a push. They are the threads that secure the team. They contribute logistical help, nourishment, strategic insight, and positive reinforcement.

Your support facilitates quick transitions and caters to your tender moments. Your crew works equally hard for the finish and suffers from sleep deprivation and exhaustion right alongside you.

The support crew is typically comprised of family members and friends. They are the team behind the team. Without them, the race is lost. They are responsible for your gear, your food, and your maps.

They endure long days with little sleep, just like you. They must navigate their way through unfamiliar territory, just like you. And, they must work equally hard to get to the finish line, just like you.

In addition to the labor-intensive duties, your support crew takes on a very important role. Their timing must be impeccable. If they arrive at a transition area ahead of your team, they must wait for you. This means they must stay awake, even though they have done all they can do for the moment, and they must be ready to take action the moment your team arrives. If communication with race organizers is slim, and the road to the next transition is long and nebulous, they have the pressure of showing up on-time to set up camp and break into action. Their responsibilities are myriad and carry heavy consequences. The following hats are just a few that are worn when you adopt the role of a support person.

MEDIC

Fixing feet, repairing wounds, and tending to digestive problems are par for the course as support. At least one member of the support crew should have some medical knowledge. The wild will leave its mark on the team, and the racers will need care when they arrive at a transition.

MECHANIC

Before a bike leg, each team member's mountain bike must be in full working order, equipped with extra components such as lights, new batteries, fresh water bottles, and whatever else the course dictates. An effective support crew will have at least one person who is mechanically inclined, who can make bike repairs and identify potential hazards.

Likewise, if a discipline, such as sailing, is included in a race, someone should know how to rig a boat. Bottom line: your support crew should be knowledgeable in the mechanical aspects of all disciplines.

NAVIGATOR

In addition to navigating their own route, the support crew becomes more effective if they can help make navigational decisions in regards to the race course. This will aid the team, who has been pushing their limits, backed by little sleep and minimal nourishment. It will reassure selected routes and enhance overall team strategy. While the team is out in the bush, and the support crew has time to kill, they can analyze and discuss possible route alternatives to give the team a head start on the next leg.

BLAIN REEVES ON SUPPORT CREWS

Support crews must be familiar enough with the racers to anticipate their needs before they reach the transition. The goal is to have everything for the next leg ready to pick up and move. Stopping should be limited to eating and a quick rest. Most teams try to get in and get out. Support crews must be navigators and strategists, making the right decisions on the amount of food needed for the next leg, as well as equipment and clothing.

THE SUPPORT CREW

LAUNDERER

Dirty laundry is abundant throughout a race. Often, facilities are extremely limited. Therefore, creativity and a large dose of tolerance are necessary to get this job done.

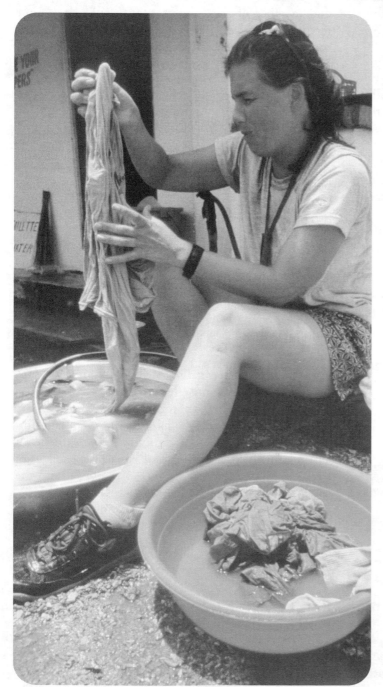

Cami Levy does laundry for team 'Spie.'

CATERER

This category is paramount to your popularity as a support crew member. The right foods must be cooked. They must be tasty, nutritious, and hot when the team arrives at the transition area. Depending on the head chef's repertoire and resources, a grill, a camping stove, and/or a good old-fashioned campfire may be used.

When a team makes their way to the transition area, they have high hopes and eager appetites. They look forward to a good, hot meal, and it is the responsibility of the support crew to come through for the racers. Soups and stews are common foods eaten at transitions. If it is possible, homemade foods add well-appreciated touches to the adventure racer's buffet.

PSYCHOTHERAPIST

Perhaps the most important role a support crew plays is in the emotion department. Positive encouragement and supportive words provide valuable fuel, which allow racers to keep pressing forward.

The support crew experiences a unique race alongside the main race. They must take care of themselves, but be able to focus on the needs of the racers. This is a hefty task, which doesn't appeal to every adventure racing enthusiast. Elite racers, such as Cathy Sassin and Rebecca Rusch, have been on both sides of the competition and agree that racing is much easier than supporting the racers.

However, there are many individuals that have made a primary hobby out of crewing for support. It is a great way to learn about adventure racing and experience an adventure that is less physical than the one the racers undertake—only in terms of heart rate and lactic acid accumulation.

In 1999, pro mountain biker Chris Scott raced the Beast of East as a solo. His mom was his support crew. "He asked me to help out with the race," said Mrs. Scott. "I thought I was going to be on the registration desk."

THE COMPLETE GUIDE TO ADVENTURE RACING

CONQUERING 'THE BEAST' WITHIN

AN EXCERPT FROM HIS ACCOUNT OF THE BEAST OF THE EAST
BY BLAIN REEVES

As I reached the checkpoint, my support crew greeted me, with "Your bike was run over but we're working to get it fixed." My first reaction was disbelief. In fact, I just disregarded what they said and told them what I needed packed in my backpack. Then it finally hit me. In my current condition, low on fuel and dehydrated, and under the realization of what had happened to my bike, I was beginning to have serious doubts about being able to finish the race. But could I quit that easily? I knew my body wouldn't have any heartburn with that decision. My mind wondered if I would be able to look at myself in the mirror the next day. I saw months of tough training going down the tubes. My mental outlook was dropping quickly.

As I tried to get ready for the bike leg, I assisted where I could in fixing my bike. I quickly realized that my own bike would not be traveling with me on this first bike leg. Luckily, after seeing what had happened, team 'SEAR's support crew helped my crew. Team 'SEAR's crew knew that I wasn't going anywhere on my bike and instead of watching me be eliminated early from the race, they loaned me one of their own support crew bikes. The Beast is unique in that it has different divisions within the race, which eliminates much of the cutthroat competition that other races have. Adventure racing for the most part is the athlete against the course, not the athlete against the other athletes. I believe the camaraderie among racers in adventure racing is unlike any other sport. The race course is designed to teach the racers about humility, while pitting them against the best that Mother Nature has to offer on the course.

As I entered the transition area to get my bike, support crews greeted me with cheers. It's a great feeling to get cheered at each transition. It's like hitting the finish line each time. That's one of the perks of expedition-level adventure racing.

ASSISTANCE CREW TIPS

The following advice comes from hours and hours and years and years of experience from two of the best in the business. Their wisdom is valuable. Use it to enhance your next supported race.

FROM ANNE WILSON

Being an assistant is challenging, but also very rewarding. When crewing for a team, it is very important to get to know all of the team member's preferences on food, their allergies, medical history and special needs. It is a good idea to spend some time getting to know them before the race starts, so you can see what motivates them or discuss the fears they may have. You will also find that some people need to be pampered and others just want their gear accessible, so they can do their own thing. The most important thing a support crew member can do is stay positive and organized and keep the team motivated.

PRE RACE TIPS

• Bring extra individual and team mandatory gear.

• Bring good cooking supplies (pots, pans, serving spoons, serving bowls, seasoning, utensils, cups, plates, bowls, coffee pot, and thermos).

• Bring lots of garbage bags, all sizes of zip locks, duct tape, baby wipes and antibacterial soap. If you are going to a foreign country, buy the team's favorite foods before you go.

• Buy food staples (i.e. peanut butter, bread, rice, oats, dried milk, dried potatoes, dried fruit, noodles and either dehydrated or canned meat).

• Bring some prepackaged dehydrated food (Mountain House is the best).

• Label everything with colored tape. Give each member on the team a different color, so it is easier to sort through.

• Type and laminate required individual and team gear lists for each section, so you can have a reference guide when organizing gear.

• Make a name tag for each person and laminate it, so you can put it next to his or her stuff. (This makes it a lot easier for them to find their gear right when they come into a transition area.)

• Bring sturdy gearboxes and if they don't already have good handles or wheels—make some.

• If mountain bikes are used in the race, bring bike tools and learn how to do quick repairs. Also, know how to build a mountain bike after it has been in a bike box.

• Bring a big tent and a few tarps for laying out gear and making shade.

• Find out about the place you are racing in, (i.e. language, helpful phrases, food, and culture).

• Either pack all of the gearboxes yourself or watch to see where everything is packed, so you can find your things easier. It is also good to label each gearbox with duct tape and put what is in it.

- Bring a Discman, car adapter and CDs for those long car rides to transition areas.

DURING THE RACE TIPS

- At transition areas, try to get the team out as quickly as possible and actually time how long they have been there. Look for signs of dehydration, altitude sickness (at high altitudes), or heat exhaustion.

- Always go as fast as you can to the next transition area, even if you know you will be waiting there for a few days. You can never predict how long a team will take.

- Try to keep food and gear organized and easily accessible.

- Lay out the team's gear on tarps and give each person some space to change and go through their gear.

- Lay out medical supplies on another tarp, so you can attend to their medical needs quickly when they come into camp.

- Have them drop their dirty gear in a pile away from the new gear they are picking up, so it's less confusing when they are repacking their backpacks.

- Make everyone show you their individual and team mandatory gear before they leave.

- Try to find cold sodas for your team when it's hot and hot coffee when it's cold. (Sometimes the simplest things bring the most joy.)

- At the finish line, bring hot food and sodas or Champagne to congratulate your team with.

GENERAL TIPS

- Help out other crews when you can, they are your best support system when you are in a race.

- Tell your team to be brutally honest with you about how they feel and what they like and don't like.

- Don't take anything personally during a race. Things may be said by your teammates because they are under an enormous amount of stress.

- Always tell your team they are doing great and motivate them in any way you can.

FOOD TIPS

Seasonings	Jelly bellies
Pasta	Cheetos
Rice	Snickers
Bread	M&M's
Dehydrated potatoes	Peanut butter and jelly
Oatmeal	Nutella
Canned meat	Dried fruit pretzels
Canned fruit	Chips/Salsa
Veggies and spaghetti sauce	Mixed nuts
Soup and pasta mixes	Ensure powder
String cheese or baby bells	Granola
Beef or turkey jerky	Protein bars
Trail mix	Fruit snacks
Pringles	Granola bars
Pop tarts	Chocolate-covered espresso beans
Famous Amos cookies	Energy gels
	Electrolyte drink mixes

MEDICAL TIPS

- Always have out Chap Stick and sun block for teams when they come in.

- Take a wilderness first-aid class.

- Bring inhalers for asthma.

- Bring BodyGlide to prevent blisters and chafing.

- Bring a good first-aid kit and know how to use everything in it.

- Know how to fix bad feet and blisters.

- Bring cough drops, Thera flu, Tylenol cold and sinus, Imodium, Benadryl, antibiotics, an Epipen epinephrine for allergic reactions, cold and heat packs, 2nd skin, tape, sterile compress, and a mix of bandages.

THE SUPPORT CREW

ROLF DENGLER'S VITAL LIST FOR SUPPORT

- Waterproof tarps (2-3 large, 1 extra-large).
- Parachute cord (2,000 ft.).
- Rope (lots)/straps (climbing webbing-color lengths) for tying the equipment down etc. Carabiners help too!
- Colored electrical tape (for marking).
- Big coolers (2—Dry food/Wet food).
- Tools (pliers/needle-nose/tin-snips/tire-wrench/etc.).
- Big thick clear trash bags and duct tape (8-10 rolls).
- Bailing wire & bungee cords (all sizes) and an off-road vehicle tow rope (this tow rope literally helped us at least 7 times in inclement weather and roads)—about $25.00 at an auto supply store like Pep Boys.
- Zip ties very helpful (just large size—they can be cut down)!
- Get to checkpoint early to get a good parking spot! Don't park all the way back—you'll get blocked in).
- Team needs to know: Where do they walk to for checkpoint timekeeper?
- Team needs to know: Where have teams been leaving?
- Team needs to know: What time did the last team come in/leave ... what place are they/we? (There will be a large board for support crews to view team stats at most CPs (checkpoints), ACPs (assisted checkpoints), TAs (transition areas).)
- Team needs to know: Dark zones and times (where/when).
- Cold food vs. warm food? Warm preferred, but not too hot. For better digestibility, food should not be too "chunky".
- Try to get cook time down so that they never wait (tough at times).

- Always know where each team member's gear is. Always.
- Have ready pre-prepared race bags (food) on arrival. Have bowls/cups/knives/forks ready!
- Have all necessary gear separated and out for transition.
- Try not to let the team think at checkpoints. Keep the team moving!
- Have tents/tarps set up for team to rest/sleep/stay out of the wind regardless of current weather.
- Make sure you can get all food and supplies in town before checkpoints.
- Get all sewing/wood work/welding done before race (may not be necessary).
- Know how to get to each checkpoint without flaw.
- Have enough money changed so there is no massive money-exchange bank search.
- Break all large bank notes and currency.
- Extra-large plastic equipment boxes for racers seem to be the most manageable, rather than soft bags for handling and protection.
- Find out where and when support can help the team (carry kayaks to the water, etc.) The race organizers may not let you, so you'll need to ask.
- Have all maps laminated—or at least bring the lamination supplies to the race.
- Wash the team gear whenever possible.
- Have plenty of safe and treated drinking water available.
- Get water and other supplies before the other teams buy it all. In Ecuador, it was a race against time beating teams to the stores for water. There's always time to relax but no time to waste in the race against other support teams.

RAID GAULOISES, ECUADOR 1999

June 1998, approximately 3:00 AM, Canaan Valley 24-hour mountain bike race.

I'm there assisting a team. Bodies and bikes everywhere. Mike Nolan (a rider) says he wants me for the Raid Gauloises in Ecuador—never heard of it. Expenses paid! This ends the conversation. About a week later, I call him. Does he remember talking to me? Is he serious? He is. So he visits and explains to me, my wife and all just what is involved. I'm hooked. My wife and kids think I'd be crazy not to go. So it starts. I'd also met Don Mann at Canaan. I'd read/heard about him—a crazy Navy SEAL who bikes 18-hour/24-hour races solo. What kind of person does that? Navy SEALs—don't they go around killing people? Don't they all look like Rambo? The answer to all the questions above was—No.

About two months later, I'm on a short trip to rural New Jersey on vacation to see a relative, which coincidentally is the same weekend as the Nor'easter adventure race and team 'Odyssey' is there. I committed to "take a look" as time allowed. So I arrive at their campsite in the dark as the team preps to leave. I'm greeted with the news that my contact is off the Raid Gauloises trip, so I immediately figure my prospects for Ecuador are down the toilet. But, I'll stick around anyway. I'm there and they (Don Mann, Chris Burgess, John Kainer, and Joy Marr) seem friendly. They are also deadly serious and extremely focused. Walt is their official helper, and after brief introductions, we're off in my car with their equipment and me—the driver—being put to immediate use in transporting some of them.

Three days later, I get a chance to call my wife. I apologize and explain what I've been doing and that

THE SUPPORT CREW

no, I'm not finished yet, but am on the last leg with at least 250 miles on the car, and may be back for dinner (which turned out to be midnight).

In the meantime, I'd pretty much been awake the entire time. I'd seen team 'Odyssey' (my team) lead Salomon Presidio, a team made up of the best adventure racers in the world, and finally finish somewhat behind. However, there were lots of smiles on their faces and they were convinced that they'd stuck to the whole route in what was somewhat of a chaotic race. The highlights: beautiful weather, moonlit nights, ghost-like canoeists on the Delaware River in the dead of night, fixing John Kainer a peanut butter and jelly sandwich at 5 AM (that he still talks about), meeting fascinating people and surprising myself that I had the energy and stamina to assist during the whole thing. I was also delighted to find that I could get along with Navy SEALs, who were sufficiently impressed with my abilities and told me that, "I was their man," for Ecuador. About five weeks later, I'm at the greatest adventure race in the world, in Ecuador.

I don't speak Spanish and have not been to a foreign country since 1968. Scary stuff. And once the team starts, I have to ensure we're at the transition spots to support the team. What happens if we break down or get lost? Fortunately, I have a wonderful, worldly companion—a former surgeon, Parker Cross, who is the team doctor/second assistance person. Maybe he's number one and me number two. Who cares? Our goals are the same—do whatever we can to give our team whatever support they need to do well.

But just what does that mean? What exactly does an assistance person do? Assist, of course. You dedicate yourself to the fact that, irrespective of how well or poorly your team is doing, your role is to facilitate their performance during the time they are with you. You are a faithful servant. Your team should know what their personal needs are and you have to satisfy those needs, regardless of whether you like it or not.

PLANNING

You should be involved and become a part of the team, with a clearly defined role that you are comfortable with. What are the team's expectations of themselves? Do they fit in for you? How competitive are they? How about you? Where are you going? How are you getting there? Who is paying for it? Etc., etc.

EQUIPMENT

An event like the Raid has lots of mandated equipment, some of which may not be easy to get a hold of (e.g., life preservers that satisfy a European specification that may not have a direct U.S. equivalent). There are lots of questions that need to be resolved ahead of the event, and everything should be field-tested prior to the race. The more familiarity the assistance crew has with all of the equipment, including personal gear, the better. But you will also have to learn each individual's needs. Does that person want you to access his or her own stuff, and how feasible is that? Clearly, some boundaries should be established and understood long before the event. The assistance crew should also have input into selection of communal gear that they would be expected to operate. For example—tents. Do you select one big enough for everybody, or do you set up several tents? In my view, a larger one makes sense. But, it may be more vulnerable in severe weather.

SHELTER

You'll need to be able to cover an area of at least 20 square feet. Ideally, your shelter should have roll-up sides, a ground sheet to cover the inside, and it should be high enough to stand up in, with sufficient anchorage to withstand high winds and inclement weather.

KITCHEN/FOOD PREPARATION

If you can't cook, you'll have to learn! You will have to operate stoves and all of the paraphernalia needed to fix a meal for about seven people, and you have to clean up afterwards with no help from the racers.

They will either be asleep or gone. Obviously, this is a really big deal and your reputation rests on how well you can do this. Equally important is your timing. You should have a rough idea (maybe 4-5 hours or less) of when your team will arrive at the transition area. Having their meal ready to eat is a major plus. They will be looking forward to it, so don't disappoint them!

I have vivid recollections of fixing a sizeable stew on a single stove burner at altitude in Ecuador, burning what I suspected was diesel fuel, while completely envious of the other crews who had four burner stoves and bigger pans. Nonetheless, I succeeded in getting complimented from my team on my fare. I later spent most of the night in sub-zero temperatures with my Capilene, fleece, and Gor-Tex pants around my ankles in a dangerously windy latrine with the most awful diarrhea! So—cleanliness, boiling water, and thoroughly sterilizing utensils with bleach has to be a top priority. Your racers might be the fittest they've ever been in their lives, but a dose of ill-prepared food could do them in. You have been warned. Some teams, such as 'Air France', were like a traveling delicatessen, and with minor persuasion, were very generous in sharing their bounty. Learn to be a scrounger for food. Throw away nothing (provided it's edible). It may be a lifesaver later.

—Peter Tempest, team 'Odyssey'

In the 1999 Elf Authentic Adventure, the support crew for team 'Epinephrine/Pharmane' had trouble with their Jeepney (leftover WWII vehicles used for public transportation in the Philippines) and had to substitute a dump truck as a short-term rescue!

The moment the race course is revealed, course strategy begins.

EXPERIENCE LAYS THE PAVEMENT FOR THE FUTURE

The best way to learn about racing is to gather the "dos and don'ts" from experienced racers. The lessons they have learned can save you time and needless mistakes. Read on!

PACE

Your racing intensity should rarely reach your maximum potential, particularly so that the few times when you need to give everything you've got, you have that extra energy to spare. In situations such as sprinting to the finish line, busting up the last steep grade on your mountain bike, negotiating ornery rapids, or making a time cut-off, you will need to turn it on. If you are wasting yourself throughout the course, you may not have that extra oomph to spare and you may burn out before the race is over.

Generally, your pace should revolve around 70 to 80 percent of your maximum output. This intensity is predominantly based on how you feel. Strive for a rate that you can maintain for many successive hours. You should find a pace that you feel you can maintain all day. A general rule of thumb, for a multi-day race, you should be going at a level you feel you can sustain for 4 hours.

For sprint races or one-day races, your pace will be faster than a two-day race. Likewise, your pace for a five-day race will be slower, and if you are out for more than a week, your pace will vary from the shorter races.

The key is to pay attention to your intensity while you train. Get in touch with how it feels to go 70, 80, and 90 percent, so that you can control your intensity while you race.

Of course, experience will provide the best answer to the ultimate pace debate. After competing in several races of varying lengths, you will have a good idea of the pace that feels good, the pace that allows you to finish, and the pace that possibly wins the race.

Also, remember the 100-meter rule. If your team is spread out beyond 100-meters from each other, you are breaking a fundamental rule in adventure racing. Adventure racing is a team sport and when you spend most of the race further than an earshot from each other, you are no longer engaged in team competition. Safety can be severely compromised and team dynamics get wrecked. Stay together.

ESTIMATING LEG—HOW LONG WILL IT TAKE TO COMPLETE THIS ONE?

If you have done your homework and have spent significant time training with your teammates, you will have a pretty good idea of how long it will take to conquer each discipline. When you plot your checkpoints and strategize your course, try to estimate how long it will take to finish each leg. Then, add at least a quarter of your estimated time to allow for surprises in terrain, inclement weather, or breakdowns of gear or the human kind.

DON'T FORGET...

* Secure water bottles to your pack straps. You will spend less time restocking and treating water supplies if you can simply scoop water into a bottle as you walk by or through a stream. The water can purify in your bottle while you drink from your bladder.

* Bring two tanks—one for water and one for a sports drink. Try to drink your carbohydrate and electrolyte replacement mix every fifteen to twenty minutes, and drink water as often as possible.

* Trekking poles serve many purposes. They save your legs and feet as they distribute the load you carry around the course. They also assist in water crossings and trekking on shifty surfaces. And in an emergency situation, they can serve as a makeshift splint.

Stay together. After all, adventure racing is a team sport!

TIPS FROM DEB MOORE, ULTRA DISTANCE MARATHON RUNNER

STRATEGY

There are four guidelines/goals that my orienteering and adventure teammate Liz Jennison and I have found to be very valuable in adventurous competitions:

1. Eighty percent of life is just showing up, but the other twenty percent is sticking it out!
2. Make sure they don't have to come look for you.
3. Give it your very best.
4. Go for the win.

Multi-day team adventure competitions require extensive planning, team coordination and often big bucks. Getting to the starting line is by no means a small feat. Give yourself a pat on the back for getting there at all. But getting there is only the first 80 percent.

A while back, I overheard an interesting comment that I want to share with those just starting in the sport. A soon-to-be first time racer asked Tom Possert, champion ultra runner and adventure racer (second place Eco-Challenge Maine, first person to do the 350-mile Iditasport Extreme on foot, and recent winner of Cal Sports Eco-Adventure race), "How long should it take a first-timer to finish a six-day adventure race?" Tom's response was: "Most people don't finish their first adventure race." A look at the finishing rates show a lot of teams, experienced or not, don't finish. How can you stack the odds in your favor? For two to three-day races, the following are critical, while in longer races even more factors enter in:

1. DON'T GET LOST.
2. DON'T GET DEHYDRATED.

Over the last few years, this has become an increasing problem in ultra-running. It's especially important for people new and inexperienced, as well as those more experienced to know about. *See the hydration section in chapter 10.

3. DON'T DESTROY YOUR FEET.
4. DON'T DROP IN THE DARK.

Whoever said: "It's darkest before the dawn," was

not just talking about lack of light. For competitions of 24 hours or longer, dealing with no or minimal sleep is a real challenge. Between about two and five AM, sometimes called the witching hours, the body really wants to sleep. Blood sugar levels are typically the lowest in the body's 24-hour cycle and your brain normally uses this time in REM sleep to help organize and store information from the previous day's experience and information. Although physical activity tends to help many people be able to literally stay awake, there are still a number of different effects you might experience. Racers often report feeling out of sorts, brain dead, dopey, or having hallucinations. You may find it difficult to concentrate and very easy to make mistakes. This is the time your brain can generate lots of very good reasons to drop out. BUT DON'T DO IT! Many of these feelings will subside with the first light. My doctor friends tell me that the light at dawn triggers the production of biochemical signals to wake the body up and get going again. The more experience you have with sleep deprivation, the better you'll get at recognizing it for what it is and doing what works best for you. Although sleep deprivation is an individual thing, there are different strategies you can consider.

Sleep in multiples of your sleep cycle. People tend to go through several multiples of their REM sleep cycle in a normal evening. For many, it takes their bodies 60- to 90 minutes to get through a full REM cycle. In multi-day racing, we have had the best luck sleeping in 90 minute segments. For me, getting a full REM cycle reduces the tendency for hallucinating at night. When feasible, timing your sleep break to start in the dark and finish at daybreak seems to trick the body into thinking it has had more sleep than it actually did.

The length of the race will influence the amount of sleep you need. In a 24-hour competition, expect to go non-stop; no sleep breaks unless someone is really in trouble, i.e. falling asleep on his feet. In a two-night competition, I find I do best with one 90-minute nap right before daybreak on the first night, then pushing through the second night (when you can smell the finish) with no sleep. In longer races, three hours sleep per 24 hours seems to be enough to keep me thinking pretty clearly. It can be taken in parts, one at night and one in the day or one three hour nap, depending on the team's condition and race cutoffs.

In the Beast of the East, where our team goal was to finish, we allowed ourselves three hours sleep per 24 hours (for the first four days) except for the last night/day where we pushed straight through for the last 30 hours with no sleep. The last few hours on bikes and in a canoe we had to work hard not to nod off without realizing it. (Recognize that elite, experienced teams often go with much less sleep.)

To get the most efficiency from our sleep breaks we ate and drank as much as we could right before we went to sleep, so our bodies could be digesting lots of calories while we slept. We also made sure our feet got a chance to dry out, to help prevent trench foot.

Seize the opportunity and be flexible. Look for smart times and safe places to sleep. Don't sleep close to a critical cut-off unless absolutely necessary. Get to the checkpoint, then sleep. Because you can never be sure how long it might take or what Murphy's law events may impede your progress when trying to make a cut-off. Some places are safer to sleep than others, especially if bad weather or heavy rain/flooding is possible. Be alert. Sometimes stopping sooner or pressing on a bit is wiser.

In a race where crews are allowed, it's a luxury if you can sleep at a transition point where you know you won't oversleep because they'll wake you up. It can also be very time-efficient for them to repack your packs with food and gear, fresh water, etc. while you sleep.

TIPS FROM DALE BLANKENSHIP, TEAM 'NOMAD'

1. Learn about your race coordinator. If your trail runs out, it may be because you have a sadistic race coordinator. If you are on the right trail, and it peters out, find the major terrain feature generally following your cardinal direction. Check your map for collecting features and catching features (an altimeter really helps here), then start bushwhacking until you pick up the trail again or get to another linear feature.

2. When using tip number one, don't forget to offset.

3. Burn times for headlamps are never as long as the manufacturer claims. Always bring extra batteries.

4. It sucks being cold. Fleece balaclavas can smash down nicely into your pack, and are very warm.

5. Feet like to be aired out. If you stop while on the trail, take your shoes off and air the dogs; your feet will love you for it.

6. Check your mountain bike closely before every race. Trying to find the bolt that holds the rear suspension onto your bike in the middle of the night really stinks.

7. Pumping large quantities of water through your stomach can flush out your system and lead to cramping. A good fluid replacement powder is a must. (I learned this one the hard way, but didn't believe myself, so I learned it again the hard way.)

8. It's easy to get sick of energy bars if that is all you eat for two days in a row. Take a treat with you. But if it's hot, don't take candy bars unless you also carry a freezer.

NATE SMITH'S TIPS

1. Always use baby powder between the tires and tubes on your bike when you set it up for a race. This almost always alleviates the problem of pinch flats and allows you to run your tires at a comfortable pressure.

2. Hydrate. Hydrate. Hydrate.

3. Always use your race equipment several times before an actual race so that you are used to it.

4. Don't try anything new during a race. If you don't routinely do it, don't do it during a race.

5. If you are not 100 percent healthy, STAY HOME!

THE COMPLETE GUIDE TO ADVENTURE RACING

EARRING DOUG JUDSON—CAPTAIN
TEAM 'BALANCE BAR/ESPIRIT DE CORPS'

Just a quickie on adventure racing tips from someone who has made every mistake in the book over the many races I've done. The magnitude of these events continues to amaze me no matter how many I do. And despite the lessons learned from each race, you can never get it quite right. So, here goes my top ten tips on pulling off a successful adventure race—from first-timer to experienced racer:

1. Wear tights or leggings because you will be chewed up by the terrain, bitten by creatures, torn up by thistles, sought out by poison sumac, ivy, and oak, and sunburned beyond belief.

2. Make sure everybody has a vested interest in the race in order for you all to have the same motivation. For example, get everybody to bring in a sponsor. That way, everyone feels the need to have the same goal during the race—whether it be finishing or kicking butt.

3. Put duct tape on your trekking poles so that it's handy when you feel your shoes are digging into your bones and you just can't go anymore. Be sure they are handy, easily accessible, and you can use them on the fly.

4. Always set two watches if you pull over to sleep. That way there is no fiasco when you intend to sleep for one hour and end up sleeping for six. It is very frustrating (from first-hand knowledge)!

5. Never try out new equipment, techniques, or strategies during the race. Always stick to old school, unless you tried it out beforehand.

6. Never let go of the rope during a rappel. No matter how hot it gets, no matter how badly it burns and blisters your hand—hold on for dear life.

7. Never let a teammate sleep in the boat. It slows down the whole team, oftentimes forcing the boats to be bungeed together, which saps the team's energy. Struggle through it, finish it off, and sleep on land. You can bungee when everybody's paddling together to go faster, but sleeping more than five to ten minutes at a time in the boat is a no-no.

8. Pick your teammates ever so carefully. If someone bails just before a race, don't just go out and grab somebody and hope for the best. Get references. Look up their resumes. Talk to people they have raced with. Talk to your potential teammate extensively. Then train with him beforehand. By no means should you simply take his word that he is on the same wavelength and has the same drive, because most people will not be honest with you about what motivates them. This could ruin your race.

9. Use caffeine, chocolate-covered espresso beans, mind games, incessant laughter, and occasional slaps in the face to keep yourself awake during the night. When the sun comes up, life is good. Until then, keep active, blink a lot, and look at your surroundings and the nights get shorter and shorter.

10. Have fun. Have a personality out there, show emotion, and enjoy the race. Get caught up in the moment. Have pain, fear, and cry. Have joy and laughs. Have frustration, then vent. Life is about expression, not being stagnant. Adventure racing is about feeling, embracing life and adversity, and making the best of trials and tribulations. So by all means, don't be afraid to live.

DAN O'SHEA'S ADVENTURE RACING RECOMMENDATIONS

FOOT CARE

Expedition adventure races are won and lost, not by seconds or inches, but by feet. The ability for a team to steadily move forward over days of nonstop racing is contingent on the condition of an adventure racer's most abused body part—his feet. Subjecting one's body to long-term physical exertion and exposure to the elements is compounded at foot level. Every step becomes a reminder of the masochistic idea of completing a nonstop, multi-sport, multi-day race with no end in site. "Prunes", "hamburger meat" or "smoked dogs" are just a few of the anecdotal adjectives describing a typical racer's feet after day two or three of a long race. Taking one's shoes off after a particularly long, wet and arduous hike can be the confirmation of one's worst fears. Every seasoned adventure racer has experienced these dog-day afternoons during a race and most will go to extremes to prevent a painful reminder in their next race.

PREVENTATIVE MAINTENANCE

The first step in avoiding blisters is to toughen up your feet. Racing and endurance running will condition your feet to the rigors of a multi-day race. Aside from racing and running, walking barefoot is the best way to toughen up one's feet. Though not always feasible, walking shoeless on hot asphalt will build up calluses and a second layer of skin. An excellent training technique for those living near a beach is to hike barefoot with your backpack during the heat of the day. The sand, the sun and the heat will braise and bake a second layer of toughness.

The next step is to pick the proper shoes and ensure that they are well broken in before the race. Most experienced racers use nothing more than a trail running shoe over an entire adventure racecourse with the exception of the high altitude/technical sections. For the expedition, multi-day races such as the Raid Gauloises, Elf Authentic Adventure or Southern Traverse, I recommend one reserve pair of racing shoes or one size larger than your starting race pair. Your feet will swell significantly over the race due to edema (trauma) and blood pooling in your lower extremities. There are many suitable brands out there and I will only comment on shoes that I have raced with personally. Salomon has tied its destiny to the sport of adventure racing and is on the cutting edge of adventure racing products and shoes. Its original shoe, the Raid Runner, has evolved into the Raid Wind, and both are excellent shoes in terms of support, stability, and durability. The next generation shoe is a waterproof version called the Raid Wind with ClimaDry.

I comment on the waterproof version because of its relationship to a critical blister factor—moisture. Water is the number one factor in accelerating blister damage. Moisture softens the skin, degrades the shoe's fitting, and can increase friction. Keeping one's feet dry (though rarely feasible) is critical in preventing the onset of blisters. In addition to a pair of waterproof shoes, the use of gaiters can aid in keeping one's feet dry and preventing dirt from entering the shoe. Gaiters are typically used by skiers to prevent snow from entering their boots and can serve the same protection against dirt for adventure racers. Dirt can be a source of both friction and infection as abrasions occur. Another insider secret is the utilization of two gaiters, one inner and one outer, to provide double protection from the elements. Outdoor Research makes the best gaiters on the market and they have two models perfectly suited for this purpose. The Flex-tex gaiter is half-boot size, stretch fitting and waterproof, and it snugly covers the shoe from the laces to the lip. Covering the outside, the Gor-Tex Mountain Gaiter provides a second layer of protection.

'MED ARTS PHARMACY'—LESSONS LEARNED

EFFICIENT RACING

Many aspects of adventure racing are going through a lot of changes in this rapidly maturing sport. After years of racing, one thing really sticks out to me year after year—teams are getting better. They are quicker and continuously astound race organizers by completing legs of races much faster than ever anticipated, and as a result, they are finishing entire races in amazing times. But one question seems to always plague teams after finishing a race, no matter how well they did: "How can we do better?"

What a loaded question! I have picked up on some very simple but continuously overlooked answers to this question. However, more specifically, teams should ask how they can race more efficiently. First, we need to know exactly what we are dealing with. This is a team sport, and the word "team" changes everything. It makes a challenging event at least ten times more challenging. We are dealing with individuals with different personalities, fitness levels, and athletic backgrounds. It is important that each person contributes their individuality to the team's knowledge, race philosophy, expertise in the disciplines, and personality. But the kicker here is that each person must also accept the same from others. I've seen more teams self-destruct because of this time and again. Every member of a team must remain very open and try not to hold anything back—and not just in preparing for the race, but for the entire, non-stop, mentally and physically exhausting event. This is much easier said than done.

It takes a lot of inner strength not to be bull-headed when a small disagreement arises, especially when extremely fatigued. Team conflicts take so much energy and are such a waste that a team will be doomed from the start. A good understanding from all team members is really the most basic building block to be successful and perform well, and may be the greatest challenge a team will face.

With this basic but often overlooked "team psyche" understood by all members, working on efficiency will come much easier. Physical fitness and proficiency in disciplines is very important, but it is sometimes over emphasized by many teams. I have seen teams with only adequate physical abilities finish days ahead of teams consisting of world class athletes. Why? They are efficient. It

does absolutely no good to finish a leg ahead of everyone else and then spend hours at a checkpoint fumbling around with gear and trying to recover. You will be passed and may not even finish the race. I am mainly talking about the expedition-type seven to ten day races. They are long, and correct pace is a crucial key to success. I don't know of many races where the team that burst out in front went on to win the race. Ultra runners have a good concept of this. The steady, proficient runner may not start out in the load pack but six hours later they are starting to pass people that have crashed and burned because they didn't pace themselves.

A team that understands this pace concept and can hold back the urge to charge ahead too fast has already established a big advantage. But remember the "team psyche" concept—all members must have the same idea, or conflict will surely arise.

Now comes the fine-tuning. We have a great team performing as a solid unit at a smart pace. They don't get lost for the whole race and everyone stays healthy and strong and has no real problems with the physical disciplines, only to finish a whole day behind the winners. They didn't even get stuck at any dark zones. Now we can look at the simple things that are often overlooked. And no, it has nothing to do with sleeping less, but it does take a lot of discipline and awareness.

First, most teams stop way too often. They often rationalize that because the race is so long, ten minutes here and there will make no difference. I have fallen into this trap before and so have many, many other teams. It is simple math—ten minutes three times a day for eight days is four hours. But if there are five racers, it is usually more like twenty hours! Twenty hours of wasted time, and I'm not referring to sleep or the necessary stops at transition areas.

This is where it is absolutely crucial for team unity and discipline. Each time a team stops for any reason, they are very vulnerable to getting sucked into these "time traps". A five-minute stop so someone can fix his feet easily turns into fifteen minutes or longer. To make matters worse, an hour later the team has to stop again so someone can get some food out of their pack, and this five-minute stop turns into ten minutes. I've been in situations where this went on for twenty hours, stopping for every reason in the world. It is really hard to avoid doing this, especially when dealing with tired

STRATEGY

people experiencing their highs and lows at different times. But it is crucial that each break is used very efficiently to avoid this string of continuous, disorganized stopping.

I think the best way to control this is having a team leader who is aware of the time and what needs to be done, helping direct his teammates to utilize time efficiently. This is not necessarily the same person throughout the whole race, but the person who is feeling the strongest and is most capable of directing others and keeping track of time. A good team will naturally switch roles and each person will know when they have to step up and help guide the group. The important thing is that everyone else will accept this. A team where everyone depends on one person to call all the shots is in for trouble.

I've seen teams like this out on the racecourse. Everything is going great until the "leader" gets sick or is fatigued to the point where unsafe decisions are made. Once that person is unable to perform as a leader, the team is helpless—no one else can seem to get things under control. The worst case is where everyone sees the chance to become the leader, which can result in conflict and a complete breakdown of the team. Awareness and discipline are key. Be aware of your team's situation and be disciplined enough to allow the roles to change.

The team leader may very well be the same person throughout the entire race, which is fine, but be aware that this is a heavy burden for a single person to carry and a team may be wiser to shift this weight around occasionally.

I need to stress that the team leader is not the team dictator. Someone screaming out orders and cutting down their teammates will quickly break down the team, but it happens in every race. Also be careful not to have too much democracy in the form of attitudes on the team, where everyone feels they can do whatever they want whenever they please, because that is exactly what will happen. If someone wants to stop, they will—because they feel just as in charge as anyone else. The worse thing you can do is suddenly stop without letting your team members know. I've always dreaded hearing a teammate say, "Just go ahead, I'll catch up." This is not a good habit for a team to get into. First, they almost never catch up without the rest of the team waiting or slowing down, and second, this person risks getting separated from the team or even lost. It can happen very easily at night in thick terrain with no trails. Don't take any chances. They will only slow the team down in the long run.

Plan your stops ahead of time as an entire team with one person (the leader) seeing that you stick to the plan.

This same principle can be applied to just about every situation encountered during a race and will save a lot of time and energy.

CHECKPOINTS

During a long race, there may be more than 20 or 30 checkpoints. Save just five minutes at each checkpoint and you've just shaved two to three hours off your race time. The checkpoint in a race is like a light at the end of a tunnel—reaching it (and finding it) is like a small victory in itself. A team's emotions and adrenaline kick in, the pace picks up, and the checkpoint is finally reached. This is where discipline again plays a vital role. I have seen and experienced the following most common scenarios many times. First, everyone crowds around the race personnel and bombards them with questions. And they're always the same, "How far are we behind the leaders?", "How far is the next checkpoint?", "What place are we in?" After all members finish the interrogation, some sit down to rest, others eat some food, and the navigator studies the map for the next leg. Maybe after ten or fifteen minutes, if they are lucky, the team will finally get reorganized and ready to move on. This is the wrong way to arrive at a checkpoint.

A plan should be made before the checkpoint is reached. If everyone is feeling fine and no one needs to stop, then one person checks in and gathers any information from the race officials while everyone else moves through the checkpoint. At this point, the navigator should prepare the maps for the next leg and be ready to continue on. If it is determined that a stop is necessary, then a time is set and everyone does what they need to do. Again, this is all planned before the checkpoint is reached.

WATER STOPS

Finding, treating, and filling water bottles eats up a lot of time, but water is one of the most crucial necessities in an adventure race. Water stops should not be overlooked as potential "time wasters" and should be approached in an efficient manner. Not everyone runs out of water at the same time, nor do they drink it at the same rate—this would make things too easy. Proper hydration is so important during a race and running out of water should never happen to a smart, properly prepared team. At water stops, everyone should fill up, and it usually works best if two people fill everyone's containers, while the others take care of other things. Comments like, "I still have half a bottle" or "I should have enough until the next checkpoint," are setting your team up for possible disaster. Water stops take time, especially if the water needs to be treated. So, if a stop is made, fill up and top off every container, otherwise you will need to make more of these time-consuming stops than necessary. If someone runs out of water before everyone else—share! Don't let a teammate risk dehydration—utilize all the water your team has efficiently until a planned stop is made.

GEAR

Ninety percent of racers bring too much gear. The more gear you have, the more time you will waste fussing around with it. I've cut my gear nearly in half since my first race and I am still bringing too much. Obviously, if it is a cold weather race or a race with many disciplines, you will have more gear, but no matter the situation, you probably have too much. This really comes down to what an individual is comfortable with, and only experience will teach someone how to be comfortable with less. It's like a security blanket. Just knowing you have those extra three pairs of shoes or five fleece jackets "just in case" can be very soothing and can give you peace of mind. But it always ends up being a burden and waste of time at transition areas—rifling through piles of clothing and misplacing things, when you could be resting. At the end of the race you will look at what you brought and say, "I didn't use half this stuff." The bottom line is that it affects the efficiency of the team as a whole.

More experienced racers learn to minimize their gear, but be careful not to take this too far. Too much gear may cost the team some time, but too little may mean the end of the race altogether. Racers are learning to cut corners and take advantage of loopholes in mandatory gear regulations, which can indeed reduce the amount and weight of gear, but it can sometimes backfire. I've witnessed teams being evacuated from high mountain glaciers only because proper warm clothing and sleeping bags were foolishly left behind. There is a balance here, but no matter how hard you try, you will probably bring too much gear.

STRATEGY

CAMERA

A picture may be worth a thousand words, but it may also cost a team hours of time.

Whenever a teammate mentions that he's going to bring a camera on the race course, I get nervous and think about a recent adventure race where we had a camera with us. I thought nothing of it until I was enjoying some of the great photos we had taken. I noticed that almost every picture represented a significant amount of "down" time. When the camera came out, it was almost like an automatic invitation to take packs off, eat, change clothes, or just stand around waiting for the pictures to be taken. Out of curiosity, I added up the extra time that taking these pictures added—four and a half hours! These were not planned stops, they just happened whenever a good photo opportunity came up. And worse yet, the time was not used efficiently at all. I mentioned this to several other teams and they realized the same thing had happened to them. A camera can provide great memories, but be aware of this potential "time trap". No matter how hard you try, bringing a camera and taking pictures on the race course will take away from your efficiency. If a team is racing to win, it makes a difference. A team racing to finish, where time is not so key, doesn't really have to worry as much.

FEET

If there is one subject that is addressed more than any other in adventure racing, it is foot care. And the reasons are valid, for if your feet fail, the race is over. The feet undergo such incredible abuse that it is nearly impossible for an entire team to escape having to deal with foot problems during a race.

The amount of time a team spends fussing around with their feet during a race is incredible, even for a team whose members' feet are in relatively good shape. On average, each person probably spends several hours just on foot care. For a team of four or five people, this adds up real fast. Foot problems have become such an expected occurrence that the attitude now is that it's okay to spend a lot of time on foot care. Many teams don't see how this really eats up time and thus don't approach it in the most efficient manner.

Foot problems are going to happen and there is no question they must be addressed immediately in order to prevent bigger problems later in the race. The worst thing is to wait to fix a hot spot. It will become a blister sooner than you think and in a matter of time, you will be facing a very time-consuming and energy-wasting foot problem. The point is, time spent on preventative maintenance is nothing compared to time spent on treatment after foot problems develop. This is how teams should approach foot care.

Preventative care begins well before the race starts and this is what many racers forget. Many racers are too preoccupied with how to fix and treat problems *after* they happen. They are ready to lube, spray, wrap, tape, and inject their feet—whatever it takes. We all have different needs for our feet and everybody should know exactly what these needs are before the race starts. This will allow you to minimize time spent on foot care. You will be more aware of what your feet need and when they need care, before any real problems develop.

I've seen racers taping their feet only because everyone else is and they just want to be "safe". What a waste of time! Don't fuss around with your feet unless you know you have to. It's easy to watch other teams spend a lot of time with their feet and feel that you have to do the same. You won't fall into this trap if you've done your pre-race preparations properly.

The bottom line is to come to a race with your feet properly prepared, not just properly prepared to fix your feet. You will be amazed at how much time you can save by doing this.

We are reaching a point in adventure racing where many teams are composed of very physically fit athletes. Time records are getting shorter and teams are finishing closer together. In this sport, there is a limit to what physical fitness can do for the performance of a team. Smart teams are now looking at more subtle things they can do to gain the upper hand during a race. There is no question that a team that can race efficiently will dramatically increase their odds of performing well.

BRAD MILLER'S TIPS

1. Know your land navigation.
2. Take that extra polypro top.
3. Buy a sea kayak and paddle, paddle, paddle!
4. Experience sleep deprivation at least once during training and learn how to manage it.
5. Don't sacrifice hydration for speed.
6. Know how your body will react to long efforts (i.e. excessive swelling).

7. The shoes you race in should be the ones in which you have trained.
8. Wrangle as much info out of the pros as you can. Exploit their good nature and generosity in giving tips on equipment, strategy, and technique.
9. Dial yourself into the adventure racing "scene" as much as possible once you have decided to do a race. There is a ton of info out there.
10. Tell your friends about adventure racing. Sucker them into training with you.

TRACYN THAYER ON WOMEN ADVENTURE RACERS

- Far too many men think they will make good adventure racers and far too many women think they will NOT.
- "Women are in touch with their inner chicken, so they make more intuitive learners."

    Jackie Phelan, former professional mountain biker.

- Any outdoor woman is well-trained in the use of "natural" toilet paper. A lifetime of "squatting" pays off. However, most males that I have raced with seem to find ways to justify the weight of at least one roll of toilet paper! In the Eco-Challenge in 1996, I had a teammate sacrifice a sock to the cause, all so that he didn't need to use a leaf or a rock!
- No matter what, I always seem to get my period during a big race. What could be more aggravating?! Women do deal with more.
- Breasts and hips—they aren't only adding shape to our appearances, but they are the natural fat storage areas that keep us going strong in endurance events.

- Women tend to blame themselves for their inadequacies. Men tend to blame someone else.
- It's important for women to be athletes first, and women second. I cringe at the question, "So what is it like being the only woman on the team?" as if it is yet another obstacle to overcome.
- If someone on a team drops out, chances are it is not the woman.
- Women can practice pain tolerance in adventure races for childbirth, and vice versa.
- Women have heart and drive. I've never heard of a group of testicular cancer-surviving men coming together to raise 2.3 millions dollars for cancer research by climbing the highest peak in the Americas!
- I'm a woman, and maybe I am a bit opinionated, but we need to start somewhere to get the word out—women are just as qualified to be excellent adventure racers as men are.
- Developing mental strength has little to do with the physical strength advantage men biologically have over women.

GREG VOGEL'S TIPS

1. Training: the race is more of a mental challenge than a physical one (I am an excellent example). Mentally prepare yourself to finish.

2. Navigation will be the most important discipline in the entire race. Do not take it for granted.

3. Eat and drink constantly during a race. Know what to eat and when.

4. Biking: a tip from Chris Scott: "I used duct tape to mount power gels within easy reach on my bike. It works great."

5. Weight: get rid of everything you don't need including excess straps on your pack.

TIPS FROM JIM HERTZ

1. Prepare, prepare, and prepare.

2. After preparing and anticipating everything you can think of, be prepared to throw your game plan away and improvise.

3. Good team dynamics are more important than athletic ability.

4. Start with a one-day race, when that gets easy, go to a two-day race, and only then take on a longer race.

5. Build endurance first, which can take years, through biking and running, then concentrate on skills such as climbing, horseback riding, etc.

6. Remember highs and lows are inevitable and both will pass.

7. Never quit, except when too injured to go on.

8. Never criticize or yell at a teammate, who is doing the best that they can do. Every team member will have some problems during a race and the other teammates should help, not hinder. If the teammate's best is not good enough for the others, the time to find that out is before the race.

JEREMY RODGER'S TIPS

1. Select teammates based on their contribution to team chemistry. If they are confrontational in a social setting, this trait will be magnified in a race setting.

2. Melt your bite valve with a match onto your hydration bladder line or carry an extra. It will fall off during the race if you remove it frequently for cleaning.

3. Carry heel and lace pads with skin lube for friction control. These work especially well in the groin and heel and can double as Chap Stick. Ask any sports medicine supplier for these.

4. Travel light. Buy a pack designed for running/adventure racing so that you don't fall victim to over packing. You would be amazed at what you don't really need.

5. Train or race with other teams if possible. The more you do, the more you realize what there is to know.

6. Carry some kind of real food even if it is only trail mix. Your digestive system can only handle a liquid/gel diet for so long. It relies on some solid foods to stimulate passage of its contents from start to finish.

7. Nutrition: a well-balanced diet is a more biologically processable (and cheaper) source of nutrients than "nutrition in a box or bar". Only use supplements as supplements. Protein bars work great if used immediately following a hard training session to preserve hard-earned muscle and rebuild damaged ligaments, but should not be used during a training session. Protein is an inefficient energy source when compared to more easily processed carbohydrates. Additionally, the human digestive system can only absorb and use two grams of protein per kilogram of body weight (approximately 140 grams for the average size adventure racer). Enough is enough and more is not better in the case of protein supplements. As a general rule, use complex carbs before training, simple and complex carbs in training, and carbs, protein, and fat sources immediately after training when your cell's nutrition channels are screaming for an energy source. If you wait an hour after training, the cells have already begun to metabolize muscle and glycogen stores to correct the energy deficit.

8. Cramps: the best way to avoid cramps is to consume a carb/electrolyte source before a well-planned, progressive training program. However, you are losing more water than electrolytes while training (hence causing uncontrollable muscle contraction), so it is best to consume plain cold water (not salt tablets) to return the extracellular balance of salt and water to normal. After the race, do the same thing —drink water first. You can apply ice to cramping muscles as ice minimizes the muscle's ability to contract by slowing down nerve's conduction rate.

9. Buy a Volkswagen bus to transport your team to the races. Even better, paint something personal on the side like a flag or cartoon character.

10. Race with Odyssey Adventure Racing.

MORE FROM DEB MOORE

Caffeine is different for everybody. Many of the sport gels have caffeine and that seems to be enough for me, but some racers carry chocolate-covered coffee beans or caffeine pills. Our crews try to have coffee or soda for us in the transition areas.

Views differ on the efficiency of cat naps. It beats falling asleep on your feet (or bike) but it is easy to expend a surprising amount of time stopping, and then getting going again, for so little sleep which doesn't give your muscles or feet much time to recover. Over a long race, it can lead to poor judgment and mistakes more costly in time than a nap would have been.

STRATEGY

TO SLEEP OR NOT TO SLEEP, THE CATCH 22 OF ADVENTURE RACING

BY IAN ADAMSON

When you sleep during an adventure race, you risk losing time to other teams not sleeping. If you don't sleep, you risk losing time through poor performance and bad decision-making. How much is enough, and when is the right time to sleep?

All too often I am confronted with people that prepare for adventure races by doing expedition-length training exercises, including extended periods without sleep. There is definitely some merit to experiencing sleep deprivation and knowing how your body reacts to ultra-endurance exercise. However, a great deal of care must be taken when doing so.

John Howard, winner of every major adventure race in the world, only races two or three long races a year, at the most. Granted, he is in his forties and claims to be "too old for this sort of thing," but he keeps winning regardless. The reality is he has a healthy regard for looking after his mind and body. Rather than beat himself into the ground with non-stop multi-day training sessions, he sticks to shorter races in between the long ones (nonstop multi-day). He knows from experience how to manage his sleep and his speed. Many argue that he has more experience than anyone to draw on (which in some respects is true), however, he says you don't need to go without sleep more than once to know how it feels. Similarly, you don't need to be hit over the head by a plank more than once to know how that feels!

There are also some myths about how much sleep the top teams get. Many published articles would lead you to believe that you need to go without sleep as long as possible to be in the top group of racers. Something to the contrary is true. There is a delicate balance between the amount of sleep taken and the time to get through a course. Fine-tuning, and yes, that intangible thing called experience, is all-crucial here. Needless to say, most human bodies demonstrate a dramatic degradation in physical, mental, and emotional performance when less than two hours of sleep per day are averaged over several continuous days. There is no doubt that it is possible to operate under severe sleep deprivation, but the cost can be enormous.

The 1995 X-Games Eco-Challenge is a good example of this sleep versus performance conundrum. 'Twin Team', made up of elite, ultra runners, came in second with about three and a half hours of sleep over six days. 'Eco-Internet' squeaked in about an hour and a half later, on nearly seventeen hours sleep. Had each team known where the other was on the course, and how much sleep they were getting, the outcome would have been much different.

In the 1997 Eco-Challenge, the highly talented American team, 'SCAR', led the first half of the race, but did so on virtually no sleep. By the third day, they were quickly overtaken by the first, second, and third placed teams, each of which had accumulated about nine hours of sleep. Some of 'SCAR's team members were so tired that they were falling asleep on a jumar ascent and on their bicycles during the heat of the day. The amount of sleep actually increased with each placing in this race. Third place, 'Canterbury New Zealand', had eleven hours sleep, second place, 'Pure Energy Australia', managed fourteen hours, and first place 'Eco-Internet', had seventeen hours of sleep put away!

So what happens when we become sleep deprived? Most studies have shown that our cognitive thought processes progressively shut down, followed by other non-essential functions (non-essential to life that is), including memory loss and hallucinations, and finally death. Luckily we literally fall asleep before the death part, although large numbers of brain cells are irrecoverably destroyed long before this happens. For reasons as yet unknown, sleep is needed in humans to allow brain maintenance and regeneration. Without it, we start to lose cells by the millions (literally)—it becomes difficult to make rational decisions and logic evades us. Physically, we lose coordination and the ability to perform tasks of strength or aerobic power.

The trick with adventure racing is to get enough sleep so that we can perform safely and effectively, but not so much that we lose time to those who are sleeping less. It is a classic "stealing from Peter to feed Paul" scenario. As there are no scientific studies that can tell us how much to sleep, observation and experience are our best guide. If you look at the most successful teams in the Eco-Challenge races, 'Eco-Internet' (2x first places, 1x third) and 'Pure Energy Australia' (1x first, 1x second, 1x fifth), they generally manage to get at least two to three hours per night—every night. If you look back at the rankings for each checkpoint in Eco-Challenge Australia, you will observe that both 'Eco-Internet' and 'Pure Energy' were as far back as 25th in the first few days, but moved steadily up through the rankings as the rest of the field slowed down. You will also note that the speed through each leg did not diminish for these two teams, instead they actually moved faster in the final run leg than in the first run leg!

Another trick used by the top teams is to avoid sleeping at checkpoints and transition areas. Many teams use these areas to refuel, change gear and sleep, but catching sleep with other teams, officials, and press milling about can be difficult or impossible. You will also note that many of the stage times are won by lower ranked teams, simply because they race through a stage and then sleep at the transitions. It was a surprise to many athletes that 'Pure Energy' didn't "win" any of the paddling legs, but then it is probably also a surprise that they got almost half their sleep during these stages!

There are some sound tactical times and places to sleep. Obviously, it is easier to sleep at night since this is the natural biorhythmic time, and navigation is more difficult in the dark than in the light. Earlier is often better than later since it can get very cold in the early hours, even in the tropics, as people found in Australia. One all-important determinate, though, is how tired you are. Obviously, you don't want to bed down because you think you should; you should hit the hay when you really need to. Being extremely tired, but not too tired (experience, experience), will bring sleep on very quickly and efficiently, making the time you are stopped most effective.

How long to sleep is another area of debate. Veterans of RAAM (Ride Across America) swear by a solid four hours each night to optimize performance. There is a wealth of experience here, but they are also operating at a higher physical threshold, made possible by continuous support and no need to navigate or make intelligent decisions. Some teams seem to operate reasonably well on no sleep for about two days, then small doses of ten minutes to two hours whenever needed. 'Hewlett-Packard' leapfrogged 'Eco-Internet' in Eco-Challenge British Columbia for the first few days by not sleeping, while 'Eco-Internet' slept several times for a total of five hours and still managed to put time on them. By day four (of six for 'Eco-Internet'), they got a full nine hours sleep at a dark zone and still maintained a lead, eventually winning by almost a full day.

There are numerous tactical reasons not to sleep; however, if the navigation is mindless or there is a window of opportunity (i.e. it is getting dark and you need to get through a difficult section or make a dark zone), then obviously you should push the envelope. Other conditions may make it possible for some people to sleep and others to move everyone forward. Paddling often provides this opportunity. A raft or a two or more person canoe/kayak allows at least one person to sleep and the team to keep moving. Some Kiwi athletes have actually learned to walk while asleep, although this is a skill that has lead teams to some bad mistakes. Team 'Southern Traverse' blew a substantial lead in Eco-Challenge Utah by walking for six hours in the wrong direction, the entire team being asleep for a large part of this not-so-scenic detour.

In the end, the decisions of the team to sleep or not will be dictated by navigation, tactics, common sense, and each individual's alertness. Each combination of individuals and each different set of circumstances will create a unique situation. With experience, some good judgment, and a little thought, your team's decision to sleep or not should come easily. Quite often it is wise to sleep when you would rather not. In other cases, regardless of how tired you are, it may be dangerous or foolish to stop, or in the words of Winston Churchill, "If you find you are going through Hell, keep going."

TIPS FROM RICHARD J. CORCORAN

1. Learn from what's out there already. Talk to other adventure racing teams and subscribe to the Adventure Racing Association e-mail newsletter.

2. Practice how you'll race—the old sports cliche! Carry a light pack when you jog or bike, do workouts in the dark, wear your adventure racing gear during runs, and do an orienteering meet. Also, once in a while make sure your simulations involve sleep deprivation—it can be the toughest thing you'll face.

3. Morning or night: go with whatever generally works for you and your schedule, but try to occasionally work in both to get your body accustomed to performing at different times and to experience the dark, the cold, etc.

4. Stretching: don't forget post-workout stretching—your body will thank you!

5. Listen to your body: pain is of course part of adventure racing, but be smart. If it hurts, be careful. If it really hurts, see a doctor. And take occasional breaks, including a day off most weeks. You will actually perform better in the long run.

6. Milestones: adventure race training can be a grind. Schedule some kind of milestone every two to three months (probably a team training event) that will get you focused and test your fitness. It's impossible to train at a high intensity all year, but events and races will get you fired back up and tell you what you need to work on.

7. Schedule: coordinating a team is part of the sport. It will be a challenge to get everyone training individually and as a unit. Appoint one person as a training czar, and try to develop a master calendar. Get everyone to commit to some dates well in advance and stick to them. Also, be constantly checking up on each other's training—help and encourage each other, especially in their weaker area.

8. Don't fret: inevitably, something will happen to screw up your training. Do your best to stick to the schedule, but don't beat yourself up when unforeseen stuff happens. Shake it off and do your best. One thing we all like to do is always have a basic workout (be it a quick run, quick bike, quick lift) that takes you 30 minutes door to door! That way, if you get an urgent call that you have to be at a dinner in an hour, you can still get something useful done.

9. Pick a discipline to form your training base: in a typical week, there's usually a lot of biking and running. Most people have a favorite between the two, so pick one and make it your base discipline. Adventure racing demands a base level of fitness and it doesn't really matter how you get it, so long as you have a plan.

10. Don't forget skills: it's easy to let stuff like ascending and paddling slip. Make an effort to put these skills to work, and figure out ways to practice in weird places. My teammate, Ranch, has frequently paddled a kayak in a swimming pool, tethered to the side with a bungee cord. We also know of other racers who practice ascending out their apartment windows!

11. Diet: the great thing about adventure race training is that you can eat whatever you want! You'll be hungry all the time, so carry around semi-nutritious snacks with you such as fruit, granola bars, and bagels. Then eat basic stuff like lots of pasta, protein, and vegetables. Also ask your nutritionist for advice.

12. Team events: at the end of the day, this is a team sport, so spend as much time as possible training with your teammates, even if that means just jogging together. Try to do a joint workout weekly, and try to do a team event (skills work, race simulation, long workout) at least every two to three weeks. These events are invaluable—you'll learn about your teammates and tackle problems. And it should be fun!

WISDOM FROM STEVE BOZEMAN, DOUBLE IRONMAN WORLD RECORD HOLDER

1. Know what you are signing up to do and get prepared. Proper planning prevents poor performance.

2. Prepare yourself physically and (more importantly) mentally. Regardless of the length or type of race, it is likely that the mental aspect of the race will be more challenging than the physical. There is a very simple old saying, which holds true for all aspects of our lives, "Never give up and don't quit." I also like the new SEAL saying: "Overcome, improvise and adapt."

3. Have a back-up plan. When something goes wrong, the best-laid plans go out the window. We all have plan A in every race we get ready to do—we hope to feel great the whole way and not encounter any interference. WRONG! Something will happen, either caused by the participant, someone else, or good old Mother Nature. The bottom line of any race is that you want to finish no matter what. With that in mind, what is the longest time I can be out on the course and still finish as long as I keep moving?

4. Prepare for the elements. Not always, but sometimes, Mother Nature gets in the way of the finish line.

5. Take care of your feet. Once your feet go, you're in trouble. One of my weaknesses is I get blisters easily, but I have finished the Barkley, 100-milers,

and other races on very nasty blisters. However, the blisters took my mental focus away from the race. Every step I took was hell. And, it took forever for them to heal after the race.

6. Pick and choose your races. You can't do a bunch of "ultra races" and be strong in all of them. Pick the one that is most important to you and focus on that one. If you have to, use the other races for "training" and go easy in them.

7. Stay hydrated. You can go a long way without food, but water is very important.

8. Take salt. When it's hot and you've been sweating for hours (or days), the potassium balance in your system will get out of kilter and cramps will occur, even if you're hydrating.

9. Go slow at the start. The longer the race, the slower you should start and pace yourself.

10. Learn from your mistakes. After you have failed to finish in a race, accept the fact that you're human. But, find the "root cause" of what happened that prevented you from being a "finisher" and fix it. Finishing last is better than not finishing at all. If you don't finish, then you have to wait a whole year before you can try the same race again.

ROBERT NAGLE ON SLEEP

Be conservative early on. The race gets harder mentally and physically as it progresses.

SOME FINAL ADVICE

SLEEP MANAGEMENT

Adventure racing teams often try to continue non-stop for several days in long races, believing that while they move, they are putting distance between themselves and the other teams. This can amount to a lack of sleep management. The effects of sleep deprivation after several days is cumulative and can ultimately be detrimental to a team's progress. It is better to sleep early in a race and travel faster and with fewer mistakes than to continue until the team grinds to a halt. In Eco-Challenge '97, the top teams tended to get more sleep per night than the mid-pack teams. The top placed team, 'Eco-Internet', averaged better than three hours, with other less-experienced teams getting less than an hour.

RACE FOOD

When considering food choices for a multi-day race, it is important to consider several factors. Food should have high energy density (calories per ounce), be compact (ounce per volume), provide balanced nutrition and have variety. Sports bars are energy dense, compact and balanced, but do not provide variety. Try including savory foods like beef jerky, powdered potato and spices, and trail mix. Nutritional balance will help maintain the body's tissues, facilitate repair, and allow optimal utilization of fuels. A balanced diet should include lots of fluid and lots of carbohydrates. Stored fat (and to a minor extent, dietary fat) is utilized for fuel in low-intensity aerobic activity, 40 to 60 percent of calories during an adventure race. When organizing food for a race, think diet, diversity, and density, and don't forget to test everything during training.

TRAINING FOR ULTRA ENDURANCE

A common mistake when training for ultra endurance is to train too long, too often. So how do you train for a 300-mile race without actually going the distance? There are two tricks to this: specificity and periodization. Specificity means train each individual discipline to a level that is equivalent to that which will be seen in the race. Adventure races rarely contain any single leg over about 50 miles—so this is a good distance to train for. Train up to being comfortable with paddling, running, biking (technical mountain biking) and horseback riding 50 miles each and you should be prepared for a 300 mile race. Periodization is a technique that involves cycles of build and recovery, typically four weeks long. Three consecutive weeks are used to increase distance, speed, and strength, and the fourth week is a recovery week. A typical periodized run over several cycles might be 20 miles, 25, 30, 22 (recovery), 25, 30, 35, 27 (recovery), 30, 35, etc.

WHEN TO STOP OR NOT TO STOP DURING AN ADVENTURE RACE

Top adventure racing teams stop only to sleep—period. Stopping for any other reason is a waste of valuable time. Stopping for a nap should be done efficiently. Eating, gear organization, and chatting can be done on the move before and after the snooze. Activities that require an individual to stop, such as foot care and certain bodily functions, can be done without the team being held up. If you need to go and can't do it on the go, then run ahead, do your stuff, and catch up afterwards. Foot care should be a team effort. One person should help with the feet and the remaining members should take their gear so they can run ahead and catch up quickly. Routine chores like eating and changing clothes should all be done on the move. The team's momentum should never be compromised. A five-minute rest every hour doesn't sound like much, but over ten days it adds twenty hours!

LIGHTENING THE LOAD

One of the most effective speed tricks you can do with racing equipment is to make it light. If you are a gear freak, this is a positive joy; otherwise, it is a pain in the butt. Nevertheless, it is something that can make a huge difference over several hundred miles. To start, forget the idea of carrying a sleeping bag, tent, stove or sleeping mat, unless it is mandatory. This saves approximately six to eight pounds, which may make the difference between walking and running. Once you have eliminated the luxury items, it is time to start paring down everything else. Buckles, labels, and personal items (like extra toothbrushes) can be eliminated. Climbing gear should be tailor-made and its weight can generally be halved by using spectra slings instead of daisy chains, and etrier, chest ascenders, instead of Jumars and simple harnesses. Use your imagination and try weighing the gear you discard—you might be surprised!

STRATEGY

FOOD IS FUEL

Chapter Ten

Transition areas provide opportune moments for refueling.

To effectively perform in an adventure race, it is paramount to fuel your body properly. Consequently, it is advantageous to develop a basic understanding of what happens to your food upon ingestion.

Nutrition is the foundation of human performance. Proper nutrition is crucial for optimal function. To successfully complete an adventure race, you must feed the body often with a variety of calorically dense foods. Think energy! You encounter great diversity when you are on a race course. Your entire being is challenged. And it takes a lot of energy to face those challenges. With a general understanding of nutrition for energy and the importance nutrition plays in your performance, you can help yourself get to the finish line with greater ease.

HUMAN METABOLISM

Food is fuel. Once it passes our lips, it performs many functions. The three macronutrients—carbohydrates, fats, and proteins—are of primary importance for adventure racing and give us energy to move about. Additionally, we need protein and minerals to build and repair tissue. The third primary function of nutrients is the regulation of many mechanisms, which occurs with the help of vitamins, minerals, and proteins. For our purposes, we will focus on body energy, or human metabolism.

ATP

We cannot directly use the food we eat for energy. It must go through a series of processes to be converted into a form that we can use for mechanical work. That form is called adenosine triphosphate (ATP).

Our body is a factory, which produces energy for work. Scrambling over rocks, climbing a steep incline on your mountain bike, or paddling a calm river is work. To perform our best, we must be efficient with the energy we put out.

High-intensity activity demands quick metabolism of energy (through the ATP-PC system). Once immediate stores of ATP are utilized, glycogen (broken-down carbohydrates which reside in the muscles) is anabolized to create ATP through a process called glycolysis.

Oxygen plays a key role in the fate of muscle glycogen. If oxygen is abundant during "aerobic" activity, enormous amounts of ATP are available for continuous energy (aerobic glycolysis). If oxygen is not available in anaerobic bouts, fewer ATP is produced and fatigue rapidly occurs.

As we compete, the body's energy systems interact to provide the necessary energy for work. The predominant source of your energy is determined by the intensity of your efforts. Most of the time, during an adventure race, you will be advancing thanks to your aerobic (oxygen) system.

THE THREE MACRONUTRIENTS

CARBOHYDRATES

Carbohydrates play four important roles in relation to energy metabolism and exercise performance.

PRIMARY ENERGY SOURCE

Carbohydrates are the primary energy source for the body. The breakdown of this macronutrient powers muscle contraction. Once it is absorbed by the small intestine, it is converted to glucose and used for work. If excess is present, it is stored in the liver and muscles as glycogen. When these stores are fully utilized, additional fuel is stored as potential energy tucked away under the skin as subcutaneous fat and also between the muscles.

Because of the limited capacity for storage of immediate energy, glycogen stores are rapidly depleted during exercise. The body's energy systems work synergistically to provide a steady flow of fuel for work. In endurance events, the body calls upon all energy reserves for work. Once immediate stores of fuel in the muscles and liver are wiped out, glucose is converted from body fat and is shuffled to the working muscles through the blood. In extreme endurance events such as adventure racing, adequate amounts of carbohydrates must continually be ingested to sustain the limited stores in the body.

PROTEIN SPARING

When the body lacks sufficient amounts of carbohydrates, it metabolizes protein for energy. However, protein is used primarily for tissue synthesis and repair.

This alternative is not nearly as efficient in energy production. When protein is metabolized for energy, it robs lean muscle mass, and it disturbs the predominant role that protein plays in the body.

METABOLIC PRIMER

If insufficient carbohydrates are taken in, fat metabolism also suffers. The body needs carbohydrates to appropriately metabolize fat. If carbohydrates are sparse, the body ends up mobilizing more fat than it can metabolize because carbohydrates are not present. The breakdown of fatty acid is dependent upon certain levels of carbohydrates. When lipid metabolism is the primary energy provider, muscular power is only about half compared to a normal, desired situation where carbohydrate metabolism is predominant.

The depletion of muscle glycogen causes localized muscular fatigue during activity. In addition, when carbohydrates are not plentiful, fatty acids transferred from fat stores cannot perform their proper role in energy fat metabolism and as a consequence, an increase in concentration of extracellular fluids occurs. Ketone bodies are formed creating an undesirable environment in the body. The result is a build up of acidity in bodily fluids, called acidosis, or ketosis.

FUEL FOR THE NERVOUS SYSTEM

The brain also thrives on adequate carbohydrate intake. If levels fall below normal amounts, consciousness is affected, and eventually, brain damage may occur. This is not desirable for performance or our health.

ENERGY AND EXERCISE

Initially, glycogen stores readily available in the muscles provide the fuel for exercise when we begin movement. Additional liver and muscle glycogen consequently provide up to half of our energy as we continue to perform. Lipids and a small amount of protein metabolism provide the other 50 percent. The percentage of energy substrates will vary depending on the intensity of the exercise. If the intensity is high, carbohydrates dominate. The lower the intensity, the more fat is utilized for energy.

Beyond twenty minutes of exercise, glycogen stores are reduced, and blood glucose reigns as the major fuel supplier. Lipid breakdown also contributes to a great amount of energy we use during prolonged exercise. Inevitably, blood glucose levels drop, creating a hypoglycemic state if exercise is continued. Lipid levels increase and protein contributes a higher percentage of energy. In this carbohydrate-depleted state, the capacity of work is dramatically reduced.

If you continue exercising beyond the place where liver and muscle glycogen levels severely drop, fatigue sets in. This is when we "bonk", or "hit the wall". This phenomenon is fairly common in adventure racing, because of the high intensity and long duration of

activity coupled with the great necessity to refuel on a constant basis.

The bottom line is to feed your body plenty of carbohydrates and wash them down with plenty of water during training, and particularly during a race. A diet rich in carbohydrates will maintain liver and muscle glycogen stores, allowing for adequate supplies of energy.

CARBOHYDRATE PROFILE

Carbohydrates earn their name from the atoms that comprise them: carbon, hydrogen, and oxygen. There are three forms of this macronutrient: monosaccharides, oligosaccharides, and polysaccharides. They are classified according to the number of simple sugars bound together in the molecule.

Each gram of carbohydrate is equal to four calories. A nutritionally sound body can store an estimated 375 to 475 total grams. Most of this glycogen is stored in the muscles, about one-fourth in the liver, and a mere five percent is available in the blood. This equates to 1500 to 2000 stored calories of carbohydrate, enough to fuel a twenty-mile run. Through carbohydrate loading, however, an athlete is able to almost double normal storage capacity and enhance endurance performance tolerance. The important point to remember is fatigue is directly related to low levels of muscle glycogen stores.

DAILY NEEDS OF CARBOHYDRATES

Sufficient carbohydrate intake is essential to maintain glycogen reserves for optimal performance in training and competition of endurance activities. As a general rule under average daily activities, we should ingest 10 grams of carbohydrates for every kilogram of body weight. Hence, a 150-pound athlete requires approximately 680g of carbohydrates (2727 calories) each day and a 200-pound person would require approximately 910g of carbohydrates (3636 calories).

During intense training, a steady depletion of carbohydrate stores occurs. In order to satisfy the body's requirement of glycogen synthesis during heavy training, researchers recommend 70 percent of daily caloric intake come from carbohydrates. In some cases of expedition-style adventure races, even 80 percent may be necessary. Moderate training demands a caloric equivalent of 50 to 60 percent carbohydrates in the diet. And, just as important during training, it is crucial to replenish stores after heavy exercise. After lengthy intense training, muscle glycogen stores need almost an entire day to recover to pre-exercise levels.

GLYCEMIC INDEX

Important to athletic performance is the rate at which carbohydrates are digested and absorbed by the body. The glycemic index rates carbohydrates according to the rapidity at which they are digested and converted to glucose—the basic, most functional form of carbohydrates.

Glucose, the purest form of carbohydrates, is rated 100 as having the highest and fastest absorption rate. This value creates a standard upon which all other carbohydrates are compared. High glycemic foods such as candy, white bread, potatoes, white rice, raisins, and carrots enter the blood stream very rapidly after ingestion.

Post workout meals and nutrients ingested during racing with higher glycemic ratings will be utilized by the body quite quickly. The accompanying effects of this form of feeding are the potential for blood sugar levels to catapult into a hyperglycemic state. To bring the body back into balance, large doses of insulin flow into the blood levels to dip into hypoglycemia. This situation can wreck havoc on your energy levels. Fat, on the other hand, has a very low glycemic index which, when combined with other nutrients, can slow the digestive process and regulate energy levels. The downside to this theory occurs in high-intensity exercise when ingestion of high-fat foods can cause gastric distress.

Ideally, in an ultra-long endurance race, where exercise intensities are lower, foods with moderate glycemic indexes like pasta, whole grain bread, and oranges are easier to digest and will sustain energy levels. This is due to the lower rate of energy expenditure over a longer period of time.

LIPIDS

Lipids, or fats, provide an enormous supply of "potential" energy, and protect vital organs through cushioning and insulation from the cold. Lipids also carry the largest amount of energy per gram. One gram of fat is equal to nine calories, over twice that of carbohydrates at four calories and protein at close to five calories. Lipids are also easy to transport and store and are readily metabolized.

Depending on our percentage of body fat, we have great amounts of stored energy, which enhance our energy output in endurance races. If we functioned purely on carbohydrates, we would rarely cross the fin-ish line if it were further than twenty miles. On the other hand, fat reserves can take us five times further.

During moderate exercise, energy is obtained fairly equally from lipids and carbohydrates. Once carbohydrates are depleted (typically after an hour or so of exercise), fat metabolism provides a greater percentage of energy. In exercise lasting over two hours, the oxidation of fat provides more than eighty percent of the energy used to sustain work. In prolonged periods of endurance activity such as an adventure race, fatty acids become the main source of energy

SATURATED VERSUS UNSATURATED FAT

The majority of dietary fat (more than 95 percent) comes from triglycerides. These "neutral fats" as they are known, are comprised of fatty acids and glycerol. Fatty acids can be further identified as saturated, where its chemical structure is filled or "saturated" with hydrogen atoms, or "unsaturated" meaning several bonds in its structure are open and able to absorb additional hydrogen.

Saturated fats are typically solid at room temperature. This type of fat can be found in animal products such as beef, pork, egg yolks, butter, and cheese. Plants contribute to this category in the form of coconut oil, and processed foods also contain large amounts of saturated fats. Unsaturated fats have a tendency to become liquid at room temperature. They can be found in plant sources, such as olive oil, sunflower oil, and corn oil.

LIPIDS AND PERFORMANCE

During a race, limit your fat intake during the day to maximize carbohydrate consumption. This practice will encourage greater energy as digestion and absorption of carbs is quicker than with fats. At night, when travel is slower, increase your fat intake. Your body will be able to digest this macronutrient easier and will also welcome the much-needed extra calories.

RDA OF FAT

The amount of fat you consume while racing should be a factor of experimentation. Every body is different. Focus on unsaturated fats to compliment your other foods. If you are taking in 70 to 80 percent of your total calories in the form of carbohydrates, that leaves 20 to 30 percent for fats and proteins.

If you are severely restricting your fat intake, there is one source in this department to pay attention to. It is integral to a healthy diet to consume about ten grams of linoleic acid each day. This essential polyunsaturated fatty acid provides important fat-soluble vitamins, which the body cannot produce on its own. Most foods contain some fat, so the intake of this fatty acid is usually not a worry. Even a vegetarian diet can provide sufficient levels of linoleic acid. Thirty grams of fat from sources such as nuts, beans, and oils will provide the minimum daily amount (ten grams) necessary for good health.

PROTEIN

The essential element, nitrogen, distinguishes protein from its other counterparts, carbohydrates and lipids. Together, nitrogen, carbon, hydrogen, and oxygen combine to form twenty different amino acids, which are then linked in various combinations to define the human body. Amino acids provide the major building blocks for the synthesis of tissue. The structural basis of our muscles and most of the enzymes in our muscles are made from protein.

The three major sources of body protein are blood plasma, visceral tissue, and muscle.

The primary function of dietary protein is to build up body tissues. However, protein can also be utilized for energy (although not desirable) in extreme situations. Under certain conditions, particularly during endurance events, some amino acids may be used for energy.

Steve Gurney knows good nutrition will propel you to championship status.

ESSENTIAL AND NONESSENTIAL AMINO ACIDS

Of the twenty amino acids, eight cannot be assembled in the human body. Consequently, these essential amino acids must be obtained purely from the foods we consume. Nonessential amino acids are synthesized from available sources in the body, which make up the rest of the amino acids we need for optimal health and performance.

In order for proper growth and function to occur, we need all twenty amino acids to be present in our body at the same time. Therefore, consumption of complete proteins, which contain all eight essential amino acids, is most advantageous. Conversely, an incomplete protein is of lower quality and less effective because it does not possess all eight essential amino acids.

We obtain protein from both plant and animal foods. The egg has been rated as the best source of complete protein because of the blend of essential amino acids. Fish and lean beef are rated as high-quality proteins, followed by milk, rice, and soybeans. The protein we obtain from animal sources provide our greatest supply while plant sources such as lentils, grains, and vegetables give us less of what we need. The most prudent means of meeting your nutritional needs in the protein department is to consume a variety of protein sources every day.

RDA OF PROTEIN

The amount of protein you need each day depends on your body weight. The more you weigh and the more muscle you carry, the more protein you need on a daily basis. To determine the appropriate level of intake under normal circumstances (moderate daily activity), use the following equation with the following value of protein:

Daily protein intake = body weight (kg) X .8g protein

For example, consider a 150-pound adult. First, to convert pounds to kilograms, divide total body weight in pounds by the constant value of 2.2 (1 kg = 2.2 lbs). Convert 150 pounds to kilograms by dividing by 2.2, which is equal to 68. Sixty-eight kilograms multiplied by .8 equals 54.5. So, the average daily requirement for a 150-pound adult is 54.5 grams of protein.

Approximate values:

* .8 g/kg—normal person to sustain normal tissue repair and growth.

* 1.5g/kg—endurance athlete to replace proteins lost during activity.

PROTEIN AND PERFORMANCE

Although protein takes a back seat to carbohydrate and fat intake during a race, don't ignore it when preparing your food for the course. Sandwiches made with roast beef and cheese or peanut butter and jelly are good choices. Consume larger amounts of trail mixes made with nuts at night. And if you are competing in an expedition-length race, obtain more protein in your meals at the transition areas, especially if you plan to nap after eating.

Ideally, seek the help and support of an experienced nutritionist in your area to create a sound dietary plan. It is important to remember that it may take some experimentation and adjustments to find a suitable regimen.

One of my favorite conversations with Angelika Castaneda (team 'Odyssey', Raid Gauloises, 1997) was when I said to her, "Angelika, please be sure you bring enough food for this race. We are going to be out there racing for eight to eleven days and I want to be sure you eat enough." Her reply in a thick Austrian accent was this: "Don, you do not need to worry about me. I do not need to eat much in a race this short. My body will eat from itself. I will not die on you, I will only feel like I am going to die."

At 52 years old, Angelika was one of the fittest and most competitive athletes I have ever had the pleasure of racing with.

— *Don*

THE COMPLETE GUIDE TO ADVENTURE RACING

ALL HUMANS ARE NOT CREATED EQUAL

Balance and moderation are two timeless concepts that govern everything we do in life and certainly apply to sports nutrition. Given all of the scientific information, RDAs, studies, and "expert advice", the ultimate eating plan can become downright confusing. It is best to learn as much as you can from multiple sources. Then experiment with the knowledge you accumulate so that you can determine what is right for your own body. Only you will know what truly works and what doesn't work.

Every one of us is unique in our own way. Therefore, everyone has different requirements to keep us functioning properly. Different genetic make-ups, varied lifestyle activities, training programs, fitness levels, and body mass ratios are important factors that make each one of us unique. In addition, the bio-availability of food, absorption levels, the interaction of nutrients once they make their way inside of us, and the effect of nutrition varies with every single one of us. We each have our own characteristics that make us unique. The shape of our eyes, nose, and mouth, the way that we walk and talk, and the nutrition we require for good health and optimum performance vary within each of us. Don't forget this when developing a nutritional program.

Experiment with a variety of foods, the ratio of carbohydrates to fats and proteins, and the timing of meals and snacks. Try using different foods for pre-race, post-race, and actual race time to determine what works best. Generally, for ultimate energy every day, strive to consume natural, wholesome foods such as fruits, vegetables, whole grains, beans, pasta, lean red meats, fish, poultry, and soy products. Use these foods as the foundation of your nutrition and then add your favorite indulgences, if you want more calories.

NUTRITION AND HYDRATION

FOOD SUGGESTIONS FOR AN ADVENTURE RACE

"It's not about cravings. It's about energy," are the reigning words that world-class adventure racers, Robert Nagle and Isaac Wilson, use when fueling their bodies for a race.

The food category is a fun one for many racers because an adventure race affords the luxury of some extra caloric indulgence. But don't let yourself get too out of hand in this regard. Your main priority is quality energy and high performance. You don't want to be crouched behind a rock vomiting junk food and consequently dragging your feet around the race course. You want to look forward to the food you have packed and feel good once it's in your belly.

FOOD TIPS

- Be cautious of perishable foods. Meats will be the first to spoil. Preserved foods will outlast you on the course.

- Choose foods you like and will get excited about eating. Think variety and nutrition.

- Don't get too carried away with junk food, particularly if you don't regularly eat it at home.

- Experiment with trail mix recipes. Start with GORP (good 'ol raisins and peanuts) and then create a blend with your favorite foods.

- Take along a bag of hard candy to keep your mouth moist and give you a tiny sugar boost.

- Gatorade mix and hydration powders supplemented with vitamins and minerals will keep your hydration and electrolyte levels in check. Use both on the course.

- Hot chocolate is a wonderful treat when it's cold outside.

- If you need caffeine, plan ahead with your source

and schedule—each person is different. If you just want a quick boost, chocolate covered espresso beans work wonders, but be weary—chocolate gets very messy in hot temperatures! If you are racing in a multi-day competition, let your support crew know (ahead of time) that you want coffee, tea, or hot chocolate when you arrive.

- Multi-vitamin mineral supplements are a good idea only if you take them on a regular basis. Don't decide to start supplementing during a race.

- Hydration packs are a handy lifesaver in various conditions. Keep a few packs handy.

- Every time you eat or drink, remind your team to do the same.

TRANSITION AREAS

Choose foods that are calorically dense (but not necessarily dense in weight) and preferably high in nutrition. Pack lots of carbohydrates, and consider variety. It is highly unlikely you will match your food consumption to the amount of energy you expend in a race. Your output will far surpass your input. When organizing food for a race, think diet, diversity, and density.

In an expedition-style race, the transition areas provide an opportunity to load up on calories. If temperatures are cold, hot meals such as soup, stew, oatmeal, or pasta and rice dishes hit the spot. If heat and humidity are prevalent, sandwiches, cold pasta salads, and fruit and granola are good bets.

If you plan on sleeping at a transition area, load up on calories right before slumber so your body can fully digest your meal.

FOOD SUGGESTIONS AND FEEDING FOR RACING

IN TRAINING: Ideal time to test foods you are considering for the race.

ONE WEEK BEFORE: Lots of carbohydrates and lots of water.

THE DAY OF: Calories, calories, and calories. Lots of water.

HOURS BEFORE: More calories and lots of water.

Pack variety! The following suggestions are tried and true:

- Energy bars
- Energy gels
- Trail mix
- Sunflower seeds
- Dried fruit
- Mixed nuts
- Turkey or Beef jerky
- Tuna
- Sardines
- Salami
- Sausage
- Pre-sliced lunch meat
- Crackers
- Cheese
- Bagels
- Pop Tarts
- Instant oatmeal
- Dried cereal
- Monster cookies
- Licorice
- Jelly beans
- Candy corn
- Cheese curls
- Fritos
- Pretzels
- Snickers
- Dehydrated camp foods
- Pringles
- Chex mix
- Soy nuts
- Ramen noodles
- Rice
- Pasta
- Soup mixes
- Cookies
- M&M's (any variation)
- Peanut butter
- Gummy candy
- Goldfish crackers

You need to train with the foods you are going to race with. It took me a number of races to find which foods best suited my stomach, gave me energy and did not lose their taste appeal. I like to eat one meal a day in a race. If it is a six to ten day race, I like a hot meal every other day. But whenever I am hiking, horseback riding, bike whacking, I try to snack continuously. I need to make a conscious effort to eat when I am cycling or paddling. Whenever forced to stop for a map study (at a checkpoint, repair stop, etc.), I will eat and remind my team to eat.

Personally, I don't like eating many sweets. My favorite race foods are Pringles, beef jerky, and hard candy (especially Jolly Ranchers, every flavor is delicious). I mix peanuts and Goldfish crackers together. It tastes great, provides me with carbohydrates and protein, and most importantly, I do not get tired of eating this snack over a period of days. The Jolly Ranchers taste incredible after hours of snacking on Goldfish crackers and peanuts. I keep these snacks in my butt pack, along with bag balm, Tums or Motrin, and a flashlight.

—Don

ENERGY UTILIZATION

The amount of energy you expend each hour is dependent upon several factors: your size, ratio of lean mass to fat mass, efficiency at each discipline (the better you are, the less calories you will expend), intensity (speed of work, weight of pack, and terrain), climate, and metabolism. Every single one of us is different.

The following values are estimates of energy utilization in endurance races of progressively longer distances:

1. Marathon: Approximately 2,600 to 5,000 calories.

2. 100-mile Ultra Run: Approximately 10,000 calories.

3. "A rough estimate from the Eco-Challenge British Columbia put the expenditure of the average finishing athlete at 60,000 calories, accounting for the distance (370 miles), elevation gains (60,000 feet), and pack weight (30 to 40 pounds)."— Ian Anderson

What can we learn from this? Munch away as often as possible!

There will be many times when you do not feel like eating. Use your better judgment. Or the consequences will slow you down and could take you out of the race altogether. Always have food handy. Whenever there is a need to stop, make sure you are organized. Keep easy to eat foods, like energy bars or string cheese, in a waist pack for easy access. Keep the main bag of your fuel at the top of your gear inside your pack. Tape power gels to your bike and trekking poles to rip off and ingest in an instant.

As a general rule, strive to average 100 calories per hour. If you are expending more energy, or have a larger body mass, increase your caloric consumption accordingly.

As with everything else in sports performance, experience is the almighty. Train with different foods. Experiment with your timing and volume of intake. Your first race will provide tremendous insight into your energy needs, and food likes and dislikes. Each race thereafter will alter your feeding methods.

Joy Marr, who raced in Ecuador with Team 'Odyssey' in '98 and was support for Team 'Odyssey' in South Africa in '97, always ensured that the team was well-fed and hydrated. It was amazing to race with Joy. Joy had our race meals broken down so that not only were the meals delicious, but they were well-balanced and rich in energy. While competing, in the time it took one of the guys to open a pre-packaged dehydrated meal, Joy would have a trail gourmet meal ready for us all. This food not only provided us with the much-needed energy, but it was great for our morale. Although Joy professed that she was not an athlete, she was the only member of Team 'Odyssey' who did not become sick or affected by the altitude, nor seemed at all phased by the ten-day event. I suppose the 22 years Joy spent as a white-water guide, and hiking and biking around the world, was a great foundation for a "non-athlete" to have in competing in the Raid.

— *Don*

HYDRATION

Hydrogen and oxygen blend in a 2:1 ratio to form a compound that is the single most important factor to your sports performance: water. Without a steady flow of water, our engines will choke and our wheels will stop spinning. Our body is approximately 85 percent water. One-quarter of our bones, three-quarters of our muscles and our brain, 82 percent of our blood, and 90 percent of our lungs are water.

The average adult needs at least 60 ounces of water a day to keep all physiological systems running smoothly. If he is active, he needs another quart. In extreme environments (heat and humidity), more water should be ingested, and physically demanding tasks require even more. A gallon a day (at the very least), in the case of a multi-day adventure race in jungle terrain, may be a minimal requirement.

There have been some situations where an individual has consumed too much water, causing hyperhydration. But, because of the high level of water requirements of this sport, it is an extremely low risk.

Water allows our physiological systems to function with ease. Almost all of our metabolic mechanisms require water for efficiency. When our supply is inadequate, alternate routes are created to compensate for the drought. Consequently, performance suffers because of the interruption of normal production.

When the body's water reservoir starts to go dry, three factors affect performance: overheating, disruption of chemical balance, and dehydration.

OVERHEATING

A product of exercise is metabolic heat. Under normal circumstances, our bodies handle this heat efficiently. To keep from overheating, blood flows to the surface of the skin to be cooled and our pores excrete fluids. The higher the intensity of exercise, the more blood flows to the surface, and less flows to the working muscles.

When the body heats up, core temperature skyrockets. In an attempt to stay cool, temperature regulation prevails over muscular function because the immobility of our muscles will not threaten our life the way an extreme rise in core temperature can.

CHEMICAL BALANCE DISRUPTION

Normal biochemistry is severely threatened if our body's core temperature rises only a few degrees. If our physical hub climbs past 105 degrees Fahrenheit, our life is in serious jeopardy. Temperatures above 104 degrees Fahrenheit greatly alter our physiological mechanisms. When caught in this situation, enormous volumes of blood are routed to the skin for cooling which deprives optimal blood pressure and cardiac output, and creates a suffocation of the muscles as they are deprived of oxygen.

DEHYDRATION

In average environmental conditions, we stay cool thanks to physiological mechanisms. When temperatures soar, and the air clings to your skin, staying cool becomes a great challenge.

In the heat and humidity, our blood vessels dilate and sweating increases. In an attempt to maintain an average body temperature of 98.6 degrees Fahrenheit, blood flows to the surface of the skin to be cooled. This is the body's way of cooling itself. However, as a consequence, less blood flows to and from the heart, which places greater demand on the cardiovascular system. As profuse sweating continues, dehydration may occur, causing further stress to our body.

THE PROVENANCE OF OUR EXISTENCE

The environment is inviting. It's comfortably warm and a shirt and shorts feel just right as you step outside. You commence your workout, and soon your heart and lungs are in sync with your feet. Physically, everything flows like clockwork, and your mind is at ease as your performance breeds confidence.

Then, out of nowhere, BOOM! Your attention is called to your wheels as if you just blew a tire. To add to the mishap, your energy gauge surpasses empty and you realize you are out of gas. Your brain begins to fog. Your concentration becomes hindered. Your muscles team up with your cardiovascular system as they go on strike, demanding relief before they will take you to your final destination.

You begin to stockpile excuses, questioning your fitness level, your large meal that you swear hasn't quite digested yet, and your attitude, hastily resigning to any factor that can be easily blamed.

You finally make it home, wind down, and go about your business accepting that this workout won't be up there with the "great ones".

That weekend, you head out for a long distance bike ride and your energy somehow has been sabotaged. The following Monday, your performance at work is sub par. You begin to wonder if you have a vitamin deficiency or maybe, you're coming down with a cold.

Or maybe, you could be dehydrated.

A tune-up with quarts and quarts of a compound made from two parts hydrogen and one part oxygen may be all you need to get back on track.

Water is prominent in our physical make-up and largely responsible for many metabolic functions. It is a vital constituent of every cell. It is a regulator, maintaining balance with electrolytes. Water serves as the principal channel of transportation, assisting energy production and by-product removal. It aids our senses, it protects vital tissues and, most predominantly, it regulates body temperature.

On any given day, our bodies need a regular supply of water. If we cripple our supply by ignoring its importance, we put our health in serious jeopardy.

We are finely tuned machines. When a deviation from normal function occurs, it is immediately detected and our systems jump to attention to fix the problem. Homeostasis, a balance of our internal environment, is our number one priority. Our internal structures depend on a constant balance for efficient function.

Dehydration is a result of the body attempting homeostasis during training or competition. When we become dehydrated, because of superfluous water losses from sweating, or lack of water intake, the concentration of our blood becomes denser. To offset this change in composition, water is drawn from our cells. Cells in the brain, called osmoreceptors, in turn react to the shift in our changed environment, and release a hormone called antidiuretic hormone (ADH). The ADH flows through our blood to the kidneys directing them to absorb more water and urinary function is greatly reduced.

Our survival mechanism is on full tilt. If large doses of water are not consumed, blood flow to the skin and muscles decreases, resulting in the inability to sweat efficiently. As a consequence, core temperature rises and the heart rate response goes up. Endurance suffers due to lack of hydration, which is necessary for efficient physiological function.

There is one simple solution: DRINK WATER! LOTS OF IT!

—Kara

DRINK OR DIE

In an adventure race, planning is everything. Before you begin, you plan your route, you strategize, and decide on a ration of food. Don't forget to plan your means of maintaining a steady water supply.

Locate rivers and lakes on your map and determine where you can refill your pack. To maintain adequate hydration, you should be sipping your water every fifteen minutes, striving to drink at a minimum fifteen ounces an hour. Drink water as often as possible, and sip a sports drink every fifteen to twenty minutes.

The size of your hydration pack will be based on how often you can replenish your supply and how much weight you are carrying in food and gear. The goal is to be as light as possible, but an adequate water supply is essential for your health and ultimate performance.

Strive to drink every 15 minutes while you race.

HYDRATION TIPS

- **When your urine is clear, you are hydrated.**

- **Place the tube of your bladder under your sleeve in cold weather so it doesn't freeze—it will be the first to freeze in cold weather.**

- **If you or a teammate becomes dehydrated, the entire team's performance can suffer greatly. To prevent this, do not let yourself become thirsty, do not let your lips get dry and force yourself to drink.**

- **Powdered sports drink supplementation also increases the palatability of most of the water you will find in the field. Lake water, even after it is filtered, is still lake water. The mucky taste is greatly reduced with a splash of lemon-lime Gatorade!**

TREATING YOUR WATER

When you are out in the middle of nowhere, you don't have the luxury of the modern day conveniences you typically enjoy at home—like water-treatment plants and plumbing! Therefore, you must be ready to treat the water you drink while you race. Any water you have to question the safety of should be treated. Most of the water you encounter will fall into this category.

The risk of getting sick and not finishing a race is not worth a hasty decision to play the odds and drink untreated water. More importantly, your health should be your first concern. Many illnesses are born from the seemingly pristine waters we encounter in a race.

Some of the more common problems include:

Giardiasis is the most popular waterborne illness characterized by diarrhea, vomiting, nausea, and abdominal cramps. It is spread through animal feces. Giardia is the name of the parasite responsible for this disease, which can be identified as a waterborne cyst for a portion of its life and can also be found in mammalian intestines. We get sick when the parasite attaches to our intestines.

Leptospirosis is a bacterial infection that arises if you come in contact with infected animal urine. Influenza-like symptoms occur, including fever, chills, headache, and muscular tenderness.

Shistosomiasis is spawned as parasites in snails or worms infuse your skin. Symptoms include itching, irritation of your urinary tract, asthma, and enlargement of the liver.

Dysentery is revealed by bloody or pus-filled diarrhea, and an infection in the colon. You can catch it by drinking water tainted by infected sewage.

Hookworms are a nasty means of weight loss. Parasitic larvae invade your body through drinking water or through the skin, which may cause anemia, fatigue, and possibly pneumonia.

To decrease your chances of falling prey to water born parasites or infections, treat all of your water. There are several easy methods:

Boiling water is very effective but very impractical during shorter races. If you are out for three or more days in an unsupported race, it may be necessary to carry a stove. Some experts advise letting your water boil at least five if not ten to fifteen minutes to assure victory over the microbes. If fuel is scarce, make sure your water comes to a roaring boil before declaring it safe. This is also a great time to fix soup, hot meals, and coffee, tea, or hot chocolate.

Assume all water is contaminated to avoid unwanted mishaps on the course.

Filters are effective in removing parasites and bacteria, but not viruses. It takes time to pump your water and the filter takes up considerable space in your pack, but you may find your water to be more tolerable with less "floaties". To sanitize your water, pump it through a hose into a purifying filter, which then sends it to another hose, expelling safe drinking water.

If you use a filter, take care in your method. After spending twenty minutes preparing your water, you won't be happy to find out the nose or intake/output hose has been contaminated. Not only will your "new" water be undrinkable, but your filter will be ruined.

Iodine tablets eliminate almost all of the harmful substances in water, but they take time. Most tablets require a twenty-minute waiting period to perform their magic. This method is very popular because the tablets take up as much space and weight as your ibuprofen. The only downside to this method is it doesn't take away any solids you may find in your water.

If you are in a situation where you have no means of formal treatment for your water, strain it with a T-shirt.

MONITOR YOUR INTAKE

The quickest way to fail a race is to ignore the importance of water consumption. How do you know if you are hydrated? Try not to get to the point where you are thirsty. By the time you are thirsty, you are dehydrated. Remember, two percent dehydration will impair your performance, but may not cause thirst.

In addition, pay attention to your urine. If you are well hydrated, you should urinate every three to four hours. Considering the amount of sweating you may be doing, this may be a hefty task because you lose water through your sweat.

While racing, monitor the color and consistency of your urine. Dark amber-colored urine is a sign of dehydration. If you notice even darker shades, myoglobin could be present in your urine, which requires medical attention. Strive for clear-colored urine at least once a day to confirm hydration.

MEDICAL ADVICE FOR ADVENTURE RACERS
FROM PARKER J. CROSS JR., M.D., ODYSSEY MEDICAL DOCTOR

A concern in extreme endurance events is balance of electrolytes. An athlete who loses large amounts of water and adequately replenishes his stores is still at risk. We lose water when we sweat, but also large amounts of sodium and to a lesser degree, potassium. Hyponatremia, a low sodium concentration in the blood has been a concern in endurance events lasting over four hours.

To prevent this situation during a race, which could cause confusion, coordination reduction, and possible seizures, be sure to take in salt. Many of the foods you will carry are high in sodium such as jerky, nuts, and chips. In addition, consume a sports drink such as Gatorade.

For the best results, drink plenty of water and supplement with a powdered sports drink in a ratio of 3:1. In other words, for every three packs of water you drink, consume a sports drink. If you are strong and have the room, you can carry two separate bladders as you race. One filled with water, the other with a sports drink.

NUTRITION AND HYDRATION

Chapter Eleven

The hours you accumulate in preparation for an adventure race are valuable. They will provide you with a solid foundation from which to compete. If you do your homework, your chances of crossing the finish line improve. The trick is to spend enough time within each fitness component in a variety of disciplines.

Adventure racing encompasses driving the entire being of an athlete—mind, body, and spirit—to the upper limits of existence. It is the ultimate in cross training. Physically, you vary your muscle access through the myriad of disciplines you must endure; your fluctuating speeds conjure different challenges, and the varied terrain imposes many demands on the body. Your mental abilities further the task of success in competition and your emotions play a large role in your efforts. Any way you define the sport, it encompasses variety!

TRAIN TO WIN

A viable adventure racing contestant has many years of sports and fitness experience, is no stranger to competition, possesses outdoor skills, has a great attitude, and strives to be challenged. He can adapt to new surroundings and isn't opposed to discomfort.

An adventure race will push limits above and beyond normal thresholds. Within each discipline, you can be assured that you will push harder and longer than you may have in the past. For this reason, it is an extreme endurance competition. There will be times when you feel like you have biked more than enough miles, just to discover you have twenty more to go—half of which encompasses a hill, a river crossing, and a section of bushwhacking. There will be moments when you will feel like you can't possibly take one more vertical step to conquer a steep climb. The more you can simulate these conditions in your training, the more you will be prepared, both physically and mentally, to meet the challenges of the race course.

Initially, when you first overload your system with an activity like running, your body experiences neuromuscular adaptations. The first two weeks of a new activity are predominantly devoted to establishing new neural pathways and biomechanical adaptations. Your mind and body assimilate the activity. Once you are familiar with the motion, then physiological changes occur. Sooner or later, depending on your initial fitness, you will experience progress.

The next stage of development depends on the degree of the next new overload. Run the same route every single day for a year, and you will become very efficient at running that specific route. However, if you change up your routine on a consistent basis, which is dictated by how quickly your body responds, you will

Significant overload must occur in training in order to prepare the body for the rigors of adventure racing.

consistently experience breakthroughs in your fitness to reach your desired goals.

To bring about a training response, the exercise overload must be significant to create challenge. In other words, the intensity of your activity should be high enough to elicit some sort of discomfort as your training stimulus exceeds normal levels. The resulting adaptations allow more efficient function. Because each of us is so different, we require different combinations of frequency, intensity, and time in our workouts. Therefore, specific attention should be given to each particular mode of exercise, to bring about specific results.

This follows the SAID. (specific adaptations to imposed demands) principle, which teaches us to place specific demands on the body to elicit specific adaptations. Simply put, if you want to be a good long distance runner—run long distances. If you want to be a good sprinter, practice sprinting. If you want to be a good adventure racer, simulate the demands of an adventure race as often as possible in your training.

Physiologically, if we apply a specific stress to our systems such as running long distances, we can become very good at running long distances. However, that does not mean we will automatically become efficient sprinters. Remember that specific exercise causes specific physiological adjustments, eliciting specific results.

To be specific in your training, create an overload that engages the specific muscles in a way that is unique to the activity. In addition, the activity should stress the cardiovascular system. Adaptations beyond a certain (general) level of aerobic fitness, occur specifically in the muscle used for a particular activity.

THE COMPLETE GUIDE TO ADVENTURE RACING

THE FOUNDATION

BUILDING AN AEROBIC BASE

Adventure racing activities vary tremendously in energy requirements. The long distances that are traveled dictate a continuous flow of energy over a long period of time. Most of the work that you perform is aerobic and fueled by your aerobic energy system. There will be times in a race, however, where you may be sprinting or exerting short bursts of high-intensity, which demand quick access to a large volume of energy.

Aerobic endurance is the body's ability to process and deliver oxygen to the working muscles with efficiency, in order to sustain rhythmical movement. As the heart pumps oxygen-rich blood through the arteries to the cells, energy is absorbed for work and waste products are extracted and carried away. If oxygen is abundantly available, we can carry on work for long periods of time (granted sufficient nourishment). Throughout each day, we all derive most of our energy from our aerobic system.

When the intensity of an activity becomes great enough that our breathing is severely challenged and our entire system is thrust into an upheaval, we obtain energy by quicker means to meet the demands of the activity.

Therefore, depending on the intensity of an action, energy is obtained through specific energy pathways. Brief explosions of activity, lasting five to six seconds, require immediate energy from intramuscular stores. As the exercise progresses, the intensity will drop slightly to allow a continuation of the activity, as energy is obtained from anaerobic pathways. If exercise persists beyond three to four minutes (average), the intensity drops further to the point where activity may continue indefinitely as oxygen is used for energy metabolism on a "pay as you go" basis.

In order to be efficient in each of the three energy systems, you must train each one specifically. But keep in mind, the body's energy systems work together. For the most part, you will race in an aerobic state, at a rate where you can obtain oxygen freely for energy.

As you become stronger, you will be able to exercise at a higher intensity without extreme exertion. Your "aerobic power" will improve. As your capacity continues to enlarge, your "anaerobic threshold" improves. This level of ability is the ceiling at which your body utilizes oxygen for energy and the point at which the working muscles accumulate overwhelming amounts of lactic acid. Beyond this point, energy is obtained through anaerobic metabolism and your muscles burn out very quickly. The higher your threshold, the higher your tolerance is for lactic acid accumulation in your muscles. The fitter you are, the harder you can work and still flush lactate from the working muscles. Hence, you will be able to accomplish more work because you will be able to work harder for longer periods of time.

"Racing hurts no matter if you go slow or fast. So do what you can to go fast."

THE NEXT LEVEL

Fortunately, we can manipulate our training to elicit a higher threshold. There are several methods of lactate threshold training: tempo training, fartlek training, and long intervals.

INTERVAL TRAINING

Interval training combines explosions of effort with recuperation time in a single workout. This work/recovery relationship allows you to train harder in time spurts because you slow down for periods of time.

Based on your normal workout, you pick up the pace for short bursts of time. Your intensity may vary, depending on the length of time you push yourself. If you are tempting your limits, your interval will be shorter. If your intensity is lower, your interval may be longer.

Then, when you reach momentary fatigue, you go back to the original tempo to recover, so you can perform another interval. This physical duet usually continues for at least three to five sets in one workout.

Interval training can be accomplished in any modality. Whether you are hiking, running, swimming, biking, skating, or paddling, you can be as spontaneous or structured as you want to be.

If you are impulsive by nature, parallel your personality in your training. When you feel like it, do an interval. As you go about your workout, pick two points along your route to begin and end your intervals. Your points could be trees, streetlights, the length of a pool, or numbers on your watch.

When you hit the first point, go hard. When you reach the second point, recover and take it easy. When you're ready for another one, pick two more points and go hard again. Recover, and continue until you feel fatigued.

If you require more structure in your program, you can design your intervals in precise time frames, so your time and intensity will be fixed.

For example, perform a set of four intervals at a 1:1 ratio in 60-second lapses. Because your duration of work is shorter, you can work harder. Using a watch, when the second hand reaches twelve, go hard. When it strikes twelve again, recover. When it reaches twelve again, go hard. Sixty seconds later take it easy. Repeat two to three more times.

For variety, try a 2:1 ratio, working twice as long as recovery, or 3:1, working three times as long as recovery. Or, reverse your work/rest efforts so that you rest two to three times longer than your work effort.

THE STUFF THAT MAKES A DIFFERENCE

Tempo training is the MVP of any racing program. It can make a champion out of you. But beware, it's not easy and it doesn't always feel good. The key word is tolerance, and anytime you have to push that concept, malaise occurs.

Once you have established a solid base of aerobic fitness (three to six months of consistent effort), you are ready to stir things up. To introduce yourself to tempo training, simply increase your effort in spontaneous intervals throughout your workout. You should be working hard enough that all of your focus is concentrated on the task at hand. Your muscles will feel like they are on the verge of an explosion. Your mind will try to convince the body to slow down, and your breathing will become labored. Initially, these intervals may only last for one to three minutes, and you may

only be able to do two to three per workout. As you progress, the intervals will get longer. Once three minutes feels manageable, increase the duration of your tempo intervals to four minutes, then to five, then eight, then ten, and then fifteen. Eventually, you will be able to train at a higher level of intensity throughout your session. Then you can start all over again and work toward even higher levels.

To assess your level of exertion, speak a short sentence out loud like: "I feel absolutely wonderful today." If you can say more than this sentence without taking in air, you are not working hard enough. Increase your speed. You should not be able to carry on a normal conversation because you will be breathing hard. However, you should be able to utter more than two syllables without gasping for air. This awareness of your breathing will give you a good idea of where you are in your aerobic zone. This method is quick and easy while training. You can also use a heart rate monitor to quickly calculate the performance of your heart while exercising.

FINE-TUNING

Training above your lactate threshold is extremely intense and uncomfortable. Include interval training in your program no more than twice a week. It is good to experience work in an anaerobic state. However, the majority of your training should be spent building strength and endurance.

LACTATE THRESHOLD AND VO₂ MAX

The two prized validations of athletic prowess are your lactate threshold and your VO$_2$ MAX—and there is a difference between the two. A high lactate threshold will allow you to maintain extended periods of powerful exertion while riding long, winding fire roads. It will provide opportunity to put distance between you and the rest of the pack.

Your VO$_2$ MAX represents the largest amount of oxygen your body can acquire at a maximal effort of work. VO$_2$ stands for volume of oxygen. An exceptional VO$_2$ MAX will enable you to blast over a hill and leave the other teams in your dust. Your value represents your aerobic capacity, or the efficiency of your body in the transformation of oxygen to energy. Lactate threshold embraces extended power and VO$_2$ MAX elicits powerful bursts of energy.

TRACK YOUR PROGRESS

Each week, establish a day in which you can assess your progress. For example, every Friday, schedule a time trial either on a track or a designated route that won't be interrupted. Choose your discipline and keep it constant. If you decide to cycle, ride as hard as you can through the route and time yourself. Record it immediately along with how you felt as you performed. As the weeks go by, you should get faster if you are sticking with your training program. This will also provide a psychological boost as the weeks go by and you get faster.

For the best results, keep a journal. You will be able

to see how and why you make improvements, or if you are not making good progress, you will easily identify the cause(s).You will be able to hold yourself accountable when you keep a journal and hopefully, your discipline will improve.

Include your periodization program and set monthly, weekly, and daily goals for yourself. Be realistic with your time and availability of terrain and modalities to work with. Each day, record the mode of exercise, the duration and intensity of the workout, and how you felt, including how much effort you put forth.

TRAINING

ENDURANCE

Adventure racing requires enormous endurance, which demands efficiency of both the heart and the vascular system. As endurance improves, the cardiovascular system acquires an acute ability to circulate vast quantities of blood. In addition, the muscle cells increase their ability to produce ATP (energy) aerobically. Their ability to excel hinges on their capacity to transfer energy aerobically.

In addition to VO_2 MAX, microscopic changes in the tissues affect performance. At the cellular level, mitochondria—the cell's "powerhouse"—increase in size and number and aerobic system enzymes proliferate. This microscopic metamorphosis allows us to generate more ATP through our aerobic system.

Our ability to use lipids and carbohydrates improves, muscle fibers increase their aerobic potential, and muscle fiber size may increase specific to each activity.

The most significant change occurs through the heart's ability to pump a greater volume of blood per beat as it becomes bigger and stronger. Consequently, the heart doesn't have to work as hard, and the number of times it beats per minute decreases, which places less strain on it. Increased cardiac output is a prominent factor between champion racers and well-trained racers.

When training, endurance is specific to the area of the body that does the work. For example, a cyclist will obtain a higher oxidative capacity of the lateral quadriceps (vastus lateralis), than an endurance runner because of a higher blood flow and higher power requirement from that specific body part. As a result, a cyclist is better equipped at generating ATP aerobically at the vastus lateralis than an endurance runner.

It is also important to consider individual differences when preparing and administering a training program. Each person adapts differently at varied rates. Our differences in adaptations are as distinct as the tones and inflections in our own voices!

F.I.T. PRINCIPAL

The formula that will elicit results is dependent upon three variables: frequency, intensity, and duration (time). *Frequency* refers to the number of training sessions you participate in each week. *Intensity* is the degree of effort you put into your workout. *Duration* measures the time you devote to each exercise session. The manipulation of these three factors will determine your results.

The *frequency* of your training is important when preparing for an adventure race. You have to log the miles through countless days of training. The duration of your race will influence the amount of time you will devote to training.

In your quest for higher fitness, however, don't overlook the importance of rest. Fitness gains occur while you are resting. Your systems repair themselves and become stronger for the next workout while you take a break from activity. Give yourself frequent rest days in your training program. A good practice is to pause from an aerobic workout once a week. This time-out is ideal for flexibility, stability, and balance training or to practice on a skill that needs extra attention.

Intensity reflects how hard you are working. For a proper training effect to occur, you must overload your cardiovascular system. There are several methods of measuring your intensity. The easiest and most practical gauge of intensity is the Borg Rating of Perceived Exertion Scale (RPE). Despite today's high-tech gadgets and scientific formulas for determining heart rates, eventually, it all boils down to how you feel. The

greater awareness you have of your performance and how it affects you, the more empowered you can become in your work output. You will be able to use your time most effectively, pushing when you can afford to push, and yielding when you need to take it easy.

The RPE scale correlates a subjective value to your exertion. Based on a scale of one to ten (the modified version), one equals rest, five equals a moderately difficult intensity, and ten corresponds to an extremely difficult rate of work. During your workouts, ask yourself how you feel in periodic intervals. Note the fluctuations of intensity.

Intensity is the key principal to catapult you from a plateau. Physical indications of higher intensity are faster heart rate, higher oxygen consumption (exercising just below the point of breathlessness), lactic acid build-up (a temporary burning sensation in the muscles), momentary muscular fatigue (forcing you to slow down), and point of tension—not pain.

The *time* or duration spent in each workout is mostly a factor of how much you can afford based on the other elements in your life. These elements will dictate how long race you can participate in because they will reveal how much time you have for your homework in preparation for the race.

Consider the following chart, which provides guidelines to the amount of time you should devote to your weekly training schedule based on the type of race you wish to compete in.

	Total Hours	Cycling	Running/Hiking	Paddling	Other
Sprint:	5 - 10	2 - 4	2 - 4	1 - 2	*
Weekend:	15 - 20	4 - 6	4 - 6	3 - 5	*
Expedition:	20+	5 - 7	5 - 7	4 - 6	*

*The "Other" category is subject to your personal skill development and time constraints.

STRENGTH

For movement to occur, the muscles must contract, or shorten. To do this, they must possess a certain amount of strength to overcome the inertia of the object of intention. For strength to be recognized, it must be exhibited through a range of motion.

Musculoskeletal strength is a crucial factor in your repertoire of fitness components. To become most effective in your sports performance, it is important to gain insight on the biomechanics of each discipline and then strive to replicate the movement in your strength-training program.

For example, to enhance your running, perform a standing hip extension on a resistant machine with your knee in a fixed flexed position. Your goal is to push your leg back through a contraction of the gluteus maximus and the hamstring with as much force as possible. This movement mirrors your running pattern, and with a continual increase in the load, you will find your running becomes more efficient.

Another example is a dip. There will be times during a race where you will have to hoist yourself up and over a natural object. In order to be successful, you must be able to manipulate your own body weight. The mechanics of a dip exercise are based on an upper body weight-bearing position where you are forced to move your body through your arms just as you would on a race course.

Push-ups, pull-ups, and step-ups should also become staple exercises in your strength-training routine as they parallel the challenges you will encounter on a race course. The better able you are to manipulate your own body weight, the better your chances of moving through the course with ease.

In order to improve the strength of skeletal muscles, they must be trained at a level close to their force-generating capacity. Specifically, the level of tension placed on the muscle is the determining factor when improving this fitness component. So, strive for momentary muscular failure (the point at which you cannot perform another repetition) in each set. See weight training periodization in this chapter for more details.

SPEED

"Work fast to be fast." If you expect to travel at a fast pace through a race course, you must practice traveling fast in all of the disciplines involved in a race. In addition, you must be able to "think fast to be fast." The coordination of your neuromuscular system determines the outcome of your speed. If you're not thinking fast, it will be impossible to work fast.

The quicker the central nervous system can process information, the faster you become. Jumping drills, commonly referred to as plyometrics, are a great tool for this. Add these exercises into your workouts on foot or in the gym.

Jump Squat—Stand with your feet a little wider than hip-width apart. Flex your knees and hips into a low squat position. Then, like a rubber band that has just been released, jump up as high as you can. Land back into the squat position as softly as possible. Repeat for eight to ten repetitions, performing three sets total.

Lateral Leap—Stand relaxed with your feet together. Push off your left side as you leap laterally to the right. Land with your right foot steady, then the left foot lands to complete the movement. Reverse the direction and leap with the left side lead. To make this exercise more difficult, reach up as you leap to the right and land in a one-legged squat (right leg) as you touch your left leg to the floor, crossing behind the right foot. Repeat to the other side. Perform eight to ten reps for three sets.

Scissors—Start in a lunge or split-legged position with the right foot forward. Flex the back knee to lower into a lunge then explode off the floor and extend as high as possible into the air. Land back in a lunge position with the left foot forward and repeat for three to ten reps (alternating leg leads) for a total of three sets.

POWER

SPEED AND STRENGTH

Adventure racing is about long-term work. Endurance is the almighty factor. However, in a race, power will get you to the top of a mountain, power will send you successfully ahead of the pack when you're neck-and-neck with other teams, and power preserves precious energy.

In technical terms, power is "the rate of performing work." Strength and speed are combined to produce a physical force. Time is the crucial factor when evaluating the magnitude of this force. Therefore, to develop power, push the harder gears on your bike at faster cadences, run hills as fast as you can, paddle in intermittent bouts of power strokes, and lift moderate weight loads at the gym at a faster rate (but always with control).

QUALITY OF MOVEMENT

We all have our own strategies for movement patterns. When a particular body segment is weak due to injury or lack of attention in training, we compensate for that weakness by detouring our biomechanical movements. As we deviate from a normal movement pattern, we lose efficiency and set ourselves up for further injury and neglect.

In an adventure race, function is crucial. Moreover, efficient function is most desired to get to the finish line the fastest while remaining intact. Complete functionality throughout the body will enhance your chances of getting through the course efficiently and also reduce your chance of injury in the wilderness. A weakness in spinal stability means reduced power, wasted energy, unnecessary movement, and more stress on the vertebral column. A strong core means greater cooperation of body segments, efficient performance, and less fatigue. Muscular tightness limits range of motion, affecting the extent of mobility. Limited mobility slows you down.

For a body segment to be functional, it must possess equal parts of mobility and stability. Then, effective movement is a question of balance between the two components. With proper balance, the body can consequently go on to accomplish fantastic physical feats.

Mobility is defined by an active range of motion. In other words, flexibility is needed to move efficiently with the help of stable body segments. Stability is more than strength as it allows the body to be firm in one segment while moving another with freedom of movement. The two components are interdependent. One cannot effectively exist without the other. If one component dominates the other, poor performance and injury may result.

Important sports skills such as speed, power, and agility are enhanced only when a balance of mobility and stability are present. Before the arms and legs can function properly, the core must get proper attention. The torso transfers power from one leg to the other when cycling, running, or hiking. It starts with good posture.

POSTURE

Your posture can make or break your performance. Practice good spinal alignment every minute of your athletic endeavors. Proper posture will encourage speed and strength and allow you to relax as you go. Excess muscular tension wastes valuable energy causing premature fatigue. It takes energy to hunch the shoulders and to "hold on" to unnecessary tension.

First, be aware of your body position and then develop a regular habit of awareness.

Ideal posture demonstrates a neutral position from the top of the head to the coccyx, the end of the spine. Focus on a slight retraction of the cervical vertebrae to keep the head over the rib cage, not drooping forward ahead of the body.

Allow your shoulders to relax and maintain space between them and your ears. As the stress of the activity increases and the hours increase, we tend to slouch, creating a flexed spine and sagging shoulders. Strive to avoid this position. It not only sabotages energy, but it

also makes you feel lousy and can lead to premature back and neck pain.

Lead with your chest without extending your spine. Imagine a string attached to your sternum. As you move forward, act as if someone is pulling you by that string, leading you by your chest. Don't let your spine extend; instead keep it neutral. Practice stability.

Finally, be aware of the natural inward curve of the lumbar spine and strive to keep your pelvis in neutral. An anterior pelvic tilt will lift the tailbone upward and create a perpetual shortening of the back extensors. This places undue stress on the lower back. Conversely, a posterior tilt rounds the back as the abdominals shorten and it becomes more difficult to take in optimal oxygen.

Quick and easy cues to remember are simply chest up, with shoulders back and down. Use these words as a constant mantra to keep your body in an efficient position for peak performance. It could be the edge you need over the other teams.

MENTAL FITNESS

Your mind has to become stronger than your body. Above everything else, that is what makes the difference in endurance races. When the body says NO, your mind has to say GO! This mentality is unhealthy for the body, but to get through these races, you have to find this power. After the race, you lick your wounds and recover.

Before you embark on a race, then, take some time to visualize your performance.

Negative imagery—Some racers visualize everything going wrong amidst the worst possible conditions. That way, when they get into the race and things aren't so bad, they have a stronger outlook and tend to perform better. This type of visualization can also help you to be better prepared when things actually do go wrong because you have already visualized it.

Positive affirmations—Start each race with a positive statement. Throughout the workout, use the statement or a few key words as a mantra to enhance your mental focus and engender physical victory. Whenever distracting thoughts enter your head, demolish them with your constructive ones.

Coach your body—Positive self-talk will take you further than you originally believed. "Let's go legs" and "I am powerful" are examples of motivational phrases that really work.

Think of a motivating song and play it in your head or sing it out loud.

Learn to *pay attention to breathing* for internal guidance. The process of breathing is controlled by the autonomic nervous system and controls important bodily functions. When faced with tough terrain, it is easy to get nervous and tense. Breath control can enhance your relaxation and hence, your performance.

THE ADVENTURE RACER'S WORKOUT

As we discussed earlier, the body is a great adapter. It will adjust to any demand placed on it. When we place positive stress on the body under specific training (physical conditioning) guidelines, it adapts to the challenges by getting stronger.

Subjecting the body to the same stimulus in a progressively challenging load will elicit a positive response. Over time, the system does not require as much effort as it did initially to produce the same amount of work. Hence, efficiency is established.

But, how do you adapt to a multi-day, ultra-endurance experience? How do you make the transition from general fitness training to adventure racer? Let's explore your options. Remember that there are hundreds of adventure racers out there who have alternative careers and families. They still find the time to train and are successful in a race.

Start logging miles, lots of miles. Increase the duration of your running workouts, up your cycling time, and paddle longer. Get in the gym and hit the weights—hard!

Get used to manipulating your own body weight. Perform push-ups, pull-ups, and dips as often as possible. Get outside and practice scrambling over rocks, hoisting your body up and over natural objects, and maneuvering through thick brush. The combination of gym strength and outdoor experience will give you a good edge when you get to your race.

Many racers isolate a discipline each day and then combine modalities on the weekends for longer workouts. It is also important to vary intensity and duration.

Rest is paramount. Fitness occurs in your downtime. Cells recuperate and increase their strength while you are resting. Don't risk overtraining. It will only sabotage your efforts.

How do you know if you are overtraining? You get injured easily, your motivation drops, your moods fluctuate.

Listen to your body. Pay attention to your internal cues. Your body will not lie to you, your mind will. Know when to push and when to yield. It's a nebulous line that will only become clear through time. Keep a log. You can go over your workouts and get a true account of what you have done. You will know if you are doing too much or too little and can make necessary adjustments.

SUICIDE THE HARD WAY

After competing in the Hawaii Ironman in 1980, I was intent on racing an Ultraman (3.1-mile swim/156-mile bike/ 32-mile run). I was one of the first athletes to compete in an Ironman distance event and back then, there were no specific guidelines to follow, so my training was all trial and error. To get in shape for this race, I trained three times its distance each week. Within each seven-day period, I swam 15 miles, biked over 450 miles, ran 150 miles, and since I was with the SEAL Team, I was required to do the SEAL training 5-7 days a week. I trained morning, noon, and night, and went from a strong 175 pounds to a sickly 138 pounds.

After months of intense training my ankles began to swell, my back hurt, I lost my appetite, I couldn't sleep at night, and I constantly felt sick. But I was stubborn and extremely driven to train three times the distance of the Ultraman each week. This behavior went on for months until finally, my skin started to take on a green tinge and I started sweating during my twenty-mile runs, which was uncommon for me as I didn't usually sweat when I ran long, slow distance workouts.

One night I went to take a bath but I had trouble standing and walking, so I crawled to the tub and eventually passed out. My wife took me to the emergency room where all kinds of troubles were revealed. When asked to lift my head for a spinal X-ray, I couldn't do it. My vertebrate in my neck and back were compressed causing a restrictive range of motion. They found marks, made from the shoe lace holes in my running shoes, on my very swollen feet and ankles. The blood tests discovered that my liver and kidneys were on the verge of shutting down. My left rotator cuff was torn and my left quadriceps was torn. There was severe planta fascia in both feet. My body was literally eating itself for energy. I came very close to killing myself by over-training. The overall diagnosis written in my medical report by the Sports Medicine physician on duty was: "The worse case of overuse syndrome I have ever seen." After all of that hard work training (30-35 hours a week), I wound up hospitalized and went from one of the fastest runners and cyclists in the area to a bed ridden, frustrated, very sick athlete.

When training, there is a line. And, what you want to do is try to come up and touch that line. Every once in a while, go past it to see what it feels like so you know where it is. Get close, then back off. Get close, then back off. You will never get strong until you push that line. But don't forget to practice balance.

—*Don*

PERIODIZATION

Periodization is the breaking down of a training year. The idea behind this concept is to split a time period into specific phases to manifest peak performance without the negative consequences of overtraining. Years are split into specific time periods, which are further broken down into weekly cycles in which training variables are manipulated. As competition gets closer, training volume decreases as intensity increases.

There are four phases involved in periodization:

Preparation phase is defined by high-volume, low intensity training.

First transition phase entails moderate effort in both volume and intensity. This period encompasses the pre-season.

Competition phase emphasizes low-volume, high-intensity training specific to the modalities of competition. This is "peak" time.

Second transition phase/recuperation period involves low-intensity recreational activities of various modalities. It is a time for recovery.

When designing your program, work backward from your competition. This practice will put things into perspective and paint a clearer picture of what you have to do to prepare for your race. Once you have a general layout of your workouts, you can plug them into cycles.

A macro-cycle spans an entire year of training. It provides an overview of your goals and reveals the various phases of your workout program. A meso-cycle represents a specific phase of your plan. Each meso-cycle is a preparation for the following one and typically lasts one to three months. Every week, you experience a micro-cycle, which is determined by your meso-cycle. Your performance progression is fine-tuned through specific workouts and carefully planned rest days.

ADVENTURE RACING PERIODIZATION

OFF-SEASON

GOALS

1. Recovery.
2. Injury prevention and rehabilitation.
3. Functional training—time for balance of strengths and weaknesses throughout muscular system and fitness components.

GENERAL FITNESS

AEROBIC/ANAEROBIC

1. Maintain aerobic base.
2. Minimize high-impact activity.

STRENGTH/FLEXIBILITY

1. Increase strength of opposing muscle groups to enhance body symmetry and performance.
2. Include yoga or active flexibility training.
3. Perform strength conditioning for all of the major muscle groups using light weights and high reps. *See strength-training chart for recommended exercises.

SPORTS-SPECIFIC

1. Fine-tune skills and techniques.
2. Reestablish goals and fitness levels.
3. Attend an adventure racing school.

OTHER

1. Get involved in other sports for cross training and diversity.
2. Revel in your days off!

PREPARATORY PHASE

GOALS

1. Prepare for the intensity of competition.
2. Get reacquainted with base line fitness.

GENERAL FITNESS

AEROBIC/ANAEROBIC

1. Increase the frequency of aerobic exercise from three to five times a week.

2. Incorporate intervals of long duration rest periods (i.e. 1:4 work/recovery bouts).

3. Focus on running, hiking or stair climbing (where there are no mountains), biking, and paddling.

STRENGTH/FLEXIBILITY

1. Moderate intensity training. Begin with three sets of each exercise at twelve to fifteen repetitions each. Work toward four or five sets at eight to ten reps.

2. Train to fatigue in each set.

3. As time in the gym progresses, higher rep workouts will enhance power/endurance, and lower rep workouts will enhance strength.

4. Maintain functional training.

SPORTS-SPECIFIC

1. Practice fundamentals of each discipline:

   • Ascending technique.

   • Paddle strokes (i.e. fine-tune steering ability).

   • Advanced biking techniques.

   • Hone new skills for upcoming race if it involves disciplines in which you are unfamiliar (horseback riding, scuba diving, swimming, and in-line skating).

PRE-SEASON

GOALS

1. Set-up for physiological peak during competition phase.

2. Overall conditioning becomes more specific.

GENERAL FITNESS

AEROBIC/ANAEROBIC

1. Improve lactate threshold and aerobic power.

2. Incorporate regular tempo workouts into your weekly program.

3. Aerobic ability becomes specific to length, duration, and terrain of competition.

STRENGTH/FLEXIBILITY

1. Incorporate compound weight-bearing exercises (pull-ups, push-ups, dips, lunges, and squats) performing three to five sets at three-quarter strength capacity, three to four times a week. Focus on explosive movement to train for power.

2. Include plyometric exercises emphasizing form first.

3. One to two weeks before a race, taper down to allow for complete recovery.

SPORTS-SPECIFIC

1. Fine-tune balance, agility, and stability.

2. Polish and perfect specific skills.

3. Sessions should be short, intense, and quality oriented.

4. Do not overtrain.

5. Emphasize nutritional habits, drink plenty of water, and get adequate rest.

RACE SEASON

GOALS

1. Priority number one—to peak at race time!

2. Maintenance of fitness.

GENERAL FITNESS

1. Competition provides training effect.

2. Maintenance workouts when recovered from race.

   * Run, bike, paddle to maintain cardiovascular fitness.

   * Circuit train two days a week for strength and endurance maintenance.

3. Emphasize rest and recovery.

4. Stay focused and enjoy the fitness you have worked so hard to achieve!

If you participate in adventure races throughout the entire year, choose the most important one to you

(which will probably be the one that is furthest from your home, hence requiring investments of varying degrees) to represent the peak of your periodization. Although adventure races are held throughout the year across the globe, competition time is usually in the warmer months of your home country.

WEIGHT TRAINING PERIODIZATION

As discussed earlier, periodization involves altering training variables and regularly changing a workout plan to continue gaining results. It is particularly effective in a weight-training program. Muscle development is a much more complex process than most people think. It is not simply the breakdown of muscle followed by a recovery period and a growth period, like we have all heard for so many years. Muscles do need to be stimulated for growth and strength gain. However, if they are stimulated in the same manner, the same exact way over a period of time, the growth and strength increases will slow down and eventually stop all together. An example of this would be the athlete who goes into the weight room, does three sets of eight to twelve repetitions on a 60 lb curl bar and moves on to the next exercise—and does this every workout. This type of exercise would be beneficial for a while, and that person would initially notice improvements in size and strength, but eventually that same workout would only be beneficial as a maintenance workout.

For training to be effective, you need to alter the training variables. Muscles need to be stimulated by a variety of angles to be strengthened. No one exercise can reach all of the fibers in any one muscle. With this in mind, you will need to create a set of exercises that affects each muscle differently. An example would be exercise for biceps development: you can do chin-ups, dumbbell curls, seated curls, standing curls, curls on a weight machine, one-arm curls, two-arm curls, use a straight bar, use the curl bar, or do negatives. There are so many different exercises that can be done for any one muscle group.

Training intensities also need to be varied and should be done on a weekly basis. Plan changes to your workout schedule. Change the frequency of workouts, number of repetitions, and the amounts of weight you use for each repetition. Make changes in the amount of rest you take between sets. For example, alternate fifteen to twelve second breaks between sets with three to five minute breaks. Shorter breaks are better for your aerobic training, and longer breaks are better for your strength training.

Periodization in weight training is done in phases. Phase one is the activation phase, which lasts for four weeks. During this phase, you will plan your routines and become familiar with the various exercises, how much weight is ideal, and how many reps you should be starting with. Record your weights, repetitions, and rest periods. This record will be very useful to compare what works and what doesn't work for you. Some of the more serious athletes will record their heart rates, the amount of calories they have consumed, their body weight, and the amount of rest they had the night before. It is recommended to begin phase one even if you already are in a weightlifting routine. Do not do anything heavy for the first two weeks. Prepare your muscles and tendons for the stress that you are about to place on them in the upcoming months. The worse thing you can do in this phase is to pile on a lot of weight, use bad form to get the weight up, then pull a tendon, ligament, or muscle while doing so. Those who lift as much as possible, using whatever form it takes, are thought of as ego-builders and not strength builders. The best thing you could do in this phase is to pick a weight that you can comfortably do eight to fifteen times.

Phase two, which should last four to seven weeks, is the strength development phase. This should be done two days a week as a circuit weight training routine.

EXAMPLE—PHASE TWO

Week	Set One	Set Two	Set Three	Set Four
1	50%* x 12**	70% x 8	70% x 8	80% x 6
2	50% x 12	70% x 8	70% x 4	80% x 6

*   **Percentage of maximum amount of weight you can lift.**
** **Repetitions**

Phase three is the muscular endurance phase. It should last between eight to twelve weeks. Doing sets with many reps is the best way to convert strength to applied or functional strength, required for some sports, jobs, and strenuous activities. In this phase, reps are more important than weight.

EXAMPLE—PHASE THREE

Week	Set One	Set Two
1	30-50% x 20	30-50% x 20
5	30-50% x 45	30-50% x 45
10	30-50% x 50	30-50% x 50

Increase each set by five to ten reps each workout, keeping the weight load 30 to 50 percent of the maximum on every set.

The importance of good form when lifting weights cannot be over-emphasized. This has to be standard to effectively achieve maximum benefits and to prevent injury. Do the lift as a controlled and slow movement. Do not jerk the weight up, or use muscles from different parts of the body to lift it. Weights should be lifted in one to two seconds and let down in two to four seconds.

After completing the three phases, reevaluate your workout goals and return to phases two and three to reach a higher level of strength and endurance. An effective periodization plan will take time and effort to establish, but the benefits will be apparent within a matter of weeks. When done correctly, you will be very impressed with your results.

WHERE TO BEGIN

Now, the enigma of adventure racing, "How in the world do you train for such a competition?" Honing your skills, improving your fitness in each discipline, and looking cool while doing each one isn't a small task, especially if you have a family and a full-time job outside of the adventure racing world. Start with the weekends and plan some long training sessions. For example:

- Incorporate two to three hours of ascending and descending.
- Spend two to three hours paddling on a lake or down a river—depending on which environment you will be racing, or if you will encounter both, practice paddling on the water in which you need more experience.
- Hike or trail run two to three hours.
- Go for a long bike ride that tackles a variety of terrain.
- Practice night riding and night navigation through some forested areas and also spend some time on foot for several hours.

During the week, peak twice in your cardio workouts. For example:

Monday	Run	1 hour	— Aerobic zone
Tuesday	Cycle	1 hour	— I.T.
Wednesday	Run	2 hours	— Aerobic zone
Thursday	Cycle	2 –3 hrs	— Aerobic zone
Friday	Run	1 hour	— Tempo workout
Saturday	Half-day or full-day outing		

- Sunday break from cardio and concentrate on flexibility, stability, and balance training, OR a half-day outing performing different skills than practiced on Saturday and rest on Monday.
- Does not include skills, training, or strength training.

SAMPLE STRENGTH TRAINING SCHEDULE

#	DISCIPLINE UPPER BODY	WEIGHTS (TO FAILURE)	SETS/REPETITIONS
1	DUMBBELL BENT OVER ROW	INCREASING EACH SET	15-12-10
2	DUMBBELL BENT OVER ROW	INCREASING EACH SET	15-12-10
3	WIDE GRIP LATERAL PULL DOWN	INCREASING EACH SET	15-12-10
4	DUMBBELL SHOULDER PRESS	INCREASING EACH SET	15-12-10
5	BAR DIP OR TRICEPS EXTENSION	INCREASING EACH SET	15-12-10
6	CRUNCHES	INCREASING EACH SET	25-20-10

#	DISCIPLINE LOWER BODY	WEIGHTS (TO FAILURE)	SETS/REPETITIONS
1	LEG CURL	INCREASING EACH SET	15-12-10
2	LEG EXTENSION	INCREASING EACH SET	15-12-10
3	LEG PRESSES	INCREASING EACH SET	15-12-10
4	LUNGE	INCREASING EACH SET	15-12-10

1. Warm up with a five to ten minute run at medium intensity, or until a light sweat.

2. Do one set of each discipline in order without rest, (i.e. one set discipline #1, then one set discipline #2, then one set discipline #3, etc.).

3. Repeat the cycle, increasing the weight and decreasing the repetitions for all disciplines.

4. Complete three continuous cycles so that all sets and all repetitions are completed continuously.

5. An additional cycle of eight repetitions may be included for a higher level of strength.

6. Upper and lower body may be done in separate cycles or on alternate days.

7. Cool down with a five to ten minute run starting at medium intensity and decreasing to a walk.

8. Stretch as necessary.

9. Always allow one day of rest between weight workouts for the same cycle.

10. RHR: Refuel, Hydrate, and Repair (carbohydrate, water, complete protein) within twenty minutes of exercise.

SAMPLE WEEK OF AN ADVENTURE TRAINING SCHEDULE

DAY	TIME	DISCIPLINE	COMMENTS	TIME (MINUTES)
MONDAY	AM	RUN	DISTANCE	120
	NOON			
	PM	WEIGHTS	STRENGTH-ENDURANCE	30
TUESDAY	AM	PADDLE/SKI	INTERVALS	60
	NOON	RUN	STAIRS	30
	PM	SWIM	MASTERS SWIM	90
WEDNESDAY	AM	RUN	TRACK	60
	NOON	BIKE	THRESHOLD	90
	PM	WEIGHTS	STRENGTH-ENDURANCE	30
THURSDAY	NOON	RUN	STAIRS	60
	PM	PADDLE/SKI	THRESHOLD	60
FRIDAY	PM	SWIM	MASTERS SWIM	90
SATURDAY	AM	RUN	THRESHOLD	60
	NOON	BIKE	SPIN	90
	PM	WEIGHTS	STRENGTH-ENDURANCE	30
SUNDAY	AM	SWIM	MASTERS SWIM	90
	NOON	BIKE	LSD	120
	PM	BIKE AND RUN	LONG DISTANCE	120-140
TOTALS		SWIM		270
		BIKE		300
		RUN		360
		PADDLE/SKI		300
		STREND		90
		SPEED		255 (20%)
		STRENGTH		150 (10%)
		ENDURANCE		915 (70%)
GRAND TOTAL				1320

HOMESICK WORKOUT BLUES GOT YOU DOWN?

PHYSICAL FITNESS

Are extensive travel periods preventing you from keeping an adequate exercise routine and eating correctly? If so, I may have some tips that can help you.

1. Commit to a lifestyle of personal fitness. Make a goal to work out at least three to five times a week. Decide on your own personal definition of the term "workout", and what your own personal minimum requirements of that workout are. Now, the hard part—keep this promise to yourself. When you get up in the morning, you know that you will have to brush your teeth, eat, go to work, and now you must work out.

   I made a personal goal in 1977 to work out everyday of the year. I did not miss a day. Occasionally my workouts would only consist of 50 sit-ups before the end of the day, but the exercises met my definition of a workout. I had such great success with this plan that I decided to do it every year until I reach the age of 60. It has been close to 22 years now without a day off. I credit my longevity and training/racing success in the ultra/extreme sports world to this plan.

2. Decide what your fitness goals are. Do you want to be in good all around (strength/endurance) shape or would you prefer to get really strong and cut? Maybe size and appearance are not so important to you and you really want to be in the best shape for a specific sport. In either case, you will first need to pick a direction and focus your workouts in that direction.

3. Shape your plan into a time/space module that will best work for you. You should plan to do your workouts during the times you do not have work, family, or other commitments. Most people work out best before the start of a busy day, others do best at the end of a long day. A good workout may be used as a way for you to wind down from the day. You may end up having to squeeze in a half hour routine and having it take the place of watching TV or idle/non-productive time.

4. Document your workouts in a day planner or on your wall calendar. At the end of each day, you should be writing something down that you did for exercise. I list every exercise I do and at the end of the week, I have a weekly summary. It may look like this: "Nautilus/free weights x2, running 40 miles, cycling 175, and paddling three hours." A bad week may only include: weights x1 and running six miles. I often find that a few times a week, I simply write the word "minimal". This means that I did my minimal requirements. It may not be much, but it keeps me committed to my goal. How many times have you heard buddies tell you, "After this deployment, I am really going to get in shape," or something to this effect? How many times have you seen these same people actually get into or stay in shape? This plan has to be a lifestyle change and a commitment that takes place before, during, and after deployments. It is all part of one long plan that will benefit you for the rest of your life.

5. Go to full-muscular failure. You will make the most of your time working out if you can take yourself to full-muscular failure. Occasionally push yourself to your physical limits while at the same time staying careful not to injure your tendons, ligaments, or muscles. Too many people run just to run, or lift just because they know it's good exercise. But the truth is, you gain minimal results with minimal effort and you gain serious results with serious effort. A full-muscular failure routine can often take as much as 72 hours to recover from. Perhaps you can do your full-muscular failure workouts prior to travel and during the periods of travel when you have access to the proper facilities and space.

6. Make the best of the space you have available to work out. If all-around general fitness is what you want, you should not have any problem finding a place to exercise. I have done many a workout on flight decks of ships, on decks of small patrol boats, in the confines of a tent, and in the cargo compartments of C-130s. Finding a place to work out is not a problem with the proper mind-set. An all-around fitness routine would include a wide multitude of exercises, such as anaerobic, aerobic, or isometric activities that can be accomplished virtually anywhere. If it's size and strength you're after, things become a bit more complex, but never impossible. If you cannot get to a gym, travel and deploy with a pair of push-up handles and a good strength-building calisthenics and isometrics plan. Plan your workouts so you train hard at the gym and plan your recovery and stretch/calisthenics routine during the "away from the gym" periods. If you are a distance athlete or are training for a specific sport, you will have to basically do the same plan as those going after strength and size. Run, bike, swim and train for your specific sports whenever time allows. When you do not have the facilities or space required to do your routine, plan your recovery phase and stretch/calisthenics routine while deployed. Again, it's all in your ability to follow through with your goal and to plan ahead.

There were two occasions in the past twenty years where I almost missed my workout. Once I was in a vehicle for a 40-hour, non-stop ride. Before the first 24-hour period ended, I persuaded the driver to pull over and I exercised on the side of the road for 30 minutes. The other time I was on a flight to Australia and the 24-hour period was quickly approaching, so I did my routine in the cargo space of the aircraft. I have eighteen years to go before this commitment is filled and I know I will always find a means and the space to work out.

7. Make a commitment to eat healthy foods. You will generally have two choices. You can choose to eat healthy foods or you can choose to eat unhealthy foods. Deployment and travel often are synonymous with galley food and/or junk food. The only thing worse than not finding the time or space to workout is to compound the situation by eating bad food. I am not insinuating that galley food is bad food, but sometimes there may be better alternatives. Try to stay away from foods with high amounts of saturated fat. The foods I have listed are good substitutes for junk food since they are low in saturated fat and are high in essential vitamins and minerals. I am not advocating that you completely stay away from junk food, I am just suggesting that you be more aware of what you eat and try to eat foods from the list below.

Almonds	Skim milk
Avocado	Pasta with sauce
Bagels	Brown rice
Bananas	Salmon
Wheat bread	Tomato soup
Broccoli	Sunflower seeds
Carrots	Potatoes
Chicken	Tofu
Citrus fruits	Turkey
Corn	Walnuts
English muffin	Wheat germ
Fish	Yogurt
Dried fruit	

An active adult should consume approximately 2,500 calories a day with no more than 25 percent of those calories coming from fat.

I wish you lots of luck with this plan. I have had many friends adopt the plan, and those who stayed with it have really benefited from it.

—*Don*

TRAINING TO IMPROVE EACH DISCIPLINE

TREKKING

- Get on the hills. Run them as often as possible.
- If hills are not easily accessible, perform sets of stair climbing in a stadium or tall building.

  Try these drills:
  Run up single-steps.
  Run up double-steps.
  Walk down single-steps.
  Walk down steps two to three at a time.
  Move up and down in lateral steps.
  Hop up on one leg (pause between each jump to assure footing and form).
  Jump up with both legs (pause between each jump).

- The Stairmaster Step Mill (the revolving stairs) is also a great tool to prepare for the elevation gains of adventure races.
- Work the legs in the gym. The strength you accumulate through pumping iron will keep you strong on your feet for longer periods in a race.
- Practice yoga for better balance, stability, and flexibility.
- Log the time on your feet. Alternate running with hiking and power walking.
- Practice step-ups and step-downs on a step platform which is four to ten inches high. To step up and down, keep your weight evenly balanced and your spine in a neutral position. When going up, shift most of your weight forward before transferring your back foot forward. When going down, keep your weight on your back foot until you are about three-quarters of the way into the motion.
- Once you achieve good form with the preceding exercises, add your pack and practice maneuvering with the extra weight.

COASTEERING

- Practice running in sand and water.
- Hone your rock scrambling skills.
- Incorporate bounding drills into your running workouts. To do this, try to explode off the ground (look for soft surfaces to practice on) and raise your knees high with each stride. This will exaggerate your running technique.
- Include knee raises in your program to strengthen your torso and hip flexors. Use a Roman chair or hang from a bar and raise your knees to your chest. Hold for a moment, lower your legs, and then repeat. Perform ten to twenty repetitions. To focus specifically on running, alternate bringing your knees into your chest.
- Lunges are a good exercise to increase lower body strength and flexibility, which will enhance running.

CYCLING

- Banish the "dead spot" (the six o'clock position of the revolution) of your pedal strokes.
- Strive for a perfect "spinning" motion.
- Focus on lifting your knees toward your chest or your handlebars.
- Keep your upper body stable as your lower body churns the cranks.
- Practice on rollers to teach effective spinning technique.
- Take some spinning classes.
- Time in the saddle is time in the saddle. To become most comfortable on your mountain bike, ride it—frequently.
- Leg presses, squats, and lunges will enhance your leg power and leg curls will increase your efficiency by balancing the muscle groups in your legs.
- Stretch. Pay particular attention to your adductors, IT band, and your external rotators. They are your stabilizers, which will serve you well if treated properly.

- A strong upper body only makes things easier on the ups and downs which are abundant on the trails.

- A strong torso transfers power more efficiently from the upper to lower body and from the right side to the left.

- If you cannot get to the mountains, drag a car tire three feet behind your bike to simulate the same physical challenges that steep terrain creates.

PADDLING

- Upper body strength is paramount to paddling longevity. Include dumbbell rows, pullovers, shoulder presses, chest presses, and torso rotations in your weekly regime.

- Don't forget the little guys—strengthen your rotator cuff, forearms, and hands.

- Lower body flexibility (particularly the hamstrings) is advantageous for long bouts on the water.

- A stronger torso means more paddle power.

- Work on your balance to stay upright while on the water.

ASCENDING AND DESCENDING

- Your lower body is supposed to do the majority of the work. But couple some strong legs with a powerful upper body, and you will get to the top faster and easier.

- Practice pull-ups for the torso and upper body, and leg presses and squats for the lower body.

- Agility and coordination come in handy when on the ropes. While dance classes and basketball games will improve these qualities, your best bet is to spend time in the harness.

INDOOR WORKOUTS

Ideally, the majority of your training should be done outdoors as this is the place where you will be racing. However, there are several possibilities when considering supplemental workouts inside. Thanks to indoor tracks, stationary racing bikes, bike rollers, indoor climbing walls, pools, and strength training equipment, you can put together challenging workouts that will compliment your adventure racing program.

If you live in a relatively flat city or don't have unlimited access to mountains, you can simulate steep inclines in your gym, on a treadmill, or a stair-climber. You can also take advantage of stairs in tall buildings or stadiums.

BE KIND TO YOUR BODY AND IT WILL BE KIND TO YOU

The countless hours of exertion the body endures takes its toll on internal structures. During training, we prepare the body to withstand heavy physical and mental distress. While we become stronger, it is also important to include flexibility and stability exercises. In addition, a balanced body will last longer on an adventure racing course than one that is overdeveloped in some areas and underdeveloped in others.

It is particularly wise to pay attention to the spine. Throughout a race, your body sinks into a forward-flexed position. The effects of stress, gravity, and fatigue unite and influence a rounded spinal position. In your pre-race workouts, seek a yoga studio or a yoga teacher in a health club or even a videotape for guidance to keep your muscles in good working order.

Seek stretches to loosen the hip joint, which takes a beating during a race. Also look for poses that counterbalance the stresses endured by the spine and promote better posture. Furthermore, be sure to stretch all major muscle groups, which provides temporary relief and relaxation in the bustle of exertion.

Periodic "time-outs" may be just the thing you need to keep going as Isaac Wilson demonstrates at the hands of teammate Patricia Storey (on Support Crew).

Adventure racing can be a high-risk sport. You are out there doing extreme things in remote locations for days on end. Accidents, illnesses and overuse injuries will happen when you push yourself to the limit. Oftentimes, it is the team that avoids or best handles these problems that wins the race.

HOMEOSTASIS

The premiere goal of our biological being is to establish, maintain, and protect equilibrium. Our complex systems cooperate to create a normal state under any circumstance to which we submit ourselves. In an adventure racing situation, our bodies must work a little harder to maintain this balance.

TOO MUCH HEAT

Our body temperature (specifically the core) maintains a dynamic balance between heat gain and heat loss in order to function properly. Body heat is created through our metabolic rate, muscular contractions, digestion, hormonal activity, changes in posture, and through the environment. Conversely, heat is lost through four methods: radiation, conduction, convection, and evaporation.

Equilibrium is established through the integration of vascular adjustments that shunt blood from the periphery to the core in cold temperatures and blood diversion from the core to the outer layers in hot weather. During prolonged intense exercise, the metabolic rate can elevate up to 20-25 levels above the resting state. In theory, core temperature can rise 1 degree Celsius or 1.8 degrees Fahrenheit every 5-7 minutes. Fortunately, this heat is regulated primarily through evaporation under ideal conditions.

Radiation occurs through absorption of heat. For this reason, we can be relatively warm on a cold day if the sun is out. And we can stay cool in the shade on a hot day.

Conduction is possible through direct contact. Heat is transferred through gas, liquids, or solids by means of molecular collision. For example, when on a hike in hot temperatures, relief can be obtained by laying down on a cool rock. Through conduction, the rock will absorb body heat. Water is also a great conductor. This explains the innate desire to jump in a lake to "cool off" in hot temperatures.

Convection is dependent upon airflow. This concept illustrates the difference between the amount of heat generated in an indoor studio cycling class compared to a bike ride outside. Inside, you are on a stationary cycle so you don't go anywhere, hence, convection is next to nothing. As a result, you can overheat very easily. Thankfully, fans are used to combat this situation. Conversely, air movement is increased as you move through space which is why you stay cooler on a ride outdoors.

Evaporation is our body's main line of defense against overheating. Sweating and respiration are the premiere channels that facilitate water vaporization. As body heat increases, our sweat glands secrete a salty solution that is evaporated upon reaching the skin's surface. As the skin cools, the increased volume of blood that is channeled to the surface is also cooled.

In extreme ambient temperatures, evaporation is the most effective means of cooling the body. However, when the amount of water in the air increases, the effectiveness of evaporation diminishes. For evaporation to flourish, maximum skin exposure is necessary, airflow is high, and humidity is low. The body's state of hydration also affects your ability to stay cool. This factor is easier to control: stay hydrated—stay cool.

Your clothing also plays a large role in the degree of your body temperature. Dry clothing keeps you warmer. Wet clothing facilitates heat loss. Cottons and linens soak up moisture. Technological advances in apparel today make exercise more comfortable as moisture is "wicked" from the skin, enhancing body heat or the ability to keep cool, depending on the environment.

TOO MUCH COLD

A constriction of the peripheral vascular system redirects blood to the core and limits the flow to the extremities. As a result, skin and limb temperature drops. Extremely cold temperatures promote life-threatening situations.

Muscular activity contributes a significant amount of heat. Shivering, which occurs when the core temperature drops, keeps the body warm and increases oxygen uptake. However, exercise is the best defense in extreme cold. Keep moving to stay warm!

In extremely hot temperatures, race faster in the morning and at night, and slow down during the day.

HEAT ILLNESSES

Thirst, fatigue, and visual impairment are direct signs of heat stress. If they are not recognized and treated, serious consequences can occur.

Heat cramps are characterized by muscular spasms beyond your control. They are usually a result of intense exercise and are localized specific to your activity. Dehydration is the main culprit. As hydration levels drop and electrolytes become imbalanced, painful muscular spasms result. Drink lots of water and don't forget to include your salt.

Heat exhaustion occurs as the effects of dehydration are compounded. This illness is identified by a faint, rapid pulse, a drop in blood pressure while upright, headache, and a dizzy, weak feeling. A slight decrease in sweating may also occur. If you think you are suffering from heat exhaustion, stop your activity, seek a cool area, and intravenous fluids should be administered.

Heat stroke is a serious illness, which should be treated immediately. At this stage, thermoregulation ceases. Sweating stops and the skin becomes arid and hot, body temperature skyrockets to dangerous levels, and the circulatory system is aggravated and placed in jeopardy of collapsing.

Fast medical attention is imperative. The first priority is to try to lower the core temperature. Apply ice packs, use alcohol rubs, and immerse the entire body in cold, even icy, water. The longer and hotter a victim remains, the higher the chances of not surviving are.

MEDICAL ADVICE FOR ADVENTURE RACERS
BY GEORGE WORTLEY, MD., TEAM 'ODYSSEY' DOCTOR

GENERAL ADVICE

1. You are ultimately responsible for your own well being. Take care of yourself. Do not expect race management to rescue you from any and all predicaments. Adventure racing is about making good decisions and being self-sufficient. What you choose to eat and drink, the clothes and gear you use, and the tactical decisions you make in the race will decide your well being.

2. Your body needs fluids and fuel to move forward. All too often racers forget to eat and drink in the heat of competition. Your car will not go if it is out of gas or if the radiator is dry and neither will you. Unfortunately, thirst and hunger can be unreliable indicators of adequate hydration and nutrition. Two percent dehydration will impair performance, but not necessarily produce thirst. Drink before you are thirsty and eat before you are hungry to maximize performance.

3. Listen to your body. Dealing with a problem early on can prevent a bigger problem later.

4. Bring a small first-aid kit for your team and know how to use it. Be sure to bring any long-term medication you may be taking for conditions such as asthma, diabetes or high blood pressure. The best book I have seen on treatment of injuries and illnesses that you might encounter in a remote area is *Field Guide to Wilderness Medicine*, by Paul S. Auerbach.

COLD ILLNESSES

Hypothermia is recognized by a drop in core body temperature below 95 degrees Fahrenheit. In hypothermic cases, the body is unable to warm itself after prolonged exposure to cold and wet conditions. The best way to acquire hypothermia is to work up a sweat in the middle of the night, or become immersed in water in cold temperatures and then cease movement. The best prevention is to stay dry through proper clothing selection and a moderate pace of movement, maintain nutrition and hydration, and common sense.

When you stop to eat, check your route, or fix your feet, bundle up. Put on your extra layer, your hat, and your gloves while your pace has slowed. Prevention is the best medicine.

If you suspect hypothermia is lurking in your shadow, take note of the following symptoms.

The first stage is defined by shivering, loss of fine-motor skills, and loss of judgment. This level can be easily reversed if recognized early on. Seek a sheltered area, load up the layers and huddle with your teammates. Make a fire if possible and consume high-energy foods.

The next, more formidable stage is not so easily shunned. Shivering comes to a halt, confusion sets in, and coordination is lost, which can lead to apathy, shock, and eventually, coma. Seek medical help immediately. If a teammate is hypothermic, he will not be able to care for himself. Be careful in handling him to prevent an irregular heartbeat. While waiting for medical help, get your teammate to a protected area, away from the wind, remove wet clothing, and then bundle him in warm layers paying attention to a layer of insulation beneath him. Wrap him in a sleeping bag and place heat packs in his armpits and groin area. Avoid cuddling at this point. If the victim is warmed too quickly, an adverse reaction could occur.

THE COMPLETE GUIDE TO ADVENTURE RACING

If your teammate is conscious, encourage him to drink hot liquids, avoiding alcohol and caffeine, and keep him from dozing off. Once he has recovered—his temperature back to normal—do not continue the race with him. He should be evaluated by a doctor and should continue to rest.

Frostbite is a localized area of frozen tissue. Encouraged by freezing temperatures, high winds, high altitudes, overexertion, and dehydration, it can first be detected through a tingling, numbing sensation in the fingers and toes or a burning in the nose and ears. In the first stages, the skin will be pale, cold, and malleable. If symptoms are ignored, the skin and other deeper structures will become very rigid. If frostbite is detected early, immerse affected parts in warm water (104-108 degrees Fahrenheit). In full-blown cases, seek emergency medical help. If not tended to immediately, severe tissue damage may result. In the worst cases, amputation is the only alternative.

THE "UMBLES"

An easy way to identify problems is to look for the mumbles, jumbles, and stumbles. Impaired speech, confusion, and a loss of balance and coordination signify trouble.

The lure of "getting high" is infectious. You want to go higher and higher as the mountain peaks call your name.

GENERAL GUIDELINES TO GUARD AGAINST HEALTH CATASTROPHES

1. Always ask yourself what the worst conditions you could possibly encounter would be. Visualize them, pack for them, and expect them. If you don't experience horrible conditions, be grateful and pleasantly surprised.

2. Keep your head covered whenever possible. In the cold, you will conserve heat. In the sun, you will prevent a burn, and in the woods, your head will be protected from brush, and tiny creatures with wings.

3. Stay dry.

4. Eat and drink regularly.

5. Pay attention to the environment. Be aware of how your body responds to it. The more in tune you become with your surroundings, the more prepared you will be to prevent an unfortunate situation.

6. Don't try to be a hero. Listen to your internal cues and if they nag at you, communicate to your team that you need to tend to them.

7. Monitor your movement. Strive for a pace that keeps you warm and that is manageable for a long distance. Too much exertion can cause profuse sweating, which will ultimately make you cold. It will also zap your strength. Too little effort or too many breaks slows you down and makes you cold.

At dusk, we started the final section of the course, up Mt. Tronador (3460m). In the middle of the night, we reached the Chilean border—a tiny tin shed at 2200m. The night was clear and it dropped to minus 12. We couldn't stay awake on our feet, so we stopped to sleep for 2 hours. Everything we took off froze solid, and to get back into everything, we first had to beat them against the wall to get some semblance of flexibility back into them.

— *Keith Murray, first place team, 1999 Eco-Challenge, Patagonia*

HEALTH

*High altitude travel.
Eco-Challenge (1999)
Argentina.*

ALTITUDE SICKNESS

Acute mountain sickness (AMS), or *altitude sickness*, is your body's way of dealing with a decrease in air density. The higher you go, the less atmospheric pressure is present, and the less oxygen is available. To decrease problems in high altitudes, follow these AMS prevention guidelines:

1. Eat plenty of carbohydrates and drink lots of water before, during, and after the race.

2. Ascend at a reasonable pace. The speed at which you climb is just as important as the altitude.

3. Keep in mind the higher you go, the harder it will be—each and every step.

4. Respect any signs that discourage your ascent: the weather, physiological disruptions, or gear problems. Heed these signs and turn around.

ALTITUDE SICKNESS

BY J. PARKER CROSS, JR., M.D.
MEDICAL DOCTOR FOR TEAM 'ODYSSEY'

Having trekked at altitudes up to 17,500 feet in Africa, Nepal, and Ecuador, experiencing mild to moderate problems on each occasion; and in conjunction with being a supporter for team 'Odyssey' at the Raid Gauloises team, I was prompted to learn more about altitude sickness.

As I understand it, the problem is currently divided into three general areas of concern with possible overlap: *acute mountain sickness* (AMS) which may consist of sleeplessness, loss of appetite, headache, nausea and energy depletion; *acute pulmonary edema* (APE) involving various degrees of shortness of breath on exertion, weakness, coughing, and a rapid pulse; and *acute cerebral edema* (ACE) with balance difficulties, marked headache, poor judgment, hallucinations, and impaired thought processes progressing to coma.

Susceptibility to altitude problems is very individual and may vary in the same individual from time to time, unpredictably. Being in good physical shape does not protect climbers from the difficulty.

Prevention is sought by limiting the amount of altitude gain, by "climbing high and sleeping low" in an attempt to acclimatize. Other steps include avoidance of exertion, high carbohydrate intake and hydration.

Medicines used to allay symptoms include Diamox, which helps to increase respiration. There is controversy as to the exact dosage and whether to take it prophylactically or to wait for symptoms to develop. Often climbers have to experiment to determine what is appropriate for them. Side effects are minimal and usually well tolerated by those who find relief with this medication.

Steroid therapy in the form of oral Dexamethasone may be of help, particularly for the person who does not tolerate Diamox. For those in significant distress, it can be administered IM.

For APE, Nifedipine is effective in many and is reasonable to try. Also, positive pressure breathing masks and/or Gamow hyperbaric bags can be valuable. Of course, if available, oxygen inhalation is a part of the treatment.

AMS and especially APE and ACE are serious, even deadly disorders in the absence of timely response to calculated climbing and medications. The best course of action is to descend pronto with at least one escort for the sick person. Even in descent, increased problems my occur rendering the victim incapable of self-care.

Large consumption of water and carbohydrates are a panacea to most environmental situations.

HEALTH

GENERAL FIRST AID

OPEN WOUNDS

Abrasions are caused by harsh friction that scrapes away the outer layer of skin.

Blisters are the result of friction.

Incisions are identified by sharp, even cuts.

Punctures are actually holes in the skin caused by pointed objects. Tetanus is a concern with this injury.

Lacerations are a tearing of soft tissue from sharp, irregular-edged objects.

Avulsions typically result from mechanical accidents or animal bites that tear a tissue, leaving it hanging.

Amputations are a complete detachment of a body part.

Crushing injuries involve fractured bones and damage to internal organs.

FIRST AID FOR BLEEDING

The most threatening bleeding is arterial bleeding. This blood is oxygen-rich as it flows from the heart to the body through the arteries. Bright-red blood spurts every time the heart beats. If your teammate suffers an injury that causes arterial bleeding, seek help immediately—his condition is life threatening.

Venous bleeding occurs from a vein which carries dark-red blood (dark from lack of oxygen) back to the heart. Capillary bleeding comes from the smallest blood vessels—the capillaries. Although not as rigorous a flow, bleeding is steady and the threat of infection is high.

Infection can cause problems in any situation, but in an adventure race, they can be magnified. Wounds are constantly exposed to dirt and other foreign substances, and you are usually wet from sweat, rivers, lakes, rain, or oceans. Therefore, keeping dry bandages on open areas becomes a hefty task.

Signs and symptoms of infection include pain, tenderness, redness, swelling, and heat at the site of the wound. Pus and red streaks will be evident and lymph glands closest to the wound will be swollen. An ill feeling may also occur.

It is almost inevitable that you will experience several open wounds, even if they involve nothing more than abrasions from thick brush. A fall will provoke more serious open wounds, which require more care and attention. To control bleeding, heed the following steps:

1. Wash the site with soap and water if it is not bleeding profusely. If the wound is bleeding heavily, do not attempt to wash it. This may cause further irritation and bleeding.

2. Apply direct pressure to the wound with a clean, absorbent covering. Keep the dressing over the wound. If the bleeding soaks the first cover, do not remove it—simply add a second one over it.

3. If a fracture is not suspected but bleeding continues, elevate the wound to slow the bleeding.

4. If bleeding persists, locate a pressure point, either the belly of the biceps or the groin, and apply pressure while continuing the first 2 steps.

5. A pressure bandage is the last resort if bleeding continues. This bandage will hold the initial dressing in place and restrict movement while controlling bleeding. While wrapping the wound, apply pressure to control the bleeding. Avoid wrapping it too tight to avoid cutting off circulation. Take a pulse and watch for blue fingertips or toes.

If your teammate becomes unconscious, radio for help immediately and administer CPR and/or rescue breathing. It is a very good idea to attend a course on CPR and First Aid prior to a race. The course takes only a few hours and could save a life.

TENDONS, MUSCLES, LIGAMENTS, AND BONES

The terrain you tread outdoors is uneven and in many cases, the weather doesn't cooperate, which makes for a slippery adventure. Add a load on your back, and the endless hours employ thousands of opportunities for missed steps—pure wizardry is necessary to escape a race injury free! If you don't suffer an injury, it is highly likely that you will adopt some kind of "itis".

Tendons transfer force from muscle to bone. They play an integral role in your locomotion. If excessive loads are placed on this structure, which exceed its strength capacity, an indirect injury is inevitable and normal function is compromised.

A *strain* is an injury to the musculotendinious unit. It is categorized according to the degree of severity. A mild strain is represented by minimal structural disturbance accompanied by some tenderness. A moderate strain is characterized by prominent swelling and tenderness, and a noticeable loss of stability and function. In severe strain cases, surgery is usually required to correct the injury. This extreme degree of strain demolishes the tendinous structure, greatly reduces function and evokes notable pain.

It is important to note the overwhelming possibility of some degree of strain as an adventure racer. Tissue damage to some extent is highly likely due to the continuous repetitive stress (chronic reaction) placed on the body. This damage can be present without detection for many years. It is also common to be aware of a possible mild injury (acute reaction) that comes with the attitude: put up with it and work around it.

However, it is more effective to identify the mild imbalance and correct it immediately. Rest the area, which doesn't necessarily mean an exile to the couch. For example, if your ankle is suffering, you can emphasize paddling, swimming, and strength training for the torso and upper body. In the onset of an injury, ice the area 10-15 minutes every 2-3 hours for the first couple days. Use an elastic bandage to compress the injured area, which will reduce swelling, and elevate as often as possible to encourage fluid drainage. You can remember the method of treatment by the acronym PRICE, protect, rest, ice, compression and elevation.

If your strain is severe, rest completely for a few days, or rest the affected area and train around it with other modalities.

Ligaments connect your bones, and a ligamentous injury is called a sprain. The function and resilience of your ligaments is directly related to their location and attachment.

A sprain sacrifices the stability of a ligament, causing interruption in joint movement patterns. There are three degrees of sprains. A first-degree sprain, classified as mild, will impair performance for a few days accompanied by local tenderness. A moderate or second-degree sprain causes marked swelling and can hinder performance for as much as six weeks. Mild to moderate sprains are most common and can be treated. A severe or third-degree sprain has more serious consequences, limiting performance indefinitely. Profuse swelling along with extreme tenderness and instability of the joint occurs.

A *skeletal muscle* is most likely to endure damage in an adventure race. "Acute muscular strain" results from an overload to the injured area. Overstretching or placing too high a load on the muscle can cause trauma, with the dynamics of the force in direct proportion to the degree of strain.

Mild strains barely interrupt normal function, while moderate strains are painful and result in partial function impairment due to a fragmentary muscle tear. In extreme cases of muscle strains, hemorrhaging and swelling signify a significant disruption to the tissue.

Bruises, or contusions, also represent muscle damage. Forceful compression to the tissue may result in a colorful collage attributable to mild intramuscular bleeding.

The third category of muscle strain is the result of intense exercise. One to two days after a hard workout, your muscles may become stiff and tender, and your range of motion is limited. We typically refer to this scenario as DOMS, or Delayed-Onset Muscle Soreness.

To lessen the possibility and severity of injury in the future, include strength training in your regular fitness regimen. In addition to strength, emphasize balance, flexibility and stability work. Yoga classes provide an excellent mode to compliment these integral fitness components.

In a race situation, if you experience a strain or a sprain, the PRICE method is still effective. Rest, ice, and elevate the injured area when you can. Anytime your team stops, be cognizant of the opportunity to treat your injury. If you are near a lake or river, submerge the injured area for 5-10 minutes. If you are surrounded by snow, build a pack around the affected area and rest for 5-10 minutes. Or, pack some ice into a baggie and tape it to your injury, or shove the pack inside your clothing. Next, compress the area with tape or an Ace bandage until you can have a medical professional do the job for you.

Finally, utilize your team to take the edge off and to allow you to continue moving forward as a team. Give your teammates your pack, and depending on what discipline you are in, create a towing system. If you are trekking, use your poles and short-rope to a teammate. If you are biking, set up a towing system. If you are paddling, administer treatment and then paddle if possible. In other disciplines, you may either have to use more imagination, or, if the impossible is knocking on your door, your will may be the only thing left to rely on.

COMMON HEALTH ISSUES YOU MAY ENCOUNTER IN AN ADVENTURE RACE
BY GEORGE WORTLEY, MD, MEDICAL DOCTOR FOR ODYSSEY ADVENTURE RACING

Skin problems are common during a multi-day adventure race. It is little wonder given the potential for blisters, cuts, abrasions, poison ivy, sunburn and fungal infections.

Blisters are common.

Sunburns happen. It probably will not take you out of the race, but it can make you miserable and increase your risk for skin cancer in the future. Prevent sunburn with SP-30 sunblock and do not forget the lip balm. Wear a hat. Treat the pain with Tylenol or ibuprophen. Aloe Vera gel can also help, as can cortisone cream.

Seven out of ten people are allergic to *poison ivy.* If the race course goes through poison ivy, the seven out of ten racers may develop poison ivy dermatitis. If you realize you have been exposed and can wash exposed skin with soap and water you may be able to prevent the outbreak. There are barrier creams available to prevent poison ivy but they must be applied prior to exposure and frequently reapplied to prevent contact with the offending plant oil with the skin. If you are highly allergic to poison ivy you may want to consider this. Minor eruptions may be treated with topical steroid creams but more extensive rashes will require systemic steroids either by injection or pill. We have used these in races with success and with no effect on physical performance. Antihistamine pills such as Benadryl can help with the itch but will cause drowsiness.

Yeast and fungus like to grow in hot, moist, dark environments. Unfortunately, during a race your feet and crotch match this description. There are many good over-the-counter anti-fungal creams (Monistat Derm, Lotrimin) that can help when applied two to four times a day. Athlete foot powders may not work on jock itch. Loose fitting, well-ventilated clothing may prevent this problem.

Most *minor abrasions* will heal nicely on their own if kept clean and dry. Consider applying a topical antibiotic (Bacitracin or Triple Antibiotic) to them to prevent infection. Cuts and lacerations can become infected. As a general rule, if the cut is full thickness (you can see underlying fat) and open more than several millimeters, it would heal faster and with less scarring if it were closed. Wounds should be closed within 6 to 8 hours or the likelihood of infection increases greatly. The wound should be cleaned before closing to remove any dirt and debris. Steri-strips or butterfly wound closures can be used, but will most likely not remain in place unless an adhesive such as Benzoin is first applied to the skin.

Some racers have used super glue to close a laceration when no help is available. Apply a tiny amount to the wound edges, being careful not to get the glue inside the wound. Tape or glue does not work well over joints or other area of increased skin tension. Sutures or staples will hold together better. Most medical assistance points will have someone qualified to close a wound. Never close a dirty, contaminated or infected wound. You are only asking for bigger problems. Never close a bite wound. All adventure racers should have a tetanus booster within the past ten years.

GASTRO-INTESTINAL PROBLEMS

Many different conditions can cause vomiting. Contaminated water or food are most frequent causes. Ulcers or gastritis can also cause vomiting. If you see blood in the vomit you should seek immediate medical attention.

Food poisoning may resolve in six to twelve hours. If this happens to you, try to keep drinking, even small amounts. Over the counter medications that can help include Dramamine and Pepto-Bismol. Prescription medications, such as Phenergan or Compazine, are stronger but have more potential for side effects (drowsiness, muscle twitching, and confusion) that can limit your participation in the race. Occasionally intravenous fluids may be needed to correct dehydration.

Diarrhea is no fun in the woods (or anywhere else for that matter). Contaminated water and food are the most common causes. Symptoms may last for hours to days. Imodium AD is a powerful medication available over the counter. Take two tablets for the first dose. Most often, the first dose will stop your symptoms. If not, take another pill each time you have diarrhea up to a maximum of eight tablets a day. Do not take Imodium if you have a fever or bloody diarrhea. These may indicate a more serious infection that could be potentially made worse by taking the Imodium AD.

Some athletes consume large amounts of ibuprophen and other anti-inflammatory medications during a race that may irritate the stomach. Ulcers and internal bleeding can occur. Blood from your stomach will appear black by the time it reaches the lower intestines. If you see black, tar-like bowel movements be aware that you may be bleeding internally and should seek medical attention immediately. Not all ulcers will cause pain or vomiting.

FEVER

Fever is defined as body temperature greater than 100.6°F. Fever is one of the ways by which the body responds to an infection. You may reduce a fever by taking Tylenol or ibuprophen. Most fevers are caused by viral infections and will resolve on their own. Occasionally, a fever may indicate a more serious condition. If your fever is mild and associated with a minor upper respiratory infection (the common cold), you are safe to continue participating in a race. If, however, you have a high fever (greater than 102°F)

you may need to consider limiting your participation in the race. There have been rare cases reported where exercise with a high fever has led to a potentially life threatening inflammation of the heart muscle (myocarditis). While the risk is small, the potential harm is great. Most experts advise stopping activity if you have a high fever.

RESPIRATORY PROBLEMS

Asthma is a common problem. Statistics reveal that up to 20 percent of the population has the potential for asthma. In addition to wheezes, symptoms include shortness of breath with exercise and cough. Fortunately most asthma is easily treated with medication. If you have asthma, continue to use your asthma medications. You may find yourself using your inhaler more often. Viral respiratory tract infections can trigger an asthma attack as can exercise in the cold air.

Colds and viral upper respiratory infections occur frequently. There is good evidence that ultra endurance exercise can lower the body's defenses and lead to more frequent respiratory infections. You may treat symptoms with Tylenol and a decongestant such as Sudafed. Unfortunately, antibiotics have little effect upon the viral upper respiratory tract infections.

IMMUNIZATIONS

If you plan on racing in a foreign country, seek the advice of a travel nurse and allow plenty of time for immunization.

SLEEP DEPRIVATION

A multi-day, non-stop adventure race is unique in the world of sports in regard to the amount of sleep deprivation it subjects participants to. Most racers will go as long and as hard as possible before sleeping. How well you perform physically and mentally in a sleep-deprived state can determine your finish in the race. When and how long to sleep becomes an important tactical decision.

Sleep deprivations will affect both physical and mental performance. Fatigue develops. Skilled motor performance will deteriorate. This is not a minor problem if you are descending on a steep trail on a mountain bike at 40 mph. Judgment is impaired. Team members will be irritable and less inclined to communicate.

Racers may become disoriented in a sport where orientation is all-important. Navigation mistakes are more likely to occur. Studies have shown a drop in IQ scores of 15 points when sleep deprived.

Even more entertaining are the hallucinations. My experience is that common themes tend to occur. White wolves, witches in trees and automobiles on the trail or water at night are frequently reported.

Potentially dangerous situations can develop with sleep deprivation. Seizures can occur especially in those with a preexisting seizure disorder. Psychotic episodes can also develop in some people. Experimental studies have shown that 2% to 3% of individuals can develop psychotic episodes if they go more than 60 hours without sleep. Symptoms of such psychotic episodes include screaming, sobbing, delirium and paranoid thoughts. The effects of sleep deprivation on physical and mental performance of adventure racers may be a fertile ground for research. Because few other sports cause this degree of sleep deprivation, little has been studied on this topic.

"The stares," that blank bottomless look, is inevitable in an adventure race.

FIRST-AID KIT CONTENTS

Here are my recommendations for a personal or team first-aid kit to be carried in a race:

Assorted Band-Aids

Butterfly or Steri-strip wound closures

Disinfectant (Betadine, Hipaclens)

Moleskin

Duct tape (12 inches per person should be enough)

Super glue

Small scissors to cut moleskin/duct tape

Small tweezers for removing splinters or thorns

Tylenol and/or ibuprophen

Imodium AD

Antibiotic cream or ointment

Cortisone cream

Ace Wrap Elastic bandage (3 or 4 inch roll)

Safety pins

Sawyer Extractor (if in venomous snake areas)

Any home medications

THE COMPLETE GUIDE TO ADVENTURE RACING

GORILLA HALLUCINATIONS

ECO-CHALLENGE AUSTRALIA '97
BY TRACYN THAYER

We were within hours of paddling to the finish line of the Discovery Channel Eco-Challenge 1997 in Australia. Leaving the final checkpoint from an island 8 or so kilometers from Cairns where the finish line banner flew, I was psyched to have traded boats with one of my teammates. I was now happily and confidently paddling with my husband, Norm Greenberg. He was on the support crew for my 1996 Eco-Challenge team. From that point on, we were determined to race together in any future event.

So, there we were, myself in the stern, and Norm at the bow controlling our sleek glass boat toward the finish line. It was just dark and the shadows falling on the cliffs off to our left started to create strange images and began to play tricks with my overly exhausted mind. I could have sworn I was seeing animals—monkeys and gorillas! I shook my head knowing they weren't really there, but I couldn't make them not be there. Suddenly, Norm interrupted my mind games with some of his own.

"Do you see that gorilla over there?" he asked timidly, perhaps also thinking it couldn't be real as he pointed to the same cliff that I was fixated on.

"Yeah...it looks like...a mother gorilla...holding a baby gorilla!" I replied as I relaxed at the justification that I wasn't out of my mind after all.

"Yeah!" Norm exclaimed, sealing our contentment as we continued to paddle to the finish line.

I'd had many hallucinations since the 2nd night of the race, and we were well into day 7. I'd never shared the same hallucination with someone else, however. Crossing the finish line, I realized that I'd shared more than I could ever have imagined in the weeklong race with my husband. I was content to know that I would not have to try to explain the pain, the glory, the beauty, the sense of accomplishment, and of course, the mother gorilla and her baby. Norm already understood.

A couple of days later, on a boat heading to a snorkeling trip in the Great Barrier Reef, we passed by the same cliffs we paddled by that last stretch of the race. Strange as it was, and as hard as we tried, we couldn't make out the gorillas!

DID YOU SEE THAT?

Chris Scott, a solo competitor, often amuses fellow racers and volunteers along the course with his high-energy ramblings. Upon finishing the Beast of the East Race of 1999, he asked where he was because he couldn't believe he was still in Virginia. Chris said he kept forgetting where he was, despite the fact that he experienced vivid déjà vu all along the course and made only a few navigational errors. Chris also said he shivered at night instead of sleeping because "shivering is almost like sleeping"—this unconventional technique could account for one of the best hallucinations reported in the race. While he was attempting to do a map study, Chris' family portrait kept appearing where the course was supposed to be. Guess that could account for not knowing where he was.

Dave Horton, an ultra runner well known for his run across America and his record for running the entire Appalachian Trail, was the final competitor to complete the full Mega Dose adventure race course in "91 hours/13 minutes", which he exclaimed the moment he crossed the finish line (a true runner's trait). Dave, who just took up mountain biking 6 weeks before the race said the bike sections were fun, but that he could have done without the long paddle. Having completed his first adventure race, Dave said the sport is "not as painful as running an ultra" and that the Mega Dose was good training for the Hard Rock 100-miler next month. At one point during the race, Dave picked up pieces of candy he found on the trail, only to find out after he put them in his mouth that he was eating rocks! Another example of what happens during the throes of sleep deprivation after only 2 hours sleep in "91 hours/13minutes."

INSIDE MY HEAD

On the trail, I followed a group of long, black-haired Mexican workers wearing black leather jackets. It was in the middle of the night and I hadn't slept more than 20 minutes in 4 days. The reality was, I was following a figment of my imagination. There was nothing there.

Juli Lynch and I took turns seeing rocks that looked like animals and animals that looked like rocks while training in the White Mountains for 3 non-stop days.

While paddling with Terry Schneider in the Raid-Himalayas, she looked at the rock wall lining the river and was seeing family faces in the rock.

— *Don*

WHAT HELP CAN I EXPECT DURING A RACE?

BY GEORGE WORTLEY, M.D.

Adventure races vary widely in the amount of medical help available to the racer during competition. Some will have no help at all. You will be responsible for your own medical treatment and back up. Other races will have services available at assisted checkpoints. Most of those providing the services are volunteers with limited resources. Sometimes, you may find a physician at an aid station. More often you find paramedics, nurses or emergency medical technicians (EMT's) working under the guidance of a physician.

Some teams will bring their own medical support person with all of the supplies he or she is qualified to use. It is always best to ask the Race Director what level of medical support will be available on the course. Know the rules for your particular race. In many races, you may not receive medical help outside of an assisted checkpoint without being disqualified.

Are intravenous fluids (IV's) permitted? Most races permit them. Some do not allow them or limit the amount of IV fluids received before being disqualified. The use of IV's during a race does present some ethical and liability questions. Does receiving an IV provide an unfair advantage to the racer? Are we rewarding those who did not pay attention to their hydration and nutrition and now need assistance by providing IV fluids? With limited amounts of IV fluids available, who decides which racers get an IV? Most often oral rehydration works as well, is safer and costs less. Still some racers feel the need to receive an IV whenever possible. Should race management provide this? Some sports such as Triathlon have very clear rules on IV's. They are permitted after the race but are grounds for automatic disqualification if given during the race. But, of course, most triathlons do not go on and triple several days (except for the Odyssey Double Iron and Triple Iron Triathlons).

Adventure racing has not yet evolved an organization with standardized guidelines and rules such as the Triathlon.

Race management and the Medical Director will sometimes have to make difficult decisions about medical disqualification. When is it no longer safe for a racer to continue? I always want to make this decision in partnership with the athlete and always give the athlete any possible chance to finish. A Medical Director who knows the course and the challenges that are ahead is in a much better position to make this decision than one who does not know the course. Trust us on this point. We want to do everything possible to help you finish but do not want to endanger your permanent well-being or that of your teammates. There are times when an athlete must be evacuated from the course or aid station for hospital care. That will almost always result in disqualification. Such decisions are also difficult to make. Remember that we are here as volunteers to help you. Please be as honest as you can with us. We do not enjoy disqualifying racers. Our reward is watching you cross the finish line and fulfill your dream.

George Wortley, M.D. is the Medical Director for Odyssey Adventure Racing and team 'Odyssey'. He is a graduate of State University of New York-Upstate Medical College at Syracuse and completed residency in Family Medicine in Latobe, PA. He is Board Certified in Family Practice and holds a Certificate of Added Qualifications in Sports Medicine and is a Fellow of the American College of Sports Medicine. Currently, he is Assistant Director of the Lynchburg Family Practice Residency and Assistant Clinical Professor in Family Medicine for the University of Virginia.

THE FIRST DAY OF SCHOOL...

Monday, August 17, 1998. It's 7:30 AM, I got up earlier, but chose to go back to bed since I realized it's my vacation and no one cared what time I got up. Anyway, I'm up now and writing this.

I'm in West Virginia, about 30 miles south of Beckley at a Hampton Inn. I guess I'm about 45 minutes from Camp Washington Carver, where my week at the Odyssey Adventure Racing Academy is about to begin. I'm supposed to check-in there about 6 o'clock this evening.

I got here early because, well, I just did. I'm hoping today to go ride some of the trails in the mountains around the camp and see what's up here, what the terrain is like, and have a little time to figure out what I forgot to bring so I can go get it before I check-in. I already realized I forgot a sleeping bag, which I'm not about to let anyone else at the camp know. I do think I have good experience at this part of these adventure-related sports, that being, that you should always travel to these events with enough cash to buy your way out of any problem you create for yourself. The cash allows you the ability to correct problems that arise from not knowing what you got yourself into or what you'll need. It's especially essential when you realize that you signed up for an event without thinking and find yourself surrounded with superhuman, 20-year-old endurance freaks, standing on the edge of a 500 foot drop-off, wearing nothing but a Speedo swim suit and a helmet. All of a sudden someone from Hell screams, "GO!" and your only salvation is the bus driver giving the tour of the ridge for Sister Helen's Home for the Criminally Old... who says he'll give you a lift down to the parking lot for a hundred bucks ... cash!

I got into this whole mess because of a damn TV show. You know the one. Everyone in the world saw it. The one on the Discovery Channel about Eco-Challenge Australia. I, like probably so many of the other endurance athletes that showed up the next day at Kennesaw Mountain, or wherever, to start trail running, had heard of adventure racing, maybe even read about the Raid and similar events. But we were truly intrigued when we saw the Japanese team on TV, carrying their injured female teammate through the mountains for 3 days, only to be dragged out of the ocean by helicopter in the last leg. Or, that guy who rode off some bridge into a rocky river bed, while mountain biking at night (hell, I hadn't even thought of mountain biking at night, let alone racing!). His male teammates began bitching because they needed to keep moving, while their female team member frantically tries to tape him back together. Here we decided that this was the sport for us!

So here I am at the Odyssey Adventure Racing Academy. For the last 4 months I altered my training from the standard triathlon format which has been unsuccessful for me over the last 10 years, to one that incorporates trail running and riding, night running and riding, some rock climbing and paddling. I'm sure it will probably prove to be just as unsuccessful as my previous training plans, with the exception that it requires much more time and money. Fortunately, this is what a grown man is after in a sport. Anyway, one of the reasons for coming to this camp is to learn how to properly train, so maybe I'll get something out of this after all. Other reasons for coming to this camp actually elude me at this time, except maybe curiosity. I'm not just curious on whether I can do these multi-day events, but why do I even want to try? By spending some time with other people consumed by the same demon, I will either find an answer to those questions, or at least some training partners.

At 6 PM, everyone begins to arrive at Camp Washington Carver. The group is much smaller than I had expected, which may be good, and since none of them para-dropped in, or arrived sporting nothing but a survival knife and face-paint, I think this might be OK. As a matter-of-fact, these people look relatively normal, perhaps even human. Even better, there

appears to be some people close to myself in age. Yeah, this is going to be all right, I can survive this.

As people drift in to form a group of about 20, we begin informal introductions to each other and briefing as to the week's agenda. Don Mann and Joy Marr are Odyssey as far as I can tell at this point and after 5 minutes of playful conversation. In the parking lot, I realize they have logged more mileage running/biking/paddling during the last month than I have, well, in a long time.

Don informs us that he was an active duty Navy SEAL until 77 days ago. They just got back from California where they were completing some kinda qualification for the Raid. Just last week, they competed in a 3-day race up north, The Great Noreaster, where they were in a tough paddling duel for 12 hours. Twelve hours? Christ, I've never even been in a boat for 12 hours! I've been fishing in the Gulf of Mexico off San Destin for 4 hours tops, but there was someone there to get you a Coke and we had A/C. He explained how he and Joy paddled constantly for 12 hours like it's a natural act.

So the paddling thing may be a little more than expected, but if it gets too tough I can always go into the "fake shoulder injury from the gym" mode and probably handle it that way.

As we begin to discuss the week's itinerary, I slowly begin to realize that this is not really going to be 4 days of training that concludes with a 2-day race. Of course not. Don and Joy are crazy! No, Don thinks it's best to try and simulate the conditions of a 6-day race. Therefore, we will cram intensely from early morning until late at night, so that when we enter the 42-hour race that concludes the week at the academy, we will be tired and only then will we be able to experience the fatigue of a longer race. What a great idea. I'm glad Satan, I mean Don, has my best interest at heart and has taken the time to create an agenda so tailored to my personal training needs.

About 10 PM, we all wander off to bed in our appropriate rooms in the bunkhouse. I, of course, plan to lay in bed and stare at the ceiling in nervous anticipation, in order to create the proper state of internal stress and panic I feel will best suit tomorrow's activities.

—*Joe Johnson*

CLASS IN SESSION

In preparation for the Endorphin Fix, several athletes, fresh from the Odyssey Adventure Racing Academy, were facing the reality of their first race. A few hours before the midnight commencement of the race, they were eagerly stuffing their packs with the necessary gear and food to carry them through the following two days. The challenge: to be able to actually lift the packs from the floor!

A common mistake that first-timers often make is over-packing. It has often been said that the amount of weight you carry on your back is directly related to your fears. If you are afraid of getting cold, you will carry extra clothing. If you are afraid of going hungry, you will carry extra food. Eventually, if your fears are abundant, you won't be able to carry your pack more than 10 feet, and you certainly won't get very far along the course.

Through experience, you realize the clothes on your back (if layered properly) will take you far. You discover the proper ration of food and water. You learn how to take care of your feet, and which equipment works best for your body type, fitness level and abilities.

The key word is experience. A terrific way to cram years of experience into several days is to invest in an adventure racing school. You will acquire valuable skills and techniques on all of the major disciplines involved in an adventure race. The opportunity to interact with experienced racers will equip you with valuable knowledge and experiences. And in some cases, you have the option of racing at the end of the school to put your new or polished talents into immediate practice.

Odyssey Adventure Racing Academy participants learn navigation skills.

As the sport of adventure racing escalates in popularity, so are adventure racing schools. The following reference list offers insight into some of the more widely known and established academies:

THE ODYSSEY ADVENTURE RACING ACADEMY

3 or 6 days of AR instruction and racing.

THE ODYSSEY CORPORATE TRAINING PROGRAM

Customized courses designed for the corporate-level executive.

THE SEAL ADVENTURE CHALLENGE

24 hours of Navy SEAL "Hell Week" training.

THE SEAL TRAINING ACADEMY

7 days of skydiving, open water diving, land navigation and SEAL exercise instruction.

THE SEAL CORPORATE CHALLENGE

SEAL training concepts training customized for the corporate-level executive.

Information on any of these programs can be found at www.OARevents.com or by calling (757) 425-2445.

For expert instruction and valuable outdoor experience, go to an adventure racing academy.

THE COMPLETE GUIDE TO ADVENTURE RACING

THE HUMAN EXPERIMENT

We had been on a rambling roller-coaster powered by our human engines for almost six hours in the dark. Our progress, illuminated by our headlamps and bike lights, was steady but slow as we managed to stay on the bumpy path that sketched through deep woods and cliffs. My mind kept warning me how crazy blazing down rugged trails in the dark was. Nonetheless, I was committed, and it would take an earthly disaster to stop me.

As the sun gradually made its appearance on the horizon, we realized we had taken a wrong turn and had traveled about a quarter of a mile out of our way. We had to make a 10 AM cutoff to be able to officially continue the race. We still had many miles to conquer.

Time was escaping our grips. Team Agonos had to move fast in order to remain a competitive force in the Endorphin Fix two-day adventure race, which toured the New River Gorge area of West Virginia.

The Endorphin Fix was the grand finale of a week of adventure racing training with the Odyssey Adventure Racing Academy. We spent four days learning and practicing the skills necessary to be successful adventure racers under the guidance of Directors Don Mann and Joy Marr.

I arrived at Camp Washington Carver somewhat apprehensive. I was diving headfirst into a grueling week of training with complete strangers in unfamiliar territory. Moreover, I was to become close and personal with three strangers in order to race for two days in the Endorphin Fix, which would culminate our training. "It's all part of the adventure," was my motto, which I religiously adhered to all week.

Our days were lengthy and crammed with learning. The first day was devoted to orienteering for sixteen hours—first, under a roof, then in the daylight, and finally beneath the incandescence of the moon. The second day we embarked on a hilly cycling jaunt that led us to the New River, where we practiced paddling for a solid afternoon.

We practiced various paddling techniques on a variety of watercrafts in a torrential downpour. We biked back as a spirited, soggy pack on bleak, climbing roads.

The following day was spent scaling a 150-foot rock face high above the New River. We rappelled and honed ascending techniques. By the end of the third day, we had accumulated the skills and knowledge and some experience that would enhance our upcoming race. We also managed to dissect a group of 19 academy participants into several 4-person teams and one team of two.

My teammates: Darren Letsinger from Louisiana, Bill Scoggins and Todd Walton from Virginia and I were a young, vivacious, and athletic foursome. We spent many hours shopping, preparing and packing for our forty-hour mission in the mountains.

By Friday night, we were anxious to get the show on the road. We had discussed our expectations and planned our strategy and were eager to put it into practice.

The goal of the academy was to teach us about adventure racing through preparing for a race then actually racing—all in the same week! It was a brilliant plan, except, by the time the race arrived, we had already been taxed by several contests. "It's all part of the adventure," my motto, prevailed. I could feel myself getting tougher by the hour.

As we approached a bridge that marked significant progress, we knew we were making good time. But we weren't there yet. We couldn't stop for idle matters. Efficiency was paramount as our attention lie on the clock.

In our valiant efforts to reach checkpoint 2 on the river, my pedaling capabilities were rapidly dwindling. To even things up, Todd strapped my thirty-pound pack to his chest and endured a tremendous balancing act as he muscled his way up the hill. Simultaneously, Bill and Darren synchronized their efforts to offer me an extra push of physical power and emotional support.

The staggering illustration of teamwork enabled us to get to the water an hour before the cutoff. This intensity revealed a unique blend of tenacity and desire that would define the success of our team. Consequently, the white-water paddle was

our remuneration for the sweat and tears shed on the nine-hour mountain-biking journey.

The dizzying exchange of ebbs and flows in adventure racing defines the nature of the sport. For every hardship overcome, liberation emerges. Sometimes, it is internal. Sometimes it takes on external properties. In this case, it was both. The river was sweet salvation, and my spirits were soaring with dignity. Twenty-four hours later, we crossed the finish line with pure elation.

The race became one enormous human experiment. It was a discovery of the consequences of sleep deprivation, physical depletion, and mental exhaustion. It was my job to recognize the changes in my existence and figure out how to alter my strategy to keep moving forward. We accomplished the academy course with immense determination. The last hours of the race became surreal, and somehow, we made it to Camp Washington Carver to finish what we started a week earlier.

—*Kara*

WHAT'S YOUR TYPE? RACES DEFINED

Adventure races can be broken down into four basic categories:

EXPEDITION-STYLE RACES

The Raid Gauloises, an expedition-style race, commenced over a decade ago as the first official adventure race. Five-person teams, with the help of their support crew, raced across remote wilderness with no specific stops written into the course (teams are autonomous with their rest breaks). Each Raid Gauloises boasts a challenging route that usually tours over 350 miles of terrain. In the year 2000, the Trans-Himalayan course escalated to just over 500 miles, which took 10 days for the first team to cross the finish line.

Today, many other organizations join the Raid Gauloises in production of an expedition-style race. Some of which are notable include the Beast of the East, the Mega Dose, the Eco-Challenge, the Southern Traverse, the Authentic Adventure, Expedition Mata Atlantica, and Raid—The North Extreme.

STAGE RACES

Stage races may last several days. Athletes compete all day for several days, covering hundreds of miles. They race all day, completing a "stage" of the race and then get a reasonable night of sleep between each stage at a predetermined stop. The Mild Seven Outdoor Quest in China is an example of a stage race.

WEEKEND RACES

Races spanning one to two days are held on the weekends and attract a larger participation. Greater flexibility with time away from the office, accessibility, and the shorter mileage, are features that appeal to many avid racers. The Endorphin Fix, a popular two-day race held in the New River Gorge area of West Virginia, the Odyssey One Day Adventure Race, and the Salomon X-Mountain Series, are examples of weekend races.

SPRINT RACES

Sprint races are much faster and much shorter than the other types of adventure races. The skills required to participate are not as finely tuned and you are guaranteed the right to a warm, cozy bed at the end of the day as you are usually done in 3-10 hours. The Hi-Tec Series offers sprint races in many major cities across the U.S.

The Raid Gauloises continues to push the edge of expedition-style races.

THE MILD SEVEN OUTDOOR QUEST

The Mild Seven Outdoor Quest has taken just three years to become the most ferocious endurance competition on earth. The very best from the mountain biking, running, triathlon, cross-country skiing and adventure racing worlds come together for four, very intense days of racing. One sees them fly into alpine Dali, (China) full of hope and athleticism, eager to test their mental, physical and emotional limits on the rugged local terrain. They are handpicked, with just 24 teams making the journey, so each team feels as if they have a chance at bagging the lion's share of that $200,000 (US) first prize. Their eyes fairly shine with anticipation, needing only the starting gun to begin a series of events that will be forever memorable for the agony and ecstasy it will produce.

Then, four days later, there is a champion. The other 23—if there are 23 left—are left to rumble about next year. During the following year, racers have time to reflect on lost chances, more practice, and the need to work more cohesively as a team. Some vow never to return. But most forget the vow before they reach the Dali airport.

The Mild Seven Outdoor Quest, by definition, is an adventure race. Four-person teams, each having at least one member of the opposite sex, contest a series of outdoor endurance skills over the course of four days of competition. The team with the lowest cumulative time is declared the winner. But the Mild Seven Outdoor Quest is a most ingenious form of adventure racing, quite different from its predecessors like the Raid Gauloises and Eco-Challenge. Instead of racing non-stop for four days or two weeks, like the Raid or Eco, teams race for eight hours a day at the MSOQ, then repair and lick their wounds for the night, and do it all over again the following day. The competition then is faster and more competitive, with no time for even a moment's mental lapse or rest. When a team wins the Mild Seven Outdoor Quest, created by Nick Freyer and Murphy Reinschreiber, it is an accomplishment to be savored, because the athletes are of such a high caliber.

—Nick Freyer

An aerial view of the last transition area of the Elf Authentic Adventure (1999) in the Philippines, 103 kilometers before the finish line.

THE HI-TEC ADVENTURE

The Hi-Tec Adventure Series is madness for the masses, or at least something a little more meaty than your typical cut and dry triathlon. Michael Epstein Sports Productions, the team that brought us the "Triple Bypass" and several multi-day athletic events, has turned its attention to the single day "even a working stiff can do it" mass-appeal competition. Gone are the four-figure entry fees, airline passes to exotic lands and stacks of topo maps. Instead, the race mixes mountain biking, trail running, and kayaking with special tasks to conquer in the "mystery events" including cargo nets, mud pits, rock-climbing walls and log hauling. These races, designed to be completed in 3-5 hours, are packed with plenty of fun and adventure for 3-person teams. Awards go to the top five in each category, but only the traditional coed teams score cash rewards.

Hartford, Connecticut team 'Odyssey' was represented by Alan Holmes, Mike Nolan and newcomer Celeste Harvey. All three were anxious to prove their merit after an impromptu interview with ESPN2, which turned up the performance pressure. We started the race Le Mans-style, helmets and bike shoes on, in a sprint up a hill to our awaiting Cannondales. Unfortunately, we found ourselves in the middle of 150 teams and as the race commenced, we could only bumble along with the crowd as the leaders sprinted off to clear ground. The pack would not go as one group into the single-track mountain bike course. However, as the race officials had stealthily flattened one of each team's tires—we were welcomed to special test #1. We were fortunate enough to realize the nature of the flat before ripping the tube from the rim, as was the case for many other teams. Mike whipped out his pump and we quickly inflated the tire. Problem solved.

The bike course was a five-mile loop which we rode three times. It consisted of fresh-cut switchbacks, rooted single-track, and several portage-mandating hills. Our team moved really well and suffered only one mishap—an overzealous competitor who tried to pass on the tree-lined single-track and took out Celeste and myself in the process. After a quick check for injuries, followed by downing an energy bar for refueling, we were back on the gas.

Transitioning from bike to kayak, we came upon special test #2—the mud pit. Cold and reeking, the mud pit was dispatched with speed and then we were off to the boats. The 1-mile kayak leg consisted of a maddening paddle upstream in our nearly deflated rubber kayaks to an island, turn-around and a downstream run. We pushed it hard and made up several positions (Mike only hit Celeste with his paddle twice! OOPS!).

Once we were out of the pool toys, we hit special test #3—a tangled web of vertically strung ropes. We successfully passed through as each of us used a different route according to race instructions and then moved on to the running course. The 6-mile leg proved to be a painful event. The sun was in its prime and the dampness of the ground combined for an extremely humid environment. Our team stayed close through the winding trails and pushed the pace in an attempt to make up one place.

As we neared the finish line, we managed to close the gap, but could not over-take the fifth place team. Special test #4 between our team and the finish line lie our last obstacle—lay between the cargo net. As a team, we scaled the 20-foot net, descended the far side, and crossed the finish line, hand-in-hand, placing 6th out of 150 competing teams.

—*Alan Holmes*

RULES OF THE GAME

The rules of a race are essential to the integrity of the sport and should be taken seriously. If any one rule is broken during a race, the team risks disqualification. The following rules are standard in most races:

1. Hold on to your passport.

2. Find each checkpoint in numerical order.

3. Stay together. If you are caught without your team at a distance of 100 meters or more, you will be disqualified. Other races require each teammate to stay within sight of each other at all times.

4. Obey specific course rules. Forbidden roads or course boundaries are written into the rules for a reason—they are there for your safety and protection.

5. Follow rules of navigation.

6. Be prepared with the proper gear and skills for each discipline. Major rule of thumb: Do not try out a discipline for the first time in an adventure race! You could lose a limb, or your life, and jeopardize everyone around you! It's just that simple. Learn your skills and hone them in your training sessions. Not only will you be prepared for the race, but also your enjoyment will rise.

RESOURCES

WEB SITES

Do a search on "adventure racing", and thousands of sites will appear, with more popping up every day. The sport of adventure racing is growing rapidly and new sites are turning up as a consequence.

THE ADVENTURE RACING ASSOCIATION

Adventure racing has grown at a prolific rate. Consequently, an alliance was inevitable. In an effort to compliment the growth of the sport of adventure racing, promote safe conduct, and provide worldwide resources, the Adventure Racing Association (ARA) was born. On August 22, 1997, a group of approximately fifty people gathered in Cairns, Australia immediately following the Discovery Channel Eco-Challenge to establish the association.

Presently, membership is well into the thousands. To become involved with the e-mail list, which provides a forum for discussion on equipment, training techniques, race information, and much more, send an e-mail to listserv@adventureracing.org. In the body of the text, simply write: "subscribe ARA-L." As a member, you can participate in electronic conversations and be up-to-date on the latest happenings in the sport.

ADVENTURE RACING CLUBS

The United States Adventure Racing Association (USARA) sends out a regular electronic newsletter, publishes *Adventure World Magazine*, and serves as an excellent resource and locator for clubs and races. In addition, this association was established to promote safe standards in the sport and provide free consulting to novice race directors.

Log on to www.usara.com for more information.

ON YOUR MARK, GET SET, GO

HOW TO GET STARTED

1. *Assess your fitness and skills.* Record them in a log and make a habit of documenting your workouts and nutritional schedule from that point forward.

2. *Determine your goals and objectives.* Start with your long-term goal, such as completing an expedition-length race. Then work backward with shorter-term goals until you arrive at the first race in which you wish to compete in. Break down your strategy, which will get you to the starting line of your first race. Document all of this.

3. *Assess your mental and emotional characteristics.* Determine if you are strong-willed, easy-going, stubborn, a quick decision-maker, and so on. Think about how you fit into the adventure racing picture, and how it will fit into your life. This process is important for your own fulfillment. It will provide a road map to guide you to your goals, and it will make the team selection process a bit easier.

4. *Start training!* Pick the discipline that you are most efficient at to use as an initial base in which

Angelika Castaneda

you can increase aerobic power and log the miles. Start logging lots of miles! A strong endurance background will provide tremendous support in adventure racing. In addition, vary your training modalities specific to the race you intend on participating in.

5. *Seek expertise in each discipline:*
   - Consider attending adventure racing schools.
   - Schedule lessons with experts in your area.
   - Interact with fellow adventure racers (their experience can provide enormous insight).

6. *Perfect practice makes perfect performance.* Practice, practice, practice.

7. *Accumulate as much knowledge as possible on the sport.* Immerse yourself. As is the case for anything you do in life, the more you surround yourself with the industry, the more knowledge and experience you obtain and the better prepared you are for success. Utilize the web, stay up on race broadcasts via all types of media, network-network, go to school, join outdoor clubs in your area, and spend a lot of time outdoors and training your butt off!

8. *Volunteer at races:*
   - Get the inside scoop.
   - See what works—and what doesn't.
   - Meet and network with other racers.

9. *Join an Adventure Racing Association club in your area.*

10. *Start small and build your race resume with gradual progression.*

    1-day (there are some sprint races like the Hi-Tec series that take 3-6 hours and other one-day races that last 8-20 hours). Progress to 2-day, then 3-5 day and the expedition-style races.

Ultimately, you will be an adventure racer when you believe that you are an adventure racer. That belief will fuel your desire and determination to train hard, acquire the necessary skills and knowledge, and surround you with the right people and information. If you want it and you believe in it, it will happen.

VOLUNTEERING

Perhaps one of the most important methods of learning about the sport in an up-close and personal way is to be a volunteer. You learn the ins and outs of the race and grasp a vast understanding of what it takes to succeed as a racer in a very short period of time. Through working with the race director and staff, you can witness and participate in daily operations. You can experience the "inside" of the race. You may also pick up on the motives and inspirations of the organizer.

When you are out on the course, stationed at a checkpoint, you can observe racers in action and even ask them questions (as long as they are short and sweet!). Immediately, you acquire a sense of what racing is all about and you can't help but develop an irrepressible urge to race.

SUPPORT CREW

Another meaningful way to learn about racing is to be part of a support crew for a team. You are actually part of the team this way and through the race as you provide logistical, nutritional, and emotional assistance, you overcome your own set of obstacles and create important learning experiences for the day you actually tackle the course as a racer.

FINDING COMPATIBLE TEAMMATES

A sure-fire way to find compatible teammates is to go to an adventure racing school. Attend the school with potential teammates or seek new ones at the school. Whichever route you choose, you will gain a great deal of insight in a short amount of time about your teammates-to-be.

The internet hosts myriad opportunities for matchmaking adventure racers. If you post a message with the race organization of a particular race that you are interested in, it is likely that you will connect with others in similar situations. You may find interested and willing parties at your local gym or sports organizations such as climbing clubs, running clubs, and cycling or paddling groups.

For shorter races, this will usually work to your advantage (not always though!). If you are seeking compatriots for an expedition-length race, be sure you do your homework on your team members. References are extremely valuable. Talk to past teammates. Investigate the character of your potential teammate. Look for compatibility, and your gut-instinct will inevitably trump all of your efforts.

Many adventure racers come from a background of marathons, triathlons, and other endurance sports. While this foundation enhances the physical make-up of a team, it may adversely affect the "team" aspect of adventure racing if your teammate is too accustomed to

individual competition. You can identify this characteristic quickly by simply scheduling a long training session with at least two others. If your "teammate" sticks with you no matter what, he/she is more likely to remain close throughout a race. If your teammate zooms out of sight and yearns to exhibit athletic superiority above everything else, don't bother to catch up to him/her. You will be sorry in a race.

A successful team shares:

- Similar athletic abilities
- Respect and compassion
- Comparable objectives and expectations
- Similar attitudes

Discuss strategy in hypothetical catastrophes. Discover how each team member responds to sickness, injury, an argument, brutal conditions and determine how each of you would handle yourself and how you would deal with the rest of the team. Then go out and create a stressful situation. Get out on a ropes course and experiment with how you work together. Train in the rain and mud to see how each team member handles it. Get out at night and practice navigation. If you get lost, find out how easy it is to get back on track as a team.

The adventure racer who can adapt positively to adversity is the one you want on your team.

OBTAINING SPONSORSHIP

To obtain a team sponsor, you have to become a salesman. Share your passion with potential sponsors and sell them on what you believe in.

Create newsworthy stories about your team. Discover unique qualities about each team member and about the team as a whole. Then, seek the attention of the media. Get the word out that you are racing and that this fact is important!

Become proactive in this quest:

1. Come up with a perspective of the race and your team.

2. Write a story and submit it to multiple publications and other media sources.

3. When approaching a sponsor, let the company representative know what they will gain from their sponsorship.

4. Assure maximum exposure of the company. Place their logo on all of your race gear. Make the company name your team name. Promote your team and the company by conducting informative lectures workshops about adventure racing.

5. Race for a charity.

Seek companies who are already interested in the sport or connected somehow to adventure sports— sports gear manufacturers and distributors, nutrition companies, medical/first-aid companies, travel companies, shoe companies, etc. There are, however, hundreds or thousands of corporations who are not related to the sport who will sponsor your team if you get them interested.

To sell your team, in addition to your write-up about your unique team qualities, compile a portfolio of articles written about the sport, television networks that have covered top races along with viewership numbers, and statistics on the sport.

The entire team must get involved. If you divide your efforts, your chances of conquering by finding a sponsor will improve. And, everyone will have a greater investment and commitment to the team. This process will make your team stronger as you practice teamwork.

Once you feel you have established a solid base of team members, create a website. Include bios of each team member, informative stories (first person perspectives are more interesting) on unique experiences and other interesting facts, and lots of pictures. This will help your team obtain sponsorship and once you find a sponsor, your website will provide a visible outlet to promote your team and the company sponsor.

Once you have a sponsorship agreement, try to keep it to create recognition in the sport. It will also allow you to develop a deeper relationship with the company. Send your sponsor pictures of your team racing in gear with the company logo attached to it. Keep them updated with the sport and your team's involvement. Regular communication is key to long-lasting relationships.

Team Agonos prepares for the gear check hours before the Endorphin Fix 2-day adventure race in West Virginia.

TEAM DYNAMICS

If a team fails, it is usually because of navigational errors or team dynamics. Dynamics are the trickier of the two. The human race is a unique species. We possess a gamut of emotions, many of which are extremely fragile. We may require high maintenance to assure an adequate existence. Or, we may have easily adaptable personalities (which lend quite nicely to adventure racing). Personalities mesh with some people and clash with others.

Unfortunately, upon first impression (or the fifth, tenth, or fiftieth encounter), we may not recognize the potential for disaster when the going gets rough. "You don't know your team until you come out of your comfort zone," explains Dave Zietsma, founder of the raid—The North adventure racing series in Canada. Therefore, it is prudent to train often as a team, immerse yourselves in challenging situations, and get to know each other's strengths and weaknesses—both physically and mentally.

Adventure racing is a team sport. You start the race as a team, you find every checkpoint together, and you finish as one unit. As part of one cohesive union, each team member does whatever it takes to keep the team moving forward with the greatest efficiency. If one teammate gets hurt, the others fall in line to offer support. The strongest member may carry the injured member's pack. A towing system, if feasible and not a hindrance to the injury, may be rigged to compensate for the injury. Use your creativity when faced with challenging situations.

In a race against the clock, the last thing you want to do is rest or sleep

anymore than is absolutely necessary. However, if a teammate is hurt, it is better to take extra time to get that person back on his/her feet and finish the race versus hastily pushing on and risking disqualification because he/she cannot go on. Be patient but efficient.

In addition to the physical measures, don't forget the importance of emotional support. An injured teammate not only suffers the physical pain but also the burden of slowing the team. Sometimes, all it takes is some encouraging words or even a pat on the back. A good story or a few jokes can also keep the air positive. Remember that you are part of a team. If one member is down, the entire team falters. By the same token, the team can work together to bring a wounded member back up.

SIMPATICO

Before you confirm a team, make absolutely certain you like your teammates. Ask yourself if you trust them. Be honest with yourself so you can be honest with them. Question whether you will want to spend a week in the bush with them.

Discuss each teammate's objectives and then how they mesh into the team. Will you be pleased to cross the finish line no matter where you fall in the rankings or are you yearning to be in the top five? Are you out to win or simply in the race for the experience? If each person doesn't share similar goals, you may be heading for trouble.

It's a good idea to team up with athletes of similar fitness levels. This practice will allow you to stick close together. Nothing is worse for team morale than continuous separation. If you are in a situation where two teammates are constantly further away than an ear shot, you will eventually lose team harmony. Not to mention the fact that it is against the rules to be further than 100 meters from each other at all times.

Generally, as an adventure racer, you should be adept in all of the disciplines. Every year, assess your abilities and rate them on a scale. One through five is a quick and easy scale where: 1 = poor, 2 = adequate, 3 = fair, 4 = good, and 5 = excellent. Then when you are putting together a team, you can get a good idea of the strengths and weaknesses of the group.

Try to fill out each discipline with a strong leader. In other words, find a strong paddler. Find another who really knows backcountry. Look for a strong, experienced mountain biker. Search for a good mountaineer with confidence on the ropes, and of course, you need a good navigator.

It is also a good idea to choose personalities that enhance yours. Make fun a priority for everyone.

Once you gather an attractive mix of talent, skill, and compatible personalities, set several dates to train together. As mentioned earlier, it is paramount to know each other's fitness levels and experience some team dynamics before you race together.

THE VALUE IN ADVENTURE RACING

BY DAN O'SHEA

If life is a search for meaning, then to what lengths do men and women go to find value in their existence? Most individuals find their personal motivators in the day-to-day doldrums of work and home. Driven by a paycheck, promotion or sales commissions, they work to live for the new SUV, the mortgage payment and other financial obligations. Many constantly seek something tangible, fixing a material value to their position in life. These individuals find their incentives in the extrinsic rewards of power, status, money, and image.

Then, there are those for whom the behavior is the reward. Intrinsically inspired by personal growth and learning, achieving goals, enhanced personal relationships and being a part of something greater than oneself. These are individuals looking to be a part of a higher community, a team. Committed to a common cause, a team is two or more people who work together toward a specific goal. A team implies a sense of shared mission, collective responsibility and alignment with others. If an enriched life of shared values is what these individuals strive for, then where do they find it? For many, it is in the sport of adventure racing.

"What are the lessons learned from adventure racing teams?"

All teams need driving motivation to bind them.

For some adventure race teams it is to win, for other teams to merely finish. Reaching these goals requires tasks that must be successfully accomplished by each member of the team. The roles and responsibilities of each team member define these tasks. Each member has an understanding of their job requirements and how they support the team's goals. Every member of a team must commit to a common mission and agree upon realistic goals to achieve that vision. If one member of the team wants to win and the others just want to finish the race, that team will fall apart.

Strong adventure teams learn that being part of a team means acknowledging weaknesses as well as strengths. "Who is the best navigator? Strongest on the bike or in the water?" The best teams find a way to mesh each individual's weaknesses with team strengths to move quickly through the course.

Like all high performing organizations, successful teams achieve high levels of performance through shared leadership, purpose and responsibility of all team members working toward the same goal. The stronger the degree of trust, competence, and commitment within the members, the greater the team. The basis of any team's strength is the foundation of their operating values.

Adventure racing has been called "life" itself. If this is true, then what are the "life" values this endeavor provides?

ADVENTURE RACING VALUES

TEAMWORK

Adventure racing is a team sport. No one finishes an expedition adventure race alone. Like team sports or military training, one quickly realizes that you require other members of your team to overcome these challenges. An adventure racer learns that he or she must succeed individually to be of use to his teammates. One must be skilled in the technical aspects of the sport's varied disciplines, from navigating by map and compass, mountain biking, paddling, navigating, mountaineering, etc. If one member is struggling due to a lack of food or water or just plan exhaustion, others must recognize and address this immediately. It might mean giving up your last Snickers bar, water from your Camelback, or carrying some of their weight for them. Like the weak link in a chain, in adventure racing, your team is only as fast as your slowest member is.

Adventure race participants learn the value of drawing on collective strengths in order to accomplish personal and team goals.

PERSEVERANCE

An adventure race requires individuals to find inner strengths they never thought they had in order to endure its challenges. Adventure racing will find limits of your physical endurance and force you to face your greatest enemy—the enemy of self-doubt within each of us. Adventure racing measures an individual's courage in their ability to continue despite the lack of sleep, throbbing muscle pain, or adverse weather conditions. It's called "fire in the gut" and it is all about unwavering tenacity. It is telling that "I can't" voice inside your head that "I will," as you put each step forward despite the discomfort. As in life, the failure occurs when one listens to that voice and no longer tries, accepting defeat. Those who learn to persevere despite physical suffering or mental exhaustion raise their personal expectations to new levels and learn that there are no limits to the power of the human spirit.

Adventure racers realize that most limits in life are self-imposed.

ACCOUNTABILITY

Adventure racing is a competition that requires individuals to travel hundreds of miles over mountains, across deserts, on rivers, lakes, or the ocean, nonstop for a week to ten days. The extremes of adventure racing force one to be accountable, not only in terms of individual experience, but in collective team preparation. Since the pace of every team depends on each individual's proficiency, strength and speed in every race discipline, any training shortfall by a teammate will become readily apparent over the course of the race. If one does not properly train for the competition's multi-sport events, it will affect the entire team's performance and threaten everyone's goal of finishing the race. In order to contribute fully to the team, one needs to be able to answer to oneself first.

Adventure racing forces one to be accountable to oneself and to others.

RESPONSIBILITY

Everyone on a team is a leader and leading involves responsibility. Each racer is expected to be technically proficient in all adventure racing tasks and each member is assigned special duties on behalf of the entire team. Each team must have a captain to make team decisions based on consensus, a navigator who can lead the team on the best route, a medic who looks after the welfare of the team, and a "sergeant" who keeps the team moving. Yet every member must be able to perform these "team" duties if others falter during the course of the race.

Adventure racing is the ultimate experience in accepting and sharing team tasks in order to reach team goals.

RESPECT

All members on an adventure race team are essential and must depend upon each other to accomplish the collective goal of finishing the race together. Each serves as a cog in the wheel required to propel the team toward the finish. Losing one element (member) of the system (team) can cause the machine (race) to break down. Everyone will "hit the wall" at some point during the race and others must be ready to support that member until they are back up to speed. All members of the team must be conscious of this fact and respect the combined strengths and shortcomings of others. Equally important is respecting one's own limits. Many racers try to write a check their body can't cash. Nothing is more terrifying than coming face-to-face with an individual's own worst enemy—oneself. Conversely, nothing is more empowering than conquering this fear and continuing despite the voices in one's head.

AWARENESS

Expedition adventure racing is more than just a metaphor for life. It is a sport, which forces a lifetime of highs and lows, euphoria and suffering, victories and defeats, upon a team of individuals within the space of a week of racing. What each person takes away from his or her experience there is up to the individual. That experience however is a collective one and dependent on many factors. Rarely will a team's race strategy last longer than one day after the gun goes off. How a group deals with the inevitability of Murphy's law that things will go wrong, is a measure of the team's collective strengths. It is not the individual pieces but the sum of the parts. Expedition adventure racing demands a universal commitment from and to every member of one's team. Adventure racing is not about one person; it is about a group of individuals coming together as a team to overcome something greater than the individual parts. An expedition adventure racer's quest for life's meaning is a journey of investigating the values of their sport through a shared experience with their teammates.

In life as in sporting endeavors, there are spectators and there are competitors. The spectators watch the action in the stands and pontificate, speculate or stare in awe at the exploits of the players. It is the man (and woman) in the arena who is the doer, the protagonist, the heroes and heroines in our world. In word and deed they ascend the great heights, overcome the daunting challenges, and lead the followers to the vision. These individuals included Columbus, going to the end of the earth, Hillary, summiting Everest, and Bannister, breaking the four-minute mile. Despite the naysayers, they all prevailed and continue to do so. That spirit continues today in extreme endurance events inspiring mountaineers to attempt new routes above 6,000 meters, sending kayakers down previously unrunnable class VI rapids, or expeditions to Antarctica.

An expedition adventure racer does not look in awe at endurance record holders or listen in disbelief at tales of human struggle and survival. They reflect in quiet agreement and respectful appreciation for the sacrifices of their peers. They share in common a life driven by passions not possessions. For those in the arena, it is the experiences that provide value in living.

COOKED ONION

As I sat in my own heap of sweat, dirt and racing gear, I munched on a roast beef and cheese sandwich and marveled at my surroundings. Twelve hours into the inaugural Ford Escape Wild Onion Urban Adventure Race, I found myself at rest and quite content on the "EL", an elevated train that winds through the city of Chicago. Concrete walls whizzed by as nearby passengers stared in wonderment at the filthy trio my two teammates and I comprised. We hardly resembled your typical passengers, but then, this wasn't a typical day in Chicago.

On a normal Friday night, it is rare to witness packs of three people running through the city streets burdened by mounds of gear and sugary gel caked around their lips as they dissect rule books and piles of maps. After all, Chicago is a sophisticated city. Equally, adventure racers are rarely exposed to Dunkin' Donuts and taxi cabs during their outdoor excursions. The Wild Onion was a very different race within a very different sport.

The race began at the North Avenue Beach Club on the shore of Lake Michigan. The colder-than-normal-for-early-October evening air stung our ears and noses as we gathered gear for the first few disciplines. Our task as a team of three racers and one support crew was to tour the city by our own power and return to the same spot where we started in less than 24 hours. On cue, at the sound of the gun, we ran through the chilly city streets and up the 103 flights of stairs of "Mt." Sears Tower. What we potentially missed in elevation gain and loss in a race set in rugged wilderness, we made up for in intensity. We were also granted the opportunity to witness every team as the entire race contingent climbed and descended the stairwells.

Upon our triumph of the man-made mountain, we ran to the Daley Plaza Center where we penetrated underground tunnels that traced confusing paths beneath the loop. Our world was transformed as we slogged through the mire, carefully avoiding pockets that threatened to swallow us with one misplaced step. Fortunately, volunteers were strategically stationed to decipher the labyrinth in an effort to avoid losing teams in the sauna-like passageways once used to transport coal.

As we emerged from the city's basement, the frigid outdoor air stung our melting bodies. The unforgiving air and the desolate channel were clear signs that activity was best saved for the summer season during normal business hours. But the essence of adventure racing is to experience unique situations in equally unique environments. Although we were in an urban setting, we were subject to uncultivated exposure.

Our primitive purpose within a civilized landscape conjured myriad opportunities. I found if I became immersed in my immediate task, my team was isolated in foreign territory performing heroic duties. We were on an important mission. We were on a treasure hunt.

However, a quick glance over my shoulder assured me we were far from dangerous lands and actually quite close to home as we paddled the Chicago River at Midnight.

Bound on dry land again as we deposited our canoes with race officials, we continued to trace the river, this time on foot. Although the river squeezed through residential property and underneath city roads, we were given explicit directions to stay off "cut grass and pavement." This meant a cold slog through the knee-to-waist deep waters or climbing up, over, and through the growth that hugged the water.

We found intermittent footpaths that afforded easy travel. But when we weren't so lucky, we carefully slid along muddy ledges. We swung from tree to tree and climbed over fences and sometimes we were forced to wrap our bodies around the chain-link barriers that protruded over the water. Ironically, civilization was usually within a stone's throw, but setting foot on it meant disqualification. This requirement catered to the adventure that was the prospect of the unknown with territory with which I was quite familiar.

This blend became the theme of my adventure.

As we continued to race, we rode our bikes along forest preserve trails, which shielded any sense that we were in an urban environment. Occasionally however, we would pop out onto busy roads and thrust back into the chaos of the city. Eventually, with the aid of a 20-minute train ride, more navigation through the loop (this time on a Saturday morning), and some lakefront riding, we deposited our bikes on the South side of Chicago and set out for a long stretch of coasteering.

Heading North along the rocky coast of Lake Michigan, the winds seemed determined to erase our facial features. They tantalized the waters, which consequently provoked our steps and became a constant obstacle in addition to the precarious path of boulders and concrete slabs. Travel could have been easy if we were only allowed to move over several yards west of what was required. However, the florescent orange spots frequently placed along our route were under watchful eyes of the race officials and too many infringements would force us off the course.

All I had to do was look to my left for reassurance from the familiar skyline of Chicago. But if I stayed focused on the rocks and the coastline, I was once again engaged in an adventure, far from recognizable surroundings. The secret mission continued.

A quick jaunt on in-line skates knocked me back to urban reality only long enough, however, to be thrown back into my adventure as my team and I secured ourselves in sea kayaks and headed north on the open waters of Lake Michigan. The relentless winds conjured man-eating swells, which we negotiated just long enough to dodge the dangerous conditions.

Our final significant undertaking was located at the end of Navy Pier, a year-round tourist attraction in Chicago. We climbed the interior of a six-story tower and then skimmed the external walls with the aid of a rappel system. The cheers and applause of family, friends, and curious onlookers fueled our flickering energy as we laced up our skates and rolled to the finish line.

Throughout the adventure race, I discovered parts of Chicago for the first time. I developed a new appreciation for the urban setting, which I had formerly protested as an inhabitant in my quest for adventure sports. I truly realized the essence of adventure. It's everywhere—if you simply open your mind.

—Kara

BEYOND THE HORIZON

As is the case in any project, sport, or aspiration in life, you start small and build big. A gradual progression of quality effort and experience will create the champion you wish to be. When you admire world-class athletes, don't forget the endless hours of dedication they contributed to earn titles and shelves of trophies. Do your homework and you will be fondly rewarded. We wish for you to have many years of safe and enjoyable racing ahead of you—good luck!

DON MANN

Don Mann has been racing in multi-discipline sports for over 25 years. He has dedicated most of his life to training and racing, and as a sports trainer and race director, he's helped thousands of others to do the same. Don has competed in well over 1,000 endurance competitions. He served 20 years in the US Navy as a SEAL, and has a B.S. in Social Sciences, a B.S. in Criminal Justice and an M.S. in Management. Don is also the founder of Odyssey Adventure Racing, currently the largest adventure racing/multi-sport organization in the United States, which produces more adventure races and multi-sport events than any other US sports organizations.

KARA SCHAAD

Kara Schaad is an international sports/adventure travel writer and a health and fitness trainer. In 1996, she was voted one of Chicago's top 50 female athletes. She has competed in a variety of adventure races from the one-day Wild Onion urban competition in Chicago, to a five-day expedition-length adventure race in British Columbia. She was a member of the first team to graduate from the Odyssey Adventure Racing Academy and successfully finish the Endorphin Fix two-day adventure race in West Virginia. In addition, Kara traveled to the Philippines to witness and write about the inaugural Elf Authentic Adventure in 1999. As the Fitness Columnist for the *Chicago Sun-Times* for two years and a Reebok Master Trainer for five years, Kara has reached over one million people with her fitness expertise. Kara has a B.S. in Exercise Science.

Berger, Karen. *Hiking and Backpacking, A Complete Guide.* New York, NY: W.W. Norton & Company. 1995.

Birch, Beryl Bender. *Power Yoga, the Total Strength and Flexibility Workout.* New York, NY: Simon & Schuster. 1995.

Boga, Steven. *Orienteering, The Sport of Navigation with Map and Compass.* Mechanicsburg, PA: Rodale Press. 1994.

Burkr R., Burke. *Serious Cycling.* Champaign, IL: Human Kinetics. 1995.

By the Editors of Bicycling Magazine and Mountain Bike Magazine. *Bicycling Magazine's Complete Guide to Bicycle Maintenance and Repair Including Road Bikes and Mountain Bikes.* Emmaus, PA: Rodale Press. 1994.

By the Editors of Mountain Bike Magazine and Bicycling Magazine. *Mountain Bike Magazine's Complete Guide to Mountain Biking Skills.* Emmaus, PA: Rodale Press, Inc. 1996.

Colgan, Michael. *Optimum Sports Nutrition, Your Competitive Edge, A Complete Nutritional Guide for Optimizing Athletic Performance.* New York: Advanced Research Press. 1993.

Forgey, William M.D. *Wilderness Medicine, 4th Edition.* Old Saybrook, CT: The Globe Pequot Press. 1994.

Gordon, I. Herbert. *The Complete Book of Canoeing.* Old Saybrook, CT: The Globe Pequot Press. 1992.

Grant, Gordon. *Canoeing.* New York, NY: W.W. Norton & Company. 1997.

Graydon, Don and Kurt Hanson. *Mountaineering, the Freedom of the Hills.* Seattle, WA: The Mountaineers. 1997.

Huthinson, Derek. *The Basic Book of Sea Kayaking.* Old Saybrook, CT: The Globe Pequot Press. 1999.

Krauzer, Steven M. *Kayaking Whitewater and Touring Basics.* New York, NY: W.W. Norton & Company. 1995.

McArdle, William D., Frank I. Katch and Victor L. Katch. *Exercise Physiology, Energy, Nutrition, and Human Peformance.* Baltimore, MA: Williams & Wilkins. 1996.

Randall, Glenn. *The Outward Bound Map and Compass Handbook.* New York, NY: Lyons & Burford, 1989.

Seidman, David. *The Essential Sea Kayaker, A Complete Course for the Open Water Paddler.* Camden, ME: Ragged Mountain Press. 1992.

Seidman, David. *The Essential Wilderness Navigator, How to Find Your Way in the Great Outdoors.* Camden, ME: Ragged Mountain Pess. 1995.

Sobey, Ed. *The Whole Backpacker's Catalog, Tools and Resources for the Foot Traveler.* Camden, ME: Ragged Mountain Press. 1999.

Tawrell, Paul. *Camping and Wilderness Survival, the Ultimate Outdoors Book.* Shelburne, VT: Paul Tawrell. 1996.

Williams, Melvin H. *Nutrition for Fitness and Sport.* Dubque, IA: Wm. C. Brown. 1983.

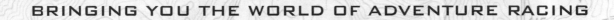